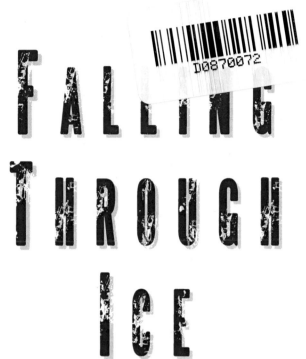

# FALLING THROUGH ICE

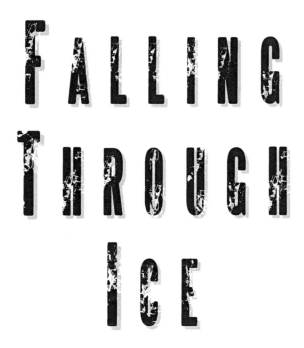

# FALLING THROUGH ICE

CAROLYN HUEBNER RANKIN

WITH

ROSETTA D. HOESSLI

# FALLING THROUGH ICE

BY: Carolyn Huebner Rankin with Rosetta D. Hoessli

Copyright © 2011 by Carolyn S. Huebner Rankin
All rights reserved.

Published by Crossover Publications LLC, 870 N. Bierdeman Road, Pearl, Mississippi 39208, www.crossoverpublications.com
(601) 664-6717, Fax: (601) 664-6818
Randall M. Mooney
Publisher

Library of Congress Control Number: 2011922173

ISBN 978-0-9819657-7-2
Printed in the USA

Inspirational
Narrative Non-Fiction

Cover Concept & Direction: Randall M. Mooney
Graphic Arts & Layout: Matthew Mooney
Background Images: 123RF.COM

# *In Memory of Daddy:*

## George Edward Shaw
### (1917-1973)

Whose unconditional love gave me the foundation to withstand
the storms of my life and whose example of faith
gave me strength to rebuild after they passed.

## *And to his God and Mine:*

## The Lord Jesus Christ

Who was with me through it all, and

Who redeemed and restored my life.

# ACKNOWLEDGEMENTS
## by Carolyn Huebner Rankin

To my husband, James, and my daughter, Audra

and to Ronni; my gratitude for your talent
and friendship cannot adequately be expressed.

*And for their love and support in my life...*

Leola Seay

Texas Ranger & Mrs. Jerome H. Preiss

Dr. & Mrs. George G. Meyer

Douglas K. Hawkins, Ed.D

Florence & Woody Burns
(Hurricane, W.Va.)

Rev. Jim Franklin
(Lesage, W.Va.)
and his listeners and friends

Pete and Chico

...and the kindness of others far too many to list here.


Blessings, Carolyn

# ACKNOWLEDGEMENTS
## by Rosetta D. Hoessli

For Kevin, my heart.
Thank you for the electric typewriter you bought me in 1976.
Thank you for making me laugh during the good and bad times
of our last 37 years together.  Thank you for just being you.

There's no one on earth I owe more to than my parents, Tommy and
Wanda Thompson.  I love them both more than I can say.

Thank you to my daughter, whose generous spirit and loving heart
comforted me during the process of this book.  She is my treasure.

Although I appreciate Jim Rankin's formidable editing skills,
I'm more grateful for his prayers than I can say.

Retired Texas Ranger Jerome Preiss was my shining light during
the dark days of Carolyn's imprisonment.  He always said, "Just hang
in there, kid, and don't be afraid to tell the truth.  The truth will
always win out."  He was right.

Terry Burns, with Hartline Literary Agency, has been an incredible source
of encouragement and motivation.

Carolyn and I have traveled a long and sometimes painful road together.
Yet, for all that, I wouldn't trade the journey for the world.  She has
more courage and strength than anyone I've ever known.
I will always treasure her friendship.

Finally, I want to thank God from the depths of my soul.  I prayed for
words and He gave them to me.  I hope I have used them well
and that He is pleased.

God bless, Ronni

# AUTHOR'S NOTE

What follows is a work of non-fiction.
The events and experiences presented
are all true, documented and faithfully
rendered to the best of my ability.
Some conversations presented are
taken directly from tape recordings.
However, others are not meant to
represent verbatim accounts; rather,
they are written to evoke the true
feeling and meaning of the
conversation, in keeping with the
spirit and mood of the event.

The reader should also know that
some of the names and identities
presented have been altered to protect
the privacy of the innocent…
and the guilty.

Other Books by Carolyn Huebner Rankin:
Healing Music
© 2010
Crossover Publications, LLC

# PROLOGUE

I was uneasy. This morning was too beautiful, too sunny and warm for what was going to happen today in New Orleans, Louisiana. This day—September 9, 1987—demanded heavy gray skies and buckets of rain splattering against steaming, narrow streets. The bustle of unconcerned people going about their everyday affairs, the tooting of taxi horns, the gusty exhaling of air brakes on slow-moving buses—all this cheerfulness and normalcy seemed almost a sacrilege. Still, in a perverse sort of way, I welcomed it. The situation in which I found myself was so unreal that it somehow appeased my confused sense of order to see that the world was still functioning right on schedule.

Now, sitting in the New Orleans Federal Courthouse and awaiting the arrival of the Honorable Morey L. Sear, I gazed longingly at the exit sign over a side door, then looked around the courtroom and struggled to come to grips with why I was here. Reporters leaned nonchalantly against the walls, already scribbling away on legal-sized note pads; I recognized two from my hometown of San Antonio, Texas. Like vultures, they had swooped in to cover this story. They were circling their prey, waiting until Carolyn Huebner was helpless and vulnerable so they could rip her from the pedestal upon which they had placed her themselves.

Carolyn and I sat close together in the front pew, thighs touching, and I could feel her uncontrolled shivering, as if her body was turning to ice. I gripped her hand and winced at the cold, clammy texture of her flesh—like that of a dead woman left for days beneath the murky waters of some Louisiana swamp. Carolyn's terror was an insidious, contagious force in the tense, restless courtroom. I could feel it swelling in my own throat, filling my lungs until every breath was a struggle. Like Carolyn, I was choking on it.

"Do you think I could step out for a minute?" I whispered to the elderly man seated on my other side. "I just need to…"

When retired Texas Ranger Jerome Preiss shook his head and held up a warning finger, I subsided in automatic obedience. I never argued with Jerome. There was something about his snapping dark eyes and the set of his thin lips that made me feel like I still needed a babysitter, yet I had never known anyone so gentle. We even called him *PoPo*, like his own grandchildren.

Jerome Preiss had come to New Orleans to lend affectionate support to this young woman he called only *The Kid*. Six-foot-two, less than one hundred eighty pounds, Jerome was all leather-skinned and mahogany-tanned, as wiry and taut-muscled as an adolescent but showing every one of his sixty-five years. To me, he was the only person in this courtroom who made sense, whose quiet stability in the midst of our shared terror and confusion was as soothing as a walk by the beach. Instinctively I reached for his hand and forced back grateful tears as I felt his rough and calloused fingers close over mine.

"All rise for the Honorable United States District Judge, Morey Sear! The federal court for the Eastern District of Louisiana is now in session!" The bailiff glared around the room, apparently on the lookout for anyone not willing to give the elderly, black-robed judge the respect due him. Finally satisfied that his audience was properly awed, he added absently, "Please be seated."

As the courtroom quieted and came to order, the interminable docket-calling began. In a last-ditch attempt to control my shrieking nerves, I forced my mind to wander into the past, allowing it to flit through one scene, then another, then another, focusing on nothing in particular as I tried to understand how this could have happened and wondering, as always, what I could have done to stop it...

Ah, now there was a question. As close as I was to Carolyn, as much as I knew about her past, why hadn't I told anyone? I had seen it coming, but I hadn't tried to stop it. I had simply removed myself from Carolyn's bizarre environment and counted myself lucky to be out of it.

Still, who would have guessed that the beautiful Victorian mansion on Elm Street in San Antonio could have housed so much inner misery, so much torment? Certainly not me—not in the beginning, anyway. In the beginning I had actually been intimidated by the younger woman's intelligence, experience, and the respect she had earned from her peers in her chosen field of locating missing children. Her office walls had been lined with gold-edged Awards of Appreciation from a dozen grateful charities and certificates of completed college hours in the study of criminology, investigative techniques, and child abuse.

It seemed that I couldn't open a newspaper without seeing Carolyn's face somewhere in it. I couldn't turn on the television without hearing her voice. Carolyn was San Antonio's Golden Child, a champion for abused children upon whom reporters could always rely for a statement that rang with truth and power and conviction. Carolyn Huebner seemed obsessed with the limelight, reveling in any kind of attention at all, devouring media worship with the greed of a starving child. She was a reporter's dream, a fellow 'crusader's' role model—and her own family's nightmare.

Even as late as last night, at the candlelit restaurant in the Canal Street hotel where we were all staying, Carolyn had agreed to give one last interview to her close friend, San Antonio newspaper reporter Bobby Edmonds. In spite of the fact that Bobby had brought along Brian Wood, an old pal of his from New Orleans whom no one had ever met before, Carolyn had spoken openly and with great emotion, determined to present her side of the story before "all the other journalists have it garbled and unrecognizable, resembling nothing even close to the truth."

It would probably be her last terrific quote.

I cast a sideways glance at the trembling Carolyn Huebner and wondered what the reporters thought of her now. Today she looked far more like a well-dressed society matron than a criminal, but either description would have been accurate. How would they describe her when their stories came out?

I could picture the articles now, with the possible exception of Bobby's *Exclusive*. The reporters would say she was short, chunky, with a cascade of red-gold curls tumbling past a moon-shaped face. That was poetic enough. They would describe her flawless milky-white complexion and intelligent blue-gray eyes. They would give her that much. But would they ever mention a hearty laugh that seemed to start in her toes and work its way up, punctuated by giggles and sometimes unfeminine snorts of pure enjoyment? Probably not. Would they say that she was hot-tempered, tempestuous, fiery? Maybe—that wasn't too flattering. It was for certain they wouldn't say she was soft, loving, passionate, loyal and generous to a fault. She had never let them see that side of her.

And who would know—except me—that she was a Child-Woman without a home, without family, without identity…

Still, I thought bitterly, even with all this knowledge about Carolyn Huebner, you didn't go to anyone. You didn't try to stop her. You never confronted her. You never told her she needed help. You never said a word—not to Larry, not to Leola… You just left her, like everyone else. She called you her Best Friend and the Sister She Never Had, but you weren't. Not really.

Even as those now-familiar waves of guilt washed over me, I knew, deep in my soul, that no one could have halted the tremendous force of Carolyn Sue Huebner's twisted emotions. They had hurtled, like a runaway train, down the tracks of her life toward inevitable and absolute destruction. That train had left the depot years earlier, when Carolyn was only six and living a storybook-perfect life back east in White Oak, Pennsylvania. That train was guaranteed not to stop until those emotions exploded, demolishing whomever and whatever stood in their way. And had I stayed, they would have destroyed me, too.

One had only to look at Carolyn's husband, Larry, to see how much damage she could do. Good old Larry, I thought, a man more misunderstood and ridiculed than anyone I had ever known. Although he was pale and perspiring now, he was usually ruddy-complected and completely composed. Plump and balding, he looked like any other middle-aged businessman. He was calm, controlled, analytical—all necessary qualities to make him a successful executive in one of the largest oil companies in the country—and so often the bane of Carolyn's passionate and headstrong existence. Fire and Ice, I had labeled them, Opposite Ends of the Emotional Spectrum…

"The United States of America versus Carolyn Sue Huebner."

Carolyn jumped, dragged in an audible shaky breath, and managed to get to her feet. She stood, head bowed, then walked slowly toward a podium placed in the center of the courtroom. I looked away, unable to bear the sight of her humiliation and quiet panic. She seemed so tiny standing there, so lost, so confused. I could feel the intense interest of the reporters in the back of the room. God, how hungry they were! Vultures, I thought again, just like black, circling vultures.

"Mr. Simno, are you here in representation of Carolyn Sue Huebner?" the judge asked, interrupting my thoughts. He leaned back in his chair and folded his arms in front of him.

George Simno nodded, taking Carolyn's elbow as he stepped closer to the podium. "I am, Your Honor."

"Very good." From his high perch of respectability and enormous power, Judge Sear squinted nearsightedly down at Carolyn and frowned. "Mrs. Huebner, the United States government has charged you with *Conspiracy* and *Solicitation to Commit Murder*. You must enter a plea of Guilty or Not Guilty. What is your plea?"

Instinctively, I moved closer to Larry. His hands were clenched into fists in his lap—I covered them with my own shaking fingers and willed him to look at me. When he didn't, I tried to force a mental message into his brain:

*Stop this now, Larry. You can do it. You know it's the right thing to do...*

But the silence went on and on. Carolyn seemed lost in thought, a million miles away from this courtroom. Finally, she straightened her shoulders and tilted her chin in a pathetic attempt at dignity. Her response was low, but firm.

"I *am* guilty, Your Honor."

Judge Sear released a gusty sigh and shook his head, seemingly unable to square the image of this small, quaking woman with that of someone capable of committing so heinous a crime. I could sympathize with him; I couldn't do it, either. Yet there it was, right in front of us, in black and white. Carolyn Huebner was who she was, and she had done what she had done.

"Mrs. Huebner, do you understand that by entering this plea of Guilty on this the ninth day of September, 1987, you have waived your right to a trial by jury and that whatever sentence is handed down by this court is final and irrevocable?"

Carolyn winced, bit her lip, and looked away from him. I understood that every fiber of her being was screaming in rejection of the finality of this statement. Yet Carolyn whispered again, "Yes, Your Honor, I understand."

It took enormous effort for me to stay seated, and Carolyn's determined words cut through my memory like a saber: *I'll do seven years for that little girl, Ronni. I'll do whatever it takes to protect her...*

To protect *her*, I thought now, and who else?

Judge Sear's voice brought me back to the present abruptly. "And still you wish to enter a plea of Guilty?"

"Yes, Your Honor."

I sagged in the pew and turned my pleading, bewildered gaze toward Larry. He met my eyes for a single instant before he looked away. Drops of sweat lined his forehead and trickled down the side of his face.

"All right. Colleen, please place it in the record that the United States Government is represented here today by United States Attorney Mr. John Volz and Assistant United States Attorney Mr. Lance Africk, and that Mrs. Carolyn Sue Huebner is represented in court by her attorney of record, George Simno, Esquire. Let the record also show that Mrs. Huebner has entered a plea of Guilty to the separate charges of *Conspiracy* and *Solicitation to Commit Murder*— specifically by the use of interstate telephone lines. Finally, let the record show that Mrs. Huebner has been duly informed of her rights and the consequences of her waiving those rights, and that she has agreed to same. Now, Mr. Volz, is the government prepared to present the facts in this case?"

The facts in this case! I thought indignantly. What do they know about facts? They know what they *think* are facts, what *seems to be* facts...

As John Volz arose, I leaned forward intently for a closer look. While the man who had been Carolyn's nemesis for the past few months was rather handsome and non-threatening, I knew him to be ambitious and determined, even treacherous in his blind desire to see Carolyn Huebner behind bars...

"The United States is ready, Your Honor."

"And you, Mr. Simno?"

George Simno straightened to his full six-foot-six inches and nodded, "We're ready, Your Honor."

"You may proceed, Mr. Volz."

I closed my eyes and took a deep breath as John Volz prepared to present his opening statement. In just a few moments, it would be all over.

"The United States versus Carolyn Sue Huebner is a cold and calculated case of attempted murder, Your Honor, and sadly, it is one that Carolyn Huebner herself cannot dispute. The facts are here—on tape—and in Mrs. Huebner's own statement. This is nothing more than a case of a disgruntled wife hiring a contract killer to murder her husband in order to inherit his very sizable estate. But she made one enormous mistake. Thank God." Volz paused for dramatic effect. "Carolyn Huebner hired an FBI informant to kill her husband, a man whose only crime in nine years of marriage had been to love and support his wife far beyond the call of duty, and the FBI stepped in just in the nick of time.

"If it hadn't been for the FBI, Your Honor, Larry Edward Huebner wouldn't be sitting in this courtroom today. Although he seems to have difficulty admitting it—and I don't blame him, Your Honor—he would have been murdered in a back alley, stabbed to death at the instigation of the very woman who is in this courtroom today, pleading for mercy from the United States government.

"This man needs to be protected from the dictates of his own foolish heart, and so does society. If we don't protect him from Carolyn Huebner, Your Honor, who will?"

This guy meant business, and his case seemed so simple it was almost embarrassing. There was another side to this story, but who was ever going to hear it? Who would ever believe it?

The answer seemed to whisper like a mocking echo through the silent courtroom: *No one…no one…no one…*

"Mr. Simno, are you ready?"

"Yes, Your Honor." George Simno's deep voice was confident and reassuring. He put an arm around Carolyn's shoulder. "We're ready."

"You may proceed."

"Your Honor, we do not deny the facts of the state's case. They are undeniable. Nor do we deny that Mrs. Huebner's husband, Larry Edward Huebner, was the intended victim. That, too, is undeniable. However, we do deny that this case is as cut-and-dried as it would appear, and we assert that the defendant's state of mind had everything to do with how and why this incident occurred. We also assert that her work with law enforcement in particularly heinous child abuse cases, as well as her own childhood experiences, contributed to her emotional confusion and…"

*Blah, blah, blah…* I closed my eyes. No matter how hard he tried, no matter how good his intentions, no matter how effective an attorney he was, George Simno was not going to be able to make this senseless case sound reasonable—at least, not in a fifteen-minute theatrical soliloquy. It was almost painful to listen to him try to sum up Carolyn's story, and it was all I could do to stay in my seat. Finally, in desperation, I forced my mind to wander away from the courtroom…

It didn't matter what he said, anyway. Carolyn was determined to keep every secret she had to keep, no matter what it cost.

The judge's voice brought me back to the present. "I am going to call a brief recess at this time," he said, glancing at his watch. "Your attorney has given me a package to study, Mrs. Huebner, which I assume to be letters and character references and so forth. Although I don't usually allow packages like these to influence my decisions in any way, I do promise to give it my full attention. Court is adjourned for thirty minutes."

It was finished. As I stood in the hall outside the rapidly emptying courtroom, sheltered between Larry and PoPo, I stared in uncomprehending disbelief at the elevator doors as they opened and closed slowly, reverberating with a terrible finality through the vacating courthouse. Part of me longed to race upstairs to that place the bailiff had called the *holding cell* so that I could take Carolyn in my arms and comfort her before the terror became too overwhelming, but the rest of me refused to move.

*If I go up there, if I see her, it'll be the last time. Maybe if I stay here, if I don't move, maybe they won't take her...*

I heard Larry's gentle voice from far, far away. "Ronni, come on. I'm so sorry. We have to go. We don't have much time."

And then the tears started. After three months, they finally streamed unchecked down my cheeks. As the elevator doors slid open once more and I followed PoPo and Larry inside, my only reality was the salty taste of tears on my lips.

When the elevator doors closed, the words exploded from me, "PoPo, I don't understand! Mr. Simno promised they'd let her go home with us today and we could put her in a hospital where she could get help! He promised there was no way they'd send her to Lexington Penitentiary, not with that first judge sending her home in the beginning and letting her stay with me! PoPo, that other judge even let her go back to Pennsylvania to see her mother all by herself! And the prosecution swore to us that they wouldn't argue for any prison time if she'd just cop a plea, but they did, PoPo! They out-and-out lied to us! And how could Judge Sear say that her past and her work didn't have anything to do with what happened? Didn't he read those reports? My God, PoPo, you read them! We all read them! He's not a stupid man..."

PoPo grabbed my shoulders and shook me. "Stop it, Ronni! Pull yourself together! Carolyn's gonna be countin' on you—just like always. You can't let her see you like this!"

I was sobbing now. "I can't help it, PoPo! I don't know what to do! What can I do?"

"Lose the drama, kiddo, and calm down. You'll do whatever you gotta do. And you gotta be strong now, you hear me?"

I gulped back a fresh flood of tears as the elevator jerked to a halt on the top floor of the courthouse. I stepped out and stared at two enormous metal doors before us. A buzzer blare was so deafening that I jumped and grabbed PoPo's arm; the metal doors slid apart. PoPo clutched my elbow and steered me into a large stark-white room. The doors slid closed behind us.

Claustrophobia seized me and I was filled with an icy, overwhelming panic. Somewhere behind these walls, maybe even behind bars, was Carolyn. They had taken her from the courtroom, hand-cuffed like some escaped serial killer. Didn't they understand that Carolyn couldn't be locked up? She had to have the doors open, the lights on. She had to be able to get out...

I couldn't think, couldn't breathe, couldn't focus on anything that made sense. The law enforcement officer who walked toward us now was moving too slowly, as if he were under water, and his fleshy face seemed stretched, distorted. What was he, anyway? A sheriff? An FBI agent? A U.S. Marshal? Why was he smirking like that? He had no right, no reason...

"Are you here to see Carolyn Huebner?" He pronounced her last name *Hoob-ner*, like anyone else who didn't know her from Adam.

Larry stepped forward, his hand outstretched. "Yes, sir. I'm Larry Huebner." He emphasized the correct pronunciation: *Heeb-ner*. "I'm her husband."

The officer made no move to shake his hand, but stared intently at Larry's pale face. I knew what he was thinking.

How could this man be crazy enough to sit on a witness stand in front of God and everyone and beg for his wife's freedom? How could he say, so reasonably and with such quiet assurance, that he understood his wife? How could he be so certain that she had simply snapped under the pressure of her work and her own past?

*How could he know, beyond any shadow of a doubt, that she had never intended to kill anyone, that she had deliberately laid a trail of mistakes that guaranteed her own destruction, not his?*

Yet Larry Huebner had uttered those words on a witness stand less than an hour earlier and set himself up to look like a fool in front of a disbelieving world.

If this officer had one ounce of insight, I thought bitterly, he'd know that Larry Huebner was a long way from a fool. He'd realize that ridicule was a small price to pay compared to what he'd lose if his wife told the truth...

"I know who you are," the officer said, obviously unimpressed. "Who're these other folks?"

Larry flushed brick-red in angry humiliation and dropped his arm to his side. "This is retired Texas Ranger Jerome Preiss. He sits on Carolyn's Board of Directors for Texas Child Search, Inc. And this is Ronni Hoessli, Carolyn's chief assistant and her best friend."

"Fine. You're just going to have a few minutes once she's through with her attorney, so get your goodbyes together now."

"Seed," PoPo muttered under his breath as the officer swaggered away. I stifled a hysterical giggle. That was what PoPo called every low-life scumbag on the street: a *seed*. It seemed particularly appropriate now.

"Mrs. Huebner wants to see someone named *Ronni*."

Startled, I turned to see a heavy-set woman in a gray uniform standing beside a large door I hadn't noticed before. I took a deep breath.

"That's me. I'm Ronni."

The woman's stern features relaxed as she gave a sweet smile that brought fresh tears to my eyes. She looks kind, almost maternal, I thought gratefully. That's good. That's important. *Carolyn's been looking for a mama for as long as I've known her…*

"In here, Ronni." She held the door open. "Make it quick, honey."

The room wasn't any larger than a phone booth, and my five-foot, one-hundred-pound body felt cramped as I sat on a tiny bench attached to the wall. I gazed blindly through a glass window in front of me. It didn't even register that Carolyn was sitting there.

Her sharp voice shocked me. "Are you listening to me, Ronni?" I sat up straight and met those blue-gray eyes obediently. "It's going to be all right. They'll let me out in three months, you'll see. I'm only going to Lexington Penitentiary for a medical and psychiatric evaluation, remember? George says the judge had to do this. We had so much publicity he couldn't just let me walk out. Do you hear me?"

I stared at her, marveling at her control. Was this the same woman who had sobbed her heart out night after night in my home just a couple of months ago? Was this the same woman who had flown into a panic because a light was off or a door was closed? Was this the same woman who seemed to regress into a spoiled ten-year-old when a phone call wasn't returned or a meeting didn't go as planned?

No, this was the Carolyn Huebner who had so awed me the very first time I met her. This was the Carolyn Huebner who was intimidating, strong and utterly invincible.

*Where in the world had she come from? For that matter, where in the world had she been?*

"I hear you."

"Okay." Carolyn's voice softened and she placed one hand against a square screen in the center of the glass. I pressed my own hand against it. "Ronni, I've got to say this fast. I want you to know how much you've meant to me. I've never known anyone in my whole life who's been as good a friend to me as you have." Her voice cracked for the first time and she looked away. "Don't leave me, Ronni. I need you now."

"I'm here, Carolyn. You know that. I'll always be here."

"You'll look after Larry and Audra for me, won't you?"

I nodded.

Carolyn pressed her hand even harder against the screen. "There's one more thing, Ronni. It means more to me than anything else in the world."

Blinded by tears, I could only whisper, "What?"

"Write my story. Please, Ronni. No one else knows me like you do. I want people to know my story. I want people to know who I am. I want people to understand how this happened. I don't want to go down in history as this crazy woman who tried to kill her husband. Not after everything I've been through..." Her voice trailed away.

"Please, Ronni...please help me. You're a writer—you can do this. You know what happened. You were there. If you don't write this, it won't get written. I'll never allow anyone else that much access to my life."

I felt invisible shackles snap shut around my heart, locking me into a promise I was terrified to keep. Yet I knew she was right. Carolyn's story had to be told by someone who had walked beside her and witnessed how it had all come about.

"The truth, Ronni. I want you to tell the truth."

I stared at her. The whole truth *couldn't* come out. Carolyn had just copped a plea so that it *wouldn't* come out. Everyone—except her husband—had told her that she could win this case, but Carolyn couldn't go before a jury and tell the world what she didn't want anyone to know. Not even for her own freedom would she do that.

Carolyn Huebner had allowed herself to look like a cold-blooded killer, and for what? For whom? How many people had she taken the fall for?

*Her husband.*

*A frightened little girl.*

*A tortured mother.*

*Even...me.*

Yet Larry could have stopped it. All he had to do was tell the truth.

"I will, Carolyn," I said quietly. "I promise I'll write it. Later. But I'll write it."

That evening, as I sat between Larry and PoPo on the flight home, I had no idea of the challenges awaiting me. And when my family met me at the San Antonio Airport, I thought I was safe, secure in their love, immune from the tragedies and chaos that made up Carolyn Huebner's life.

It wouldn't be long before I discovered that nothing could have been further from reality. No single living person could tell Carolyn's entire story. At least, not back in 1987.

Because no one—not me, not Larry, not even Carolyn Huebner herself— knew the truth.

As I read these pages now, from a safe distance in the winter of 2007, I find the story so far removed from all of us that I can hardly believe it happened.

But it did happen—and I couldn't write about it then, no matter how badly Carolyn wanted me to. It was too painful; too much had yet to be explained.

And, although I never would have believed it back then, the story wasn't finished. In fact, it had just barely begun.

But more important than anything else, no one could tell the story except Carolyn herself...in her own words, using her own voice, living in her own memories...

# PART ONE

*The past is never dead. It's not even past.*

**~William Faulkner~**

# CHAPTER ONE

The early-morning sunshine streamed through a large bay window, bathing six-year-old Carolyn Sue Shaw in its warmth as she stood in the middle of the bedroom she shared with her big sister, Maureen. Humming softly to herself, Carolyn rocked her favorite baby doll in her arms before she finally stooped to place it tenderly in its cradle. She sat on the floor, crossing her pudgy legs Indian-style, and moved the cradle gently back and forth, back and forth, like she had seen her mommy do.

Carolyn looked around the room. It was her favorite room in the whole house, maybe because her daddy had built just about everything in it. The double-sized pedestal bed with the bookshelves behind it, the little seat in front of the window with all the stuffed animals on it, even the chest of drawers with the antique music box on top of it were all built by her daddy. And Carolyn had helped her mommy decorate it in that frilly lavender and white with the splashes of royal purple Mommy had called *accent colors*. Carolyn liked that term, *accent colors*. It sounded important.

She turned her attention back to her baby. "Now, Cindy, you have to go to sleep," she scolded softly, stroking the doll's white-blonde hair out of its staring glass eyes. "You kept me awake all night. Mommies have to sleep, too, you know."

"Good morning, Carolyn. How're we doing this morning?"

"Daddy!"

Carolyn jumped up and flung herself into her daddy's outstretched arms, immediately enveloped in a giant-sized bear hug. She inhaled deeply, savoring all the aromas that made him who he was—that Brylcreem gook he put on his wavy black hair, the faintly sweet fragrance of that green stuff he splashed on his face after he shaved. No one else in the world smelled quite like her daddy.

She leaned back in his arms, fixed wide blue-gray eyes on his face, and frowned. "You didn't wait for me to come get you up. Why not? I always come get you up on Saturday mornings."

Not meeting her steady gaze, he shrugged and squeezed her tightly again. Carolyn felt a tiny tremor of something she couldn't quite identify flutter in the pit of her stomach. She clung to him as he carried her across the room and sat on the edge of the bed. Twisting in his arms so that she could cuddle comfortably against him and still look up at his face, Carolyn waited for him to speak.

The silence stretched on and on and the sunlight grew warmer and warmer. Finally, bored and drowsy, she closed her eyes, stuck her thumb in her mouth and listened to his heartbeat through his scratchy wool sweater.

"Sleepy?" he asked tenderly, dropping a light kiss on top of her red-gold curls.

Carolyn nodded and spoke around her thumb. "Cindy kept me awake all night."

"Again?"

"Umhmmm."

"Why do you think she doesn't mind you?"

"Dunno."

"Maybe it's 'cause you still suck your thumb. Mommies don't usually still suck their thumbs."

Carolyn jerked her thumb out of her mouth, giggling. This was more like it. Nothing got her daddy out of a mood faster than talking about her babies, and he was sure in a mood now. She couldn't remember him ever holding on to her like this, like he didn't want to put her down, like she was the only person in the world he wanted to hold on to. It was a good feeling, the best.

"I wasn't sucking my thumb last night and she still didn't listen."

"Maybe she saw you doing it some other time."

"Nope. She never sees me."

"Carolyn, I have to tell you something, and you have to be a real big girl about it."

She felt that funny tickle in her tummy again, like a bug flittering around in it, only now she recognized the feeling. She was scared. Something in her daddy's voice scared her.

"I won't suck my thumb anymore, Daddy, I promise..."

"Carolyn, be real quiet and listen to me." His arms tightened around her again. "Your mother's coming to pick you up in a little while and you're going to go spend the whole night with her. Won't that be fun? It'll be just like the big-girl sleepovers that Maureen goes to. You'll have your own bag, and you can take your baby, and..."

Carolyn wrenched away from him and jumped to the floor. She faced him, arms stiff at her sides, hands balled into tiny fists of defiance. "She's *not* my mother! And you said I *never* had to go with her! You promised!" Carolyn's small, round chin quivered. "I won't go!"

"Carolyn, that's enough."

Subsiding immediately, she took a step backward, popped her thumb in her mouth once more, and watched him warily. This was a tone she recognized, the tone that told her she couldn't argue with him. He didn't use it very often because she could almost always get whatever she wanted, but every once in awhile she heard it and then she knew she might as well give up.

But, no matter what, her daddy never, ever broke his promises. Carolyn was so confused her head hurt. She had overheard him and Mommy lots of times when they were talking about that crazy lady—they said really bad things about her, too—and Daddy had promised Carolyn would never have to go with her. Now he said she had to go, and she was supposed to be happy about it, and it didn't make any sense because Daddy never broke his promises...

It was because she sucked her thumb. That's what it was. She broke her promise to him about sucking her thumb, and now he was breaking his promise to her. Well, she would show him she could do it. Carolyn held her thumb up and inched her way back to him.

"You can put quinine on it," she told him, her voice quavering just a little. "I don't mind."

He groaned and gathered her close to him again. As she wrapped her arms around his neck, Carolyn's heart almost stopped because she could feel him shaking. That was worse than anything else because her daddy never got upset like other people. He was stronger than anyone else in the whole world and nothing could happen that her daddy couldn't fix...

But maybe this time something had, and maybe now it was her turn to make it better. He had asked her to be a big girl, and maybe she could be, even if she didn't feel like it inside. Carolyn tried to put a big-girl smile on her lips before she pulled away, so he would see it when he looked at her.

"Will you help me pack my bag, Daddy?"

His snapping black eyes looked larger than usual because they were all watery with tears, but he nodded silently. Carolyn kept that big-girl smile planted on her face. She marched to the closet and took out a small suitcase that had once belonged to Maureen. Suddenly she stopped, stood stock-still, and stared at the floor.

"I love you, Daddy," she whispered. Then, without even thinking, she blurted, "Why don't you want me to live with you anymore?"

She felt his big hands on her shoulders. He turned her around slowly and knelt before her so that they were almost nose-to-nose. "You know better than that, Carolyn," he said firmly. "I didn't say one word about you not living here anymore. You're my best girl, my favoritest person in the whole world. Don't you even think I don't want you to live here anymore."

"But the judge said so, didn't he? That's why your lawyer was here last night."

"The judge just said we needed to give your mother a chance, that's all, and he's probably right. Maybe I just wanted to keep you to myself too much."

"But I told the judge I didn't want to go!"

"This was a different judge, sweetheart. Someone even more important than the judge you talked to. You never talked to this judge."

Carolyn cocked her head to one side, aggravated. "Then how can he tell me that I have to see her if I never talked to him?"

"Because it's his job to make hard decisions about little children. He has to do it all the time."

Carolyn shook her head firmly. "I don't see why he has to make them about me. I'm fine right here."

"I know, and I'll see you first thing tomorrow morning..." His voice cracked.

Carolyn's eyes filled. She couldn't keep playing this big-girl game. It was too hard and she was too scared.

Her thoughts tumbled over themselves as she struggled to understand what was happening in her life. But it didn't make sense or else she was just too little to understand it. Mommy said that to her sometimes: "You're just too little to understand, Carolyn..."

Then the doorbell rang and Carolyn's heart hammered so hard in her chest that it seemed to close her throat. She gulped.

"She won't hurt me, will she, Daddy?"

He stroked her hair tenderly and shook his head. "Of course not, angel. I promise."

Carolyn stared at him, hard, and tried not to think of those words: *I promise... I promise...* Those words used to mean something, but not anymore. They didn't mean anything anymore.

"And I get to come home in the morning?"

He nodded, "First thing."

"Okay." That was black and white. That was something she could understand. Carolyn reached out and patted his cheek tenderly, with an odd maturity. "I love you, Daddy," she whispered again. "I love you really lots."

"I love you, too, sweetheart. Now, let's get you packed, shall we?"

"You do it, Daddy." Carolyn walked to the cradle and lifted her doll baby out of it. "I have to get Cindy ready to go. Mommies don't leave their babies behind."

The lady sauntered up the sidewalk toward them and kicked a red tractor out of her way. She ignored it as it fell on its side. Carolyn didn't like the way she looked at all. She didn't have a friendly face. Her hair was a yucky brown, baby-fine and stringy, and she was too fat. As Carolyn thrust her thumb back into her mouth, she felt her daddy's fingers tighten around her other hand.

"Well, good mornin', y'all. It's sure a beautiful mornin', ain't it?" The lady's slow drawl was whiny, nasal, like she had a bad head cold. "You ready to come with me, Car'lyn?"

Carolyn shook her head fiercely and pressed her cheek hard into her daddy's leg. As she sucked frantically on her thumb, he stroked her long red-gold curls absently. He was calm, unhurried and deliberate. "We're going to be just fine, aren't we, sweetheart? You're going to go with Rose without any fuss, aren't you?"

*Rose.* It was the first time Carolyn had heard the lady's name. She hugged her doll a little closer.

Then her daddy asked in a voice so quiet that Carolyn recognized the threat in it immediately, "Who's that man in your car?"

Carolyn squinted against the sunlight, trying to see who he was talking about, but she could barely make out the shadowy figure behind the steering wheel. A police officer that she hadn't noticed before stepped closer to the lady.

"Uh… Excuse me… Mr. Shaw? George?" The police officer's face was scrunched up sort of funny, like he felt sick to his stomach. "George, this document says you've got to let Carolyn go with her mother. It doesn't say she can't have a male companion with her." He held out a single sheet of paper. "Do you want to see it?"

"I've seen it. I know what it says better than you do."

Carolyn's eyes filled. She popped her thumb out of her mouth and peeked around her daddy's leg.

"I want my mommy."

"I'm your mother, Car'lyn," the lady butted in, putting her hand on Carolyn's shoulder, "and that's what you'll call me, y'hear? You'll call me *Mother.*"

Carolyn shrugged away from her and glared up at her, tears now streaking down her cheeks. "Will not! My mommy's not ugly like you are!" She held her daddy's leg even tighter. "I know who you are—you're the bad lady! Where's my mommy?"

Her daddy knelt before her again and caressed her cheek with a hand that was ice-cold. "Mommy has a headache, Carolyn. You know how she gets those sometimes." He looked up at the lady. "Why don't you let her call you *Rose* to begin with? I don't think she's ready…"

"I don't care what you think. And what you think ain't really important to Car'lyn anymore, either. It's what *I* think that matters, and what I think is that she's gonna call me Mother."

He got to his feet, keeping a comforting hand on Carolyn's head, and spoke to the lady in a level, expressionless voice. "You have her back here by ten o'clock in the morning, and you have her back here in good shape. If she says one thing to me that I don't like, you won't have the legal system to deal with. You'll have me. Do I make myself clear?"

Carolyn looked up at him anxiously, noting how that little muscle in his jaw was working like it always did when he was upset. She didn't understand why he was so upset, but it was like he was going to shimmy himself right out of his own skin.

The lady seemed to notice it, too, because she tried to give a smile that was supposed to make her look nice but didn't. "Don't worry about her, Mr. Shaw. Car'lyn's my daughter. I've grown up a lot. I wouldn't hurt my own child."

Carolyn shivered as an icy chill swept over her body. That lady was crazy, calling Carolyn *my own child*. She was crazy and that's all there was to it. But there was nothing Carolyn could do about it. She had promised her daddy she would be a big girl, and that's exactly what she was going to be.

Without a word, Carolyn stepped away from her daddy, picked up her overnight bag, and lifted her face for his kiss. "Bye, Daddy. I'll see you in the morning." She held up her doll. "I'm taking Cindy with me, okay?"

"Okay."

"Tell Mommy I hope she feels better."

"I will."

Carolyn looked at him closely and the tears she saw in his eyes scared her half to death.

Carolyn squirmed to her knees in the back seat of the car and stared out the rear window. The morning sky was a solid steel gray and a faint mist blanketed the earth. Tears threatened but she bit them back, still mindful of her promise to be a big girl. She wouldn't cry, not where her daddy might see her, and not where this lady might think it was funny. The figures of her daddy and the policeman, standing like statues on the lawn, grew smaller and smaller. When the car turned a corner, Carolyn couldn't see them anymore at all.

She turned around and huddled in a corner of the back seat trying to be very quiet, like invisible, so she wouldn't bother the lady and her friend up front. The radio was playing softly and Carolyn picked up Cindy; maybe if her baby could hear the radio, she wouldn't be so scared. She knew Cindy was scared and that made her feel better, more like a big girl because she was going to have to take care of her baby. Carolyn's own mommy had told her lots of times that "mommies can't ever show how scared they are because it isn't good for the children." That thought made Carolyn feel much stronger. She didn't want to do anything that wasn't good for her baby.

"Hey, kid!" The man driving the car had a booming voice that seemed to explode from his feet. Carolyn jumped and hugged Cindy tighter. "I've got an ice cream cone up here with your name on it, but it's melting. Don't you want it?"

Carolyn started to shake her head, but her stomach rumbled and reminded her just how hungry she was. Daddy had offered her a little bowl of cereal earlier, but Carolyn couldn't eat it, and besides, she really loved ice cream. She reached out, took the cone from the lady, and slowly licked the dribbling chocolate from the sides.

"No, you can't have any," she whispered to her baby, rubbing her cheek against the doll's tousled curls. "You're too little."

"Who on earth are you talkin' to?" Rose demanded. She twisted around in the front seat and stared at Carolyn. "Don't tell me you go around talkin' to yourself."

"Aw, leave the kid alone, Rose. She's talking to her baby there, aren't you, kid?"

Eyes wide, Carolyn nodded, licking the ice cream more frantically as she struggled against a boulder-sized lump in her throat. The man didn't seem too bad, but the look on Rose's face was unlike anything Carolyn had ever seen before. Her lip was curled up funny, kind of like her dog Buster when he snarled, and her eyes were narrow—almost slits—in a face the color of cookie dough. Carolyn took a big bite of the ice cream cone and scrubbed at her chocolatey chin with a corner of Cindy's dress. "Don't you tell me what to do, John Goldstein," Rose flashed back in a low voice. "Where were you when I needed you, anyway? Sittin' out here in this car, just watchin' while I got turned loose to the lions! I needed you there with me, didn't I? You're my lawyer, aren't you? But no! You're sittin' here in this car, leavin' me alone with a man that hates my guts... Hell, he coulda killed me and you wouldn't of stopped him."

"Watch your mouth in front of the kid," the man said, yawning. "She's a good kid."

"Drop dead, Goldstein. You don't know nothin' about kids."

Carolyn almost swallowed the ice cream cone whole. "Don't you say that about my daddy!"

Suddenly, completely without warning, Rose's arm shot over the seat like a streak of lightning. She grabbed a handful of Carolyn's hair. "Let's get a few things straight, you little snot. Number One, he's *not* your daddy. Number Two, I'll say anything about him that I want to. And Number Three, don't you ever sass me back again!" She tightened her grip in Carolyn's hair and yanked her head to one side. "Do you hear me, little girl? Don't you ever sass me back again!"

Carolyn squeezed her eyes tightly shut against the excruciating pain in her head, but she didn't whimper and she didn't struggle. All she could think about was the freezing ice cream dripping into her lap and staining her new overalls. Now she was really going to get in trouble when she got home...

"Let go of her hair, stupid," the man said calmly, pulling off the busy street they had been traveling on and slowing down. "Leave the kid alone. You're going have us in trouble before we even get her out of Pennsylvania."

Carolyn's head swam as Rose released that fierce grip on her hair. Her nose felt funny, like if she blew it she wouldn't know for sure it was there, and the back of her throat felt real thick, like her tongue had become part of it. She closed her eyes slowly and listened, almost entranced, to the sound of her own deep, even breathing.

She was floating around in her head. Her body felt like it didn't weigh anything. She was part of the seat, and the seat was made out of cotton balls. The white softness enveloped her, covered her up, became one with her. The uneaten ice cream cone fell to her lap...

And then there was nothing.

Shivering, Carolyn came awake slowly and found herself lying on a chilly hardwood floor. She was in a tiny room about the size of her mommy's kitchen pantry and eerie shadows danced over the walls, created by fading sunlight that barely managed to penetrate the filthy window above her. A lumpy mattress was thrown into the middle of the room.

Carolyn had never been so hungry in her life, but her stomach felt all topsy-turvy like when she took her first roller coaster ride. Her mouth tasted nasty. She tried to run her tongue over her dry lips, but it was too fat and stuck to the roof of her mouth. Carolyn rubbed her eyes groggily and squinted, trying to see through the creeping darkness.

It was then that she noticed the heavy chain wrapped tightly around her left ankle and connected to an old metal radiator like the one Grandma Rankin had in the basement of her farmhouse. Frowning, she touched the chain and tried to understand why it was there. She wriggled her foot and tried to slip her thumb between the chain and her ankle, but a lock firmly secured it. They had given her enough chain to walk a little, but that was all. Why would someone want to lock her up? She jerked at the chain angrily and pain shot up her leg. Her eyes filled with tears.

The window above the radiator caught her attention. Moving carefully so that the chain wouldn't rub her ankle raw, Carolyn climbed on top of the radiator and eased herself to her knees. Making a tiny fist, she rubbed against layers of dust and dirt on the glass and peered outside. Even though she was confused and terrified, she caught her breath in wonder.

Miles and miles of water, bathed in a glorious sunset of pink, lavender and gray, stretched as far as she could see. Ships and boats were all lined up near a tall bridge that crossed over the water. Although a single straggly tree was right outside the window and the backyard was flat, dotted by little brown tufts of dead grass, Carolyn scarcely noticed. She was mesmerized by the water.

Carolyn had seen pictures of the ocean before in her daddy's set of *National Geographic* magazines, but she had never realized how big it was. It made a lot of noise, too. The rhythmic roar of rushing water pounded against the earth, then rumbled and splashed as it rolled away again. It was a soothing, almost hypnotic sound unlike anything Carolyn had ever heard before.

She pulled her fascinated gaze from the ocean and squinted, peering harder into the gathering darkness as she sought some familiar landmark. Her home had been nestled in tall trees, her neatly-trimmed backyard creeping right up to the edge of deep woods, and there had been jagged mountaintops visible from her front sidewalk. Here, there seemed to be nothing but sky and water.

None of this made any sense. Why was she chained to a radiator in a place she had never been before? As she squirmed down from her cold metal vantage point, something bitter burned the back of her throat. She was hungry and she had to go to the bathroom and she was going to throw up.

Carolyn tried to whistle, but it came out in an empty puff of air. She tried again, fighting tears. Daddy always whistled when he got scared, and he said he learned it from the little boy in *The King and I*. Carolyn had seen it at the picture show with her daddy last year and she had learned to whistle that very afternoon. But today it didn't seem to help. She just couldn't whistle now.

A fresh wave of nausea washed over her, bathing her in a film of icy perspiration. Carolyn gagged, fighting it. Finally, in an attempt to get warm, she curled herself into a tight fetal position beside the radiator and stuck her thumb in her mouth, sucking frantically. She was so hungry, but her stomach cramped and lurched like she was going to get diarrhea. That nasty bitterness burned her throat again.

Carolyn closed her eyes and willed herself to think of something else. What could she think about? She was too scared to think, too lonely, too hungry, too sick…

As she lay with her ear against the floor, soothing herself with her own suckling noises, Carolyn could hear clanging sounds beneath her, like silverware hitting dishes. Deep voices rumbled, followed by high-pitched laughter, and for a moment it sounded to Carolyn like someone was having a party. She could hear a type of music she never heard before. Carolyn concentrated hard, trying to figure out why all this felt so familiar.

*Jack's Soda Fountain*! Her thumb popped out of her mouth and her heart actually seemed to leap into her throat. Maybe she wasn't so far from home after all! *Jack's Soda Fountain* was only a couple of miles from her house. Her daddy used to take her there every Friday after he closed his hardware store.

As a sudden rush of strength and energy flooded her body, Carolyn pounded a balled-up fist against the floor. "I'm here! I'm here! Help me... please... help me..." But her shriek had been no louder than a whisper, the banging of her fist no stronger than the patter of soft rain drops.

Although Carolyn's head spun with the effort, she managed to focus on the sounds beneath her. There was food down there—she could just about smell it. There were grownups, too. Someone would help her; someone would find her daddy and take her home. There was music, people laughing—kind people who wouldn't let Rose keep a little girl chained to a radiator...

All she had to do was get down there.

Then Carolyn remembered the water, the lack of mountains and trees, and she knew she was a long way from home. Nobody downstairs knew George and Betty Shaw, or *Jack's Soda Fountain*, or anything about a little girl lost.

The tiny room was pitch-black now. Even the shadows on the wall had disappeared. Yet somehow, to Carolyn, the darkness seemed to develop a pulsating life of its own. Her imagination, always creative and visual, slammed into action.

What was it her daddy had told her? Carolyn fought to remember. *Your imagination is playing tricks on you.* That was it! She could hear his voice even now, right here in this room. He was chuckling as he poked in the corners and felt his way through the darkness. *See? There are no monsters here, no bogeymen. They wouldn't dare come and bother my Carolyn!*

But her daddy wasn't here now to stop them. Maybe her daddy had kept them away all those years... and now they had found her.

Carolyn squeezed her eyes tightly shut. Maybe if she couldn't see them, they couldn't see her. But she knew she wasn't alone in this room. Things came out in the darkness, ugly things, bad things. Like cockroaches. They were afraid of the light—Mommy said so. Snakes liked the dark, too, and so did spiders.

Snakes were behind the walls. Carolyn knew it. She could feel it. In just a minute they would slither right up to her and wrap themselves around her, their little pointy tongues darting in and out of their mouths, teasing her, hissing... And the spiders! She knew all about spiders. They were black with hairy bodies and big eyes and they built silky houses that felt creepy against your skin and got tangled up in your hair. Spiders didn't like strangers to come to their house, and Carolyn was a stranger, and this was their house...

The chain clanked against the floor as she tried to pull her legs even closer to her trembling body. Desperately seeking even the tiniest glimmer of moonlight, Carolyn stared at the little window above the radiator. But it was black outside. She had never seen a night so dark. Still she stared, keeping her eyes away from the walls that hid the snakes. Then, slowly, a grinning white face appeared at the window...a little man with big teeth...

Carolyn buried her face in her arms, squirmed, twisted, whimpered…beyond loneliness, beyond hope, beyond terror. Her mommy's voice came then, whisper-soft in the darkness as it floated around her head, enveloping her in a cozy, warm, silken blanket. "Think of something nice, Carolyn. When you're really scared, think of something nice…"

Even as Carolyn looked around frantically and reached a small, trembling hand out into the darkness, the voice faded away. But Carolyn remembered—she and her mommy had done this before. Together. During the bad times. She could plant a picture in her brain, a picture of what she wanted most, a picture of where she felt most comfortable, and she could go to that place. No one could stop her, and no one could make her leave.

Carolyn closed her eyes and concentrated, hard. She saw the picture. It was tiny, like at the end of a long, long tunnel, but it was sharp and it was focused and it was real.

It was a picture of her house in White Oak, Pennsylvania. It was small, red brick, built on the side of a hill. A little red tractor was overturned in the grass. Mommy and Daddy stood on the sidewalk with her dog, Buster, between them. They all stared down the street, watching for her. They were like statues as they waited.

Leading up to them, winding through the tunnel, was a Yellow Brick Road, just like the one in *The Wizard of Oz*. Carolyn moved herself from the pitch-black room into the tunnel and began walking toward the house. Night turned into day and the house was bathed in the pink-and-blue radiance of a glorious sunrise. Mommy began to wave slowly, as if she couldn't quite believe her eyes, and Daddy started to run toward her, his arms outstretched, as Carolyn came closer and closer to the house. He engulfed her in that giant bear hug and he smelled so good, like Brylcreem and aftershave lotion.

With lightning speed, Carolyn whizzed out of the picture and slammed back into the pitch-black room, hitting the floor with an audible thud. Tears came and she whimpered again, curling herself into an ever tighter ball as she tried to blend into the darkness and make herself invisible. She fought for the picture, but it wouldn't come back. There were too many spiders and snakes and white-faced little men with big teeth…

*Come back. Come back. Oh, please come back …*

# CHAPTER TWO

"Well, I've made my decision, Rose, and that's just the way it is."

Carolyn came awake with a jerk. The man's angry voice was so close it sounded like he was in this tiny room with her, but she knew she was alone. She was too tired and weak to lift her head, yet she tried hard to listen and understand. She didn't know who this man was, but he was angry, so maybe he was on her side…

Rose's whiny, bored voice interrupted Carolyn's hopeful thoughts, then shattered them completely.

"Oh, don't be ridiculous, Redmond. Why do we have to go through this every time I turn around? Just let me get away from you for five minutes and you start screamin' about how you're never seein' me again. Well, I got your precious little bastard, Deanna, don't forget. And you can bet your last buck I'll see to it that your wife's family finds out…"

"Don't waste your breath. They already know. They understand. It's over, Rose."

"You're full of crap."

A child's high-pitched voice giggled, "Mommy, that's a bad word! You said a bad word!"

Carolyn was instantly alert. There was another little girl here, someone who might help her. Maybe she didn't want to be here, either. Maybe she was stolen from her mommy, too.

"Shut up and go to your room."

The man cleared his throat. "Don't talk to her like that."

Rose laughed. "Who're you to tell me how to talk to her? You're leavin', remember?"

"She's still my daughter."

"Huh! Maybe."

"I can't believe what a slut you are."

Carolyn tucked herself more tightly into the corner, trying to get away from these angry voices. She had never heard big people talk to each other this way. People were kind in her house, even though her mommy and daddy sometimes argued just like other grownups did. But they didn't call each other names and they didn't talk ugly to little children.

Rose was screaming now. "You'll think *slut* when I get through with you, Redmond Kincaid! You're not gonna come in here and saddle me with a kid and then just skedaddle…"

"I'll pay for her."

"You're not kiddin' you'll pay for her! Up to the day you die, you'll pay for her!"

Glass shattered against the wall. "You listen to me, Rose Lovell! I've cleaned out one full bank account getting that kid of yours back—don't talk to me about owing you one single thing! I don't! Whatever I do for Deanna now, I do because she's my daughter. I don't do it for you. Even if my wife *is* in a nuthouse, she's twice the woman you'll ever be! I'm sorry to tell you this, baby, but you're just not that good!"

Carolyn heard a low, throaty chuckle, then sounds of people moving around the room. The little girl they called Deanna cried out, "Mommy, what're you doing?"

"I told you to go to your room!"

There was the crash of a chair hitting the floor, then the sound of someone running. A door slammed. Carolyn squeezed her eyes tightly shut, waiting for something, anything. There was nothing but silence. Then a gasp, a moan, a sigh…

"I hate you," the man said softly, "I hate you…" His voice cracked and he groaned, low in his throat. "Oh, how I hate you…"

"I know, baby, I know. Come to Mama, Red, come to Mama."

Carolyn relaxed and crawled to the lumpy mattress in the middle of the room. Her chain clanked against the floor and rubbed hard against her ankle, but she ignored it. She was so tired, so very, very tired. She curled herself into a ball on the mattress and closed her eyes.

The rhythmic squeak of an old sofa in the other room lulled her to sleep…

*Buster is barking, tugging at her shoelaces, running back and forth to show her that special place where he has hidden his favorite bone. The sky is cloudless, pristine blue, and the early autumn air is chilly, crisp, nipping at her nose until it's numb. Daddy is in the driveway, working on Maureen's old blue clunker, and Mommy is sitting on the front porch, a cup of coffee in one hand, a cigarette in the other. Carolyn feels cozy and warm on the inside, full-tummied with a breakfast of pancakes and orange juice. She runs across the lawn, shrieking with laughter, Buster hot on her heels. Music drifts from Maureen's car radio…*

Carolyn awoke with a start. Moonlight flooded through the little window above the radiator, casting her own shadow against the wall. She lay very still on the lumpy mattress, waiting for the dream to return, yearning, longing for it. It had been so real, so vivid, that even the fragrance of Mommy's morning coffee still lingered in the air and cigarette smoke actually tickled her nose.

Then she noticed an empty plate beside the mattress, but she had no memory of eating. An empty glass lay on its side near the plate, but she had no memory of drinking. Someone had brought the food and drink into this room, but Carolyn never heard a thing.

Carolyn shivered violently—she felt icy cold from the inside out. She wrapped her arms around her knees, trying to hold in body warmth, and realized that the mattress beneath her was wet. Her fanny felt mushy and burned as if it were raw. Her chin quivered as she fought humiliated tears. She was a big girl, but she had wet the bed—and pooped in her pants. Carolyn eased her thumb into her mouth, closed her eyes, and once again tried to sleep, tried to find the dream...

It comes more easily now. The Yellow Brick Road is clearer and so is the little house built on the side of a hill. Carolyn skips toward it, happy, smiling, singing to herself. Buster scampers beside her, pausing to pee on first this bush and then another, but he doesn't look like Buster anymore. He is small, with black curly hair, like Toto, and he can sing, too. Carolyn can hear the words, clear and sharp: *There's no place like home...There's no place like home...*

Suddenly, amidst a cloud of smoke and a clap of thunder, the Wicked Witch of the West appears on the Yellow Brick Road, blocking Carolyn's path. Her black cape billows as an icy gust of wind lifts it; Buster growls and shows his teeth. Carolyn looks at the witch and it has Rose's face, and Carolyn is paralyzed, rooted to the road, because she knows she can never go home again.

In a flash, the scene changes and Carolyn is riding her little red tractor down the hill. She is going to visit Grandma Rankin at her big old farmhouse, and they are going to play tea party. Little Jimmy Rankin will be there and Carolyn will have to put up with him, but that's all right because Jimmy's always there and he's not too bad for a boy. She sees him standing outside, tall and red-haired, waving to her, and she waves back...

Then, Carolyn is curled spoon-fashion against Maureen's warm body in the big double bed they have always shared. Their heads rest on ruffled pillows, and a lavender comforter covers them. Stuffed animals line up on the window seat and watch over them, and Cindy is crying in her cradle. Carolyn can hear Mommy fixing breakfast and Daddy singing in the shower down the hall...

Carolyn stands with the little children's choir in front of the congregation, singing *What a Friend We Have in Jesus*. Daddy sits in the front row, nodding in time with the music, a proud smile on his face as he gives her a thumbs-up every once in a while. Mommy sits beside him in her pretty blue hat with the flowers on it and Carolyn feels all warm inside because they are so pleased with her.

This is her family. These are the people who love her.

Suddenly lightning crashes through the roof of the church and splits the congregation down the middle. There is fire and smoke and screaming and crying as people run around trying to find their children. But all the children are gone. They have vanished into the smoke as if they had never been born at all... everyone except Carolyn. As she stands alone, a jagged crack tears through her forehead, then breaks away, slowly, until her entire face is split down the center. Her eyes change shape, her mouth is ripped, blood gushes...

Carolyn jolted awake and sat straight up on the mattress. She screamed and screamed and screamed.

No one came. The nights and days blended together until they were all the same to Carolyn and she completely lost track of time. But it didn't matter. She dreamed of food, but she was no longer hungry. She dreamed of toilets and bubble baths, but she no longer cared that she lay in her own poop. She dreamed of filled water pitchers, but she was no longer thirsty.

Carolyn stayed in the middle of the mattress, curled up in a tight fetal position, and stared, almost hypnotized, at the small window above the radiator. Sunlight streamed in as best it could, struggling to illuminate the little room, but it looked more like a gold and yellow rainbow to Carolyn than real sunshine. She couldn't remember what real sunshine felt like. She was always cold to the bone.

Carolyn often heard the deep voices of men coming in and out, always followed by that rhythmic squeak-squeak-squeak in the room next to hers, but some sixth sense of self-preservation kept her from crying out. Whatever was going on in there couldn't be good because Rose laughed a lot and seemed to enjoy it too much. That in itself was enough to keep Carolyn quiet.

Only Carolyn's imagination kept her going. She relied on it like her daddy had relied on prayer. When the hunger pangs became nauseating, she visualized her mommy's dinner table covered with her favorite dishes—fried chicken, mashed potatoes, gravy, and a green bean casserole—and ate until she was full. When her tongue grew parched from thirst, she pictured the icy little stream that ran by the Rankin farmhouse and drank until her lips were moist and soft. When the itching and burning on her bottom became unbearable, she imagined herself in a tub of soothing water like the one her mommy had put her in when she had the chicken pox, and the throbbing went away.

Carolyn survived by going to those warm, comforting places in her own mind. Only there did she find a release from terror and hunger and pain...

"Holy crap, what on earth is that smell?"

Rose stood in the door way, her fingers splayed against her lumpy hips, and looked around the room, her nose wrinkled in disgust. A little girl with black curly hair peeked around her and made a retching sound.

"Yuchhh! She's nasty, Mommy!"

Carolyn curled up tighter, her knees almost tucked beneath her chin, and squeezed her eyes tightly shut, trying to become invisible.

"Shut up." Without any anger at all, Rose slapped behind her. "Go to your room."

"Mommy…"

"Now!"

Carolyn felt the hot tears squeeze from beneath her closed eyelids. One ran unchecked into her ear. She didn't move.

"Hey, kid, you hungry?"

Carolyn's stomach jumped in response, but she shook her head.

"No? Well, you been in here for almost a week. I was gonna take you downstairs for some real food. You don't wanna go?"

Carolyn's eyes flew open. Downstairs! The soda fountain was downstairs! She didn't care about the food—she honestly wasn't hungry. But there were people down there. Someone would see her. Someone would know…

"Don't go gettin' any bright ideas, kid," Rose continued lazily. "You say one word to anyone and I'll beat you to death and no one'll ever miss you. You understand what I'm sayin'?"

Tongue-tied with terror as well as excitement, Carolyn managed a nod. Rose came into the room and threw open the little window. A soft breeze that smelled like salt and felt strangely heavy ruffled Carolyn's hair. As she turned her face toward it, trying to breathe deeply of the fresh air, the stench of her own body turned her stomach.

The sounds of the ocean were thunderous with the window open, but Carolyn felt an immediate kinship with it. They were the sounds of life happening outside: waves rushing in and rolling away, children shrieking on the sand, birds screeching overhead. Fighting nausea, Carolyn concentrated on the new sounds that told her she was still alive.

"Get off that bed, kid. I can't take you anywhere 'til I get you cleaned up."

Carolyn bit back a cry of pain as she straightened her legs and tried to ease herself into a standing position. Every muscle shrieked its resistance to movement, but Carolyn was equally determined. She would get out of this room, no matter what it took. Rose squatted to unlock the chain around Carolyn's ankle.

"Leg's asleep, huh?"

Weak-kneed with hunger and the strain of standing, Carolyn shook like a leaf in the wind. She watched, fascinated, as the chain fell to the floor, a harmless pile of metal that no longer held her captive. Yet for just a moment she missed it.

She felt naked without it, even fought an urge to grab it and put it back on. It had become a part of her, like her baby doll or the thumb she immediately popped in her mouth.

Suddenly, moving so fast that Carolyn squealed in terror, Rose grabbed a handful of the red-gold curls that cascaded down Carolyn's back and jerked her head sideways.

"You got puke and crap in your hair. How'd you get puke and crap in your hair? We gotta cut it all off, that's all. C'mon, kid, march!"

"No!" Carolyn planted her feet on the floor, willing her trembling body to stand firm, and thrust her chin out defiantly. "I can wash my own hair! I can! Mommy taught me how!"

"Look here, you little snot!" Rose jerked her up and shoved her face so close to Carolyn's that they were eyeball-to-eyeball. "You ain't got no mommy but me, you understand? I'm your mommy, and I'm gonna cut your hair!"

She grabbed Carolyn by the arm and dragged her kicking and flailing as weakly as a sick puppy down a narrow hallway, through a dark living room, and into a filthy kitchen that smelled like old grease and sour milk. She threw Carolyn into a chair and jerked open a drawer, rummaging through it until she found a pair of jagged-edged scissors.

"Now sit still, you hear me? I'm not takin' you out lookin' like somethin' the cat drug in!"

Carolyn's lower lip quivered as she fought tears of frustrated resignation. This was just another battle she couldn't win. But someday, she promised herself, someday…

Long, thick clumps of red-blonde hair showered around her and fell on the floor, still curling and shimmering as if they had a life of their own. Tears streamed down Carolyn's cheeks, burning her swollen eyes, and she gave an occasional hiccough. Rose chattered away heedlessly.

"You know, this hair should've come off a long time ago. You're entirely too full of yourself—I knew that the first time I saw you. I ain't got time for that crap. I don't know what old George and Betty Shaw told you, but it was all lies. They ain't your mommy and daddy. They're your grandma and grandpa. Your daddy's name was Art Lovell and he was a worthless piece of crap. He stole you from me and *dumped* you on George and Betty Shaw. They didn't want you. They just didn't want *me* to have you is all. Now get over here by the sink so's I can clean you up."

Carolyn drew in a long, shuddering breath and deliberately averted her eyes from the piles of golden curls on the floor. Her neck felt naked yet pleasantly cool as she followed Rose to the kitchen sink, where she was running steaming hot water. Carolyn was too frightened to even raise her hand to touch her cropped hair.

"Deanna!"

The little girl with the black curls poked her head around the door so quickly that Carolyn knew she had been standing there all the time. Carolyn looked at her with interest and more than a little envy. Her hair wasn't all cut off and she sure didn't look like she didn't get enough to eat. Carolyn didn't like the way she looked. She didn't look nice, even if she was just a real little girl. Her eyes were slitty, like Rose's, and she had her button-nose stuck up in the air like she was better than everyone else. Nope, Carolyn told herself, she's not going to be my friend...

"Deanna, go get those pants and tee-shirt I picked up from the Salvation Army and bring 'em here. The ones that're too big for you."

"Mommy, she smells nasty!"

"Go!"

Carolyn ducked her head in humiliation. No one ever said she smelled nasty before.

"Lift your arms."

In automatic obedience, Carolyn raised her hands as Rose pulled the vomit-stained shirt over her head. She left them in the air even as she stepped out of her overalls and stood in the soothing sea breeze, clad only in her cotton panties.

Rose chuckled. "You can drop your arms, kid. I'm not gonna shoot you." Carolyn didn't answer. The warm, soapy wash cloth felt wonderful against her itchy skin. Even Rose's hands were gentle. Carolyn closed her eyes and sighed.

Suddenly, without warning, agony shrieked through her body. Carolyn screamed and lunged away from Rose's tightening grip. For a moment the pain was so excruciating that she had no idea what caused it or which way to turn to get away from it. Then, vaguely, in the shadowy recesses of her mind, she realized that Rose was trying to pull down her panties.

"Will you shut up and stand still? Holy crap, Car'lyn..."

Carolyn screamed again, over and over. The pain was too much to bear. She couldn't stand it, she just couldn't. It felt like her skin was coming off with the panties, like strips and strips of it were peeling away from her bones.

Rose slapped one hand over Carolyn's mouth. With the other, she jerked the panties straight down to her ankles. Scarcely missing a beat, she placed the warm, soapy washcloth against Carolyn's raw bottom.

"I'm just tryin' to help you, Car'lyn! Be quiet, y'hear?"

Sobbing, gasping for breath, Carolyn managed to nod. She was weak, sweating, shaking with nausea and pain. Closing her eyes, she scrambled frantically in her mind to find the warm, comforting place she always went to, the place no one could make her leave.

With Rose's voice whining nasally in the background, Carolyn found it: the Yellow Brick Road that always took her home. She marched down it, stronger and healthier and braver than anyone else, until she heard nothing except her own voice whispering, *"There's no place like home. There's no place like home. There's no place like home..."*

Rose's fingers dug like claws into Carolyn's shoulder as they clambered down the rickety stairs outside an apartment building and entered a soda fountain. It was all Carolyn could do to keep from screaming and jerking away from Rose's painful grip, but her mind was too focused on the wafting fragrances of food to do anything that stupid. Suddenly all she wanted to do was eat.

"Get up on that stool and keep your mouth shut," Rose said in a low voice, tightening her grip on Carolyn's shoulder. "You're deaf, dumb and stupid, understand?"

Carolyn flashed her a look of pure hatred before she lowered her eyes, nodded meekly, and climbed up on the stool at the counter. She folded her hands in her lap and gazed down at them.

"What can I do you for, ladies?"

"A pancake special for the kid, Max, with extra hash browns. Can you do that?"

"Sure thing."

From beneath lowered lashes, Carolyn could see that the man Rose had called Max was very fat and just as dirty. He had black stuff under his fingernails, brown stuff smeared across the apron that covered his enormous belly, and yellow stuff stuck between the gaps in his front teeth. Even the silver hair dangling over his forehead was greasy. Carolyn didn't care. He had food and nothing else mattered.

"What's your name, little lady?"

"Don't waste your time talkin' to her." Rose's voice was calm but firm. "She's stone-cold deaf, dumb as a stump, and mighty hungry. Belongs to a girlfriend of mine—didn't take care of her, y'know? Dropped her off with me almost a week ago and never came back. Some people! Anyways, I haven't been able to get her to eat a thing. I'm hopin' maybe you can."

Max lifted an eyebrow and pushed himself away from the counter. "Then I better get a move on, huh?"

Rose didn't answer. She just nodded, obviously bored with his attempt at chit-chat, and rested her hand on Carolyn's knee. When the swinging doors to the kitchen had closed behind him, Rose leaned closer to Carolyn.

"You're doin' real good, Miss Fancy Pants. I guess it ain't hard for you to play stupid. Comes kinda natural, don't it?"

Carolyn nodded again and stared transfixed at the hand gripping her knee. Those fingers were a lot stronger than they looked, and that hand could come out of nowhere to knock a person's head completely around. Carolyn tried to swallow the lump in her throat. *Why does she hate me so much? What did I ever do to her? She doesn't even know me …*

"Don't you start that bawlin'," Rose muttered to Carolyn's quivering chin. "I've had it with all that snivelin'. Deanna don't do that and she's two years younger'n you."

Turning her head slightly, Carolyn bit her lip, stared out the window, and began counting the cars that went by. She did it without thinking because it was a game she played with her daddy every Friday when they went to make a bank deposit from his hardware store. She would stand at the window and read the license plates while he talked to the bank teller. The more cars she got right, the more ice cream she could eat later. She had learned to read that way and now she could count to over a hundred.

When a pickup truck backed into the parking lot, the license plate was as clear as anything. For the first time, Carolyn knew where she was. *Texas*, the plate said. She was in Texas.

Carolyn frowned, trying to hide her excitement. Where was Texas? She had heard of it because her big brother, Bobby, always wanted to go there so he could see a real cowboy. Cowboys were a big deal to Bobby. He said they rode bulls and killed Indians and broke horses. Carolyn couldn't see why anyone would want to break horses—they were so pretty and what if you couldn't fix them later? And Carolyn didn't see any horses here. All she saw were beat-up old cars and funny-looking trucks …

"Here you go, my darlin'."

Max slid a plate in front of Carolyn, then moved down the counter to clear away some dirty dishes. As she stared at the food in wonder, her stomach gave a low growl and her hands trembled. Her mouth actually watered. There was a stack of already cut-up pancakes swimming in butter and dark syrup, and a mound of stringy little potatoes off to the side. She looked pleadingly at Rose, still unable to believe she was going to be allowed to eat.

Rose's voice was so soft and sweet that Carolyn was more terrified than ever. "Go ahead, baby. It's yours."

Carolyn's hand shook as she picked up her fork and stabbed it into a piece of pancake. It seemed to melt in her mouth, and as soon as she had swallowed the first bite, she was ravenous. The more she ate, the hungrier she became. As she concentrated on getting the food into her mouth before Rose could change her mind, Carolyn was only half-aware that Max had returned to his place at the counter.

"Y'know, Rose," Max was saying in a low voice, "I been thinkin'."

"Yeah? Sounds dangerous to me."

"Naw, I do it sometimes." He chuckled, leaned his elbows on the counter, and rested his chin in his hands. He eyed Carolyn. "You sure she can't hear us?"

"I'm sure."

"Well, I been hearin' lots of noises upstairs. Know what I mean?"

Rose's fingers tightened convulsively on Carolyn's knee. "Nope," she drawled, "I don't have no clue."

Carolyn shoveled large bites of pancakes into her mouth as fast as she could, trying to ignore the pain shooting up her leg. Max was upsetting Rose, and Carolyn wanted to eat as much as she could before Rose jerked her out of the soda fountain. "Well, see, it's like this. I been hearin' lots of thumps and stuff—last night I even heard a scream or sumpin'. You didn't hear nothin'?"

Rose's grip was so tight that the bottom of Carolyn's leg was numb. "Not a thing. Maybe you're havin' them night terrors again, Max."

"Hmmm. Maybe. 'Cept I'm awake when I hear it and it's even botherin' my customers. You reckon all my customers have night terrors, too?"

"I don't know, Max. You got some mighty weird customers."

Carolyn slowed down. She was getting sick to her stomach, like she was going to get diarrhea again. She tried to ignore the cramps because she was suddenly more interested in this conversation than in eating. Keeping her eyes glued to her plate, she took smaller bites and listened intently, hoping they didn't notice.

Max leaned closer. "Y'know, Rose, I done some things in my life I ain't too proud of. But one thing I ain't never done is hurt a little kid. I just don't hold with that, y'know?"

"Sure I know. Folks like that oughta be shot."

Carolyn's heart jumped so hard she almost threw up. Maybe this fat, ugly, dirty man would help her. Maybe he would call her daddy... if she could just get to him...

"Course, you know I'm gonna believe you if you tell me there ain't nothin' happenin' upstairs. I mean, we got that kinda...friendship...right? Like, you just come downstairs—you know, later on—and tell me ain't nothin' happenin' and I'll believe you..."

His voice trailed away. Carolyn's stomach sank like a rock to her feet, and Rose released her agonizing grip on Carolyn's knee. She gave a breathy little giggle that sounded more like a whimper to Carolyn than a laugh.

Rose reached over the counter and patted Max's beefy forearm. "Well, you just don't worry about a thing now, y'hear? We're awful good friends. Fact is, once I get the kid back upstairs, I'll just come right on down and we can…talk…about it some more. How's that sound?"

Carolyn finished the last of her pancakes, struggling against tears. He wasn't talking about her after all. He wasn't even thinking about her! There was something else going on here, something Carolyn didn't understand.

"You don't need to eat the plate, too," Rose said, suddenly stern again. "Come with me, kid. I need to make a phone call."

Carolyn slid off the stool obediently. Rose took her hand and stalked toward a phone booth beside the door, muttering beneath her breath.

Carolyn stared up at her, frightened again. Rose was real mad about something, and Carolyn had to go to the bathroom. Rose kept her grip on Carolyn's hand and grabbed up the telephone with the other. Cradling the receiver on her shoulder, Rose dialed rapidly and put the phone to her ear.

"Redmond Kincaid," she said in a low voice. "It's an emergency."

Carolyn gazed out the window again, trying to look bored and unconcerned. Yet she took in everything she could about her surroundings, as well as the telephone conversation going on above her head.

She knew the ocean wasn't far from this soda fountain because even the parking lot was flat and sandy, and there wasn't a tree or mountain in sight. This Texas is sure an ugly place, she thought, watching as the wind whirled dirt and sand down the narrow street.

The tension in Rose's voice as she spoke into the telephone interrupted Carolyn's faintly interested observation.

"You gotta help me, Red. I'm in trouble and I gotta get outa here. I need some money. I gotta move. Now. Today."

Carolyn frowned, confused. Why was Rose in trouble? That ugly old man wasn't going to do anything. But Rose sure sounded scared. And where had Carolyn heard the name Redmond Kincaid before? She'd heard it somewhere, but she just couldn't remember where, or when …

"Please, Red! I'll never ask you for anything ever again, I promise. Please, Red!"

As Rose gripped Carolyn's hand more tightly, her skin felt cold and slippery. Her fear was so intense that Carolyn could almost smell it. For a moment she was jubilant—it was great to see Rose so scared. Her excitement faded immediately. Whatever happened to get Rose upset, Carolyn was going to pay for. She had already learned that.

"You can't come any sooner?" Rose was pleading. Then, "Okay, okay. I'll see you after work. Thanks, baby."

Rose hung up and turned back to Max, who was still leaning on the counter, watching them with narrowed eyes.

"I'll be down in a little while, okay?" Her voice was bright and chipper, but even Carolyn could sense her underlying panic. "You'll wait for me, right?"

"Sure thing. I ain't goin' nowhere."

Carolyn cast a longing look at the telephone as Rose pushed her out the door. She could still remember her phone number in Pennsylvania. If only there was some way she could get back down here to call it…

*If only… if only…*

But there wasn't a single *if only* that would work for Carolyn, and she knew it. In five minutes she would have a chain locked back around her ankle, and sometime tonight she was moving. No one would know where she had gone. No one would look for her. No one would care.

Nausea crashed over her like one of those thundering ocean waves, then receded and left her light-headed, weak and bathed in icy perspiration. Panicked, Carolyn stopped, retched miserably and vomited.

"Holy crap, now look what you did! Splattered all over me…"

Rose jerked Carolyn's arm and dragged her toward the stairs leading up the side of the building. Carolyn followed, legs buckling as another cramp ripped through her stomach. She cried out, gasping and panting as she struggled to go with the pain, and tried to pull away.

"Don't you fight with me, you little snot! Why did I bring you back here, anyway? I wish you were dead, do you hear me? I wish you were dead!"

Suddenly, overpowering all the pain and nausea, overshadowing everything around her, Carolyn felt rage, and hatred, and an overwhelming desire for revenge. She had never felt anything as intense as this before, didn't even understand the feelings, but they were there—and immediately the sickness was gone. Disappeared. Vanished.

Carolyn lifted her face and stared hard into Rose's eyes. For the first time in her life, without even realizing what she had learned, Carolyn instinctively understood the power of hate.

# CHAPTER THREE

They had moved again.

After the door closed behind her, Carolyn heard the sound of a key turning in the lock. She stood in the center of another tiny room, her hands clasped tightly in front of her, and looked around.

A dim light on the back porch just barely illuminated the room through a single, small window set in the middle of the wall. A rusty, wrought-iron bed with a lopsided, water-stained mattress had been moved away from the window so that Carolyn couldn't reach it, and a coffee can was in a corner so that she could do her business without bothering anybody.

She could hear Rose's whiny voice issuing orders to the short, skinny man who had helped them move here, punctuated by the soft hiccoughs of a sobbing Deanna who was looking for somewhere to sleep. Carolyn ignored the chaos, realizing it had nothing to do with her. This room was where she would stay—until they moved again.

Carolyn sat on the edge of the bed and yawned. This was a little better than before. At least they hadn't chained her up yet and she could move around when her legs started to hurt. Carolyn had always done ballet exercises with her mommy because Mommy said that's how she kept her legs strong, so Carolyn knew that was important. But she was weak now, and so tired...

Carolyn crawled onto the middle of the mattress and stretched out, listening to the thumps and curses coming from the other rooms. Deanna had stopped her crying, so she must have found somewhere to sleep. Carolyn frowned as she thought about Deanna and that scrawny little man who called himself her father. He was scared to death of Rose, and Carolyn thought that was funny, but he seemed nice enough. He even carried Deanna into the house because she was too tired to walk. Still, Carolyn might have been invisible for all the attention he paid her and she wasn't used to that. Back home, someone was always paying attention to her.

It's better this way, she told herself, popping her thumb into her mouth and curling herself into a little ball in the middle of the bed. The room was awfully damp and chilly, and Carolyn would have given anything for a blanket. But she didn't call out, keeping up a running dialogue with herself instead.

*You can't get in trouble if they don't know you're here. And if you're real quiet, maybe they'll forget you're here and you can find a way out...*

Tears rolled down her cheeks and Carolyn scrubbed at them angrily. She wasn't going to cry anymore, no matter what happened. Rose liked it too much when she cried. Carolyn could tell because she'd get this sneaky, pleased expression on her face just like Bobby did whenever he got Maureen in trouble. Even though Carolyn didn't understand it at all, she knew she didn't want to be the reason that Rose felt good. It was the only little bit of power that Carolyn had left, and she didn't intend to let go of it.

The front door slammed and Carolyn heard a car engine start, followed by the spraying of gravel against the house as the car sped out of the driveway. She guessed it must be the skinny little man leaving. Even though he was obviously scared of Rose, it was clear he didn't like her very much, either. Carolyn listened closely for the sound of Rose's footsteps, but the house was silent.

She turned over and stared at the little window in the middle of the wall. It was just too high for her to reach on tip-toe, but if she could find something to stand on, maybe she could push it up and climb out. She was too little to move the bed, and the coffee can was too short, but if there was something... anything... Carolyn's gaze wandered over the walls and finally landed on a narrow door she hadn't noticed before.

It was a closet.

Carolyn eased herself from the bed, trying hard not to make any noise, and tip-toed to the door. She held her breath as she slowly turned the knob. She didn't know what she was looking for, didn't even know what she was hoping, but she did know that the means for escape might be inside. The door creaked so loudly as it opened that Carolyn jumped in terror, expecting Rose to blast into the room. But there was no one, not a sound except the panicked thudding of Carolyn's own heart.

She took a deep breath and peered into the tiny, pitch-black closet. She couldn't see a thing. Breaking into an icy sweat as she felt through the darkness, she swallowed a shriek of fear as her fingers touched the velvety softness of a spider's web. Quickly, before she could jerk her hand out, she began to pretend that she was playing her favorite game, *Pin the Tail on the Donkey*, and continued feeling inside. There was nothing.

She stepped one bare foot in, then the other, and moved her body to the right. There was a scraping sound as her hip pushed something against the wall. It was a chair. It was small and rickety, but it was still a chair.

Carolyn held her breath again as her little fingers curled around the seat and she tried to pick it up. She lifted it a few inches off the floor and took a couple of steps backward, then set it back down. Concentrating harder than she had ever concentrated in her life, Carolyn strained to hear some sound of activity in the house, some sign that Rose was there and awake. The silence was heavy and threatening; Carolyn was afraid to trust it. But she had no choice. She had to get that chair to the window.

Carolyn lifted it again, took a few steps backward until she was out of the closet, set the chair down, listened. And this was her pattern, over and over, as she inched the chair across the dark room toward the little window: lift, take a few steps, set it down, listen. The house remained silent.

She was hot and breathless by the time she reached the window, but she didn't care. She placed the chair smack against the wall and looked up at the dim light coming in from the back porch. It seemed so high, much too high, but maybe... just maybe...

Carolyn climbed onto the chair, squirmed to her knees and slowly eased herself to her feet, trying to hold herself steady by placing her hands flat against the wall. The chair creaked and wriggled as Carolyn planted her feet unsteadily in the center of the seat, but it held her weight. She moved her hands up the wall toward the window, straining to reach the sill until finally her fingers touched it. Carolyn caught her breath, standing on tip-toe as she strained to reach the glass. She could push it up, she knew she could. And there was no screen. If she could just figure out a way to pull herself up there...

Suddenly the room was flooded with light. "What d'you think you're doin'?"

Carolyn lost her footing and crashed to the floor. The chair toppled over and she smacked her head hard against the wall. Dazed, she stared up at Rose, who stood in the doorway with that bored, smirky expression on her face.

Carolyn swallowed against the lump of fear forming in her throat. She wasn't going to cry, no matter what. Her chin quivered and she looked away. Fully expecting to be jerked up off the floor by her hair, Carolyn steeled herself, but Rose didn't move. Suddenly, out of that awful stillness, Rose began to chuckle, low in her throat. It was a lazy, easy sound, unconcerned and mocking. Carolyn looked at her quickly, warily.

"So you thought you could climb outa that window, did you? Even found a chair! Hmmm...you're smarter'n I thought you were. 'Cept...not really." Rose shook her head sadly. "See...you've put yourself in a pretty pickle 'cause now I can't trust you. Ain't that a shame?" She frowned and looked at Carolyn curiously. "Where'd you think you were gonna go, anyways? Who'd you think was gonna help you? You think those stuck-up snots back in Timbuctoo give a hoot about you? Even if you showed up on their doorsteps tomorrow, they'd send you back to me. You'd better believe what I'm tellin' you, little girl, 'cause I don't want your heart broke. You ain't got no one but me anymore and the sooner you realize that, the better off you are."

Icy rage propelled Carolyn to her feet. "You're lying! My mommy and daddy love me! You're lying and I hate you!"

Rose crossed the room in three steps. She grabbed Carolyn's arm and jerked her close, shoving her face down to Carolyn's. Her eyes were slits of rage and her breath was foul as she spat, "*I'm* your mommy, you understand me? *I'm* your mommy!"

Carolyn turned her head, fighting tears. "No, you're not… You're not…"

"That's it! I've had it with you, you little snot! You come with me. I'm gonna show you who's boss around here and you can scream 'til you're blue. Ain't no one gonna hear you out here…"

Rose slapped her, hard, and Carolyn's head jerked backward. Then, without warning, she found herself being dragged out of the room, down a narrow hall, through a filthy kitchen, and out onto the back porch. Rose shoved her against an old, dilapidated washing machine—just like the one Grandma Rankin had in her basement. Carolyn eyed it warily.

"Give me your hand."

Carolyn clasped her hands tightly together in front of her and shook her head fiercely, eyes bulging with terror. Her heart hammered.

"I said, give me your hand!"

Rose jerked Carolyn's hands apart and grabbed her right arm with steely fingers, cranking a lever on the side of the washing machine at the same time. Two rollers at the top spread apart. Struggling against Rose's iron grip, Carolyn stared at the rollers in fascinated horror. Rose pulled her hand closer and closer toward the rollers, laughing maniacally as Carolyn shrieked and fought and wept in panic.

"You gonna call me *Mommy*?"

"No!"

Carolyn's fingers touched the rollers.

"Call me *Mommy*, you little snot!"

"No!"

Rose grunted in speechless rage, then jammed Carolyn's right hand between the rollers and cranked the lever furiously. The pain was excruciating as the rollers slowly closed on Carolyn's fingers, flattening knuckles and squashing tender bones until she couldn't see or feel anymore. The back porch light swam before her eyes, blurred and blended with a midnight-black sky. Sweat and tears poured down her face, mucus streamed from her nose, bitter vomit erupted, splattering Rose, the washing machine, the floor…

Jumping backward with a curse, Rose released the lever but retained her grip on Carolyn's arm. She pushed her face up close. "*Now* are you gonna call me *Mommy*?"

Carolyn sagged, whimpering. Her eyes were glassy with shock as she stared at Rose, struggling to focus. Everything looked so strange, so swirly…

Rose's voice blasted through Carolyn's head. "*Are you?*"

The excruciating pain was slowly dissipating, gradually replaced by a banging, throbbing ache where her fingers had been. Carolyn gazed toward her hand curiously. Still jammed between the rollers, it no longer felt like part of her body. It was as if it had been cut off and left to dangle in the old washing machine.

"Oh, what the... I'm too tired to mess with you anymore." Rose cracked the lever the opposite direction, opening the rollers. "Just remember this, Miss Priss. The sooner you call me *Mommy* like you're supposed to, the sooner we can stop foolin' around. This is gonna keep happenin' to you 'til the cows come home if you don't learn your place."

Before Carolyn could even respond, Rose jerked her away from the washing machine and dragged her back through the house. Unresisting, practically unaware, Carolyn stumbled behind her, fighting tears as the pain slowly began building, throbbing, pounding again...

Rose kicked the bedroom door open and shoved Carolyn inside. Carolyn fell against the bed and slid to the floor, cradling her hand against her chest. Her entire body shook; she felt like she was trapped in ice. Rose stomped across the room, grabbed the rickety chair, and stalked back to the door. She glared at Carolyn.

"And don't you go gettin' any more brilliant ideas, you hear me? You ever try a stunt like this again, I'll cut your whole damn arm off."

Carolyn closed her eyes wearily, no longer afraid. Rose's voice sounded funny, like a distant, tinkly little bell. From very far away, she heard the door close and a key squeak in the lock. Realizing she was alone in the dark and grateful for it, Carolyn finally allowed the tears of pain and humiliation to flow unchecked.

She crawled on the bed and curled up, still cradling her throbbing hand against her body. The foul odor of her own vomit stung her nostrils, but it didn't matter. Nothing mattered any-more. Nothing would ever matter again.

Even Mommy and Daddy didn't matter now. They weren't here; she would never see them again. She had no home. She had no family.

There was no Yellow Brick Road.

And then, for the very first time, Carolyn saw him—a pale, gentle figure bathed in light. He held out his arms and she went to him, unafraid and trusting. Bowing his head, he held her close and stroked her hair. She could even feel his tears as she was enveloped in warmth as soft and soothing as velvet.

There was no reason for her to be frightened because she recognized him. She had seen him in church, studied him in Sunday school, listened to her daddy tell stories about him. He was no stranger. He had come to her, just like he promised.

As she snuggled closer in arms that seemed to blanket her with love, Carolyn began to sing in a whisper, *"Jesus loves the little children... all the children in the world..."*

Days and nights all ran together, and this Texas place only had two seasons—hot and cold. One day they were nailing her window closed and she was burning up, and the next day—or so it seemed—she was freezing to death. She had lost count of the number of times they had moved, usually in the middle of the night. Time just didn't matter anymore because it went by, all on its own, filled up with black, empty places that Carolyn didn't understand.

All she knew for sure was right this minute, and right this minute they were moving again. At least, she thought they were. Rose's new friend, Harold Something-Or-Other, was running through the house, yelling and screaming bad words at everybody, and Carolyn could hear the screen door slamming and suitcases thudding as they hit the front porch. Carolyn sat still in the closet, trying to be very, very quiet, praying that they would forget her in their rush to leave.

But she knew they wouldn't. They would *never* forget her—they needed her too much. Carolyn didn't know the reasons *why* anything was happening; she only knew what *was*. And what *was* was that they needed her to be hurt. They needed her to be terrified. She could tell that by the way Rose smiled when she stuck Carolyn's hand in the wringer and Carolyn started screaming. She could tell by the way Harold's eyes got funny right before he socked her in the face and knocked her clear across the bedroom. She could tell by the way they both giggled when they brought her rice and water for supper and waited for her to throw up.

Even little Deanna got into the act. She was just a baby herself, but she seemed to have a mean streak just as big as her mother's. Carolyn's daddy would have said that she couldn't help it—children are what they see—but Carolyn didn't think that was a very good excuse. Deanna would come into Carolyn's room and act all sweet, and then, when Carolyn wasn't ready for it, Deanna would start screaming at the top of her lungs that Carolyn had punched her, and then Rose would crash in—

It seemed to go on and on and on, over and over again. The same old thing.

What seemed to make Rose the maddest was that Carolyn just wouldn't call her *Mother*, but Carolyn couldn't understand that. Why should she? Rose *wasn't* her mother. Carolyn Sue Shaw just couldn't have a mother like Rose, she couldn't! Her mother lived with her father in a brick house in Pennsylvania, and they were looking for her. Carolyn was as sure of that as she was sure of her own name. They would never stop looking for her. So, since Rose wasn't really her mother, then maybe this time they'd all just forget her and leave her in this closet and let her real mother find her…

No, that wouldn't happen. They wouldn't forget her. Carolyn stayed mixed-up all the time, but she wasn't mixed-up about this. All she had to do was wait. They'd come for her, and they'd move again, and it would start all over.

Carolyn closed her eyes, leaned her head back against the wall, and waited for the commotion going on in the house to fade. It would; she knew it from experience. She could make it go away. Usually the man in the white robe came to her right before everything else disappeared. Carolyn looked forward to seeing him because he talked to her, he *really* talked to her, and the most important thing he told her was that she wasn't alone. She still didn't know what he meant by that—after all, she had never been more alone in her whole life—but it made her feel much better to hear him say it. Carolyn took a deep breath and waited…

"C'mon, kid, we gotta go."

Carolyn jumped and stared up at Harold with wide, terrified eyes. His pale face, greasy with sweat, looked eerie and cruel in the shaft of moonlight streaming in from the window behind him. Her heart thundered and her stomach boiled as she slowly stood up and inched past him, waiting for the blow that would crash into her head and knock her down. But he didn't hit her. Instead he grabbed her arm and jerked her up close, squatting in front of her so that they were nearly nose-to-nose. His breath smelled foul, sort of like sour milk.

"Now you listen to me, kid, and you listen good! I'm sick and tired of you screamin' and wakin' up the whole neighborhood so that we gotta move every time I turn around. We're goin' back in the woods where you can't bother no one, so you might as well quit your hollerin'. Ain't no one gonna hear you where we're goin'. I can kill you up there, little girl, and ain't no one ever gonna find you. I can cut you up in a million tiny pieces and feed you to the hogs. Don't think I won't do it."

Carolyn cringed with terror and turned her face away from his nasty breath, battling tears. He *would* do it, she knew he would. He was mean enough, bad enough, crazy enough, and Rose wouldn't stop him. No one would stop him.

Even so, Carolyn didn't know what he was talking about. She never screamed. She never cried. She never talked to anybody. Why did he say that she was the reason they kept moving?

Instinctively, Carolyn glanced around the dark room, looking for the man in the white robe. Where was he? Why didn't he come now when she needed him? How could he say she wasn't alone—and then leave her? Even as Harold grabbed her arm and dragged her down the hallway, Carolyn's gaze darted everywhere, looking for him. No matter how many times they moved, no matter what time of the day or night, no matter what the circumstances had been, he had always come with her. She had always been able to see him. Now he was gone.

Harold pushed her into the back of his beat-up station wagon, slammed the doors shut, and climbed into the driver's seat beside Rose. As he started the car and slowly pulled away from the old house, Carolyn squashed her nose against the rear window, still looking for the man in the white robe. But there was no one. An overwhelming sense of deep loneliness washed over her and a single tear finally trailed down Carolyn's dirty cheek.

For the first time, Carolyn realized how cold and windy it was outside. Her bare feet felt like ice, and the chill crept right through her thin tee-shirt, freezing even her bones. She looked around the back of the station wagon and spotted Deanna curled up inside a sleeping bag, warm as fresh toast, but there was nowhere for Carolyn to rest. Finally, teeth chattering and so cold that she didn't care about the consequences, Carolyn inched her body closer to the faintly snoring Deanna and shut her eyes.

The warmth and soft, rhythmic breathing of another person against her made Carolyn feel like a member of the human race again. It brought back comforting memories, growing fainter and fainter as time passed, of those warm, cozy nights spent in a high-pedestal double bed with Maureen.

As Carolyn drifted into the softness of sleep, she saw him again—the man in the white robe. He held out his arms to her, and she went to him, and she wasn't cold anymore.

Harold had lied. They weren't moving at all, Carolyn discovered, but merely visiting his mother, Lavinia, for the Christmas holidays. It didn't seem to be Rose's idea of a good time, but Carolyn didn't mind that. Rose never had a good time. So, while Rose sat around and complained that the old farmhouse had no running water, no electricity, and she was sick and tired of eating pigeons, Carolyn reveled in her first taste of freedom in almost two years.

Lavinia was kind of scary looking—she reminded Carolyn of the Wicked Witch of the West—but she wasn't unkind. She allowed Carolyn to watch her as she boiled her clothes on the ramshackle back porch to get them clean, and absently answered all of Carolyn's persistent questions about the strange animals that seemed to wander at will into the yard. Carolyn's favorite was an armadillo, a sort of silver-skinned, accordion-looking thing on skinny legs that she had never seen back home in Pennsylvania.

Lavinia was too old, tired and overworked to really talk to Carolyn, but she protected her just by being there, and Carolyn was grateful for it.

The house itself was simple. It was nestled in pine trees so tall that the yard was always dark and shadowy, as if it was going to rain, and there were rolling hills in the distance. Carolyn could imagine that she was back home, surrounded by trees and mountains, and the games she played by herself reflected that.

And that was the real beauty of this place. She could let her stifled imagination run free. She wasn't chained to anything, she wasn't watched every minute, and Harold Whoever-He-Was seemed thoroughly cowed by his mother. It was this knowledge that alerted Carolyn to the fact that she could escape if she wanted to.

It happened two mornings after their arrival. Rose and Harold were arguing in the kitchen, as usual, and Carolyn walked in to announce she was going to the outhouse to use the toilet. Rose glared at her and Harold took a step forward, like he was going to grab her, but Lavinia held up a coffee pot and nodded.

"You go on, child, and hurry it up. Folks is comin' in droves shortly and everyone's gonna hafta go. 'Sides, we're eatin' in just a minute."

"Yes'm."

Carolyn walked slowly out of the house, even though every muscle in her body urged her to run. But she couldn't run anymore, not like she used to. She lost her breath too easily and her legs seemed to give out. Now she moved with a peculiar shuffling gait that didn't seem to get her anywhere very fast. Once at the outhouse, Carolyn cast a last glance over her shoulder to be sure no one was watching.

She was alone. For the first time in nearly two years, she was free. Carolyn drew in a deep breath and walked through the fringe of tall pine trees.

Darkness enfolded her like a shroud, and her tattered sweater was no match for the icy December morning. As she walked quickly through the woods, naked branches, like teasing fingers, tickled her hair and scratched against her cheek. Carolyn held her breath and peered through the eerie shadows, fighting an overwhelming terror.

In the distance she could see a tiny, cinderblock house nestled in the pines. Heart pounding, she headed toward it, ignoring the trees and shadows and unfamiliar forest sounds as she focused on getting there. Someone would help her, someone *had* to help her. All she had to do was get there. All she had to do was let someone know how much trouble she was in.

The pine trees opened into a small clearing. Carolyn stood uncertainly in misty shadows that no longer seemed threatening. Now she was protected, hidden, invisible. But she had to go, had to…had to… She took one tentative step, then another, then another, until she was lurching in that painful shuffle across the grass toward the tiny house.

She halted in front of three steps that led up to a rotted porch and took another deep breath. The picture that sped through her mind was one of the wicked witch's house in *Hansel and Gretel*. No other fairy tale scared her as much as that one. For just a fleeting second, she could hear that old woman's cackle as she danced around a huge black pot, filled with screaming children in scalding water…

Fighting tears of pure panic, Carolyn climbed the stairs and made her way carefully toward a front door that stood half-open, hanging crazily on rusty hinges. Someone was home. In just a few minutes she would be safe. Rose would be a bad dream. There wouldn't be any more chains, or hunger, or pain. She would be safe. Whoever lived in this house would let her call her mommy and it would be all over. In just a few minutes.

And then she came face-to-face with it—the biggest, blackest, hairiest spider in the whole wide world. It was so huge she could even see its eyeballs as it clung tenaciously to its silky web. It was so huge that all it had to do was open its mouth and it could swallow a little girl whole. It was so huge that it could wrap its hairy legs around her and squeeze her until she was dead. Carolyn took a step backward, gawking in terror. Spiders. She hated spiders.

"Hey, little girl, come on in."

Carolyn jerked in fright, gaping at the man standing in the doorway. He was the biggest, fattest man she had ever seen in her life, and he had lots of hair on his chest and belly. Squinty eyes. No front teeth. He took a step toward her.

"C'mere, kid."

He was naked.

Carolyn screamed, turned and ran. She raced back through the clearing and into the woods. She ran until she couldn't run anymore. She ran until she couldn't breathe.

She ran toward Rose.

She ran toward chains and hunger and pain.

She ran toward what she knew.

# CHAPTER FOUR

Carolyn spent Christmas day peeking through a keyhole in a locked bedroom door at Harold's brother's house, watching as the family gathered and opened their presents. Only Deanna received real toys, probably from her daddy, Carolyn thought, and she wouldn't share them with the other children.

The other children weren't all that interested Carolyn. There were several, boys and girls who must have belonged to all the strangers in the room, and a stabbing loneliness pierced the soul of the little girl watching through the keyhole. How she yearned to play with them, to run in and out of the house with them, to shriek and laugh and pull pranks with them. It didn't matter that their clothes were ragged and their noses ran. Nothing mattered except that they were children, just like her...

Carolyn didn't understand why she was locked away in this unfamiliar house, and old Lavinia apparently didn't understand it, either. In fact, she and Rose had had a huge fight about it the night before, and Carolyn had held her breath hopefully, but Lavinia had lost. That was kind of unusual, at least in Carolyn's mind, because Lavinia ruled her impoverished domain like the wicked witch she resembled, but no one could budge Rose when her mind was made up. No one knew that better than Carolyn.

"I'm tellin' you, Livvie, the guy's lookin' for her!" Rose had declared. She pointed a red-nailed finger at Carolyn, who had been huddled in a corner of the kitchen, trying to get warm. "Why else do you think we're up here? Listen to me, old woman..."

Harold had slammed a beer bottle on the table and Carolyn jumped. "Shut your mouth! That's my ma you're talkin' to!"

"Holy crap, Harold," Rose said wearily. "I told you before. We got to hide out up here for a while, and I don't want that little brat runnin' around where everyone can see her. Now, if you want to go to Bubba's for Christmas, that's fine with me. But Car'lyn stays away from everyone, you hear me? George Shaw has someone snoopin' around out there—I can smell him—and I ain't gonna have her flappin' her jaws to anyone who'll listen!"

Harold sighed and took another swig of beer. He wiped his mouth with the back of his hand and gave a loud belch. "You might as well drop it, Ma. You ain't gonna win. 'Sides, who cares? The kid's nothin' but a pain anyways."

Carolyn didn't care about the argument. They argued all the time. All she cared about was that one sentence: *George Shaw has someone out there...* Nothing else mattered but that one sentence. Her daddy hadn't forgotten her. Her daddy was looking for her. She had known it all along. Nothing else mattered.

Except Lavinia's next question.

"Why don't you just let her go?"

Silence stretched for eons; Carolyn held her breath. Her heart began to pound when Rose finally answered, in that dangerously low voice, "Why don't you mind your own bus'ness?"

Lavinia's eyes narrowed into slits of fury. "Man, you're a piece of work! This here is my house you're stayin' in. This here is my food. Who do you think you are, comin' in here and tellin' me to mind my own bus'ness? Long as I'm standin' on my own kitchen floor, I'll tell you what I think—and you'll listen, by God! This kid is crazy and you don't even know it! She ain't even in the world half the time—what good is she to you? What's the point, Rose? That's what I wanna know. What in hell is the point?"

Now, peeping through that keyhole and racked with loneliness, Carolyn was still happy. Lavinia and Harold were both mad at Rose, and Daddy had somebody out there. Rose's little world was caving in, just like Carolyn had prayed it would, and it wouldn't be long now. Her daddy would find her and she could go home...

The door opened and Carolyn fell back on her rump, startled. She stared up at Rose's glowering face, once more scared silent.

"You come on out here, Miss Fancy Pants. You can sit in that rockin' chair in front of Bubba's new TV. Livvie'n I hafta take the others back to her house for a while. Don't you move, you hear me? And don't you say a word to no one. Harold'n Bubba'll be back in a minute."

Nodding quickly, Carolyn scrambled to her feet, sidled past Rose without touching her, and plopped herself into a child's rocking chair. She stuck her thumb into her mouth and stared blindly at the new television set. It was turned off, but she stared at it, anyway.

"Oh, here. I plumb forgot." Rose tossed a yo-yo into Carolyn's lap. "Yep, it's yours. Merry Christmas."

Carolyn stared at the cherry-red yo-yo. Then, in spite of herself, her gaze shifted to Deanna's stack of presents in the corner. Hastily, before Rose noticed, she stared back down at the yo-yo in her lap.

Rose leaned against the wall, cocked her head to one side, and studied Carolyn intently, as if she had all the time in the world. "Y'know, kid," she said finally, "you'd get more presents if you weren't such a brat, you know that? It's the truth. Deanna ain't a brat. She minds me."

Carolyn kept her head lowered and said nothing.

"Why don't you mind me like Deanna?"

Carolyn didn't answer. She stared so hard at the yo-yo that it blurred before her eyes.

"Crap." Rose moved away from the wall and sauntered to the door. "We'll be back. Don't you move from that chair, you hear me? Harold'n Bubba are just outside."

Carolyn nodded, fighting tears, trying to gulp away the terror that was rising in her throat. Rose was bad, but Carolyn knew Rose. Harold was different. Nobody knew Harold... Nobody knew what he would do. And Bubba...

Carolyn heard the truck doors slam shut. She heard the children laughing in the bed of the pickup as it sputtered and choked its way out of the yard. She heard the gears grinding as it traveled down the dirt road beside Bubba's house. Then, finally, she heard the silence.

Carolyn had come to fear silence, even as she longed for it. Silence meant she was alone, and she had learned that being alone was good. Being alone meant that no one was yelling at anyone else, no one was tormenting her, no one cared where she was or what she was doing or even if she was dead or alive. But silence had also become a warning, a little nudge somewhere in the back of her mind that told her something bad was going to happen. Silence always came before something bad...

Carolyn began to pray in that small, sing-song voice that always comforted her. Monotonously, robot-like, she rocked back and forth in the little chair, in perfect rhythm with words that were more like a chant than a prayer. They were words that lifted her, transported her far beyond her surroundings, moved her away from anyone who could hurt her.

"Jesus, take me home. Jesus, take me home. Jesus, take me home." Carolyn closed her eyes and continued to rock. "Jesus, take me home..."

"Come with me, child." The voice was clear, whisper-gentle.

Carolyn's eyes flew open and she looked frantically around the room. Was someone here? Had someone spoken to her? No, she was alone. It was just a thought. She didn't know where the thought had come from, but it was so clear, so vivid and real, that it might have been a human voice talking to her. But it wasn't human, and it wasn't in the room. It was speaking inside her head.

And then Bubba's awed whisper broke the spell. "What's she doin'? Who the devil is she talkin' to? She do that all the time?"

Instinctively, Carolyn tried to flatten herself against the rocking chair and become invisible, but it didn't do any good. Harold lunged through the front door, covered the floor in three giant strides and kicked the rocking chair all the way across the room. Carolyn screamed and crashed into the new television screen, shattering glass. Wood cracked and splintered and hit the walls—but the chaos only seemed to fuel Harold's rage.

With measured steps, he bore down on Carolyn. She curled her legs next to her chest, whimpering, and tried to scoot backward toward the corner. Her skinny face was white with terror and blood trickled down her cheek. One eye was already bruised and closing. Harold lifted his booted foot, prepared to slam it right into her face.

"What's the matter with you, you crazy sonuvabitch?" Bubba hollered. "Look what you done to my new TV!" He knelt before the busted television, practically in tears as he tried to pick up the splintered glass. "Look what you done, Harold!"

As Harold turned away from her, now just a putrid, scrawny shell of himself, Carolyn curled up in a ball in the corner and waited for whatever was going to happen next. Somehow it didn't matter anymore.

A blue and lavender light beckoned at the end of the tunnel. Carolyn wasn't afraid as she floated toward it. She knew it would be warm when she reached it, soft and soothing like soapy bath water, and she knew the angel would be there. He was always there, and he always held out his arms to her, and she always went to him.

As she neared the brilliance, Carolyn was filled with wonder. The angel seemed to fill the tunnel with the pastel light—the radiance flowed from his white robe and his uplifted arms. Beside him stood a woman she had never seen before, a woman as beautiful as he was handsome, a woman young and glowing with love.

Carolyn floated toward them and landed softly in a cloud of silver. The woman held out her arm; Carolyn put her tiny fingers in the woman's hand trustingly.

The woman's voice was sweet, like a gentle lullaby. "Hello, Carolyn. We've been waiting for you."

Carolyn's heart soared. "Who are you?" she whispered. "I've never seen you before."

"We're your friends, Carolyn. We've always been here."

"Always?"

"Always."

"Come see, Carolyn," the man said gently. "We have something to show you."

Suddenly, like a velvet curtain, the light parted. Carolyn caught her breath. Trees with golden leaves stood tall in the sun. A delicate bridge crossed over a pond that sparkled with diamond-brilliance in soft lavender; shiny fish swam and flipped in the water. Large white lilies floated on top, petals curved upward like praying hands. All around was smooth grass and the air was filled with a soft, sweet fragrance. Carolyn looked around her, wide-eyed in disbelief. There was no place on earth so beautiful, so peaceful. This wasn't earth, she decided instantly. This was heaven. The angels had come and taken her away to heaven…

And then she saw them—birds with silver bodies that shimmered in the light and wings so transparent they looked like spiders' webs covered with dew. There were animals, all kinds of animals, wild and free and unafraid. It was like a magic forest that had come to life in her favorite dream.

Carolyn stepped toward the bridge and peered down at the water, laughing as the fish swam beneath her reflection. She glanced over her shoulder at the angels.

"Can I come back?"

"Any time you want to," the woman answered. "We've made this place just for you."

Somewhere far, far away, Carolyn heard someone calling her name. Her throat closed with terror and her head began to pound. She was dizzy and her ears rang as she was ripped from the light. In the distance, millions of miles away, she could hear someone screaming.

And screaming.

And screaming.

Then, somehow, Carolyn was wrapped in the angels, protected by their love and strength and warmth.

She didn't know the screaming was hers.

Somehow, to Carolyn's great relief, Harold disappeared. Then, late in 1966, when Carolyn was eight years old, Rose Lovell married a man named Beau LeBlanc. He drove a *Tom's Peanuts and Candy* truck and Rose met him one day when she bought Deanna a Snickers bar. Carolyn liked him because he wasn't mean to her and there was nothing scary about him. He was healthy-looking, handsome and blond. She also liked him because he did his best to keep Rose away from her.

Of course, Beau couldn't do very much because he worked most of the time, but Rose seemed a little bit cowed by him, which might have been because she was expecting a baby and really wasn't feeling well enough to fight with anyone. Whatever the reason, Carolyn was grateful.

If Beau took her outside so she could get some fresh air, Rose just turned her head, tightened her lips and said nothing. If Beau allowed her to play alone in the backyard, all Rose did was make sure that Deanna stayed inside so that Carolyn had no one to play with. Rose didn't even argue when Beau brought Carolyn a horny toad stuck in a matchbox as a little present, although it was pretty clear she didn't like the fact that he hadn't brought anything for Deanna.

She didn't even make fun of Carolyn for being so excited about the horny toad. She just nodded and went on about her business.

After all that Carolyn had been through, these brief moments of childhood normalcy were gifts from God.

The truth was, Beau explained one evening as Carolyn helped him pick up trash in the backyard, he had come from a huge French Catholic family. So he liked kids and was really looking forward to the new baby on the way. Carolyn didn't say anything, but she wondered if he had any idea what kind of person Rose really was.

Yet Carolyn didn't really have to wonder; she already knew the answer. He knew perfectly well how scary Rose was—he had called her on it a dozen times. He had even told her once that if she hated Carolyn so much, she ought to just send her back where she came from. Carolyn had held her breath, waiting for Rose's response, but she hadn't said a word. He had also listed all kinds of terrible incidents to Rose during arguments, trying to make her feel bad...

Like the time she'd put Carolyn in that big old freezer on the back porch and locked the lid closed. Beau had come all undone, hollering about how Carolyn was going to suffocate and there were spiders in there and what did Rose think she was doing?

But he hadn't left her.

And then there was the time when Carolyn had just lost her mind and started screaming at Rose, calling her a pig and a rat and all kinds of other things. Well, Rose had grabbed her up and carried her outside and tied her to a tree and set her fanny right over a fire ant bed. Rose had been smart enough to bring Carolyn back inside before Beau came home, but apparently she hadn't counted on him checking on Carolyn to see why she was screaming in pain and then taking her to the bathtub to clean up the ant bites. Rose and Beau had an awful fight after that.

But he still didn't leave her.

And Carolyn knew that when push came to shove, she couldn't count on him any more than she could count on anyone else. He was like every other man that had ever come to live with Rose. She had *something*, that was for sure, and she always won. Carolyn had seen it a million times: Whatever this *something* was, it turned ordinary men into mush and they did whatever she told them to do.

Beau was like everyone else. If Rose told him to do it, he did it.

The only person Carolyn trusted even a little bit was Aunt Kat, a sweet older lady who was somehow related to Rose. She told Carolyn that her name was *Katherine Mattair*, but that people she liked called her *Kat*. Carolyn felt really important to be able to call her *Aunt Kat*, like she was part of a real family.

Aunt Kat lived in a home in Houston and had flowers in her yard. What Carolyn remembered most was that Aunt Kat was the tallest woman she had ever seen, with the prettiest brown, wavy hair, and she wasn't afraid of Rose like everyone else was. In fact, the tables were actually turned and Rose seemed scared to death of Aunt Kat. That really impressed Carolyn.

Rose would probably have never taken Carolyn all the way out there, but for some reason she couldn't see her brother, Junior, if she didn't visit Aunt Kat's house. So she had swallowed her fear and hauled Carolyn out there at least three different times.

Carolyn would never forget the first time she had met Aunt Kat. Aunt Kat had taken one look at the dirty little girl and informed everyone that she was going to give her a bath. And she had done just that—even though Carolyn kicked and screamed and threw a hissy fit big enough to beat the band, or so Rose said. Carolyn didn't remember throwing the fit, but she did remember Aunt Kat telling Rose, "You need to send this child back to her people." She also remembered sleeping in a real bed that night and every subsequent night until they left, and Carolyn loved Aunt Kat for that.

Carolyn had only seen Aunt Kat three or four times since she had first left Pennsylvania, but Carolyn had always felt safe with her.

Like everyone else, though, Aunt Kat seemed to have disappeared and Carolyn was on her own. Again. In fact, Carolyn sometimes thought she had imagined the older woman's kind sweetness, just like she seemed to so often imagine everything else that was pleasant.

But pleasant occurrences were so few and far between in Carolyn's life that she fixated on them and built them up in her mind to be far more important than they actually were. Like the time that they had all visited Beau's family, who lived out in the country in a big, old house surrounded by a fence, animal pens and a horse corral. Beau's mama, a short, fat lady with a whispery voice, had bathed Carolyn in an old washtub on the front porch, wrapped her in a pair of too-large long underwear, tucked her into bed and gave her a kiss goodnight. Carolyn lived and re-lived this sweet moment as often as she could. For the moment at least, it seemed to bring her back into the human race.

For the most part, though, Carolyn remained alone, isolated and abandoned in a room she shared with no one except the voices that only she could hear.

It might have been midnight, the sky was so thick and dark, but the wind was only beginning to howl through the naked trees in the backyard. To Carolyn, it started out like a baby's whisper and ended up like a freight train screaming right through her head. At first she was fascinated by it all; then she was scared to death and ran to the house. Beau had let her go outside, and now someone had to let her come back in.

Carolyn banged and banged on the back door, struggling to stand upright and not be blown right into the ditch—Beau called it a *bayou*, but it looked like a ditch to her—that separated the backyard from the little road that ran alongside the bay. The wind blew cutting shafts of rain into her face, blinding her, and thunder crashed all around her so violently that the rickety steps beneath her bare feet actually shook. Still Carolyn pounded on the door, tears mingling with the rain on her face, and her high-pitched shrieks of terror were lost in the thunder and the wind.

The door remained closed. Carolyn grabbed the knob, pushed and pulled and rattled it, banged her open hand against the door again. She was frantic, desperate, terrified, unthinking. Lightning shot straight down from a pitch-black sky and struck a huge old tree across the road. As the branches snapped and crackled and lunged toward the earth, Carolyn leaped from the steps, threw herself to the ground, and rolled beneath the house.

It wasn't much quieter here, but at least it was dry. For the moment. Carolyn lay very still on her belly, adjusting her eyes to the darkness beneath a house that creaked and groaned with every blast of wind. The dirt was cool on her bare legs. She felt safe here, like a baby still sleeping in its mommy's tummy, and the explosive violence of the storm seemed very far away.

Something soft and warm rubbed against her arm. Its fur was damp and it shook with fear, but its purring was loud and rhythmic and soothing. Carolyn reached out to stroke the mama cat that had chosen to have her babies in a big old washtub beneath the house. She was completely safe now. Animals had always been her friends.

The rain was pounding against the house and the thunder was constant— a deep rumble that barely seemed to explode before another rumble started—and the old house shook as if it would be ripped right up off the foundation and tossed like matchsticks into the air. Carolyn crawled to the washtub where the kittens were huddled together and climbed inside.

Carolyn lay on her side and pulled her knees up to her chest, trying to keep warm. To protect her babies, the mama cat jumped in, too, and curled up close to Carolyn's face.

Her purring never stopped, but Carolyn could no longer hear it over the raging storm outside. It sounded like the whole world was coming to an end, like one of those nuclear explosions Bobby was always talking about had actually hit the house and was blowing it straight to hell.

When a huge clump of dirt smashed into the side of the washtub and the kittens started squealing in terror, Carolyn's panic returned. She was going to die out here and no one would ever find her! The ocean was going to fill up higher and higher and roar right under the house and sweep her away, out into that black nothing she stared at night after night. Carolyn squeezed her eyes tightly shut, waiting. The wind would pick her and mama cat and baby kitties right up out of the washtub and sling them back down into the water, and they would all fall down, and down, and down... They wouldn't be able to breathe because the air would be water, and the water would fill up their noses and mouths and throats and chests and lungs and...

"Carolyn, do you want to come with me?"

Carolyn's eyes flew open and she gasped with relief at the musical sound of those familiar voices. Her two angel-friends stood there, right at the foot of the washtub, the man-angel filled with light, and the beautiful lady who always came with him. This time, though, they brought silence, a peaceful kind of silence that sounded like a spring morning, a velvet kind of silence that admitted nothing but the soft chirps of bluebirds with gossamer wings and the gentle slap of fish playing in a lily-covered pond.

Carolyn floated in a cloud lined with silver and whispered words of comfort to the frightened animals. They didn't understand how their home could be soaring through a storm that didn't make any noise, over rain that wasn't even wet, but Carolyn understood. The angels were carrying them far above the thunder and the lightning and the wind, and there was nothing to be afraid of.

They had come—and she hadn't even looked for them.

"Rub-a-dub-dub, three men in a tub," she whispered, petting one particularly frightened kitten. "Rub-a-dub-dub..."

Suddenly sunlight streamed over the washtub as it bobbed up and down, making its way gently over the bayou toward the road. Carolyn lifted her head, peeked over the side, and her heart pounded so hard she thought it would burst. She was free! The damp ocean air breathed softly against her face. The storm had ended so quickly she thought she must have imagined it—and the sun was warm on her chilled skin. Carolyn looked around for the angels, but they were gone.

The washtub bumped up against a shallow place in the bayou and Carolyn climbed out, trying to see where she was. The highway was to her left and that wasn't too far from her house, but it was far enough that she would have time to run before Rose knew she was gone. Someone driving a car on that highway would stop and pick her up and take her to a telephone. She could call her daddy, and her mommy would come get her and everything would be all right.

"You little brat! Do you know what a scare you gave me?"

Rose's voice whined out of nowhere and her fingers reached out to clamp down hard on Carolyn's arm.

Carolyn no longer knew how much time had passed or exactly how old she was. She didn't know how tall she was or what she looked like. She didn't remember going to school and she had no friends; she was an outsider looking in on the life that everyone else led. But her memories, still vivid and brilliant, kept her strong and gave her hope.

She still remembered her daddy, her knight in shining armor. She still remembered her mommy, the most beautiful lady on earth. She still remembered Maureen and Bobby, the best playmates ever. And she still remembered going to church with them all: Daddy so handsome with his hair all slicked back, Mommy smelling so sweet that Carolyn couldn't get close enough to breathe her in, and all the kids standing straight in the pew together, everyone on their very best behavior.

Now, alone in her room, Carolyn could hear their voices whenever she wanted. She could see her family, touch them, even talk to them. They were so real to her that Carolyn had no desire to leave what she had come to think of as a safe area, even when Beau invited her to join him and the others in the living room. The solitude was where she was most comfortable and where she felt she was among friends.

Besides, Carolyn could sense that her time was coming. It wouldn't be long and she would be free. Even though she didn't have much to eat, she knew she was growing taller, while Rose was growing fatter and lazier everyday. Rose didn't seem to care as much whether Carolyn was in her room or somewhere else as long as Carolyn didn't bother her. Carolyn was positive that it would soon be her moment.

Every night when she said her prayers, Carolyn made a single promise to God: *When I get out of here and I grow up, I'll do everything I can to help other children go back home. I promise, God. Just please, please help me get out of here…*

It wasn't a deal—Carolyn knew better than to try and bargain with God. It was a promise, and she meant it with all her heart. God was going to take her home to her mommy and daddy. It was going to happen. It was going to happen soon.

When it did, and when she grew up, Carolyn knew she would keep her promise.

# CHAPTER FIVE

Carolyn eyed the broken broomstick leaning against the wall in the living room. How many times had Rose hit her with that thing over the last three years? She couldn't count them all. She couldn't even remember. But she remembered the pain and the humiliation and the helplessness. She remembered because she carried those feelings with her all the time now. They were as much a part of her as blood and bone.

But now something new had been added, something that boiled beneath the pain and the humiliation and the helplessness, seething like an evil, dark, lurking Presence. It was Rage. It was Hatred. It was Power.

Those feelings didn't bother Carolyn. In fact, she enjoyed them because they kept her from being afraid. Nothing mattered to her anymore, and she recognized that because of her unconcern, she finally held some control over what happened to her. Rose was sick now, real sick, bloated with another baby she could hurt, so Carolyn knew that she was stronger than Rose. She didn't know *how* she knew it; she just knew it. She was as certain of her own strength as she was that she would soon be going home.

Suddenly, without thinking, Carolyn grabbed the broken broomstick and advanced slowly toward Rose, who was resting on the sofa as usual. When Carolyn poked the swollen belly, then pushed harder, Rose opened her eyes and glared up at her.

"Put that down before you hurt someone!"

Rose grabbed the broomstick, then gasped as Carolyn pushed it even harder into her belly. Carolyn couldn't tell if the gasp was from pain or fear or both, but it sent a surge of adrenalin and power through her that almost took her breath away.

"Let go of it." Carolyn's voice was low and steady. It didn't even sound like hers. "Go call my mother."

"Are you crazy, girl? Put that damn thing down!"

Carolyn didn't miss the uncertainty in Rose's eyes or the little tinge of panic in her voice. It was empowering. It pushed the Rage…

"Go call my mother. Right now."

"I don't remember the number," Rose whined, eyeing the broomstick warily. "How can I call her if I don't remember the number?"

"I remember it." Carolyn spouted out a series of digits as easily as she could have quoted the alphabet. She jerked her head toward the telephone on the little table beside the sofa. "Call her."

Rose stared at her for endless seconds, locking eyes, and something in Carolyn's face seemed to spur her to a decision. She eased herself into a sitting position and reached for the phone.

"You know what, Car'lyn?" she said in a friendly voice as she dialed, "I think you might just be right. You ain't happy here and I can't control you anymore. Well, I could, I guess, but I just don't care. You ain't been nothin' but a pain to me ever since you came—and I ain't been nothin' but a good and lovin' mother to you. Hello, Miz Shaw? This is Rose."

Carolyn's heart stopped, and the small hand holding the broken broomstick began to shake. Tears threatened, and she swallowed hard. She bit them back and turned her head away so Rose couldn't see how afraid she was. She fought for the Rage and the Hatred, but they were gone. She felt little and weak again, scared that she didn't matter, terrified that her mommy wouldn't want her.

"Tomorrow it is then. Let me know the time so we can get her there, will you? Sure, sure," Rose chuckled. "Naw, I ain't changin' my mind. I don't want her around here no more. Fact is, I'm havin' another baby and I just don't have time to take care of all of Car'lyn's problems. You're welcome to 'em, that's for sure. She's a sick kid. I don't know what you did to her, but..." Rose held the receiver away from her ear and chuckled again. "Huh! She hung up on me. How d'ya like that?"

Carolyn was shaking so hard she could hardly stand upright. "Is she...will she...I mean..."

Rose glared at Carolyn as she hung up the telephone. "We're takin' you to the airport in the mornin'. But you better not let me see you run at her or call her *Mommy* or anything else, you hear me? You better not make any scenes that make me look bad."

Carolyn nodded, wordless. Joy battled disbelief and terror that this was all a dream. It wasn't really happening. But it *was* happening. Carolyn Sue Shaw had made it happen.

Now in March 1967, three years to the month that Rose had first taken her from the front yard of her little house on Mohawk Drive, her mommy was coming to bring her home.

Like so many other times in the last three years, Carolyn had no memory of arriving at the airport. She didn't remember how she had gotten there or who had taken her. That morning played like a series of movie scenes that made no sense, like so many different occasions in the past. All Carolyn knew was that one moment she was locked in a room, and the next moment she was sitting alone on a bench inside a bustling airport terminal, rejecting a concerned policeman's offer to buy her a doughnut and some orange juice.

When Carolyn saw the small, beautifully dressed woman standing uncertainly in front of a customer service booth across the aisle from her bench, she wasn't sure at first that it was her mommy. It wasn't until the lady spotted Carolyn and seemed to recognize her that she started walking toward her, and then Carolyn was absolutely positive. No one else in the world moved as gracefully as her mommy, like she was gliding above the floor. As Carolyn soaked in that vision, she was so scared she didn't even try to stand up. What if it wasn't real? What if she was just dreaming, like so many times before?

Carolyn waited patiently as the lady continued to walk toward her.

Finally the lady stopped, knelt down in front of her, and cupped Carolyn's face in her hands. As they looked at one another for the first time in three years, the child's eyes were wide with disbelief. Tears streamed down the lady's cheeks as she whispered, "Carolyn? Is it you, Carolyn?"

Carolyn was shaking so badly she couldn't speak. She could only nod her head.

The lady gathered the tattered, trembling child into her arms. "Let's go, sweetheart. Our plane is waiting. Are you all right?"

Carolyn nodded again and stood up, clutching her mommy's hand with a grip of steel. She was embarrassed by her awkward gait as she walked beside her toward a large sign reading *Braniff Airlines*, but her mommy didn't seem to notice. They walked together down a long tunnel and entered what appeared to be an empty airplane. A young stewardess greeted them with a warm smile.

"You can sit right here by the window," she told Carolyn. "Won't that be fun?"

"Where does my mommy sit?"

"Your mommy will sit right next to you."

Carolyn grabbed her mommy's hand with both of hers and planted her feet firmly on the floor. Her throat closed with panic. She shook her head vehemently, battling tears and an overwhelming sense of terror...

*They're going to take her away...She's going to leave me again...*

Somewhere in the background of her mind, Carolyn could hear herself screaming. She watched herself fighting to hold onto her mommy with every ounce of strength she possessed as two stewardesses struggled to pull her away, but she couldn't let go. She couldn't risk it. She couldn't lose her mommy again...

Finally, in the distance, Carolyn heard a woman's trembling voice pleading, "Can't you just strap her in my lap?"

"I'm so sorry, Ma'am...it's against the rules. She has to be strapped into her own seat until we're in the air."

"Please...leave her alone...just this once, please...there's no one else here..."

Carolyn's heart pounded so hard she could hardly breathe, but still she held tight, still she fought—until finally, finally, she was allowed to snuggle against the soft warmth that was her mommy's body. When the seat belt clicked shut, locking them in together, Carolyn closed her eyes and took a deep, trembling breath.

It was over.

And then...out of nowhere...Carolyn stood before a full-length mirror in the women's restroom at an unfamiliar maze-like airport and stared, bemused and bewildered, at the skinny, gaunt-faced little girl in front of her. She hadn't seen herself in three years, but she knew she hadn't looked like this when she left. This child's blue-gray eyes were huge, haunted and black-circled like the eyes of one of the monsters in Carolyn's own nightmares. She was a stranger to herself, both inside and out, and she was scared to death.

Those eyes grew even bigger as they filled with tears. This was a ghost-child staring back at her. Before, she had been sparkling and soft and snuggly. That was what her daddy had always called her: *snuggly as a teddy bear...*

And then...with a crash...a hairbrush fell to the floor, smacking against white tile. Once more Mommy gathered her in her arms and Carolyn could feel her rubbing a cheek against her filthy, matted hair. She edged away, embarrassed. She remembered that her mommy had always liked everything to be perfect and spotlessly clean, and she knew that she certainly wasn't. But maybe she wouldn't mind...this time.

"Mommy?" Carolyn's voice came out in a breathless whisper. "Can I please call you *Mommy*?"

"Of course you can call me *Mommy*. I *am* your mommy. Why would you even ask me such a thing?"

Her mommy's voice sounded funny, kind of thick and strained like she had something stuck in her throat. Carolyn eyed her anxiously. Everything about her was perfect—her hair, the velvety leopard-skin coat she wore over her forest-green suit, her tiny pearl earrings. It had been a long, long time since Carolyn had seen such perfection.

"You look so pretty, Mommy."

"Why, thank you, honey! You look real pretty, too."

Carolyn shook her head seriously and met her mommy's gaze with eyes that seemed as old as time. "No, I'm not pretty, Mommy. Not anymore. But I will be, won't I? You'll make me pretty again."

Now the tears streamed unheeded down her mommy's cheeks and she drew Carolyn back into her arms. "You bet I will, sweetheart," she whispered. "You'll be beautiful. Just beautiful."

Carolyn nuzzled her cheek into her mommy's neck and inhaled a fragrance that was suddenly familiar. She had breathed it in millions of times during the last three years. She had slept with it, depended upon it, carried it with her into her dreams...

"Mommy, what's that perfume you're wearing? What's it called?"

"It's by Estee Lauder, sweetie. Why?"

"I remember it, Mommy! I smelled it the whole time I was gone. I could even go to sleep and smell it."

Her mommy made a funny sort of choking sound, then cleared her throat and stood up. Shoving the brush back into her purse, she took Carolyn's hand and led her out of the ladies' room. They had to walk slowly because Carolyn's little steps shuffled along rather awkwardly, her knees bent toward each other, but her mommy didn't mention it. She just adjusted her own gait to match Carolyn's as she led her to the waiting airplane.

Flying home to White Oak, Pennsylvania, Carolyn dozed on and off, feeling secure enough to actually, really and truly *sleep* for the first time in three years. Yet she hugged her mommy's arm tightly, terrified that she might wake up and find she was in a dream like so many times before. And even though their flight was several hours covering thousands of miles, her mommy never even tried to remove her arm from Carolyn's tenacious grasp.

Whenever Carolyn awoke for just a few moments before she slipped back into slumber again, she stroked her mommy's arm or tried to snuggle closer into the fragrant security that seemed to surround her. She couldn't get enough of that sense of sanctuary, that childish feeling of being clean and safe and pure. It had been so long since she had touched anything delicate or smelled anything sweet that her senses were starved, greedy. She wanted to gobble up everything around her, especially her beautiful mommy, and keep her protected so that no one could ever take her away again.

Carolyn heard her mommy's soft voice coming from a long, long way off. "When we get to Pittsburgh, you'll see lots of friends and family that you haven't seen in...well, in a long time. And Daddy will be there with Maureen and Bobby. They're all so excited, honey, especially Daddy. He's missed you so much. Then, after you've taken a nice, long bath, we'll give you a beautiful haircut. Won't that be nice, sweetheart?"

Without even thinking, Carolyn plopped her thumb back in her mouth and began sucking it slowly, rhythmically, just as she had done three years earlier. It was a soothing action that she could do in time with each heartbeat, an action that made her feel safe and calm and in control.

"Are you hungry, Carolyn? You must be hungry. I'm sorry. I wasn't thinking. I was just babbling on and you must be starving."

Carolyn shook her head fiercely and tightened her grip on her mommy's arm. The very idea of food was nauseating—she couldn't remember the last time she had really eaten anything. All she wanted to do was stay where she was, safe and warm and unmoving.

"Okay, baby," her mommy said softly. "It's okay. We'll wait until we get home. Then we'll give you whatever you need, whatever you want…"

*Until we get home… until we get home… until we get home…*

Those were real words, and someone real was saying them! Carolyn closed her eyes against sudden stinging tears and swallowed hard. It was all a dream, she knew it was. But it didn't matter because it was the most beautiful, most real dream she had ever had, and she didn't want to leave it. She wanted to hold on to it forever and ever. She wanted to fix it in her memory so she could go back to it whenever she needed to, whenever Rose hurt her, or Deanna sneaked in, or some man she'd never seen before came into that house…

Still, the drone of airplane engines was louder than anything she'd ever heard before, and the fragrance of her mommy's hair was more aromatic, and the velvety feel of the leopard-skin coat was more powerful than anything she had ever managed to envision in the past. Maybe it *was* true. Maybe she *wasn't* imagining it…

Carolyn twisted in her seat slightly and stared at her mommy intently, silently.

Finally, after a long while, her mommy asked, "What is it, Carolyn? What's the matter?"

Carolyn's huge blue-gray eyes filled with tears. She reached up and touched her mommy's cheek. "Is it you, Mommy?" she whispered. "Is it really you?"

The woman with the perfectly coiffed hair and baby-soft skin just nodded and answered, "Yes, honey, it's really me. And you're really coming home. It's real, I promise."

Carolyn snuggled closer and closed her eyes.

"Go to sleep, my angel," her mommy murmured in that strange choking voice, "you just sleep…and sleep…"

Their arrival at the airport in Pittsburgh, Pennsylvania, whizzed through Carolyn's consciousness like one of those weird little dirt devils she had often seen twisting down the dusty roads of Beaumont, Texas. There seemed to be hundreds of people there, holding balloons and waving and calling out to them; it was a loving, if overwhelming, welcome for the little girl who had been gone for so long. As she clung to her mommy's hand, Carolyn tried to recognize friends and family, but for some reason their faces just didn't register for longer than a few moments.

Although Carolyn realized that these people loved her and her mommy very much and were only there to welcome them home, she was also painfully aware of her dirty, tattered clothing, her matted, filthy hair, and the scrawny, knock-kneed body she had seen in the mirror. She stepped behind her mommy, attempting to conceal herself from the inquisitive glances and pitying stares of the people greeting her, and tried to hide her tears. It was just too much, too overpowering...

And then she saw her daddy. He squatted down on the floor and stretched out his arms for her to run into them. Carolyn stepped from behind her mommy and attempted to fly into the big bear hug she had dreamed about for so long, but her legs just didn't move right. As she moved awkwardly toward her daddy in that stiff and clumsy gait, she didn't care how she looked or what anyone else thought. All she cared about was reaching his arms and feeling him wrap them tightly around her. She had *lived* for that moment and she was going to have it.

He didn't wait for her to come to him. He rushed toward her, and upon reaching her, he knelt down and gathered her into his arms. His strong, wiry body shook like a fragile branch fighting through a hurricane and she could feel his tears against her cheek. He made no attempt to hold back his sobs and Carolyn tightened her thin arms around his neck.

"Oh, Daddy, don't cry," she whispered, "please don't cry..."

Somewhere behind her she heard Bobby welcoming her home and felt Maureen patting her shoulder, but her daddy's embrace was all she really cared about. For three long years she had imagined that Yellow Brick Road with her daddy at the end of it, and she knew that that vision had kept her alive and sane.

Finally, now, it was no longer a dream.

And then...she was home...and the people were gone...and the world had finally become quiet. She was wrapped in a warm quilted bathrobe, her feet encased in pink fuzzy slippers as she sat patiently at the kitchen table. She sipped at a cup of hot chocolate as her mommy cut her hair.

Daddy sat across from her, his own hair damp from a recent shower, and every once in awhile his face would break into a goofy grin, for no reason at all that Carolyn could figure. Even though there was now some gray in his hair, a few more lines around his eyes, and the creases running from his nose to his mouth were deeper, to Carolyn he was still the handsomest man in the whole world.

Carolyn wiggled her toes in the soft slippers and gave a huge yawn of total contentment.

"Sleepy, sweetheart?" her daddy asked.

Carolyn nodded, rubbed her eyes with a balled-up fist, and touched her damp curls. Her head was spinning with weariness.

"Are you nearly finished, Mommy?"

"Just about." Mommy's voice sounded funny, tight, like a wound-up clock. "Will you please sit still, Carolyn? I don't know how in the world this hair got so nasty!"

Carolyn subsided immediately and bit her lip. Instantly her mind slammed back to the first days she was with Rose and she could hear Deanna's baby voice pipe up, "She's so nasty, Mama!"

Nasty, Carolyn thought now, I'm nasty. I'm still nasty. Maybe I'll always be nasty...

"Mommy cuts hair real nice, Carolyn," Daddy said soothingly. "She still cuts Maureen's hair and Maureen's married now! Just be patient a little while longer and you'll be beautiful. Isn't that right, Mommy?"

Carolyn could feel her mommy stiffen behind her and the scissors stopped clicking for a moment. What was the matter? Didn't her mommy want her here after all? Wasn't her mommy happy that she was home? Carolyn knew all about anger now—and her mommy was angry. About something. And she wasn't saying anything. What was she angry about?

Carolyn was stiff with fear and her voice was barely audible. "Are you mad at me, Mommy? Did I do something wrong?"

"What did you say?"

Carolyn shook her head and stared down at her fingers as they clenched and unclenched in her lap. It was like they had a mind of their own. Her gaze moved to her knuckles and fixated on them. They were flat now from being run through the wringer on that old washing machine. Carolyn could hardly see them anymore, especially on her right hand.

"She asked if you were mad at her, Betty."

"Oh, of course not!"

Mommy put the scissors on the table and knelt beside Carolyn. She took Carolyn's chin in her hand and turned the freshly-scrubbed, thin little face toward her. "I'm mad that Rose did this to you, sweetheart, that's all. I'm mad at Rose, Carolyn, not you."

Carolyn shuddered as the memories flooded through her mind again, like flashes of light in a picture show, and her chin quivered. "Rose was mean to me, Mommy..."

"Don't, baby." Mommy's face looked funny, like her features were all pinched together. She shook her head fiercely. "We're not going to talk about it,

Carolyn. Never. It's over. You're home now. We're just going to make believe it never happened, okay? We're going to pretend you never left. That way we can all get on with our lives. Do you understand, Carolyn? We're going to move forward, not backward. Now, let me finish your hair."

She stood up, once again all business. Carolyn subsided once more and stared desperately at the floor. She wriggled her feet up and down in the soft slippers, trying to enjoy the warm fuzziness against her toes, but she just couldn't concentrate on the pleasure. This room felt like it was full of ghosts whizzing and whirring by her head, like they all had something to say and were angry because they couldn't say it. Her heart pounded with the closeness of them—it was like the air was too heavy to breathe.

"There now, all done!"

Mommy dropped a light kiss on the top of Carolyn's hair and placed the scissors in a drawer. Carolyn shook her head and ran her fingers through her newly cropped curls. The action triggered a memory, and the memory slammed through her for a split second—the memory of Rose cutting her hair for the very first time, kneeling behind her in the kitchen, ripping her soiled panties from her body, and the pain, the pain… Then, just as quickly, the memory vanished…

Trying to keep the dangerous memory at bay, Carolyn looked at her mommy and daddy. "May I go to bed now?" she asked politely. "I'm very tired."

"Your room is exactly the way it was when…when you left, Carolyn," her daddy told her. "We haven't changed it one bit. And since Maureen's married, you get it all to yourself. Bobby's gone to spend the night with a buddy, so things will be nice and quiet around here tonight."

Carolyn nodded, suddenly and inexplicably frightened of sleeping alone, and she couldn't think of anything to say. Finally, for lack of anything else, she said only, "Thank you, Daddy."

"Do you want me to tuck you in?" he asked. There was laughter dancing behind his question. "Or are you too big for that?"

"Please tuck me in, Daddy." The words caught in Carolyn's throat as she asked softly, just as she had years earlier, "Will you carry me to my room?"

"I certainly will." He pushed his chair away from the table and stood up.

"You certainly will not."

There was that tone in her mommy's voice again. Carolyn slumped down and stared at her feet, wishing the floor would swallow her up. She had done something wrong, she knew it, but she didn't know what it was.

"You're much too big for Daddy to carry, sweetheart, and he's much too old. He'll just walk with you to your room, okay?"

Carolyn nodded, blinked back tears, and climbed out of her chair.

"Come on, kiddo," her daddy said softly, taking her hand. There was a little tremor in his voice that tickled at her memory and sort of frightened her, but she didn't know what it was or why it was scary. "Let's get you to bed."

The lavender-and-white bedroom was exactly the same. There was the large bay window, the double-sized pedestal bed with the bookshelves behind it, the little seat in front of the window with all the stuffed animals on it, and the chest of drawers with the antique music box on top of it. All built by her daddy's hand, with her daddy's love... In between nightmares and monster-visions, how many times had Carolyn imagined this room?

And then Carolyn saw it in the corner—the empty cradle. There was no white-haired, glass-eyed Cindy in that cradle. Her baby was gone. In that one moment, in that one split second, Carolyn finally understood the magnitude of what had happened to her in this one day. Tears of joy and heartache and loss erupted, streaming down her cheeks.

Her daddy knelt before her and gathered the sobbing child in his arms. "What is it, sweetheart? What's the matter? Aren't you glad to be home?"

Carolyn clung to him, rubbing her cheek against his scratchy sweater, and nodded. "Oh, yes, Daddy, I'm so happy! I'm sorry... I didn't mean to cry... I'm sorry." She straightened up, wiped at the tears on her cheek with the back of her hand and hiccoughed. "I'm just tired, that's all."

Her mommy patted her back, then pulled down the bedspread, plumped the pillows, and helped her into bed. "I'm sure you are, honey. You just go to sleep and we'll all see you in the morning. Everything will be much better in the morning."

"Shall we say prayers?" her daddy asked, moving closer to the bed.

Groggy with fatigue, Carolyn whispered, "Yes, Daddy. But you say them, okay?"

"You say them together tonight, all right?" her mommy interrupted quickly. "I have to check on something in the kitchen." She dropped a light kiss on Carolyn's cheek and headed for the door, like she couldn't get out of the bedroom fast enough. "Good-night, sleep tight."

Carolyn burrowed deeper into her pillows as her daddy pulled the blankets up and tucked them beneath her chin, then knelt beside the bed as he had done for as long as she could remember. She heard his soft voice in prayer for just a brief moment before she drifted into her first deep sleep in three years.

The moonlight streamed through the big bay window, dancing over the walls and bathing the empty cradle in its silver radiance. Carolyn jolted upright in her bed and looked around the room, disoriented and confused.

Where was the metal radiator? Where was the tiny window near the ceiling? Where was the ocean? She touched her bare ankle. Where was that big heavy chain?

And then she realized where she was. She was finally home again. She was in her own bedroom. Things were going to go back to the way they were before. She was going to live with her mommy and her daddy and her brother and her sister, and they were all going to love each other. She was going to have her toys and her family and her friends, just the way she had had them before.

Everything was going to be exactly the same as it had always been.

Carolyn closed her eyes and drifted back into sleep. And then somehow, as the blackness of slumber drifted over her and enveloped her in its soft warmth, her baby's round, staring, glass eyes twinkled through the darkness, accusing her of something...something she should have done...something she didn't understand. But what? And then, as Carolyn twisted away from the doll's accusatory stare, she came face-to-face with Rose's eyes—eyes that were slitty, flat, cold and dead...like fish eyes...

Carolyn jerked awake, wide-awake, and fought the scream that threatened to erupt and shatter the peaceful stillness of the sleeping Shaw household. As she looked around the frilly bedroom that had once sheltered her from the confusion and violence of the outside world, Carolyn slowly began to realize that the last three years had somehow managed to follow her into this sweet, lavender-and-white sanctuary.

But I'm stronger now, she told herself firmly, and I'm a big girl. I'm almost nine years old. I can handle this all by myself...

She had lived with the night terrors and monster-visions for what seemed to be a lifetime and she hadn't told anyone about them. She could keep quiet until she was dead if that's what it took. She would find a way. She had done it before and she could do it again.

Her mommy wanted everything to be just the way it was when Carolyn was a little girl and life was perfect. All her daddy had ever wanted was for her mommy to be happy. Carolyn wasn't too young to know what that meant. It meant that even though her mommy and daddy loved her and she was back at home, she was still lost and she was still alone.

Carolyn pulled the covers up over her head and squeezed her eyes tightly shut. Like she had so many times before, she couldn't do anything now except wait for the dawn.

# PART TWO

*I've spent the better part of my life trying to get back to my mother.*

**~Carolyn (Shaw) Huebner~**

# CHAPTER SIX

The western half of the Commonwealth of Pennsylvania had always been much more than just *home* to Carolyn—it was her whole world. Whatever any young, imaginative child wanted could be found *somewhere* in this lush and beautiful place. If she wanted to play hide-and-seek in thick, cool forests, she could. If she wanted to splash around in icy creeks, she could. If she wanted to hike up craggy hillsides, she could. It was all there for her pleasure.

During her three-year imprisonment in that dusty hellhole of Beaumont, Texas, Carolyn had remembered western Pennsylvania as spectacular autumn colors where leaves turned magenta, orange, red and even turquoise. She remembered frozen pine trees in the wintertime and breathtaking blue sunsets and rickety little bridges crossing whispering streams. She remembered Amish country and historical railroad trestles and haunted inns dating back to before the American Revolution. In the comforting recesses of Carolyn's Technicolor memory, there was nowhere else in the world more magnificent.

If western Pennsylvania was the whole world to Carolyn, then White Oak was the center of her universe. A sleepy, close-knit community, White Oak *was* Small Town, America. But it seemed to share a not-so-flattering trait with other small towns of that era: at the core of White Oak society was a self-righteous sense of decency and godliness that often seemed to obscure its compassion and humanity.

During the three years she had been gone, Carolyn had believed with every fiber of her being that all her problems would be solved if she could only get back home to her family and friends. She had been so certain that she would never need anything else. But now, nearly two years after her return, Carolyn was beginning to realize that White Oak might never be her home again, no matter how much she wanted it.

On April 2, 1967, just a few weeks after she had returned home, Carolyn had celebrated her ninth birthday. The small party, given by her family, was perhaps the biggest event of her whole life—certainly in the last three years—because she had actually been the center of attention on her big day, just like most every other kid celebrating a birthday. Her big sister, Maureen, had worked for hours on her red-gold hair, which was already attempting to grow back, and doing everything she could to make it look pretty. Her mommy had dressed her in a sweet party dress that hung far too loosely on her still-skeletal frame, but it didn't matter. Carolyn Sue Shaw was home. She felt beautiful, and, most importantly, very special.

That was in the beginning. But as time passed, attitudes began to change.

Carolyn wasn't sure what had happened or where she had gone wrong. She only knew that everything seemed different now—from *inside* her two-story brick home on Mohawk Drive to *outside* on the playground of White Oak Elementary School—and she was sure it was all her fault.

These days, Carolyn felt stupid, confused and awkward, like everyone was staring at her and she was the main topic of conversation. She knew what people in town said about her; she knew what they called her. To them, she was *that poor little Carolyn Shaw,* and since no one knew for sure what had happened to her, they just made stuff up. While people in her neighborhood were kinder to her than those strangers in town, and in some cases even protective, Carolyn really just wanted to be like everyone else. She didn't want to be singled out, pointed at, or whispered about. She just wanted to fit in.

In Carolyn's mind, she didn't belong anymore. She didn't belong in White Oak…she didn't belong in the Shaw family…perhaps she didn't belong anywhere at all.

This wasn't something that Carolyn realized immediately. It took awhile, partly because she was still too young to understand the often dysfunctional dynamics of a small town community and partly because the erosion of a marriage and the destruction of a child's psyche never happen overnight. It happens in stages, like that proverbial snowball rolling down a hill, slowly gathering power, growing ever more cumbersome and unwieldy. Yet, as the months passed, the tiny but significant changes had gradually become more and more obvious—even to Carolyn.

Like, Maureen was married now to a really nice guy named Tom, and Carolyn hardly ever saw her these days. That was hard because she had been Maureen's pet before, but now Maureen acted like she wasn't even there. Before Rose had come into their lives, Maureen had fixed Carolyn's hair and had taken her with her everywhere—even on dates she had with local boys—but now she didn't want to take her anywhere. Daddy said it was because she was a married woman now and she just didn't have that kind of time anymore.

Her big brother, Bobby, didn't have any time for her, either. But Daddy said it was because he was in college now and college boys just didn't want to hang out with their little sisters. If he did, his friends might make fun of him and that would be the end of the world to Bobby. Carolyn could understand that a little better than she could understand Maureen's rejection, but it didn't hurt any less.

Anyway, there was something far more terrible than Bobby's growing pains and Maureen's preoccupation going on in Carolyn's house.

Even after two years, Carolyn's life still seemed to be separated into sections of time she could label *Before Rose* and *After Rose.* In Carolyn's memory, life had been perfect Before Rose. Mommy and Daddy had never been cross with each other, and Daddy had a successful hardware store called *George's Supply Company* that kept him busy, and Mommy was never too tired to play house with Carolyn.

Before Rose, when life was perfect, every single Sunday the entire Shaw family had attended the beautiful red brick *McKeesport Assembly of God Church*, where one full pew had been reserved for them, and Carolyn often sang lead in the children's choir. From a special seat in the balcony and surrounded by splendid stained glass windows, she had watched her parents be baptized together. Now, After Rose, Mommy wouldn't step foot inside a church and she said lots of hurtful, bad words. Carolyn could only attend services with her daddy and sometimes her grandparents.

Before Rose, Carolyn remembered birthday parties and family picnics and occasional evening trips to the small old-style Dairy Queen with the blue neon sign perched on the roof. Daddy would drive the car into the parking lot and they would all walk to the window together to place their ice cream orders. Sometimes they ate them right there and sometimes they took them home, but whatever they did, it was an event that everyone looked forward to. Now, After Rose, it was only Carolyn who went with her daddy. Her mommy was no longer interested in ice cream.

Carolyn remembered all the family gatherings that had taken place Before Rose, often at *Rainbow Gardens*, a glorious amusement park that had a drive-in theater, a huge swimming pool, a skating rink, and a roller coaster that actually screeched to a halt in a gigantic pond. Now, After Rose, no one seemed particularly interested in family gatherings anymore.

Now Mommy and Daddy slept in twin beds, and although Mommy still met him at the door when he came home from work, she didn't kiss him anymore. That observation alone made Carolyn feel really nervous and insecure. In addition, Daddy had lost his business sometime while Carolyn was gone and now worked for his brother Artie in a place called *Dura-Kitchens,* building and installing top-of-the-line cabinets, and Mommy never wanted to play anything at all. Of course, now Mommy had a part-time job in a dress shop in McKeesport that left her more tired than usual, but Carolyn couldn't help but feel that Mommy was working not for the extra money but for the opportunity to be away from home…and away from her.

It just didn't make sense, and Carolyn knew it had to be her fault. Who else's fault could it be? It was because of her nightmares and the voices she heard and how she couldn't stand to be in a room with the door closed. It was because of the way she floated ghost-like through the house after everyone had gone to bed, just so she could check on them. Her mommy hated that, but Carolyn couldn't seem to stop it. No matter how hard she tried to lie still and go to sleep, Carolyn had to constantly reassure herself that everyone was home and safe in their beds, that no one had taken her away from them while she was sleeping…

Carolyn knew that they all tried to make things normal for her—it was obvious how hard they tried—but somehow nothing seemed to help. She had slowly gained weight and the color had gradually returned to her cheeks, but her dreams remained haunted.

Her mommy had found her a "walking teacher" because she had been shackled and malnourished for so long that she couldn't walk right anymore, but it didn't seem to matter because Carolyn could still see that old metal radiator and feel that cold, bulky chain locked around her ankle. She had had a private tutor who saw to it that she caught up academically with other children her age and she had accomplished that with very little difficulty, but still the kids didn't accept her and she didn't want to be there. Finally, a special teacher had worked with her on her verbal skills, but that seemed unimportant, too. In Carolyn's mind, no one wanted to talk to her and certainly no one wanted to listen, so why bother?

That was the hardest part of it all. When she had first returned, Carolyn was convinced that she could keep her story to herself; she would never need to bother anyone with it and she was strong enough to handle her memories alone. But, as time went by, the venomous monsters that inhabited her past had begun to gnaw away at her resolve, appearing at the most inopportune times, visible to no one else but clear as day to Carolyn.

Those monsters whispered her name when she walked through the woods, then disappeared. They brushed against her cheek in the middle of the night, then vanished. Once in a while, out of nowhere, she even heard the high-pitched voice of a little girl softly singing, "Car…o…lyn…" Sometimes she even heard a sharp "Car'lyn!" when she was doing normal things like studying in class, or reading a book, or taking a bath. It had finally gotten to the point where she was desperate to tell her story to anyone who would pay attention, but that was the problem: no one wanted to hear it.

It wasn't that they didn't have the time. It was that they didn't have the heart.

It was obvious that no one wanted to learn about her three years of hell. Her story would disturb—no, *destroy*—that picture of the perfect family her mommy seemed so determined to create for her friends in White Oak. Instinctively, Carolyn understood that and knew she had to play along.

Nothing was more important than her mommy's happiness and peace of mind, especially to Carolyn's daddy, so Carolyn did everything she could to be perfect—more for her daddy's sake than for anyone else's. She didn't argue, she never talked back, and she tried to do everything she was told. In truth, she mostly tried to be invisible, a lesson she had learned well while she was with Rose, but that didn't seem to be good enough for her mommy.

Now, when her mommy looked at her, Carolyn often saw a fleeting expression of anguish race across her face. Sometimes she even saw anger. But most often she saw cool detachment, like her mommy was no longer part of the family, like she had somehow removed herself from anything that caused her pain.

And Carolyn, for some incomprehensible reason, apparently caused her mommy more pain than anyone else in the whole world.

What had happened to the woman who had promised a terrified child on an airplane that she would always be her mommy? Where was she? Carolyn didn't know. She only knew that that warm, loving, beautiful woman was gone, replaced by a stranger who was cold and bitter and filled with rage.

Even though her daddy told her that she was imagining things, Carolyn knew she wasn't. Just in the last few weeks, her mommy had begun blaming her for doing stuff she knew she hadn't done and accusing her of saying things she knew she hadn't said. It was totally bewildering, like her mommy couldn't stand the sight of her, and it broke Carolyn's heart.

Just a few nights earlier, her daddy had found her crying on the back steps. Sitting down beside her, he had cradled her hand in his and said softly, "It's not your fault, baby. Your mommy's just trying to deal with some stuff you don't know anything about. We have to be patient with her."

Carolyn had sniffled, nodded and scrubbed away her humiliated tears with a balled-up fist, but she didn't understand. All she knew was that it was best if she stayed out of her mommy's way.

Although Carolyn would have given anything to have her family back exactly as it had been before and felt increasingly isolated from each of them as the months went by, she did have one very important ally: her beloved Viola Rankin, a sweet, lovely elderly lady that Carolyn called *Grandma Rankin*. Grandma Rankin lived down the hill from the Shaw family in a cottage that was fenced in by massive pines and tucked securely away behind what White Oak old-timers still labeled *The Rankin Farmhouse*.

Carolyn's memories of the plump and feisty Grandma Rankin and the Rankin farmhouse were part and parcel of what had kept her alive and comparatively sane for three years. But the fact that she could now physically *touch* the old lady's soft skin meant more to Carolyn than anything else, perhaps because her tangible presence reinforced the reality that she was truly home. Carolyn always looked for the old lady when she walked down Rankin Road toward the cottage, and Grandma Rankin's welcoming bear hugs never failed to fill that huge, yawning void in her spirit—at least for a little while.

Grandma Rankin was the only person in White Oak who had all the time in the world to spend with a lonely, confused little girl—a little girl whose own mommy had no time at all—and she gave Carolyn a voice where no one else would or could. In the afternoons, she taught Carolyn how to hook-latch rugs on a loom, bake cookies out of oranges, crochet, and even grow perfect African Violets. Sometimes Carolyn brought her coloring books to the cottage and spent hours coloring with Grandma Rankin's quiet and rather backward brother, Abbey, while the old woman told stories or explained parables from the family Bible that always rested open-faced on the kitchen table.

In the summers they picked blackberries together, and in the autumns, before Halloween, they gathered apples from the small apple orchard next to the farmhouse and cored them at the kitchen table. Whatever Grandma Rankin needed done, Carolyn tried her hardest to do it. But most importantly, Carolyn absorbed the old woman's vast wisdom and loving attention like Grandma's beautiful African Violets soaked up the sunshine.

The truth was, she loved to be wherever Grandma Rankin was, especially when she got to hold the elderly woman's much-loved weenie dog, Heinsy, in her lap. Carolyn couldn't figure out why other children on the hill called her an old witch and tried to make her life miserable. But, even though she was a beautiful lady with sparkling blue eyes and silver-white hair, Grandma Rankin could give as good as she got—and often did. She chased mischievous kids out of her yard with a broom, which kept them all pleasantly terrified, but never Carolyn. She always welcomed Carolyn with open arms, and Carolyn always went straight into them.

That was how Carolyn knew that her mommy had to be lying about her bad behavior. Grandma Rankin didn't tolerate evil children, so she would never put up with the kinds of wicked behavior Mommy had begun accusing Carolyn of.

"Am I ugly, Grandma?" she would ask anxiously. "Is that why Mommy doesn't love me anymore?"

Grandma Rankin would chuckle and shake her head. "Good heavens, no, child! Your mommy loves you. She just needs to get right with the Lord is all. Once that happens, she'll be fine. In the meantime, you just do the best you can."

Grandma Rankin offered unconditional love and acceptance to Carolyn, which was why Carolyn never talked to her about the past three years, no matter how desperate she was. The last thing in the world Carolyn wanted to do was show Grandma Rankin what a bad person she had become during that time— such a bad person that her own mommy no longer wanted to be around her. If Grandma Rankin didn't already know it, Carolyn certainly didn't want her to find out.

That little house was a safe and soothing place for Carolyn to be, and she visited as often as she could. If the truth were told, the quiet serenity of Grandma Rankin's cottage comforted Carolyn's often agitated spirit so that when she went home, it was easier for her to handle the increasing chaos she found within her family.

One Friday evening after school, as she walked up the stairs to her room, she could easily hear the raised voices of her parents coming from her mommy's bedroom. Sighing in resignation because there was another argument in progress that she couldn't stop, Carolyn closed her door and prepared to do her homework. As she spread her books out on the bed, her mommy's voice wafted up through the furnace register in the middle of the floor. Her words were muffled, but Carolyn could easily understand them.

"She's been home almost a year, George, and she's just getting worse. Why on earth can't you see it? She's not getting any better."

Carolyn frowned, giving up any idea she had of doing her homework, and sat right down on the floor beside the register, listening intently. Who was Mommy talking about? Was someone sick? The silence stretched for what seemed like eons; her daddy said nothing. She could visualize him sitting on his bed, head down, waiting patiently for Mommy to finish her tirade.

"Talk to me, George! I can't handle this by myself anymore. I just can't."

George Shaw came back at his wife so furiously that Carolyn was shocked, not only by his tone but by the stunning realization that they were arguing about *her*.

"What are you talking about, handling this by yourself? What do you do besides accuse her of doing things she didn't do, calling her a liar—I heard you tell her the other night that she had been nothing but a thorn in your side since the day she came here! I found her out on the back steps, crying her eyes out. How can you say that to a child, Betty? How can you be so cruel to a little girl?"

Carolyn bit her lip, waiting for the answer. Maybe she would find out now why her mommy was so angry.

"I shouldn't have," Mommy said finally. "You're right. I lost my temper, that's all. But I'm tired, George, I'm so tired. She isn't *my* child, don't you understand that? She's my *step-grandchild*, for God's sake! That means I'm too old to be her mother. I'm too old, George! I just want to be left alone now. I can't do this anymore."

Carolyn's eyes filled with tears. It was going to happen again. Her mommy was going to throw her away—she said so. She said she couldn't do it anymore. Carolyn drew in a ragged breath, laid flat on the floor with her ear pressed against the register, and kept listening. She had to. Somehow, some way, she had to try to understand.

"What can't you do anymore?" Daddy was asking quietly. "Tell me, Betty. Talk to me."

Carolyn heard the click of a lighter as her mommy lit a cigarette. Carolyn envisioned the smoke pouring from her nostrils as she spoke, trying to get control of her temper. "You're not here, George," Mommy said finally. "You don't see what I see—not that it matters. I've never known a man that can fool himself like you can. I keep telling you that she needs help. You think that because she's learned to walk again and her hair's grown out that everything is normal. It isn't, George. It just isn't."

"She needs time, Betty. She just needs our love and support."

"Oh, for God's sake!" Mommy exploded. Carolyn started, heart pounding. "She lies all the time, George! I can watch her do something, and she will look me right in the eye and swear she didn't do it. Sometimes she'll apologize, sometimes she won't. It's fine when she talks to that silly parrot that Maureen and Tom gave her—Talka talks back. But I draw the line when she starts talking to *herself* and acts like *I'm* crazy because I don't know who she's talking to! She wanders around the house during the night like a ghost. She touches things all night long. I've followed her and she doesn't even know I'm there. I've been awakened in the middle of the night by her standing at the foot of my bed, just staring at me, patting my blanket, stroking my foot. Sometimes she's sleepwalking. Sometimes she's... I don't know what she's doing. You can't close a door without her throwing an absolute fit..."

"I took the doorknob off her bedroom door," Daddy interrupted calmly, "and she's all right with that now. She can go in and out when she wants to. That's all she needed, Betty. Don't you understand that? She can't be locked in." His voice dropped. "Wherever she was, I think she was locked in."

But Mommy didn't seem to hear him. "I feel like I'm living in a madhouse, George. I can't take it anymore."

"God will provide, Betty. God heals. You know He does. He brought her back to us and He'll take care of her."

Daddy's soothing tone seemed to drive Mommy crazy and her voice escalated into a shriek of rage. "Is God going to provide a shrink for her, George? When are you going to accept the fact that *I* can't help her? That *you* can't help her? She's sick, George!"

Carolyn recognized the upcoming volcanic eruption—she heard it all the time. Mommy was working herself up into a towering, monumental fit of fury. It wouldn't be long before she was in such a frenzied state that no one would be able to control her.

"She's not sick, Betty—she's hurt, that's all! All she wants is for you to hold her! Just hold her and love her like you used to. I've seen you back away from her...like she's something dirty that you don't want to touch..."

"Of course I back away from her! You would, too, *if* you were here! She needs too much time. She needs too much, period! She's too demanding of everything, George—my time, my person—she'd take my soul if I'd let her!"

"We don't know what she's been through, Betty, but we know it was terrible. All we have to do is trust in God and wait it out."

"Really?" Mommy lowered her voice, but her words dripped sarcasm. "Why do we have to wait it out? She has a father, doesn't she? He's your own son, and you're keeping her from him! What do you suppose your precious God thinks about *that*? You know where Art lives. You know how to reach him. Do it."

"Betty, there's no way I'm sending that child all the way out to Olympia, Washington, to stay with a man she has no idea even exists! You must be mad to even think of it!"

An icy silence stretched endlessly. When Mommy finally spoke again, she sounded like steel. "You listen to me, George. You can trust in God 'til the cows come home, but I don't have time. Carolyn's mind isn't the only one in trouble here, but you can't see that. It doesn't matter to you, anyway. Carolyn's mind is the only one you care about. You don't care about mine. You're totally obsessed with this child—you always have been. You've sacrificed your health, your business, even your marriage… And now you're going to sacrifice me. If you think I'm going to stay here and let that happen, you're just as crazy as she is."

Then it was silent in the room below and Carolyn backed away in horror from the register on the floor. She stared at it as if evil itself had writhed and slithered its way up the pipes and through those opened vents.

The ghosts returned in earnest, but now they weren't imaginary. Now they were parts of scenes from Carolyn's past, scenes that made no sense to her and followed no chronological order, but scenes that she knew beyond any shadow of a doubt had truly occurred. She knew because she could *feel* the people in those scenes; she could *smell* their fragrances and *taste* their food and *touch* their flesh. Yet those scenes were strangely insubstantial, like flashes of light, snapshots in time, and the more frequently she saw them, the more confused she became…

Without warning, Carolyn sees a young child in a hospital room. The door swings open and a short, sweaty, heavy-set woman with reddish-blonde hair bursts in and shrieks, "I'm your mommy and I'm taking you with me!" The child gives a blood-curdling scream, and a doctor rushes in and grabs up the child. "It's going to be all right," he soothes her. "She's just a crazy woman." The doctor is big and tall, with black hair and a black mustache, and somehow Carolyn knows that he loves her, that she matters to him…

Abruptly, unexpectedly, Carolyn sees her mommy hiding a toddler in the basement—a toddler that bears an uncanny resemblance to Carolyn—and she sees a young Bobby hiding that same toddler in the clothes dryer. She sees her mommy pulling herself across the kitchen floor, lower than even the windowsill, from the cellar door to the kitchen counter, to get a box of animal crackers. She takes them back downstairs to the hungry toddler still hiding in the cellar...

Those memories, as clear as they were, meant very little to Carolyn because they weren't in any context; they seemed to live outside of time. So, when the memories came, what mattered most to Carolyn was that for some reason her mommy had cared enough to make a "hiding" game out of whatever was happening—and her mommy had loved the child. In these startling flashes of light, she was the mommy that Carolyn had remembered and yearned for, for three long years.

But she was *not* the mommy that Carolyn knew now.

Now, at nearly eleven years old, Carolyn had overheard an argument between her mommy and daddy that had put her in her place. While her instinct was to go to her mommy, she already knew what her mommy would say. She would ask, in that angry voice, "Why are you bringing this up to me now? Haven't you caused me enough trouble? You want to know about your family? Go ask your daddy—and leave me alone!"

She might even begin to swear and curse against God, an ever-increasing tendency she had that scared Carolyn half to death. After all, when Mommy got like that, she was raving against the loving Being that had not so long ago provided His very own angels to protect a terrified little girl locked in a closet. Carolyn had never told her about the angels, of course, but it wouldn't have mattered. Mommy would never have believed her, anyway.

Carolyn didn't want to bother her daddy with her questions, either. He seemed so tired these days. He was still handsome, of course, but to Carolyn he seemed "weary to the bone," as Grandma Rankin described it when she was talking about herself at the end of the day. He was unhealthily pale, too, against his still-black hair and snapping dark eyes, and his shoulders seemed more slumped than she had ever noticed before. Carolyn worried about him, even more so because her mommy didn't seem to care at all, and the last thing she wanted to do was give him any more heartache than he was already suffering.

But there was no one else in White Oak that she could even begin to talk to; no one else knew the answers to the questions that Carolyn had. If she asked Grandma Rankin, the old lady would tell her that all she knew was gossip and she couldn't repeat gossip and it wasn't her place, anyway. Her grandson and Carolyn's good buddy, Jimmy Rankin, was so naïve that he didn't know anything outside of what he could learn from books, so he wouldn't be any help. Even

Carolyn's best friend from school, Adriana Holt, wouldn't be able to do any more than simply listen.

For the first time since she had returned home, Carolyn needed more than just an ear. She needed answers, and she had no idea where she was going to find them.

# CHAPTER SEVEN

Soft lamplight bathed the living room in a cozy glow as Carolyn curled up in one corner of the sofa, stroking the warm belly of her mommy's white toy poodle, Jacque, as he lay flat on his back beside her, all four paws in the air. Keeping one eye on some goofy variety show that came on television every Saturday night, Carolyn also furtively watched her mommy as she applied a second coat of *Antique White* polish to her perfectly oval nails.

At just this moment, Carolyn felt safe, wanted, and like part of the family simply because her mommy occasionally glanced in her direction, giving her that familiar sweet smile.

Yet, when her mommy wasn't looking, Carolyn studied her more carefully than she had ever done before. For some reason, Mommy seemed smaller now. Just a shadow over five feet, she was still fragile and slender like the ballerina she had once been, but Carolyn at nearly twelve years old was already almost as tall as her mommy. Mommy's still-lovely skin was a little more lined than Carolyn had noticed before, her hands were slightly wrinkled, and her perfectly coiffed chestnut-brown hair—now rolled around large curlers—was lightly laced with silver.

For the first time, Carolyn realized that her mommy was right: she *was* getting older. They were *all* getting older. For some reason, Carolyn hadn't really noticed that before and she certainly hadn't thought about it. What was it like to get old? Maybe it was hard on your bones. Maybe it hurt your heart. Maybe Carolyn would be too much for *anyone* who was getting old, not just her mommy. Maybe her mommy would be angry at *anyone* who made her life any harder than it had to be these days…

No, that wasn't true, and Carolyn knew it wasn't true. She was making excuses for her mommy's unpredictable and ugly behavior because it was just too painful to admit that she, Carolyn, was the problem. Her mommy didn't mind if Maureen dropped by and took up her whole afternoon. She didn't even care if Bobby asked her to do his laundry right in the middle of the week. She was always available to them, and Carolyn knew why. They were her children, not her grandchildren.

For some reason, that made a difference.

"Hey, sweetheart! How's about my best girl joining me for some ice cream at the Dairy Queen?"

"Really, Daddy?" Carolyn pushed the sleeping poodle to one side and jumped off the sofa. She looked at her mommy anxiously. "Is it all right, Mommy? Can I go?"

Waving her hand in the air to dry her fingernails, Mommy shrugged in obvious disinterest. "Go ahead. Don't forget your jacket. It's getting cold outside."

Carolyn dashed to the coat closet and pulled her jacket off the hanger. Then, with one arm thrust halfway into a sleeve, she held her breath as her daddy asked, "Why don't you come with us, Betty? It's been a long time since we all went out for ice cream."

Mommy capped her fingernail polish with an air of finality and placed the bottle carefully on the end table beside her. "I'm in my robe, George. I have curlers in my hair. Do I look like I'm interested in getting ice cream?"

"Oh, come on, Mommy! It'll be neat." Carolyn finished putting her coat on and took her daddy's hand. "We used to go all the time, remember? Please, Mommy..."

Mommy stood up and glared at them both. "Go. Have fun. I'm staying right here."

Carolyn backed up slightly as her daddy's hand tightened around hers. "Calm down, Betty," he said quietly. "There's no need to be that way. Come on, Carolyn."

Carolyn's lip quivered and she bit back tears as she followed her daddy out the front door and down the steps to his work truck parked on the driveway. The autumn-night chill was biting enough to make her eyes water and her nose tickle—a sure sign that Thanksgiving was right around the corner. Before long the first snow would be on the ground, and then it would be Christmas.

But the thought of Thanksgiving and Christmas didn't hold any thrill for Carolyn this year. Those were family times, and even though she knew that her mommy would put on a good show for the whole neighborhood, she also knew that it wouldn't be real. The more Carolyn thought about it, the more she just wanted it to be over with.

"Hey, are you going to get in?" Daddy asked, chuckling. "It's a little cold to stand outside all night."

Embarrassed, Carolyn climbed into the truck and shoved her hands more deeply into her warm jacket pockets.

"Let's get this heater turned on, shall we?" Daddy asked once he had closed the doors, rolled up the windows and started the engine. "I didn't know it was this cold outside. Really, it's way too cold for ice cream."

Carolyn had been thinking the same thing, but she was willing to put up with any amount of discomfort if it meant she could be alone with him for just a little while.

"Oh, no, Daddy, I want to go to Dairy Queen! I'm not cold, Daddy—really!"

He chuckled and reached across the seat to pat her knee. "Well, of course we'll go to the Dairy Queen. I said we would, didn't I? We'll just get some hot chocolate instead, how's that?"

Carolyn grinned with relief and nodded as he put the truck in reverse and backed out of the driveway. Driving out of the neighborhood toward Lincoln Way, the main thoroughfare leading right through the middle of White Oak, Carolyn gazed wistfully at all the pretty houses they passed, homes that seemed to envelop happy families in soft lamplight and crisp curtains and TV laughter.

Somehow people seemed to *connect* inside these houses and Carolyn longed to experience that kind of bond with her own family once again, instead of just automatically functioning within the empty spaces that seemed to make up her life these days. In fact, the only place in which she felt truly *alive* anymore, besides at Grandma Rankin's cottage, was in the lush, green forest behind her house. This was her secret place, her hide-out where she could get away from hysterical mommies who blamed her for things she hadn't done and vicious children who didn't want to include her in their games. The cool, damp, dark solitude soothed her restless spirit; here she felt at peace with nature, connected to all the little wild animals, and free to communicate with other silent visitors that no one else could see...

As Daddy turned his truck onto Lincoln Way and headed toward Rainbow Gardens, that unique amusement park/drive-in theater combination across the street from the old Dairy Queen, Carolyn spotted the large, blue-lit ice cream cone perched on the roof.

"There it is, Daddy!"

"Yep, there it is." He turned into the parking lot behind just a couple of other vehicles and parked the truck near the window where teenaged workers took the orders. "Do you want some hot chocolate?"

Carolyn nodded happily and snuggled more cozily against the seat. As she waited for him to return, she closed her eyes, enjoying the low rumble of the motor and the hum of the heater as it gently puffed its warmth against her face. For the first time in a long time, she was completely relaxed and sleepy.

"Here we go, sweetie."

As he slid into the driver's seat and slammed his door shut, Carolyn took the cup of hot chocolate from him and blew on it cautiously, blinking against the steaming liquid. Every once in awhile she cast a glance in his direction, watching him in the headlights of other cars driving in and out of the parking lot, and wondered what he was thinking. He was obviously somewhere else, not with her, and he was obviously worried.

Finally, Carolyn cleared her throat. "Daddy?"

He jumped a little, startled, and gave her a sheepish grin. "I'm sorry, sweetie. My mind was wandering. What is it?"

Carolyn twisted in her seat so that she could meet his eyes head-on. "You were thinking about Mommy, weren't you? You always have that funny look on your face when you're thinking about Mommy."

"No kidding. What funny look is that?" He scrunched his face up like it was made out of rubber. "Is it this one?" Then he crossed his eyes and stuck out his tongue. "Or this one?"

Carolyn giggled, but sobered immediately. "No, Daddy. I'm serious. You know what I mean."

He gave a deep sigh and his handsome face grew thoughtful. "Yes, Carolyn," he finally answered with a tinge of sadness in his voice, "I know what you mean."

"So...were you?"

"Was I what?"

"Were you thinking about Mommy?"

"I was." He was silent for a long time. Finally he cleared his throat and added carefully, "And you. I was thinking about you, too."

"Me?" Carolyn's heart began thudding uncomfortably in her chest. This wasn't going to be good; she could feel it in her bones. She sipped her hot chocolate carefully and looked away from him. "What about me?"

"I'm thinking that maybe...well, I'm thinking that maybe...it's time, Carolyn."

Here it comes, she thought, fighting inexplicable panic. The rug was going to be pulled out from under her again. Why doesn't anyone ever ask me what *I* think? Carolyn wondered suddenly. Why does everyone make decisions for me? It would be one thing if they were decisions that didn't matter, but they were decisions that affected her life and no one else's.

A cold, implacable anger unlike anything she had ever felt before began to well up inside of her, building and strengthening slowly but undeniably. When I grow up, she promised herself, no one will ever again make a decision for me. I'm going to control my own life...

But right now she was young, vulnerable, tossed back and forth like a flimsy paper doll, helpless to the whims of grownups who seemed even more confused than she was. Fighting tears, she stared desperately at the lit dashboard. "Time? Time for what?"

His voice was gentle but he spoke in a rush, as if he couldn't get the words out fast enough, "I'm thinking that maybe it's time for you to meet your real father, Carolyn."

For the first time, Carolyn allowed those words to sink into her brain and sort of nestle there like an inoffensive stranger standing quietly in the corner of a huge family reunion. Maybe it wasn't so bad, she thought. After all, how many children actually had two whole-but-separate families? She didn't know of a single one.

Realizing that perhaps her daddy was finally willing to give her the answers she craved, Carolyn asked quietly, "Will you tell me about him? I don't know anything about him."

Relaxing against the seat, he took a sip of his hot chocolate before he ran his fingers nervously through his wavy dark hair. He seemed a little disoriented, like he wasn't sure where to begin.

"Well, Carolyn," he said finally, "you know I'm not so good with words. You just bust in and ask me questions if you want to, okay? I don't know much about your father. I didn't raise him, you know."

"Then where did he come from?"

Daddy chuckled. "Well, he didn't crawl out from under a rock, that's for sure. A long time ago—before I even knew your mommy—I went out to California and married a nice lady named Clara Hudd. We had two boys together, Arthur and Gary. But our marriage didn't work out and we got a divorce. I left my sons with Clara and moved back here to Pennsylvania, where I met your mommy at some family gathering. Her name was Betty Norton at that time and she knocked my socks right off. She was a beautiful lady, and she had been married to a very nice man named Frank Norton who got hurt in World War II and just never got over it. Anyway, she and Frank Norton had a daughter together named Maureen, but their marriage didn't work out, either. Eventually, Betty and I got married. We had a son together and named him Bobby."

Daddy ran his fingers through his dark hair and looked at Carolyn apologetically. "You might get real confused here, Carolyn, but all that's really important is this: Arthur, my son with Clara, is your real father. We named him after my brother, but we call him *Art* instead of *Artie*. He lives in Olympia, out in Washington State, with his wife, Lorene, and their three boys—who are actually your half-brothers. So, Clara and I are actually your real grandparents, not Betty and I. Do you understand so far?"

Carolyn was getting a headache, but she nodded.

"The lady you've always called *Mommy* is your grandmother, too—but *only because she's married to me*. In other words, she has no blood ties to you like I do. I think they would actually call her your step-grandmother. And her daughter, Maureen, isn't really your big sister. She's just your aunt by marriage. Since she isn't actually my child, she has no blood ties to you, either. And our son, Bobby, isn't your big brother. But he *is* your true uncle by blood because he *is* my son... Sweetheart, I'm so sorry. Are you following this?"

Carolyn stared at him, a troubled frown on her face and her eyes clouded with confusion. "I'm trying, Daddy," she answered finally. "Go on."

He took a deep breath and dove in again. "Meanwhile, back in California, Clara married a terrific man named Bob Lovell. He raised my sons, Arthur and Gary, like they were his own. Even though I always sent money to help support them, they took Bob's last name, *Lovell.* I didn't argue about that because Bob was always so good to them and I was happy that he cared enough about them to give them his name. So your real father's name is *Arthur Lovell,* instead of Arthur Shaw, and you were born *Carolyn Sue Lovell,* instead of Carolyn Sue Shaw. Do you understand that?"

"I think so."

But none of it made much sense to Carolyn. She wasn't even quite sure why it mattered. As far as she was concerned, she was Carolyn Sue Shaw and she would always be Carolyn Sue Shaw, no matter how many different names people tried to give her. When she had finally come home and Daddy had taken her to his bank to open a little savings account, they first had to get her a social security number—which they registered in the name of *Carolyn Sue Shaw.* So, as far as she was concerned, that was that. George Shaw was still her daddy and would always be her daddy, Betty Shaw was still her mommy, and Maureen and Bobby were still her big sister and brother—blood ties or not.

Still, for a moment Carolyn felt like she was lost in one of those bizarre amusement rides where crazy mirrors gave back crazy reflections totally unlike reality and nothing was what it seemed to be. In one fell swoop, everything in Carolyn's life had become an illusion.

There was only one reason for her daddy to tell her all this stuff, she reasoned, and that was to try to explain why her mommy didn't want her around anymore. Did he honestly think that the "no blood ties" between her and Betty Shaw actually had anything to do with anything? Carolyn couldn't believe that. It just didn't make any sense. When Mommy had hid her all those times before, there were no blood ties. When Mommy had tried to protect her from that crazy Rose, there were no blood ties.

Yet now, suddenly, blood ties mattered.

Even though she was only eleven years old, Carolyn was old enough to understand that the very deep love she had always shared with the woman she called *Mommy* had nothing to do with blood.

Then, Carolyn took a deep breath and asked the only question that did matter to her, the only question she truly wanted answered. "Who is Rose, Daddy?"

Now he would tell her that Rose wasn't who she had said she was, either. Now he would tell her that that fishy-eyed, pasty-faced woman was just a cruel, insane human being who had "no blood ties" to the child she had stolen. Nothing else mattered to Carolyn but that they shared no blood…

Her daddy gave a huge sigh and closed his eyes. "Rose is your real mother, Carolyn. Her name was Rose Mattair, and she was only seventeen when she met your father. Art was in the Navy and stationed down in Corpus Christi, Texas, and they…"

Carolyn began to shake. She held up one hand and shook her head firmly. How many beatings had she endured because she had refused to call that woman *Mother*? All that had kept her going during those years were her memories of her family in White Oak, Pennsylvania, and the absolute certainty that this woman was, in truth, a complete stranger who had shown up one morning to steal a child away…

"I don't want to hear anymore, Daddy. It isn't important, okay? Forget I asked."

"Carolyn, I…"

"Really, Daddy, forget I asked." She turned her head away and stared blindly out the window. "Mommy's right. We should move forward, not backward. I don't ever want to talk about this again."

"That's fine, Carolyn. In fact, I completely agree. But there's one more thing."

Her eyes stung with tears as she shrugged. She didn't care anymore. It didn't matter.

"Your young dad wants to talk to you, Carolyn. How do you feel about that?"

"My young dad?"

Carolyn was puzzled. Somehow she had never given one moment's thought to her *real* father. It was like he was just out there somewhere, unimportant to any part of her life.

Daddy chuckled. "Well, I'm old and he's young. We have to separate your dads somehow, don't we? Anyway, that's how I've thought of him for a long time: I'm your old dad and he's your young dad. Is that okay?"

Carolyn's half-grin was bitter and a little self-mocking as she looked at him. "You're asking me?"

"Oh, come on, Carolyn, don't be that way! I know how you must feel, like we grownups have really fouled everything up in your life and you have nothing to say about it, but that isn't true. Sometimes things happen that are just out of our control and we can't do a cotton-picking thing about it. But now your young dad wants to get to know you and I think it's a good idea."

"You do, really?"

"I do. Really."

*Sure you do. You think it's a good idea because it's what Mommy wants. She wants me gone. She said so. She wants me gone, so you want me gone… Anything to make Mommy happy.*

Carolyn shrugged again. Once more she would wear a pretend face, a face that belied what she was really thinking, how she really felt. She was an expert at doing that and she could fall back into that habit at the drop of a hat. For three years no one had known how frightened, lonely and hurt she was; for another three years she had honed the art of running from the truth into a perfect science. She could certainly do it again.

"It's okay with me, Daddy," she said finally. "If that's what you want, I'll be glad to talk to him."

His face actually went pale with relief. "Really? Do you mean it?"

"Of course I mean it. He's my young dad, isn't he?"

"That's the key, Carolyn! He's young—and he was very, very young when you were born. Sometimes we have to forgive people for the mistakes they made when they were too young to know better…"

Carolyn didn't want to hear anymore, especially if he was going to start talking about forgiveness. It was easy enough for the grownups to forgive; they hadn't been stolen and locked in a closet and tortured day in and day out. For Carolyn, living alone and lonely in the anguished memories that no one wanted to hear about, it would be a different story.

But she didn't voice these thoughts and instead fought a losing battle to crush the anger that continued to build. Once more hiding her emotions behind that comfortable façade of nonchalance, she said only, "Sure, Daddy. Can we go home now?"

"Hey, kid, happy Thanksgiving! How's it goin'?"

"Fine, thanks. It's going just fine."

"Good, good! You know, I'm glad you let your dad call me."

Carolyn thought his voice sounded way too hearty—kind of like a Santa Claus in a McKeesport department store who really wishes he was somewhere else—and she wrinkled her nose in distaste. But she didn't let on and tried to sound just as friendly.

"Well, he thought it was time we talked, and I said it was okay with me."

"That's sure grown-up of you, Carolyn. I mean, lots of people wouldn't have talked…I mean, after everything that happened…"

"It's okay," Carolyn interrupted firmly. Her stomach was beginning to churn and she wanted nothing more than to get off the phone. "It's over now."

"You're right, you're right!" His voice grew louder with relief. "Listen…we'd all really love it if you could come out here and visit sometime. What do you think?"

"Gee, I guess that would be okay …" Carolyn's voice trailed away. "I don't know what to call you," she said suddenly. "Should I call you…"

"You just call me *Art*. That'll be fine with me. Pop has been your dad all these years and we can't change that overnight, now can we? That's something we'll have to work on."

"Okay…Art," she answered, suddenly shy. "Thank you."

"Sure, kid. Listen, you call me again, any time. And you think about coming out here to see us. I got three little boys here that would love to meet you, and Lorene would love to have a little girl to fuss over, and I got a lot of years to make up for. You think about that, okay?"

Carolyn's emotions immediately went all topsy-turvy. She was terrified yet thrilled—excited that maybe some other part of her family actually *wanted* her, that there were other kids that might actually *look forward* to playing with her, that there was even another woman out there in the world someplace that would actually *enjoy* fussing over her. Not like her mommy here in Pennsylvania who couldn't get away from her fast enough…or her daddy who didn't know what to do with her…

But what if this Art-person was lying? After all, he had once gotten with that crazy Rose-lady and made a baby, which just showed that he wasn't all that smart…and maybe he was just as wicked as she was…

The truth was, Carolyn didn't know what to think. She wasn't old enough to understand grownups and why they did the things they did, but she *was* old enough to understand that they could lie, and even be selfish and cruel if it would benefit them in some way. She had experienced all that first-hand…

"Hey, are you still there, kid?"

"Yes, sir, I'm sorry. I was just thinking."

"It's okay. You're pretty shocked, aren't you? I would be, too. Listen, let me talk to Pop a minute, okay?"

"Yes, sir." Carolyn put her hand over the receiver and spoke to the silent figure beside the office window. "Daddy, he wants to talk to you."

Daddy turned and walked toward his desk. He seemed so much older, sort of slump-shouldered and tired, and there was such a deep sadness in his dark eyes that Carolyn had to look away from him. It was like no human being could carry so much pain and not break in half.

It's my fault, Carolyn thought for the umpteenth time, it's all my fault. Her daddy could have his life back with the woman he loved if there was no Carolyn around to ruin it for him.

Maybe next summer, after school is over, I'll go out to…where did he say it was? Washington State? Maybe next summer I'll meet my real dad, and my real brothers, and my real grandmother… Maybe it won't be so bad.

It was obviously time to find out what else an unfamiliar world held in store for little Carolyn Sue Shaw. Maybe next summer...

In early days of June, 1970, not long after Carolyn had turned twelve years old and school was finally out, she found herself on an airplane heading from Pittsburgh, Pennsylvania, toward Olympia, Washington. But this visit to Art's family hadn't really been her idea. It was more like she had run out of options.

It had come about because Mommy had found Carolyn down at the baseball field near the Rankin farmhouse, playing ball with a group of boys. This wouldn't have been any big deal under normal circumstances, but Mommy got it into her head that Carolyn was doing dirty stuff with the boys and demanded that Daddy get her out of the house before everyone's reputation (especially Mommy's) was completely destroyed. Daddy had somehow managed to calm her down, but Carolyn understood the trade-off.

"Just send me out to Art's place, Daddy," she said later that evening. "He wants me to come."

Daddy looked at her miserably. "Just for the record, sweetheart, I know you weren't doing anything wrong."

But that record didn't matter, Carolyn thought now, gazing blindly out the airplane window as they circled the runway, preparing to land. Her daddy hardly ever thought she did anything wrong. It was her mommy who seemed more determined everyday to believe that Carolyn was trouble and worthless and nasty.

And no matter what Carolyn did, she couldn't convince her otherwise.

Carolyn pulled her thoughts away from White Oak, Pennsylvania, and focused instead on the amazing landscape below. Even from this height she could see how green and thick the forests around the city were—apparently no one cut down a tree out here. Also visible were looming, snowcapped mountain ranges, and lots and lots of water.

Except for the water, Carolyn reflected, Olympia, Washington, seemed quite a bit like Pennsylvania.

The pilot's deep voice crackled through the microphone. "Welcome to Olympia, Washington, the capital city of this beautiful state. Off to your left and in the distance you'll see the magnificent Olympic Mountains, and that body of water straight below is the Puget Sound. We hope you've enjoyed your flight and we look forward to seeing you again..."

Once the plane had landed and Carolyn had disembarked, she stood in the waiting area and looked around nervously. She was alone, just like the last time she had been in an airport, and once again she was waiting for someone who might or might not accept her. It seemed to be a staple of her life, being passed around from person to person to person...

"Hey, kid! You're Carolyn, right?"

Carolyn jumped, startled nearly out of her wits, and met the snapping dark eyes of a man who bore a strong resemblance to her daddy. Art, too, was slightly built, with a head of thick black hair and a wide, friendly grin—but there was something about him that immediately left her ice-cold. Following behind him, hand-in-hand, were two little boys, and bringing up the rear, a toddler on her hip, was a sweet-faced, brunette woman that Carolyn assumed was their mother. *Lorene*, Art had called her.

This is my father, Carolyn thought suddenly, trying to come to grips with that realization. These are my half-brothers. This is my stepmother...

"Come here, guys! Let me introduce you to Carolyn!"

Once again his voice was too loud and enthusiastic, just like that Santa Claus he had first reminded her of, and she realized that he was actually more nervous than she was. It was a comforting thought.

"This skinny kid is Tommy," Art was saying, "and he's the oldest." He pushed 'the skinny kid' toward Carolyn. "Behind him is Derek, and the rug rat hanging on Lorene is Jon. Oh, and this is Lorene."

The sweet-faced woman drew Carolyn toward her, adjusting the toddler to settle more comfortably on her hip. "Welcome, sweetheart," she said in a rich, maternal voice that Carolyn immediately responded to. "I'm so glad we could all finally meet."

"Yes, ma'am. Thank you, ma'am."

"Well, let's get your bags and head for the old homestead, shall we?"

Art's bombastic laughter actually made her teeth hurt, and for some reason her heart wouldn't stop slamming in her chest. She couldn't remember ever having had such a negative, volatile reaction to meeting someone for the first time, but she knew that she had—at some point, somewhere...

When it came to her, Carolyn stopped stock-still in the middle of the airport and stared up at the man who had called himself her father. The last time she had felt like this was on a chilly spring day in her own front yard, when a pasty-faced woman with clammy-cold skin had taken her by the hand and said: *"Howdy, Car'lyn! I'm your mother! Beautiful mornin', ain't it?"*

# CHAPTER EIGHT

The Lovell house was white and wood-framed, located in a modest, older section of Olympia, Washington. Like the rest of the city, the neighborhood actually *felt* dark because of the lush, green foliage that seemed to grow everywhere, unchecked and wild. The sky, or what Carolyn could see of it, was gray and overcast.

"They don't call this *The Evergreen State* for nothing," Art said, setting one of Carolyn's suitcases down on the front porch. He opened the door and gestured for her to enter the small house first. "It rains just about everyday out here, did you know that?"

Carolyn shook her head and walked into the living room. She didn't think that the lack of sunshine was anything to be proud of, but apparently Art did. He had a goofy grin on his face that made Carolyn want to smack him. She set her other suitcase down and waited for the rest of the family to troop in behind her.

When they did, they were all silent, as if awaiting further orders. Carolyn had never seen three children so quiet. Tommy, the oldest boy, held her overnight bag in his hands, shifting his weight uncomfortably from one foot to the other.

Carolyn looked around the modestly furnished living room and frowned. There was something wrong here, she thought, but she couldn't quite put her finger on it. The inexpensive, dark wood end tables on either side of the sofa were polished to a deep sheen, throw pillows obviously lovingly cross-stitched by hand were perfectly placed in the middle of it, and the hardwood floors were so highly waxed that Carolyn figured she could probably see her own reflection in them. It was a perfectly kept home, just like her mommy maintained back in Pennsylvania, but still... there was something wrong.

Art's friendliness suddenly disappeared as he turned to his oldest son. "Take Carolyn's bags to your room."

Tommy grabbed a suitcase. "Yes, sir."

"Oh, I can get it," Carolyn objected. "Here, Tommy, let me..."

"Tommy'll do it," Art stated flatly.

Carolyn subsided immediately, but the little spark of anger that seemed to have moved permanently into her psyche months ago began to simmer. She recognized a target when she saw one, having been one herself many times, and Tommy was definitely a target for his father.

"Oh, and listen, Carolyn, you're gonna have to sleep in the boys' room," Art continued. "We've only got two bedrooms in this little place. But they've got bunk beds in there and you can have a top bunk. That'll give you some privacy."

"That's okay. Thank you."

"Lorene, put Jon down and start dinner. I'm sure Carolyn here is starving. Right, kid?"

"No, sir. I'm fine. I ate a big breakfast."

"Well, I'm starving and that's what matters around here. Go on, Lorene! What are you standing around for?"

"Can I help you do anything, Mrs. Lovell?" Carolyn asked, a little nervous at the thought of being left alone in the living room with Art. "I'm pretty good in the kitchen."

"Really?" Lorene glanced at her husband, apparently waiting for his permission. "I can always use a little help."

"Sure, you gals go on and whip up something delicious together. I've got a couple of customers I need to call before it gets any later."

Relieved, Carolyn followed Lorene into the kitchen. Like the living room, it absolutely gleamed with cleanliness. Suddenly Carolyn realized what had disturbed her from the moment she had entered this pristine little house: it was like no one *lived* here.

And there were no toys anywhere around. There was no sign of children.

"Why don't you sit at the table, honey?" Lorene asked, busying herself at the kitchen sink. "There's really not a single thing I need help with—I just thought you might want to sit down. Would you like something to drink? I have lemonade, Kool-Aid, iced tea..."

"No, ma'am, I'm fine. Thank you." Carolyn pulled out a chair and sat down. "What kind of customers does Art have?"

"Didn't you see the old truck out in the driveway? That's Art's work truck. He has a painting business."

"No, I didn't notice it."

"He calls it *Lovell Painting*. Real imaginative name, huh?" Lorene chuckled. "But it's a good business. It gives us a good life."

"Yes, ma'am."

Lorene pulled a large frying pan out of a lower cupboard near the stove and spoke over her shoulder. "Honestly, I don't need any help, honey. Why don't you go to the boys' room and get settled in? It's down the hall, the last door on your right."

"Are you sure?"

"Of course." She opened the refrigerator and disappeared behind the door. Her voice was muffled. "You go on, sweetie. I'll call you all when supper's ready."

"Yes, ma'am. Thank you."

Carolyn scooted down the hall, worried that she would run into Art on her way to the bedroom, but he was nowhere around. Although the bedroom door was closed, Carolyn could hear hushed laughter within. She knocked on the door.

"Can I come in?"

Tommy opened the door and stood to the side, a shy smile on his sweet, rather sensitive face. "Sure. Listen, we don't have much room in here, but the top two drawers over there in the bureau are yours. Do you want us to leave while you unpack?"

Carolyn looked at him like he was crazy. "Of course not. Why would I want you to do that?"

"The bunk over mine is yours," piped up the middle child, who had been introduced as *Derek* at the airport. His wavy hair was rusty brown and his face was mischievous, almost Peter Pan-like. He had an adorable tip-tilted nose dotted by a sprinkling of freckles. "I've never slept with a girl before."

Carolyn grinned. "Well, you won't be sleeping with one now, either."

Then, closing the door, she spotted a chubby toddler seated at a small play table in the corner of the bedroom. This was the child who reminded her most of her daddy, with his black hair and large dark eyes. He also bore a strong resemblance to his eldest brother, Tommy. Derek was the odd child out; he looked like his mother.

She offered her hand to the toddler. "Hi, there. I'm Carolyn. I don't remember—what was your name again?"

The little boy chewed on his bottom lip and didn't answer. He also didn't touch her hand. He just stared up at her solemnly. Carolyn squatted in front of him so that they were eyeball-to-eyeball. "Do you know who I am?"

He shook his head.

"Well, don't feel bad," she chuckled. "Sometimes I don't know, either. But that doesn't matter. I'd still like to know your name."

"His name is Jon, short for Jonathan," Derek interrupted impatiently, "and he's only three. He won't talk to you. I'm seven. I talk all the time. Do you want to see my muscles?"

Carolyn cocked an eyebrow and got to her feet. "I think I'll pass. How old are you, Tommy?"

"Nine."

"I'm twelve. Did you say these top two drawers are mine?"

"Yeah, for what they're worth. You won't be able to get much stuff in there."

"Oh, that's okay. I'm only going to be here about a month." Carolyn added silently, *and less than that if I have anything to say about it...*

"Lucky you," Tommy muttered under his breath, shoving a suitcase toward her.

Although Carolyn didn't answer and instead busied herself by placing folded underwear and nightgowns into her two allotted drawers, she didn't miss the muted hostility in Tommy's voice. She reacted to it by instantly wanting to protect him, just as she always wanted to protect the tiniest, most vulnerable member of any group—whether it was the runt of a litter or one of society's rejects. But she said nothing, knowing instinctively that he would be embarrassed and humiliated if she made an issue of it.

Still, she filed it away in the back of her mind. It was one more strike against a man she was trusting less and less, and disliking more and more.

"Dinner, you guys!"

Tommy jumped about a foot and went pale, but Derek ambled nonchalantly across the bedroom and opened the door. "Carolyn's putting her stuff away, Pop. We'll be there in a minute."

Art glared down at his middle son. "*I'll* tell you when you'll be there," he said softly, the threat in his voice unmistakable, "and you'll be there right now."

"It's okay," Carolyn interjected quickly. She jammed her hands into the pockets of her jeans so that no one could see them trembling. "I'm all done."

Once they were all seated around the kitchen table, Carolyn waited for Art to say Grace for his family, but no hands were folded and no heads were bowed. Fried chicken and mashed potatoes were passed back and forth with such speed that Carolyn could only manage a quick, silent prayer before she had to begin shoveling food on to her plate.

"So, tell us about yourself, Carolyn," Lorene said, handing her a bowl of green beans. "What do you do for fun up there in Pennsylvania?"

"For fun?" Carolyn thought a moment and came up blank. She shook her head. "I don't really know, ma'am. Normal stuff, I guess. I sing in the choir at church if that counts."

"Of course it counts. I wish I could sing. I can't carry a tune in a bucket."

"And that's the truth," Art chuckled. "She even sounds horrible in the shower. I sure don't know where your singing gene came from. My mom can't sing, and Rose couldn't, either. But Rose couldn't do anything. She was useless..."

Desperate to interrupt Art's line of conversation, the words popped out before she could stop them. "My daddy has a really good voice."

"Your daddy?" He looked puzzled. "Oh, you mean *Pop*. I didn't know that. 'Course, it's not like I know Pop real well. He conveniently disappeared when my brother and I were real young, and I didn't see him again 'til you were about six months old. My mom, Clara, sort of went nuts after he left, I think. She's your real grandmother, you know. Actually she's an old witch. She carries her teeth in the bottom of her purse and you can hear them chatter when she walks..."

"Art, stop it," Lorene chided. "Don't pay any attention to him, Carolyn. He's just teasing."

"Yeah, I'm just teasing." He pushed a napkin-covered bowl in Tommy's direction. "Pass these biscuits to Carolyn." Then, grinning, he added, "You know, you're skinnier than I thought you'd be. As I recall, your mother was pretty hefty."

Carolyn ducked her head and stared desperately at the glob of mashed potatoes on her plate. This man was horrible and all in the world she wanted was to go home, where her daddy said Grace before meals and at least *tried* to think before he spoke. This man wanted to hurt people. Carolyn didn't know how she knew that, but she was sure of it.

"So, how *is* Pop these days? He didn't sound so good last time I talked to him. Sounds like Betty's giving him fits. Derek, pass me the salt."

"He's all right," Carolyn murmured, not lifting her gaze from her plate. All her food suddenly seemed to run together, like a river of vomit, and she struggled not to gag.

"Don't you want your dinner, sweetheart?" Lorene asked softly from the chair beside her.

Carolyn shook her head frantically, now fighting the nausea for real. "No, ma'am," she muttered, "I'm sorry... I don't feel well..."

"Aw, she's fine," Art interrupted, stabbing his green beans with his fork and jamming them into his mouth. "Just too much excitement is all. Eat up, Carolyn. You'll feel better if you get something in your stomach."

She broke into an ice-cold, clammy sweat. The room began to tilt crazily and everyone at the table started moving in slow-motion, like they were swimming underwater. Her heart pounded, slamming hard in her chest, and her throat seemed to close up. She gagged, couldn't breathe...

The chair next to her scraped against the linoleum as Lorene jumped to her feet. Carolyn could hear the water running, then felt a cool, damp rag against the back of her neck. Lorene stroked sweaty hair away from Carolyn's forehead.

"Leave her be, Art," she said firmly. "She's had a rough day. Lots of people don't fly well."

"Bull. Don't coddle her."

Carolyn's eyes stung with hot, unshed tears of embarrassment and panic, but she breathed a little more easily with each gentle stroke of Lorene's hand. The room gradually leveled out, then straightened completely. A fork clattered against someone's plate.

"You listen here, Carolyn," Art said suddenly. "I don't know how things have been for you back in Pennsylvania, but I know how they are out here. Out here we don't put up with any crap. We get up early in the morning, whether school's in or not, and we do chores before we do anything else. We mind our manners and we do as we're told and we eat what Lorene here puts in front of us. Is that clear? So don't go thinking that you can puke and get out of eating…"

"Art, good Lord!"

If Carolyn was astonished by the determination in Lorene's voice, she was even more shocked when Art immediately subsided and mumbled, "Well, I just want her to know how things are."

"I'm sure she understands. Don't you, Carolyn?"

Carolyn nodded, "Yes, ma'am."

"Would you like to call your folks tonight, sweetheart?"

For the first time, Carolyn lifted her head and met Lorene's soft brown eyes. "Oh, yes, ma'am! Can I, please?"

"Of course you can, honey. Right before you go to bed, we'll get them on the phone for you…"

"I don't want her running to Pop for every little thing, Lorene! While she's here, I want her knowing how things are…"

"I'm sure your father would want to hear that she arrived safely."

Carolyn couldn't wait to talk to her daddy. Just the thought of hearing his voice was comforting enough to help her regain her appetite and she reached for the uneaten biscuit on her plate. She even managed to give Art a little smile.

As soon as her daddy knew how unhappy she was, he'd talk to Mommy and surely they would let her come home. Surely they would.

Tears streamed unchecked down Carolyn's cheeks as she spoke barely above a whisper into the receiver. Lorene had allowed her to use the phone in the bedroom that she shared with Art, but Carolyn didn't trust him to give her any privacy for very long.

"I want to come home, Daddy, please! Please let me come home!"

"Carolyn, you've only been there a few hours…"

"But I already know, Daddy! I want to come home! You *have* to let me come home!"

"Absolutely not, Carolyn. He's your father and you have to give him a chance. For you to come home now wouldn't solve a doggone thing, now would it? And it would be rude, especially after they've opened their home to you this way…"

"Daddy, please!"

"That's enough, Carolyn! I don't want to hear it. How was your flight?"

Carolyn sighed, hiccoughed, and forced back her tears. It was over. She recognized that tone of voice; he wasn't going to listen to her anymore. She was going to have to deal with the situation in this house—whatever *that* was—all by herself.

"It was fine, Daddy."

"Well, what do you think of Lorene and your brothers?"

"Lorene's nice enough, I guess," Carolyn answered sullenly, "and they're not my brothers. They're just boys. They're okay. I have to sleep with them."

"What?"

"Well, not in the same bed. They have bunk beds, but we're all in the same room. I have a top bunk. How's Talka?"

"That goofy parrot chatters all the time and drives your mother crazy imitating everybody, but I think she's great. Are you all going to church in the morning?"

"No, sir. Well, that is, I don't think so. They didn't even say Grace before dinner."

Daddy paused. "That's too bad," he said finally. "Listen, Mommy's calling me. I'll talk to you in a couple of days, all right?"

"Can I speak to Mommy?"

There was a long pause, and Carolyn could picture him trying to come up with an answer that wouldn't hurt her feelings too badly. Finally he just said, "She's busy now, Carolyn."

"That's all right, Daddy. I'll talk to you later. Good-night."

"Good-night, baby."

When he called her his favorite pet name with such tenderness, Carolyn's eyes welled with tears again but she said nothing more and carefully put the receiver back into its cradle.

He didn't want her to come home and Mommy didn't want to talk to her. What *was* it about her that everyone seemed to hate so much? She tried so hard to please everyone, but no matter what she did, it just wasn't enough. Maybe she really *was* just too ugly to have around. Grandma Rankin always said she was pretty, but Grandma Rankin was old and maybe her eyesight was going…

Then, spotting a full length mirror attached to the back of the bedroom door, Carolyn crossed the room and stood before it.

Was she still skinny, like Art said? No, the truth was, Carolyn thought she looked pretty darned good. Her reddish-gold hair was darkening a little now and sort of gleamed like the shiny copper of a new penny, falling with a slight wave a few inches below her shoulders. She parted it in the middle and tucked it behind each ear like all the other girls did, and it emphasized what she considered her best feature—large, thickly lashed blue-gray eyes. She was developing nicely, too, or at least she thought she was…

There was a light knock on the bedroom door. "Carolyn?"

Carolyn jumped and eased the door open. "Yes, ma'am?"

Lorene came in and closed the door behind her. "Did you have a nice visit with your folks, sweetheart?"

"Yes, ma'am. Thank you for letting me call them."

"Well, of course you can call them. They're your folks, aren't they?" Lorene sat on the edge of the bed, her sweet rather plain face troubled. "I know how you must feel, Carolyn. I know how much you must miss them and how much they must miss you…"

"But Art didn't want me to call them."

"Oh, don't worry about Art," Lorene said with a conspiratorial chuckle. "He doesn't know anything about young girls. He never was one, you know? We'll just keep this stuff to ourselves. When you want to talk to your folks, you let me know. I'll see to it."

"Really? You can do that?"

"Of course I can. Why couldn't I?" She joined Carolyn at the mirror, put her arm around her shoulders and gave her a brief squeeze. "You're turning into a lovely young lady, by the way. I think we're going to have a really good time together, don't you?"

"Yes, ma'am," Carolyn answered shyly, almost overwhelmed by Lorene's maternal kindness. It was something she had longed for, for so long: a sense of feminine connection she had once shared with her own mother and lost so many years ago…

"It's bed time now, sweetie. We'll see you in the morning. I think Art said we were all going to visit Mount Rainier tomorrow and that's a couple of hours from here, so it'll be a big day."

"Excuse me, Mrs. Lovell…"

"Lorene, sweetie. You call me *Lorene*."

"Yes, ma'am. Goodnight…Lorene."

Carolyn let herself into her bedroom and climbed the ladder to her top bunk, trying not to awaken the sleeping boys. She pulled the covers up to her neck and lay flat on her back, alert and cautious, staring wide-eyed at the ceiling.

She hadn't felt this way in a long, long time, but she recognized the feeling even if she didn't understand it. Once again, Carolyn felt like a cornered animal, helpless and at the mercy of forces far more powerful than she was, frightened without any real comprehension of what was so frightening.

As she stared at the ceiling, watching moon-shadows move slowly around the room in a way she found vaguely familiar, Carolyn knew that sleep would be a long time coming…

Then, sunshine streamed in through the bedroom window and something whisper-soft fluttered against her neck, up her cheek, near her mouth…lips pressed long and hard against hers—long and hard enough to steal her breath and completely awaken her…

Carolyn's eyes flew open and she discovered Art's face right in front of hers—so close his sour breath assaulted her nostrils. She jerked backwards toward the wall and took a deep breath to scream, but the icy warning in his narrowed dark eyes kept her silent.

Carolyn sat between Tommy and Derek in the backseat of Art's cherished, completely restored, red and white 1959 Chevy Impala, staring straight ahead as they headed back to Olympia after their day at Mount Rainier National Park. She had a headache so brutal that even her eyeballs throbbed with pain and her cheekbones hurt, but she said nothing about it. The last thing she wanted to do was to draw any attention to herself—especially from Art. The man was sick, dangerous in a way that Carolyn couldn't begin to understand.

Lorene twisted slightly in the front seat so she could make the sleeping Jonathan more comfortable and glanced back at Carolyn. "You've sure been quiet today, honey. Are you all right?"

"Yes, ma'am. I'm fine."

"Are you sure?"

Carolyn nodded and closed her eyes. Pain stabbed behind her eyeballs.

"She said she was fine, didn't she?" Art asked. "She's had a big day mountain climbing, haven't you, Carolyn?"

"Yes, sir…"

"Pop," Tommy interrupted in a small, tentative voice, "I've got to go to the bathroom."

"I told you to go before we left the park. Now you're just gonna have to wait 'til we get home."

"Yes, sir." Tommy subsided immediately and squirmed slightly in his seat. As he stared out his window, Carolyn could see his lower lip quiver and her heart went out to him.

Before she could say anything, Derek dug his elbow into Carolyn's side and gave her a mischievous wink. "I need to go, too, Pop. Can we stop at the next gas station?"

"Nope, I want to get home. Pass that Pepsi bottle back to Tommy, Lorene."

Carolyn's eyes flew open and her mouth dropped.

Lorene stared at him. "You can't be serious, Art!"

"I said, pass that bottle back there. If they need to pee that bad, they can use the bottle."

"Art…"

"Don't argue with me."

Mouthing the words, *Be careful,* Lorene shrugged and handed Tommy the Pepsi bottle. Taking it, he looked at Carolyn with pleading, tear-filled eyes. She immediately understood and turned away from him, staring fixedly out of Derek's window as they sped past giant fir trees lining the highway.

Finally, Tommy managed, "I'm done, Pop. What should I do with the bottle?"

Art ignored him. "What about you, Derek?"

"Aw, I can hold it, Pop."

"Okay. Tommy, roll your window down and throw out that bottle."

"Oh, for crying out loud—there's way too much traffic!" Lorene objected. "That bottle's going to hit someone!"

Art acted like she hadn't even spoken. "Do it, Tommy. I'm not carrying pee in this car all the way back to Olympia."

Tommy sagged in his seat like he knew he was already in for it, but he did as he was told and rolled down his window. Taking a deep breath, he threw the urine-filled Pepsi bottle out the window as hard as he could—and watched as it sailed straight into the windshield of the car behind them.

"Now you've done it, Art," Lorene said in disgust. "Now you've really done it."

"Good Lord, Tommy—can't you do *anything* right?" Art glanced nervously in his rearview mirror. "How hard is it to throw out a stupid bottle…"

"Pull over, Art. That man's flashing his lights at you. I think his windshield is cracked."

"Shoot. Now look what you've done." Art maneuvered the Impala out of traffic and drove onto the shoulder, closely followed by the other car.

"You did it, not Tommy. Just tell the guy you'll pay for it and let's go."

Once he had let himself out and walked to the back of the car to talk with the other driver, a red-faced man furiously gesturing toward his windshield, Carolyn gave Tommy's knee a comforting pat and closed her eyes. Her headache was so painful now that the inside of the car actually seemed lined in some kind of a weird pink haze. This was one of the craziest families she'd ever seen and all in the world she wanted to do was get away from them. She just *had* to figure out a way…

Art got back into the driver's seat, slammed his door so forcefully that the car shook, and eased it back into traffic. "I'm gonna take the cost of that man's windshield out of your allowance, Tommy," he said, his voice quivering with rage. "You'll be a hundred years old before you get it paid back, but you can bet your bottom dollar you'll pay it!"

A shudder went through Tommy's thin body, but he said nothing. He just sat there, quiet and still and obviously terrified. Yet when Carolyn opened her mouth to defend him, Derek nudged her, shook his head in warning, and put a finger against his lips.

Not another word was spoken all the way back to Olympia; even Art withdrew into the throbbing silence of his own fury. Yet, for the first time, Carolyn wasn't concerned about Art, his anger, or even the danger he posed to her. She was far more concerned about the frightened child seated next to her— and the ugly, awful memories that the little boy's panic was slowly awakening within her.

Carolyn had only been in Olympia for nine days, but it might as well have been nine years. It wasn't only that she missed her family or that her daddy seemed determined to keep her in Washington for as long as he could, but that her every waking moment, whether Art was home or not, actually felt *menaced* by some unseen threat that Carolyn couldn't explain to anyone. She could only *feel* it.

Outsiders who didn't know what was happening every single sunrise in the Lovell household might have claimed that she was over-imaginative and maybe even lying, but Carolyn knew better.

There was something wrong with this man. There was no reason for him to let himself into her room every morning before anyone else was up and awaken her with a long, hard kiss on her mouth. Her daddy had certainly never kissed her that way. But that's what Art did—every single morning.

Carolyn had tried everything she could think of to keep him away from her. She tried to stay awake all night, but that was hopeless after awhile. Then she tried to wake up before he came in, but she was too exhausted from trying to stay awake all night. She tried to sleep closer to the wall or with her hand over her mouth, but nothing she did worked.

All that made the visit bearable was Lorene and the three little boys, but Carolyn knew she had to get back to Pennsylvania and her daddy. It was the only way she would be safe.

Art's angry voice exploded into her thoughts. "Did you hear what I said, Carolyn?"

She jumped. "No, sir. I'm sorry."

"I said, Clara's coming all the way up here from Escondido, California just to see you. That's over a thousand miles away. What do you think of that?"

"Clara, sir?"

"My mother." His voice was thick with revulsion. "The old witch I told you about. The one with the teeth at the bottom of her purse. I tried to keep her from coming, but she won't hear of it. She's determined to get her hands on you and I can't stop her… She's crazy. Crazy."

Carolyn stared at him, puzzled. For some reason, his words didn't register. His face blurred, distorted…then actually began undulating right in front of her eyes. She backed away in horror, unable to fight the torrent of razor-sharp images that flooded her memory; she struggled against the panicked nausea his words created: *She's determined to get her hands on you and I can't stop her… She's crazy. Crazy…*

Then, somewhere in the distance, Carolyn heard shrieks and weeping, like someone far, far away had gone completely insane with hysteria and shock and terror…but she didn't know who it was or where it was coming from. The bitter taste of bile burned the back of her throat, then disappeared as she stepped away from the chaos and into the comforting embrace of that long-ago, long-forgotten light.

# CHAPTER NINE

Carolyn sat in her daddy's truck, waiting for him to join her for a Sunday afternoon drive. They had attended early services at church this morning—without Mommy, of course—and it had turned into such a beautiful summer day that neither of them could stand the idea of staying indoors. She was so excited that she had changed from her Sunday clothes into shorts and a tee-shirt in ten minutes flat.

Taking an afternoon drive with her daddy was one of Carolyn's favorite things to do, partly because she had him all to herself for a little while, but also because she didn't have to be on guard all the time to be sure he remained convinced that she was as normal as any other thirteen-year-old girl. He would be too busy driving out in the lovely Pennsylvania countryside to pay all that much attention, and she could be secure in the knowledge that her secret was safe.

At least for another day.

Carolyn hadn't realized that she even *had* a secret until after she had returned home from her visit with Art and his family last summer. She had been frightened and upset—but so what? She had been frightened and upset before, and she got over it. But this time had been different. This time, without any warning at all, she had somehow stepped away from Art Lovell's hate-filled voice right back into her bedroom in White Oak, Pennsylvania—and she had no idea why or how that had happened.

She had lost an entire block of time.

Carolyn was afraid she was losing her mind, or maybe she had already lost it and just didn't realize it. Whatever the case, she didn't know what she could do about it except keep it a secret and try to continue presenting her "normal" face to the world.

This wasn't always easy, especially when her mommy accused her of some socially unacceptable crime that she knew she hadn't committed. But now, sometimes, reaching way back into the furthest, darkest corners of her mind, Carolyn wondered exactly *who* was crazy: her mommy for accusing her, or Carolyn herself for *perhaps*, just *perhaps*, not remembering anything about it...

Even Daddy seemed different these days. His job took more out of him than it ever had before, so he was very nearly exhausted at the end of the week, and he never seemed to have much to say—to Carolyn or anyone else. She sensed a sorrow so deep within him that there was nothing she could do to help him and it broke her heart, especially since she felt so responsible. Although he was as genuinely sweet to her as ever, he sometimes seemed sort of distant now and he wasn't quite as accepting of her behavior as he had been before.

Of course, part of the reason for his rather chilly attitude might have been because Mommy was hardly ever home anymore and he seemed really frustrated about that. When Maureen and Tom had welcomed a beautiful baby boy into their home in January 1971, Mommy seemed to have practically moved in with them. Daddy accused her of being "obsessed" with the new arrival and ignoring everyone else who needed her, but she didn't seem to care what he thought. And, although Carolyn missed her mommy, she couldn't help but be relieved by her absence just because the house was so quiet and peaceful when she was gone.

Still, since her daddy's affection was the only real constant Carolyn had ever had in her life, she was now terrified that she might actually do something wicked enough to lose it. That thought had never before occurred to her. His love for her had always been unconditional and she had believed that it would always be hers. Now she wasn't so sure.

So, she was thrilled when Daddy asked her if she wanted to take a drive somewhere. It had been so long since they had been together like that, just the two of them.

"Here we go, ready or not." Daddy climbed in beside her, started the truck and backed down the driveway.

Carolyn turned sideways in her seat so that she could gaze out his side window and watch his face at the same time. Every once in awhile her love for him was almost overwhelming, enough to bring tears to her eyes, and when it was a perfect day like this—cloudless blue skies, music playing softly on the radio, just Carolyn and her daddy—even the fleeting thought of not having him in her life was painful enough to take her breath away.

He glanced over at her and grinned. "What are you staring at? Oh, I know. Your old dad's getting older by the minute, right in front of your eyes."

Carolyn smiled shyly and looked away. After they turned on a fairly new two-lane highway at the outskirts of town, the bustling little suburb of White Oak disappeared behind them and was gradually replaced by endlessly rolling hills and acres of lush, healthy cornfields. There wasn't another vehicle anywhere. It was like Carolyn and her daddy were the only two people in the whole world.

"I guess you're glad school's out, huh? I know this year has been sort of hard on you."

She stiffened and glanced at him out of the corner of her eye. This wasn't the direction she wanted their conversation to take. She needed to keep it lighter. "Not really," she said, her voice sounding normal enough. "Jimmy Rankin says that eighth grade is hard on everyone."

"*Little* Jimmy Rankin? Since when do you care what he says?"

"Well, you know how smart he is. If he says that eighth grade is hard on everyone, then I figure it probably is." Blushing, Carolyn gazed out her window.

"I wish I was as smart as him. All the kids make fun of him because he's so smart."

"There's nothing new about that. They've always done that, haven't they?"

Carolyn nodded. Jimmy Rankin was practically a genius, or at least she thought he was, and the other kids had always been jealous because he was smarter than all of them put together. Plus, he had always been very tall and husky, with red hair and pale skin, so he was the perfect target for jokes. When the neighborhood children were very young and busy playing childhood games, he never joined in. He was too fascinated with medicine and space travel to waste his time on ordinary kid stuff. He preferred to spend his time reading books, building spaceships out of boxes in his garage, and filling his room with model airplanes and toy skeletons. But that was what Carolyn liked about him. He wasn't like anyone else and he didn't care.

"Are you still going to marry him when you grow up?"

Carolyn giggled. "Oh, Daddy, don't be silly! I just said that because I always have to stand up for him. Anyways, I was just kidding."

"Oh, I see. Okay."

Carolyn glanced at him again just to be sure he wasn't teasing her. She knew that Daddy was fond of little Jimmy Rankin—even though Jimmy's father was known to chase women, drink too much and get a little more belligerent than Daddy liked.

"Daddy," Carolyn asked suddenly, "how did you know you wanted to marry Mommy?"

"I just knew, sweetie."

"But didn't you feel that way about Clara, too?"

He didn't answer right away. "Now there's a question," he said finally. "I guess I did. I was young, stupid, just out of high school. I didn't want to take a job in the mill like my father. So I had this crazy idea to go to California and become a movie star. Pretty big dream for a twenty-year-old kid, huh? Anyway, we just hooked up and before I knew it, we were married. And then we had two boys, one right after the other."

"Oh."

"I don't mean to make it sound like it wasn't important, Carolyn. Marriage is one of the most important things you'll ever do in your life. I just made a bad decision."

"Sure, Daddy. I understand."

"Do you?" He drummed his fingers against the steering wheel for a moment before he said, "I guess Art holds it against me that I wasn't there when he and his brother were growing up, huh?"

Carolyn took a deep breath and stared blindly out at the cornfields rushing by her window. The last thing in the world she wanted to do was talk about Art. "I don't know, Daddy. He never mentioned it."

"I tried to make it up to him, you know…when he brought you to us."

Carolyn focused hard on a single fluffy cloud that looked like it was hanging suspended just above a small farmhouse far in the distance. She said nothing.

Her daddy didn't seem to notice how quiet she had become; he appeared lost in his own memories. "I'll never forget the day he showed up on our doorstep with the prettiest baby girl I ever saw in my whole life," he said quietly. "You were about six months old, and Art told me that the Navy had called him back from overseas because Rose had left you alone in their apartment and disappeared. He had taken you to Clara at first and she kept you for awhile, but finally he had no choice but to bring you to us. Mommy and I loved you from the moment we saw you."

Carolyn's eyes burned from staring out at the cornfields so hard and for so long; she thrashed around in her mind for something else to talk about. She'd heard that story before, at least bits and pieces of it, and she certainly didn't want to discuss it this afternoon. As far as she was concerned, it had nothing to do with who she was now. Daddy's voice broke the lingering silence. "Sweetheart, can I ask you a question?"

She was relieved that he seemed to want to change the subject, too. "Sure, Daddy. What?"

"What happened at Art's house? Why were you so crazy to come home?"

Carolyn's scalp actually began to tingle with hot, nervous perspiration. She stared blindly at the dashboard in a panicked attempt to buy time. That had happened a year ago! Why in the world was he asking now? It was such a dangerous subject…

"Tell me, Carolyn. It's all right."

She shook her head. It wasn't all right. She couldn't tell him about Art's morning kisses, or the way he treated his children, or even how threatened she felt every time he was near her. She couldn't tell her daddy anything. After all, Art was his son.

"I just missed you," Carolyn finally managed. "I just wanted to come home."

"Sweetheart, I can't believe that. I heard you over the phone—you were hysterical. I had no choice but to let you come home. It wasn't fair to Art and his family to insist that you stay with them. But I need to know why. I need to know what happened."

Desperately grasping at the only real memory she had about that day, Carolyn blurted, "He said that Clara was coming and she was an old witch and she put her teeth in the bottom of her purse and they chattered when she walked..."

"Wait a minute, honey, hold on! You mean, Art's *mother*, Clara?"

Nodding, Carolyn was almost sick with embarrassment. It was too silly to repeat. He chuckled. "Well, Clara's a lot of things, but an old witch with chattering teeth in her purse? That's goofy. Why would that bother you so much?"

Carolyn knew how crazy it sounded. But she also knew she truly didn't have any answers, and she didn't have them because she couldn't remember. She had to say *something*, no matter how lame it was, no matter how much trouble she got into. She couldn't tell him the truth.

"I was just so...home...sick..."

The words died on her lips and her voice trailed away. Incredulous, Carolyn caught her breath in wonder. What she saw out her window was surreal, unbelievable...but she gazed at an image that grew more and more vivid the longer she looked at it: An extraordinarily tall man, dressed all in white and arms outstretched as if he were feeling the silks, hovered above the high stalks of corn. He appeared out of nowhere, perhaps out of the sun itself. As he walked through the field, his entire body seemed to radiate a light so intense and so loving that it actually hurt to look at him.

Incredibly, Carolyn felt no fear. Instead she was overwhelmed with joy. She *knew* him. She pointed toward the cornfield. "Do you see him, Daddy?" she whispered. "Do you see him?"

Daddy slowed the truck a little. "No, sweetheart, I'm sorry. I don't see anyone. Who do you see?"

"I see Jesus, Daddy." Tears of pure elation trickled down her cheeks. "I see Jesus."

Like a visitation from heaven, this radiant image was far more powerful than the angels that had appeared to her during all the bad times. This was as if God Himself was sharing with her a revelation that most people never get to see, and for His own purposes. Carolyn had never doubted the existence of Jesus, but suddenly He became far more than just a story from the Bible or a vibrant stained-glass image in their church windows. He lived, and He had just given her the most powerful spiritual moment of her thirteen years.

Then, as suddenly as it had appeared, the luminous figure moved backward above the corn and vanished.

"Oh, how beautiful He was!" Carolyn breathed. "Oh, Daddy, do you believe me?"

He stroked her cheek gently. "I do, sweetheart. I absolutely believe you."

Carolyn rested her forehead against the cool glass of the car window and closed her eyes. If she lived to be a hundred years old, she would never, ever forget the glory and magnificence of this compelling vision and the peace it brought to her spirit.

She would keep it in her memory and in her heart forever.

Before Carolyn knew it, it was winter, and 1971 was nearly over. Winter in Pennsylvania could be treacherous: windy, icy and freezing cold with snow drifts up past the window sills. But it could also be beautiful, especially down on Rankin pond. This small, spring-fed body of water was nestled in a deep valley situated between two craggy mountains. In the heart of winter the pond was frozen completely over—except in the one spot where the spring water bubbled up. Here the ice remained thin and was the only dangerous area in an otherwise perfect place to show off one's skill at ice skating.

Carolyn was a pretty good ice skater and an even better show-off, especially when little Jimmy Rankin was around. As they trudged side-by-side through the snow toward the pond—Carolyn with her skates draped casually around her neck, Jimmy with some space book in his jacket pocket—Carolyn was a little surprised at the way her heart suddenly sped up when he put his hand against the small of her back to guide her through the tall trees.

She glanced at him out of the corner of her eye. They were both bundled up against the cold, so Jimmy looked even huskier than usual. The fact was, she didn't know why she had ever thought of him as *little* Jimmy Rankin. Jimmy Rankin had never been little. He had always been taller than she was, even when they were barely out of diapers, and these days he towered over her. His red hair seemed to be darkening as he got older and now it glistened like burnished copper in the sunlight. Hazel-eyed and wide-shouldered, he was actually kind of cute…

"Hey, Carolyn…wait up."

Jimmy put his hand on her shoulder to halt her determined trek through the snow and turned her slowly toward him. She looked up at his face, her blue-gray eyes wide with sudden confusion, and her breath caught in her throat. He had never looked at her with so much tenderness before. He had never seemed so…*in charge*…

"You know, Carolyn," he said softly, "I'd fight for you. I know you don't think I would, but I would. I'd fight for you."

Carolyn gulped. For the first time ever, she was so acutely aware of how much bigger and stronger he was that she couldn't even breathe. Yet she wasn't frightened. At that moment, all she wanted in the world was for him to touch her.

As if he had read her mind, little Jimmy Rankin cupped her face in both his gloved hands. Her legs went weak and she closed her eyes. As he kissed her, she was surprised at how soft his lips were, how sweet and natural his scent was… Finally, when he stepped back, Carolyn opened her eyes and stared up at him, stunned.

He looked more than a little proud of himself as he gave a crooked grin. "What's the matter?"

She ran her tongue over her lips, still tasting him, and shook her head.

"Well, do you want to stand here all day or do you want to skate?"

Suddenly shy, Carolyn ran past him and reached the pond a good five minutes before he did. Panting, she plopped herself down on the huge trunk of a fallen tree, put on her skates with shaking fingers, and then headed out over the ice. As she sped around the pond again and again, leaping over that dangerously mushy place in the ice, she felt exhilarated, invincible.

"Carolyn, be careful!"

Jim's warning floated away on the wind. Grinning, Carolyn tossed her head as she skated past him. "I'm fine, scaredy cat!"

Rushing adrenalin made her careless. She jumped, high, but even before she came down on that delicate place in the ice, she knew she hadn't jumped far or high enough. She crashed right through it and into water so freezing cold that her breath was immediately sucked from her lungs. Her heavy clothing dragged her down into the water, deeper and deeper. She couldn't even scream as she struggled to climb back onto ice that kept breaking under her weight…

"Here, grab this!"

The voice seemed to come from miles away, like it was disembodied, but a sturdy branch appeared from nowhere. Jimmy's pale face loomed above her. Carolyn's head throbbed and pounded and spun as she fought for air, but still she managed to grab the thick limb and hold on like it was life itself. As he began to edge backward on the ice, pulling her, Carolyn's fierce grip on the branch helped ease her out of the water, inch by frozen inch. Finally, chilled to the bone, paralyzed by terror and exhaustion, she sprawled motionless on the ice. She was barely aware of Jimmy removing her skates or massaging her feet. She couldn't breathe, couldn't feel anything at all, anywhere…

"Get up, Carolyn!" Jimmy grabbed her beneath her armpits and heaved her upright. "Come on! We have to get you home! Come on!"

Soaked clear through, Carolyn had never been so cold in her whole life. All she wanted to do was lie down and rest a minute, but Jimmy just wouldn't allow it. He pushed, prodded, poked and practically dragged her toward home; he did everything he could to keep her walking.

Just before they reached her house, Carolyn stopped and gripped Jimmy's arm. She was nearly frozen solid, shaking with cold, and her teeth were clattering so hard she could hardly breathe, but she had to speak. "Th-thank you, Jimmy…"

He guided her down the driveway and toward the basement where Mommy had suddenly appeared outside. "Don't mention it." His voice was calm and unemotional, like he hadn't just saved her life. "Hi, Mrs. Shaw. Carolyn fell through the ice on the pond."

"No kidding. I can see that. Thank you, Jimmy."

"Yes, ma'am. I'll see you later, Carolyn."

Carolyn nodded, hardly aware of him. She was far more aware of Mommy's arm encircling her shoulders, propelling her into the basement, and pushing her toward the shower that her daddy had installed there just for these types of emergencies. Mommy turned on the hot water and tested it until she was comfortable with the temperature. "Let's get you out of these wet things," she said, tugging ice-covered clothing away from Carolyn's nearly frozen body. "Good Lord, Carolyn, your skin is as red as fire!"

Carolyn was shaking too violently to answer, but she didn't care. She couldn't remember the last time her mommy had been concerned about her, or had spoken to her without accusation or anger, and she was going to rejoice in this moment. Even if she got pneumonia and died, it would be worth it.

"I'm going to go upstairs and get you some clothes, Carolyn. You stay in this shower until I get back."

Carolyn nodded, luxuriating in the water as it beat against her and gradually brought her body back to life.

Christmas vacation came and went. The New Year's celebration welcoming the arrival of 1972 exploded on the streets of White Oak and died out. Valentine's Day passed with the usual hearts and flowers. Life kept moving forward and Carolyn moved along with it.

Yet, as she did, she wondered if she would ever fit in anywhere—at school, at church, even in her own neighborhood. It just didn't seem like she would ever find a place for herself in this town where she could blend in and be like everyone else. She wished she could be more like Jimmy, who didn't seem to care what anybody thought about him, but she knew she just wasn't as strong-minded as he was. She *longed* to be accepted and maybe even looked up to a little, but that was never going to happen.

Of course, Jimmy didn't know how much she admired him. They had never once mentioned to each other the kiss they had shared, and the fact that he had become her hero that day was just another one of Carolyn's secrets. It was weird the way that afternoon had slid into a private compartment in her memory, like she could take it out and enjoy it whenever she wanted to, but she never shared it with Jimmy or anyone else.

It was a cinch that Jimmy wouldn't be in the hot water *she* was in now, primarily because he wasn't stupid enough to let some kids talk him into doing something he knew he shouldn't do. Carolyn, on the other hand…

Well, Carolyn had stood guard in the bathroom while a few girls she didn't even like stole a couple of smokes before the bell rang, and Carolyn—as usual—got caught. She got a week's detention while the real culprits were sent to class with tardy slips. But all that mattered to Carolyn was keeping this disaster from her folks.

Carolyn didn't even want to *think* about the fit her mommy would throw if the word got out that she was on detention. So, she did the only thing she could think to do: she accepted a ride home after detention from a local high school boy. It was another cardinal rule broken, but she had to do it because he could get her home early enough that no one would become suspicious.

Holding her breath, Carolyn got all the way home without anyone spotting her. She got out of the car without anyone being the wiser. She stood on the curb for just a moment, watching as the car traveled just a little too recklessly down the icy street… She stared in disbelief and horror as the car slid sideways—right into Jimmy Rankin's front yard.

Carolyn dashed into her house, praying it was empty, and slammed the door shut. "I'm home!" she shouted. "Anyone here?"

There was no answer and Carolyn almost fainted with relief. For once it looked like she might actually pull this off…

But, not five minutes after they had finished supper that night, there was an awful commotion on the porch: banging on the front door, ringing the doorbell over and over again, hollering obscenities…

"Good Lord—what in the world?" Daddy threw his napkin on the table and stomped toward the door. "Hold on just a cotton-picking minute!"

Mommy stared at her from the opposite end of the table, her face frozen into a mask of both fear and blatant dislike. Carolyn was compelled to meet those furious eyes; she couldn't look away. She had seen that expression somewhere before, at some other point in time, but she couldn't remember exactly who or when…

"What have you done?" Mommy's question was posed in a dangerously soft tone and Carolyn recognized the threat. "What have you done to embarrass us this time?"

Before she could answer, Daddy's outraged voice blasted through the house and brought Carolyn to her feet. "You're drunk, Rankin! I can't understand a word you're saying! Just get off my porch and go home!"

Carolyn was thoroughly confused. What did Jimmy Rankin's father have to do with anything? Nothing that she knew of, but she also knew she was going to have to face the music, anyway. Carolyn took a deep breath and headed for the living room, her mommy marching along right behind her. Daddy blocked the screen door with his body, but she could see Mr. Rankin, red-faced with rage and far too much alcohol, attempting to stand upright on the porch.

"There she is!" he roared, swaying and jabbing a finger in Carolyn's direction. "That tramp almost got my Jimmy killed today and I wanna know what you're gonna do about it!"

"Watch your mouth, Rankin," Daddy answered calmly. "I told you to go home. We'll talk when you sober up."

Carolyn gasped as her mommy's fingers gripped her wrist so fiercely her hand went numb. "What's he talking about, George? What's happened to Jimmy?"

"Get out of here, Betty, and take Carolyn with you. Nobody did anything to Jimmy."

"Don't you dare tell me what to do in my own house, George Shaw!" Mommy's grip tightened on Carolyn's wrist and she moved closer to the front door, pulling Carolyn with her. "What are you talking about, Mr. Rankin? What happened to Jimmy?"

Rankin glared at Carolyn and almost fell over in his haste to explain. "She nearly ran my Jimmy down in my own yard today! He was standing in the driveway and that car nearly slid right into him! I'm sick and tired of these snot-nosed kids messing with my family! By God, they were trying to kill him!"

Carolyn gasped. For the first time she understood what he was raving about, but he had it all wrong. Where had this story come from? Jimmy Rankin hadn't even been anywhere around…

"Don't be ridiculous," Daddy said flatly. "I'm sorry that Jimmy could have been hurt, but Carolyn takes the bus home from school. She wasn't in anybody's car."

"Aha!" Rankin jabbed the air again. "Ask her why she's not taking the bus after school right now! She maybe wasn't in the car right that minute, but she was in it earlier all right! Fact is, she probably put them up to it!"

Mommy's voice was desperate. "For God's sake, George, the neighbors…" Still gripping Carolyn's wrist with those fingers of steel, she gazed steadily at Mr. Rankin. Her haughty, disapproving expression could have easily leveled a bigger man. "Now you listen to me. If you don't get off our property, I'm calling the police. We'll deal with this situation in our own way, and we'll deal with it alone. Now get out."

Rankin opened his mouth to object, then thought better of it and backed away from the front door. He stumbled and weaved his way down the porch steps, then turned around to face them. "You see that you do, Mrs. Shaw. If you don't, you can be sure that I will."

Carolyn couldn't win. This was the last straw. Her mommy was on a rampage, and her daddy had withdrawn into his study, pale and silent and broken. No one cared about Carolyn's side of the story, or that the kids at school had targeted her for years, or that the school's punishment certainly didn't fit the crime.

What everyone really seemed to care about were the neighbors.

Mommy had been white-faced with rage, shrieking hysterically behind Daddy as she followed him to his study. "I've had it, George! It's either her or me! Now! This minute! She goes or I go!"

But Daddy hadn't said a word. He just looked at her and quietly closed the door in her face. Mommy whirled around and stalked into her bedroom, slamming her own door shut. Carolyn stood alone for a time, her heart hammering, summoning all the courage she was going to need to do what she had to do.

Finally, she knocked on the study door. "Daddy? It's Carolyn. Can I come in?"

"Sure, baby." His voice was muffled. "Come on in."

The pet name brought tears to her eyes, but she managed to swallow them and open the door. As Daddy sat behind his desk, his face buried in his hands, she saw his tears falling onto the polished mahogany. To see her daddy cry was one of the scariest moments of her life, but she stood silently in front of him, her hands folded, waiting for him to collect himself.

After a few minutes, he was able to wipe his eyes with a handkerchief, look at her sheepishly, and even smile a little. "I'm sorry, baby. I'm really sorry." His voice cracked and he glanced away from her. "I just don't know what I'm going to do about your mommy."

Carolyn had never loved her daddy as much as she did at that moment: he had actually apologized to her, which no one else had thought to do. But she had also never seen him in so much pain and she knew, right then, that she would do whatever she had to do to take that pain from him.

She tilted her chin with determination and took a deep breath. "Send me back to Art, Daddy."

He frowned and shook his head. "Absolutely not. You don't like it there, Carolyn. I don't feel good about that."

"No, it's all right, really! I'm older now. I'll try harder, Daddy. I can do better, I know I can."

As she saw the hope dawn in his dark eyes, Carolyn knew she had done the right thing. For some reason that she could never understand, she had cost him an immensely valuable part of his life, although she had only meant to bring him joy. Now she had an opportunity to make it up to him and, by God, she was going to do it...

*Even if it killed her.*

# CHAPTER TEN

Carolyn was determined to make it work this time, if for no other reason than that she knew she had run out of options. No matter how badly she missed her daddy and wanted to go home, she was all too aware of the explosive chaos her presence seemed to trigger within her whole family. She was like the detonator on a time bomb, and that had to end. It wasn't really her decision, anyway. Once she had made the offer to Daddy, and her mommy had learned of it, Carolyn's life in White Oak was over. The very next evening she found herself on an airplane flying to Olympia, Washington.

Carolyn had been a little insulted at the speed with which she had been dispatched from the Shaw household, but the more she thought about it, the more convinced she was that it was probably for the best. Although school wouldn't be out for another four months and she hadn't been able to say good-bye to any of her friends, she knew that the sooner she left the house on Mohawk Drive, the sooner everyone could get back to normal—whatever *that* was.

It really didn't matter, anyway. Upon Carolyn's arrival to his house, Art had informed her in no uncertain terms that she might as well consider herself the newest member of the Lovell family. "Your life in Pennsylvania is finished," he told her. "I'm your father now."

Although Carolyn's stomach lurched the first time she heard those words and she couldn't quite understand why, she managed to bite back what she was sure he would have considered a smart-alecky response and just nodded. It wasn't until later that she realized his words simply reminded her of Rose's constant refrain: *I'm your mother… You call me mother… Betty Shaw is not your mother…*

This time, though, Carolyn refused to blame Art Lovell for a painful period in her life that wasn't his fault. After all, she told herself, he was opening his home to her now, which he certainly didn't have to do, and he had every right to try to ease her into his family. She wanted to cooperate in every way she could. What little future she could visualize depended on it.

Besides, life had improved for the Lovell family during the eighteen months that Carolyn had been away—at least, financially. Gary Lovell, Art's brother, had moved up from southern California and joined Art's contracting business, so *Lovell Bros. Painting* was now emblazoned in large letters across the side of their work truck. All three boys now wore braces, no small monetary feat. They had also purchased a much larger home in an upscale part of Olympia.

Carolyn really enjoyed the new house. Located near a church that none of the Lovell's ever attended, their rather contemporary residence had a large, well-maintained back yard surrounded by a tall privacy fence. Lorene kept the home as spotless as ever, but this time Carolyn noticed that the boys were finally allowed to play within its walls. The front family room, with its huge windows and highly polished hardwood floors, even contained slot car race tracks and a toy box.

Tommy, ultra-cooperative kid that he was, turned his bedroom over to Carolyn without complaint and moved in with his younger brothers. It was a starkly furnished room with only a twin bed, a chest of drawers and a night stand with a lamp, but that was perfectly all right with Carolyn. She could add her own touches as she went along. What mattered most to her was that Art no longer came into her room in the mornings like he had before. There were no more unwanted hard kisses on the mouth and no more little boys sharing bureau and closet space with her. This time she had her own alarm clock and got herself up for school, so she was able to enjoy complete privacy.

Art also seemed determined to be a good father to the young girl he hardly knew, so Carolyn always tried to respond in kind—especially when he went out of his way to do something nice for her. Like, only a week or so after she had arrived, Carolyn's daddy sent her a surprise she had never in a million years expected: her beloved parrot, Talka, was delivered in her cage to the Lovell family. Instead of making a rude comment about the arrival of a pet bird that no one had ever mentioned to him, Art had simply disappeared for a few minutes, returned with some tools and a short ladder, and headed straight for Carolyn's bedroom. Hearing hammering from that vicinity, the whole family crowded at the door and watched as Art put the finishing touches on a large hook that now jutted from the ceiling.

"There you go!" he said in satisfaction, stepping down from the ladder. "Your bird will be right at home up here. What's her name again?"

"Talka. She's an Amazon parrot. I've had her since I was ten."

"Well, she's a beauty, that's for sure."

Carolyn gave a shy smile. "Thank you, Art. I really appreciate this. Really."

"No problem. Oh, and listen, go see the old man next door. He's got stacks of newspapers and magazines in his garage probably going back fifty years, so you'll have a built-in supply for whenever you need to clean the cage."

"Which will be every night," Lorene added firmly. "She's pretty, but I don't want her stinking up my house."

"I've always cleaned it every night," Carolyn answered. "I love taking care of animals. It's my favorite thing to do."

And so the days began to merge together with the natural ebb and flow of normalcy that most people don't even notice, but Carolyn appreciated that gentle rhythm. For the first time in years, she felt just like other kids. Like them, she had chores after school, did homework in her bedroom, talked on the telephone with Kelly Sheridan, her best friend down the street, listened to rock'n'roll music on the radio, and wore jeans and tee-shirts nearly all the time. For the first time in years, Carolyn didn't feel like she was living on the edge of calamity, jumping from crisis to crisis, constantly trying to prepare herself for the next catastrophe. For the first time in years, she could actually be a kid.

Carolyn and Lorene also began building a sort of tentative mother-daughter relationship that was based on their own personalities, and not on Lorene trying to take Mommy's special place in Carolyn's heart. They cooked and sewed together, even creating matching dresses in Carolyn's spare time after school, and sometimes Carolyn set Lorene's shoulder-length hair on hot rollers so it would be curly like Art liked it by the time he came home. They shopped and talked together, just like Carolyn and Mommy had once done, and Carolyn was nearly happy.

Now, whenever she thought back on her fear of returning to the Lovell home, she was almost embarrassed at the way she had overreacted to Art's teasing a year earlier. He seemed different now, much less uptight (even though he was still very strict with his sons), and Carolyn thought that perhaps Lorene had spoken with him about the difference between raising boys and girls. She didn't know what had brought about the change in him, but she was grateful for it. Now, strangely enough, when Tommy came into Carolyn's bedroom to confide in her about his father's sometimes too-rough treatment of him, Carolyn was surprised to find herself, if not out-and-out defending Art, at least trying to explain his side of it.

Probably the only thing about Art that completely unnerved Carolyn was the way he carried a small automatic pistol with him everywhere he went, usually in a shoulder holster he wore under a jacket or jammed in his back pocket, and he liked to be sure that people noticed it. He even had a small closet-sized room next to her bedroom that was filled with all different kinds of pistols and rifles. To Carolyn's amusement, Art called this *The Gun Room*—once again showing his lack of imagination, she thought.

Anyway, quite often in the evenings, through the wall separating her room from *The Gun Room*, she could hear him running some kind of a machine that he claimed counted bullets. It didn't make any sense to her, but no one else in the family seemed to think twice about it.

It wasn't even all that hard being the new kid in the eighth grade at the local junior high school. At least she didn't have to live down being *poor Carolyn Sue Shaw* like she always had to do in White Oak. At least in Olympia, no one gave a hoot who she was, one way or the other. Consequently, she was—at least in this one sense—able to start all over. For the first time in ages, she could be herself without having to constantly lug her past around with her. It was an advantage that Carolyn tried to remember, especially when she was reminded of everything else she had left behind.

Like when she received letters from her daddy, begging her to let him hear how she was. Since it was too hard to tell him how she really felt, she just didn't answer at all. Even after he sent her a check for fifty dollars to buy school clothes, then followed *that* up with the surprise arrival of Talka, she couldn't find a spare minute to send him a thank-you note. I'm just too busy right now, she told herself. I'll find time next week...or the week after...

One evening in early March, just a few weeks after she had arrived, Carolyn received an audiotape from her daddy that she really dreaded hearing. She knew what he was going to say, and she put off listening to it for as long as she could. She went next door to the old man's house to get a stack of newspapers for Talka's cage, ate dinner with the family, finished her homework, took a shower, and finally said good-night to everyone. Only then did she go into her bedroom. She closed the door firmly behind her, popped the tape into her recorder, turned it on—and caught her breath at the sound of her daddy's beloved voice.

Once again, tears of loss and homesickness rolled unchecked down Carolyn's cheeks. She had tried so hard to put her love for him into a special, hidden compartment, that she had nearly succeeded in forgetting just how much she missed him. And now his voice sounded so tired, so beat down and worn out, that it broke her heart.

"Carolyn," he began, "I've been looking in the mail, hoping you'd answer the letter I sent you shortly after you left. But I guess you're mad at your old dad for sending you out there because you haven't so much as written him a line. I don't even know if your bird got there all right. I thought you could at least write me a little note and say, 'Thanks, Dad, for the money for clothes that you sent along with that letter.' After all, if a man sends fifty dollars, he'd at least like to know that it got there. So I guess you're mad at me."

Battling tears, Carolyn switched off the recorder. Daddy's voice was so clear on the tape that he might as well have been sitting right next to her; she could actually *see* the hurt and disappointment on his face. And even though she knew she should have thanked him immediately and she owed him an apology for not doing that, she didn't understand why he kept saying that he had *sent* her out to Art's house. He hadn't *sent* her anywhere. She had *asked* him to let her go. So, whatever happened to her from now on, it was her fault, not his.

She turned the recorder back on. "I didn't send you out there on account of the explosion we had the night you got in trouble with Jimmy Rankin and that business. The only thing that explosion did was make me realize that I haven't been fair to you. I shouldn't have tried to raise you without having a normal home life to offer you. I actually owe you an apology.

"If I'd been smart back when Rose decided that you should come home from Texas, I would have made arrangements for you to go live with your young dad while you were already used to being away from me and Mother. But I thought that if you came back here, your mother might get her problems straightened out and she would go back to normal. It turns out I was 100% wrong. It's just a doggone shame that I didn't realize this sooner. If I had, all this heartbreak and aggravation would have been over with a long time ago."

Frowning, Carolyn shut off the recorder again, pulled back the bedspread and climbed in bed, plumping the pillows behind her. Was he saying that the only reason he had brought her home was to help her mommy get back to normal? That couldn't be true; she knew better than that. He had brought her home because he loved her, period.

She clicked the recorder back on. "But your mother, rather than getting better, is getting worse. What if you were living here and she had a complete nervous breakdown? You'd still have to pull up roots and go to Olympia and stay with your young dad. And this could happen any time. So we might as well make the break now while it's our choice, rather than having to do it during an emergency."

Carolyn sniffled and scrubbed at the tears on her cheeks with her fist. Everything was about her mommy, just like it always was... She pulled her attention back to her daddy's voice.

"I'm not saying this to knock your mother. You're nearly fourteen years old and you can take facts straight from the shoulder. Another big issue is you. To move you back here wouldn't be accomplishing much, Carolyn. You have personality problems you brought back with you from Texas, and you haven't done much about overcoming them. You don't even seem like you care. And I might as well tell you that unless you prove to me that you can get along where you're at without causing any problems, there's no use coming back here."

Carolyn shut the recorder off with an angry snap of her wrist. She had tried so hard to be perfect, to be everything that they wanted her to be, that she had completely lost sight of who *she* was. In fact, she didn't even *know* who she was. But ever since her return from Texas, her mommy hadn't believed a word she said or trusted her one single inch... Yet now her daddy was accusing *her* of causing the problems...

Carolyn took a deep breath and turned the recorder back on. "You better just make up your mind that you're not gonna give anybody out there a hard time, and do exactly as you're told. Try to make people like you, Carolyn, whether you want something out of them or not. I've seen you be nice to people if you're gonna work them for something, but you gotta get in the habit of being nice to everybody, not just somebody you want to get something out of."

Wow, Carolyn thought, he's talking about somebody I don't even know. Simmering anger was gradually replacing her confusion. She honestly couldn't understand what she might have done to make things better in her home, but she did recognize that it was truly best for her to be gone.

She turned her attention back to her daddy's voice. "So, that's the story," he said. "I'm sorry it had to be this way. I want you to communicate with me. If you want to say something to me, put it in a letter. Put it on tape. But you're not gonna get anywhere by not communicating with me because I'm the only one that can say whether you can come back here.

"There isn't anybody in this world that loves you any more than your old dad, and his heart's been broken over this thing as much as anyone else's. But if you think that making life miserable for the people out there is going to get you back here, you're wrong. It isn't going to work that way this time. When you left and started talking about coming back when school was out in May or June, I didn't make you any promises and I don't want you saying that I did. All I promised was that when that time came, we'd talk about it. And that still holds good."

Daddy's voice died away and the tape whirred on for a few empty, silent seconds before it ran out. Carolyn sat upright in her bed, stock-still, clutching the covers with shaking hands, trying...so hard...to understand. He was actually angry with her for behaving like a spoiled, scheming child, but she wasn't aware of ever having behaved like that. What were the words he had used?

*Try to make people like you, regardless of whether you want something out of them or not...*

Those words just didn't make any sense to Carolyn. She remembered a few times in the past when her daddy had seemed a little more irritated than usual with her behavior, but nothing like what he seemed to be accusing her of now. This was different, and she knew it. Her daddy's voice on this recording was telling Carolyn that she had nowhere else to go, that he didn't want her, that no one wanted her, and that she had to make it work with Art and his family this time or else...

Or else, what? Carolyn wondered. Or else she could live on the street, or under a bridge. She could live anywhere—except in White Oak, Pennsylvania...

Restless and wide-awake, Carolyn climbed out of bed and put the recorder in the nightstand drawer, then went to the closet to pull out a few newspapers to place in the bottom of Talka's cage. She had forgotten to clean it earlier in the evening and Lorene wouldn't be happy about that, so she decided to get the job done now. Quickly, trying to be as quiet as she could, Carolyn began separating pages of newspapers, not really paying much attention to what she was doing until one large photo caught her attention, then another, and another, and another… A nude man straddled a large-breasted woman. A young girl fondled an older man. Two naked women lay tangled up with each other…

Carolyn's eyes widened in disbelief and she gulped. She had never seen anything like these pictures before and there were several more she didn't even look at. All she knew was she had to get rid of them, and fast. If she didn't, Lorene and Art would go through the roof and God only knew what would happen then.

It was hard for Carolyn to believe that the old man next door actually *looked* at this dirty stuff, but obviously he did. He had probably forgotten that they were in those piles of ancient newspapers out in his garage, and of course Carolyn would never bring it up to him because it would probably embarrass him to death. Since there was no way she could get the photos out of the house at that very moment—someone would hear her leave—she had to find someplace to hide them, at least in the meantime.

Carolyn did the only thing that she, a scared thirteen-year-old kid, could think of to do. She stuffed the nasty pictures under her mattress and went to bed.

"You filthy little creep! Get her out of here, do you hear me? Get her out!"

Heart pounding and cotton-mouthed with terror, Carolyn couldn't move. She couldn't even cry. She stood rooted to her bedroom floor, staring transfixed at the scrunched-up dirty pictures Lorene was waving around in the air like a madwoman. Art shoved past Carolyn and grabbed his wife's arm.

"Shut up and calm down!" he shouted, almost as red-faced as she was. Then, more quietly, he ordered, "Give me those." Lorene handed him the photos without another word.

Carolyn backed away and closed her eyes. This was it. It was over. Hearing the bedroom door open, she felt the presence of three curious little boys and, at that moment, wanted nothing more than for the floor to swallow her whole.

Art didn't even look up. "Get out of here," he snarled, rifling through the pictures with a disgusted look. "Right now. Get out."

The boys backed out hastily and closed the door. Carolyn stared down at her feet, fighting panic and nausea and struggling to breathe.

Then he asked, "Where did you get these?" His voice was so soft and gentle that a chill of terror raced down Carolyn's spine.

"The old man next door," she whispered, fighting tears. "You told me to get newspapers from his house for my bird…"

"I don't care where she got them," Lorene interrupted furiously. "The point is, she got them and she hid them under her mattress and I won't have her in my house around my boys one more minute! Do I make myself clear? I wouldn't have even known about them if I hadn't come in this morning to change the sheets and flip the mattress. I don't care where you send her or how she gets there! All I care about is that she's gone! I don't even want to hear her name again!"

Art completely ignored his wife's tirade and looked at Carolyn curiously. "Why didn't you bring these straight to us? You wouldn't have gotten in any trouble at all if you had brought them straight to us."

Tears streamed down Carolyn's cheeks as she shook her head. "I was scared you would think I was nasty..."

"Get her out of my house," Lorene interrupted again. This time there wasn't an inch of give in her voice. "Drive her down to Clara's tomorrow. Put her out on the street. You find a place for her. I don't care. I don't want to hear another word about it."

Ashamed to her core and feeling as filthy as slime, Carolyn hung her head.

Late the next night, it was cold and pouring down rain by the time Art pulled into the dark parking lot of an inexpensive motel on the dingy, neon outskirts of Portland, Oregon. While Carolyn waited in his station wagon, Art went into the office to see about vacancies. Although she was dull-witted and heavy-eyed with exhaustion, she was still alert enough to realize that he was wide awake and filled with so much enthusiastic energy that he made her head hurt. But it wasn't until he came out of the office and walked toward the car, jaunty and whistling and holding up the room key, that Carolyn grew worried.

Then, back in the car and driving toward the side of the motel, Art said with a soft chuckle, "I could only get one room and it only has one bed. But we'll make do, won't we?"

Carolyn swallowed hard and nodded. She couldn't say a word. She realized that she had been wrong and she didn't truly know this man at all. Still, she had seen evil before—many times. And this man was evil.

Once inside the tiny room, Carolyn placed Talka's cage on a small round table in the corner, fed her, and draped the coverlet back over the cage. Then, as quickly as her shaking fingers would let her, she grabbed a long flannel nightgown out of her suitcase, undressed and stepped into it.

Carolyn didn't turn around when she heard Art come in, close the door and lock it. Numb with fear, she stared at Talka's cage as he removed his jacket and walked to the nightstand beside the bed. She remained rooted to the floor when she heard the clatter of metal as he put his gun on top of it. She didn't turn around when he pulled back the covers, and winced when the bed squeaked as he sat on the edge of it. When his shoes hit the floor and she heard the rustling of the rest of his clothing as he undressed, every sound seemed to reverberate through the room, somehow magnified and far too loud. Then, suddenly, he flicked off the lamp beside the bed, throwing the room into dark shadows. The neon lights across the parking lot flashed on and off, blue and red, and the pounding rain drove hard against the roof.

Carolyn's heart hammered in her throat, nearly strangling her, but she didn't know what she was so afraid of. She only knew that she was afraid of *something*—something so malignant and menacing and malevolent that she couldn't move. She couldn't breathe.

She had no choice but to climb into bed, pull the covers all the way to her chin, and try to ignore his body next to hers. She closed her eyes…waiting…waiting…waiting for *something*.

When he spoke, it was like an electric shock exploded through her. "You owe me this, girl," he said softly. "Lorene isn't here and I'm by myself… You owe me this."

And then, suddenly, she knew exactly what was going to happen and why that gun was there…

She struggled to roll away from him, pulled her knees to her chest, took a deep breath to scream—and felt one hand clamp tightly over her mouth. The other pressed hard against her throat. Bile burned the back of her tongue, set it on fire, choked her… "Don't make a sound, you little whore, and don't try to act like you don't know what I want," he whispered, his lips close to hers. His breath was sour, hot against her face. "I saw those pictures you had. You're no innocent little kid. So, you're gonna put out now, you hear me? You're gonna put out now and you're gonna like it."

Carolyn turned her face away from him, tears snaking down her cheeks, and shook her head. "Please, no… I've never… I've…"

"Shut up. You're a pro. I know a pro when I see one. But remember this: there's a gun right here. You try anything funny and I'll kill you."

Then, suddenly, without warning, calloused hands grabbed her arms, pinned them back against the pillows… Lips moved…down…over soft skin, childish breasts… Once again she was back there, closed in and locked up, trapped in a dark and tiny room from which she could never escape. She tried one final plea, one last time. "Please, don't… I might…get pregnant…"

"No chance. I been snipped."

Fingers entwined themselves in her hair…jerked hard… A sweaty knee shoved her legs apart. Pain shot through her, ripped her in two…

And then, far in the distance, she heard a child… screaming and screaming, begging and crying and pleading for mercy, cursing and swearing and praying… There was laughing, groaning…a whisper, a moan….

That night was cold, and black, and endless. And as it went on and on and on, she came to know who he was. He was the grinning, white-faced monster that had haunted her nightmares for as long as she could remember, oozing out of the walls of all those closets and living in the shadows of her life…

And then, finally, the man satisfied his every perverted fantasy with a child that, without him even knowing it, was no longer there.

"You know, Carolyn, I've been thinking." Art maneuvered the car on to Interstate 5, heading south, and popped a piece of gum in his mouth. "I think I'm going to take you to Reno. You know where Reno is?"

Carolyn shook her head and stared blindly out the window. She didn't care where Reno was. She didn't care where anything was. She didn't even care where *she* was. All she cared about was the burning pain somewhere deep inside of her, between her legs…

"Are you listening to me?"

Carolyn nodded but said nothing.

Art's voice was friendly, conversational. "Reno's in Nevada and prostitution is legal there. Do you know what prostitution is?"

Now Carolyn looked at him, big-eyed and cotton-mouthed.

"I asked you a question. Do you know what prostitution is?"

She nodded and fought tears.

"Good."

He slid his arm across the top of the seat so that his jacket opened and she could see his shoulder holster and the metal of his pistol. She couldn't take her eyes off that gun. If there was just some way she could get her hands on it, she'd blow his head off right then and there…

The laughter in his voice jerked her back to reality. "I could make a ton of money off a kid like you. 'Course, I need to teach you a few more things, but men really dig young stuff, you know? 'Specially *old* men."

He caressed her cheek, slowly, gently… Carolyn jerked away from his touch. Her body felt cold, like it was encased in ice, and her heart thudded and pounded and slammed in her throat. He *couldn't* do that. He *wouldn't* do that.

Yes, he could… yes, he would…

"You couldn't take me to Reno," Carolyn managed finally. "People would notice. What about your mother? What about Lorene?"

"What about them? Lorene won't care what I do with you—especially if I send her some of the money I make off you. And I lied about my mother. She don't even know we're coming." He chuckled, obviously satisfied with himself. "So, no one's going to care what I do with you. What do you think about that?"

When she didn't answer, he continued, "Must be sad to not have anyone in your corner. Sad for you. Good for me…"

Carolyn remembered Daddy's tape, and his firm words letting her know in no uncertain terms that she had no home with him, and she knew that Art was right.

She was alone. Just like before. Just like always.

Carolyn moved closer to the car door, as far away from him as she could get, and leaned her forehead against the ice-cold window. She closed her eyes and began to pray.

*Please, God, please wreck this car… Just kill me now… Please, God…*

"Are you hungry?"

Carolyn stared at him. This man was more than evil. This man was insane.

"Guess not." Art shrugged carelessly and tossed his gum out the window. "We've got about five hundred miles 'til we get to the Reno exit off this highway, somewhere near Sacramento, I think. That'll give me about eight hours to decide what to do with you. I don't have to make a decision 'til then."

Five hundred miles…eight hours…locked in this car… alone with this man…

"Don't start thinking that you can get back to Pop. He's already told me that Betty don't want you, so he can't have you living back there… And if you're thinking you can tell anyone, just forget about it. Who's gonna believe you?" Suddenly Art's voice sounded strangely soothing, almost compassionate. "But I'll take care of you. I'll take real good care of you. You'll see…"

And so Carolyn began to pray once again, over and over, monotonously, rhythmically, in time with the sound of tires rolling down the highway: *God, please wreck this car and let me die… Please wreck this car and let me die… Please wreck this car and let me die…* Still, the miles kept passing and the wheels kept turning and Art's voice kept droning on and on and on.

But then, easily, without warning or fanfare, she heard another voice, a softer voice, a sweeter voice that she recognized. For the first time in years and like an old friend, she welcomed the shelter and love that the familiar voice offered.

Finally, safely enveloped in defensive armor, Carolyn stepped back… moved away…and disappeared.

# CHAPTER ELEVEN

When Carolyn awakened in a sweet blue-and-white bedroom that was completely unfamiliar to her, she wasn't exactly sure what day it was. When she heard her name called by an older woman she wasn't sure she had ever met before, she made her way through a large stucco house toward the kitchen and got to share her first cup of coffee with the grandparents she had never known.

And when she finally realized that Art Lovell was gone, she was nearly sick with relief.

But at least she knew why. She had total recall of the cheap motel in Portland, Oregon, what had happened in that ugly room witnessed only by her parrot, and even Art's threats to sell her in Reno. If she lived to be 100 years old, she would never forget one single detail of that nightmare.

What she couldn't quite remember was how or when she had come to be here, with these people, in this town.

Yet, if there was anything that Carolyn had learned during the last eight tumultuous years of her life, it was how to conceal from others any confusion or loss of memory that she might experience. So, unlike most teenaged girls who couldn't keep quiet about anything, she was an expert at keeping secrets.

For as long as she could remember, Carolyn had kept secrets. But she had kept them because she was positive no one wanted to hear them—not because she had given a promise, or she was afraid of trouble, or any of the other reasons that children usually kept secrets. The stark truth was, Carolyn would have given anything to blurt out every single secret she had, but she knew that was impossible. Especially now.

Now, suddenly, things were different.

Now she had a secret so huge and so frightening that she couldn't tell a soul about it, not *ever*. Now she had to go through each day as if everything in her life was normal. Now she had to push her secret into the deepest recesses of her mind where it could remain hidden from her own view as well as everyone else's.

Carolyn wasn't sure how she was going to accomplish this. The violation of her young body, as well as her psyche and her soul, was horrific enough. But the fact it had been perpetrated by a man she was supposed to be able to trust was a betrayal so vile and so vicious she was afraid she couldn't bear to keep it to herself.

But she had no choice. Art had been right when he said that no one would believe her. And she certainly couldn't tell her daddy. Art was his son, and his heart would be broken if he realized that he had actually *sent* her into a situation so evil and traumatic. Besides, Carolyn yearned to return to him and White Oak. If he knew her secret, he would never be able to look at her the same way again and she could never go live with him.

Finally, and maybe even more important than anything else, was the disconcerting reality that once again she was missing a large block of time...

On the rare occasion that Carolyn actually allowed herself to think about the full scope of her life, she was overwhelmed by the magnitude of all her secrets. She had to hide her deepening sense of shame and abject humiliation behind an attractive and intelligent exterior of coolness, accomplishment, and complete control. She had to hide what she had come to think of as her *missing time episodes* behind self-denigrating jokes about early senility, daydreaming, and absent-mindedness. In fact, whenever she really allowed herself to think about it, she recognized that the real truth about her entire life had to remain hidden from public view.

But Carolyn was nothing if not a survivor. She decided that the only way to deflect dangerous questions from nosy people was to lose herself in the casual, laid-back lifestyle of a teenager living in Escondido, California, and try to be exactly like everybody else. Fortunately, this project turned out to be far easier than she had anticipated.

Eventually, and for the first time in years, Carolyn's days began to pass smoothly. Unlike the rather turbulent weather in Pennsylvania and Washington, it almost never rained in southern California, so she was able to enjoy balmy breezes, cloudless skies and white-sand beaches. She attended a nearby junior high school in which the classes weren't too difficult and she fit in with no problem at all, and her best friend, Lisa McKenzie, lived on the corner. She even had a cute boyfriend named Doug Kenner who was seventeen years old, lived right across the street, and drove a neat car that he proudly called a *Studebaker Golden Hawk*.

Most importantly and for the first time in years, *both* of her adoring grandparents, Clara and Bob Lovell, owners of a successful contracting business in Escondido, trusted her and gave her nearly total freedom. Both of them cared a great deal about the young granddaughter they hadn't seen in so long and they didn't try to hide it.

One Saturday morning Bob Lovell, a tall, slender man with thinning salt-and-pepper hair, pulled out a chair at the kitchen table and sat down with a large cup of coffee. Clara leaned toward Carolyn, a sweet smile on her tanned face. "Are you happy here, sugar?" she asked suddenly.

Carolyn nodded emphatically. "Oh, yes, ma'am!"

"I'm so glad. I missed you that time when you went out to Art's house— I drove over a thousand miles to see you, did you know that? I was so upset when Art said you had already gone back to Pennsylvania that I got right back in my car, turned it around, and came home. I sure as heck didn't want to spend any time with *him*." Clara paused to catch her breath, then stood up and began to clear the table. "You know, I don't get to see my grandsons at all, so I still can't believe Art brought you down to us. He's a piece of work, isn't he?"

Carolyn's mouth went dry and her heart thundered in her throat. She couldn't speak.

Clara poured herself another cup of coffee, then returned to her chair and sat back down. "Can I ask you a personal question, sugar?"

Carolyn managed a wary nod.

"I was just wondering how Miss Palerno's group rap sessions are going after school. Are they helping you, do you think?"

Carolyn wasn't sure what she had been afraid that Clara was going to ask, but this question was unthreatening enough. "I think so. Yes, ma'am. The kids are nice and it helps to have someone to talk to."

Of course, Carolyn didn't tell Clara that she was very careful what she told her group or how much she told them. She complained about chores and curfews and boyfriends during each session like everyone else, but she never went near the nitty-gritty of her life. She treasured her obscurity within the student body far too much, and the last thing she wanted was to once again become *poor Carolyn Sue Shaw* to a bunch of kids she didn't even know.

On the other hand, Carolyn was learning a great deal about coping mechanisms—some good, some not-so-good—from others in the group. Marijuana was fast becoming the cool method of hiding or running from pain, she discovered, but Carolyn knew she wanted no part of that. Cigarettes and alcohol were much easier to get and far more enticing. Sex also seemed to be an outlet that everyone was whispering about, but Carolyn already knew more about sex than any ten kids, or at least she thought she did. She had no desire to increase her knowledge. Besides, Carolyn had discovered her own coping mechanism, and it was just the thing. It allowed her to function so perfectly within whatever society she happened to be part of that no one ever suspected that she was in fact running just as hard and as fast and as far as she possibly could. If a painful emotion or a frightening memory popped up that she didn't want to deal with, Carolyn just took on another job, another chore, another responsibility. This particular coping mechanism was actually nothing more than simple manic activity, but it was so effective that she found herself envied and admired by people less efficient and energetic than she was learning to be.

And, Carolyn discovered, admiration and approval from her peers and teachers was far more important to her fragile ego than anything else they could give her.

Clara looked more closely at Carolyn, but she didn't pursue the subject. "Do you hear anything from George these days?"

"Yes, ma'am. I talked to him last night."

"How is he?"

This was the perfect opportunity for her to break her news even though she hadn't planned it, so Carolyn plowed ahead.

"I don't think he's well. Actually, I *know* he's not well. Clara, I asked him if I could come back for a visit when school lets out at the end of next week. He said I could."

"But you've only been here for two months, Carolyn! I thought you were going to stay with us. I was looking forward to it…"

"Well, I wanted to, you know, but he needs me to take care of him. I could hear it in his voice."

Strangely enough, that was a completely true statement. Even though it hadn't been that long ago since her daddy had sent her the audiotape that had sounded almost intimidating and made her so angry, Carolyn had picked up on the note of vulnerability and even weakness in his voice during their phone conversation last night. So, even though she wasn't sure exactly what was wrong in his life, she had no doubt that her daddy needed her now.

Clara leaned forward and covered Carolyn's hand with her own. "Sugar, George is Betty's responsibility. His *wife* needs to take care of him, not you."

Yes, ma'am, you're right, Carolyn thought, but she won't…

Bob pushed his chair away from the table and stood up. "You have to let her go, Clara. George raised her. If she's worried about his health, she needs to go home."

Clara ignored him and tightened her grasp on Carolyn's hand. "Sugar, look at me."

Carolyn met Clara's swimming eyes and fought back her own tears. These dear people had been so good to her and offered her so much that, had she been able to stay, she might have even learned how to be happy. But she couldn't stay. Something dark, perhaps even dangerous, was calling her back… and she had to answer that call.

"Listen to me, Carolyn," Clara said gravely. "If you ever need a place to come to, you come here. Do you understand me? You have a home here."

Carolyn nodded and squeezed the older woman's work-roughened hand. "I will, Clara. I promise. I'll be back."

Within just a few weeks of Carolyn's return to Pennsylvania in the early summer of 1972, George and Betty Shaw separated.

Immediately, like the little caretaker she was fast becoming, Carolyn abandoned any notion she might have had about ever going back to California.

Finally, since it was so obvious that she was determined to remain in White Oak, Clara and Bob Lovell sadly shipped Carolyn's belongings—including Talka the parrot—back to her.

In the beginning Carolyn stayed with her mommy simply because she didn't want her to be alone and thought that they might actually learn to be friends, but it was wasn't long before she realized that this arrangement would be next to impossible. Carolyn seemed to be a lightning rod to Betty Shaw's explosive and inexplicable rage. Together, these two females were like oil and water.

By early 1973, the situation had become untenable.

"She hates me," Carolyn told her daddy during a weekend visit to his small apartment located on the second floor of a close friend's home. "She really hates me."

To her surprise, he didn't argue. He simply nodded. "That's probably true. Do you want some hot tea?"

"What do you mean, that's probably true? What kind of thing is that to say?"

He chuckled and prepared two cups of hot tea before he answered, "It's a true thing to say—but it's not personal, Carolyn. Don't take it personally. I don't. She hates everyone. Including me. Including God. Everyone."

"She doesn't hate Maureen."

"That's because Maureen reinforces her anger. Maureen is exactly like her—she's just a little duplicate of Betty Shaw. But you're not like her at all."

He placed steaming cups of hot tea on a small table and sat down, watching her as she bustled around the living room, plumping up throw pillows and straightening pictures on the walls. She was the perfect image of efficient domesticity.

He smiled. "Come sit down, Carolyn. Relax."

"This place is a mess, Daddy! I don't know how you can live here..."

"It's not a mess. Come sit down. You're making me a nervous wreck."

Carolyn stopped instantly and joined him at the little table. She sipped her tea carefully, silently studying him. Her eyes filled with tears.

He didn't look like himself, and the way he looked scared her to death. His formerly ruddy complexion was now pasty-pale beneath his thinning dark hair, and there was a faint bluish tinge to his lips that Carolyn had never noticed before. He seemed lethargic and apathetic, like he was living right on the brink of total exhaustion. Even the slightest bit of exercise left him breathless and perspiring.

"I'm moving in here, Daddy," she announced suddenly. "You need me to take care of you."

He looked surprised and slightly offended. "I don't need any such thing! I'm perfectly capable of taking care of myself."

Carolyn immediately backed up. "Well, what I meant was, Mommy obviously doesn't want me with her and you need some help. So I'm moving in here. If you don't let me, Daddy, I won't have anywhere else to live."

"Oh, don't be so dramatic, Carolyn! Of course you'll have somewhere to live."

"Where?" she countered. "Maureen's house is too small and anyway she's going to have another baby soon. Besides, she doesn't like me, and Bobby doesn't want me. Do you know that I've never even been to his house?"

"I know, sweetheart." He drained the last of his hot tea. "So you want to move in with me?"

"Can I, Daddy?"

"You know you can, sweetie. I'd love the company."

And so, once again, Carolyn moved. Finally situated in her daddy's little apartment, she attended to him with the same kind of love and concern his own mother might have lavished upon him, but she didn't resent the time it took. He had cared for her for so many years and loved her so unconditionally that she was perfectly willing to do for him anything that he needed her to do. Although he wouldn't talk to her about his health problems, choosing instead to gloss over them, she knew there was something wrong. She just didn't know how serious it was.

Carolyn tried to keep her own life a secret from him just so he wouldn't be bothered. She hated the local high school with every fiber of her being because she was still ostracized. Many kids were beginning to use drugs, and some of the boys even tormented her in unspeakably nasty ways. Still, she tried hard not to burden her daddy.

Eventually, Carolyn recognized—and accepted—that no matter what she did, no matter how hard she tried to be absolutely perfect, she could never be anything more than a thorn in this good man's side. It was clear that he needed to be rid of her.

When she finally told her daddy that she needed to leave, he didn't argue. He just nodded, took her in his arms, and held her silently for a long, long time. As she clung to him, fighting tears while she listened to the rhythmic sound of his breathing, she suddenly recalled with painful clarity another time...another place...when he had held her exactly this way...

On that morning, when she was only six years old, he had held her like she was the only person in the world that he wanted to hold this closely. She had sleepily nestled her check against his chest, feeling warm and secure and loved...

And then he had disappeared.

"No, Daddy, don't! Don't do it! Please, Daddy, don't..."

"Carolyn, you've got to stop being so dog-gone dramatic!"

His words crackled through the telephone like he was on a different planet instead of just across the country, but she could still hear the amusement in his voice. Tears streamed down her cheeks as she took a deep breath and tried to calm down.

"Okay, Daddy... I'm better now." Her voice quavered and she cleared her throat. She had to sound supportive, upbeat, in control of herself. "So you're gonna have this surgery on your heart..."

"They do it all the time, Carolyn, really!" he reassured her again. "There's not one thing for you to worry about. And Mommy says that I can come home as soon as I get better, so we can all be a family again. Just like it was before, Carolyn. Won't that be wonderful?"

Suddenly Carolyn felt like she was a million years old and he was the infant. Was there anything this man wouldn't do for Betty Shaw? Was there anything this woman could tell him that he wouldn't believe?

*How could he love her so much? What had she ever given him in his life that he was willing to die for now?*

"When you first come home from the hospital," Carolyn asked hesitantly, "who's going to take care of you?"

"Some people in my church are going to check in on me every day, but I won't go home too soon. Don't worry about me so much, sweetheart! I'll be fine."

Carolyn frowned, swallowing anger and fear. "You're going to go home from the hospital and be by yourself? Mommy's not going to look after you?"

"Mommy has to work, sweetheart, you know that. And she doesn't need to be saddled with a sick man. The important thing is, we'll all be together again very soon."

Carolyn shook her head and thanked God that her daddy couldn't see her face. There was no way that Betty Shaw would ever allow them to be a family like before, but apparently he needed to believe that she would. And if it would help him to get better, Carolyn would play along.

"I want to come home, Daddy. I want to be there when you come out."

"Absolutely not. You just got back there and it's too expensive for you to be flying back and forth all the time. I want to know that you're happy there in California, Carolyn. I want to know that things are good with Clara and Bob, and that you're doing well in school and hanging out with your friends..." His voice trailed away and he was silent for a long moment. "I'm very tired, Carolyn," he finished finally, "and I don't want to worry about you anymore. I love you way too much."

For the first couple of weeks after that conversation with her daddy, Carolyn stayed busy every single day and tried not to think. But, like so many years before, the nights were a different story. The nights had become so thick with memories close to her heart that she could almost taste them. The nights were long, and dark, and nearly unbearable. Even though she struggled to believe that everything would be all right, she knew, deep down inside, that she would never see her daddy again. And even after his surgery was declared successful, Carolyn couldn't shake that ominous feeling of dread.

Finally, disgusted with what she was beginning to see as some kind of a sick desire to actually bring about the worst, Carolyn joined Doug, Lisa, and some other friends for a day-long outing to the Del Mar Fairgrounds, about twenty-five miles away. The weather was perfect, like most every day in California, and the party-time atmosphere was filled with the screeches of hungry seagulls and the tinny, player-piano sounds of carnival rides. It was one of Carolyn's favorite places in the whole world, especially when she could walk through the grounds hand-in-hand with Doug and trade good-humored insults with her best friend… But today it didn't feel right. No matter what she did or how hard she tried to have a good time, nothing felt quite right.

Then, without any warning, Carolyn's heart seemed to stop beating. She couldn't breathe. She felt encased in ice, from her head all the way down to her toes. She managed to reach a concrete bench nearby and sit down, oblivious to all the bright colors and loud music and whirling carnival rides around her. Suddenly she was alone and enveloped in thick, black silence; everything felt cold and hellishly isolated…"Carolyn! Carolyn!" Lisa's voice came from far, far away. "Carolyn, are you all right?"

Carolyn came back to herself slowly, laboriously, like she was swimming through warm, thickening gelatin. She looked into the worried faces of her friends, for a moment not even certain who they were. Finally, her eyes filled with tears and her entire body began to tremble.

"I'm sorry," she managed to whisper. "I have to go home now. My daddy is dead."

Carolyn sat cross-legged on the floor in her bedroom, staring blindly into a full-length mirror on the wall, and hardly recognized herself. Her shoulder-length hair was wild and tangled; her eyes were red-rimmed and swollen; she was pale with fatigue and shook from head to toe. Even though she needed to pack for her flight back to White Oak, which was leaving in a few hours, Carolyn felt numb and paralyzed.

Just as she had the night she was locked in that closet in Beaumont, Texas, so many eons ago, Carolyn felt alone and deserted on a vast and ruthless planet. And even though she was fifteen years old, she was no less frightened now than she had been back then. With her daddy no longer a part of the world, who was going to teach her how to live? She had so much more to learn! She knew she could *survive* just about anything—she had already proved that. But knowing how to *live* was something entirely different.

Clara opened the door without knocking, entered the bedroom and squatted down beside Carolyn. As she put her arm around the young girl, her own grief was obvious; their bloodshot eyes met in the mirror. "I've asked Bob to fly out with you, sugar," she said softly, "and he's almost ready to go. Are you packed yet?"

Carolyn shook her head slowly. "I don't know what to do, Clara," she whispered. Her chin quivered. "What should I do?"

Without another word, Clara helped Carolyn to her feet and led her like a dim-witted child toward the bed, then gave her a gentle push. "You sit down, baby. I'll pack for you."

Carolyn obeyed and closed her burning eyes, allowing Clara to fuss over her in a way that seemed to make her feel better, and finally stopped thinking. She followed directions automatically and had no memory of following them. It was as if everything in her world had completely shut down. She even boarded the airplane without realizing it.

The late-night flight back to Pennsylvania was uneventful, quiet, and filled with slumbering passengers. Although Carolyn couldn't sleep, she was grateful for the darkness that concealed the tears that kept rolling down her cheeks; the intense silence was only occasionally broken by a sporadic snorer sleeping in the seat behind her. This cocoon-like atmosphere was comforting to the young girl who couldn't seem to feel anything and was dreading the moment when she would begin.

Yet, regardless of how unreal the present seemed, Carolyn's memories were still vivid and vital: the little town of White Oak loomed ahead for her like a bad visual effect in a scary movie. There wasn't a soul left there now who wanted anything to do with her. At least, she didn't think there was. Her daddy had been the glue that held them all together, whether they had ever appreciated it or not. Now, with him gone, they could all scatter in every direction. And once again little Carolyn—big-eyed and hungry—would be left alone, standing on the outside of the Shaw family, looking in.

But maybe not, she thought suddenly, feeling a flutter of hopefulness. Maybe Mommy will need me now. She twisted in her seat, trying to stretch her legs, and stared out the window into a pitch-black, starless sky. Maybe, with Daddy gone, she'll realize how much we all need to be together now. Maybe she'll know how much I love her and she'll love me back...

Carolyn closed her eyes, suddenly sleepy, and the unexpected fragrance of Mommy's Estee Lauder perfume wafted through the air, tickling her nostrils and her memory. As she dozed off, Carolyn felt loving arms gather her close, just as on another airplane so many years ago, and she heard the whispered words, "Of course you can call me *Mommy*. I *am* your mommy..."

# CHAPTER TWELVE

The moment Carolyn saw her big brother Bobby standing in the airport lobby waiting for them, the tears rained down her cheeks once more. And then, when he held out his arms, she rushed into them without reservation, without even thinking. This rather short man with dark, thinning hair and a slight paunch strongly resembled his father, and was the same individual who, as a youngster, had defended little Carolyn from anyone who even looked slightly threatening—but who had teased her unmercifully himself whenever he got the opportunity. This was also the man who had pretty much disappeared once she had safely returned home, not because he was disinterested but because he had gone away to college, joined the Navy, got married and had his own life to live.

"Come on, baby girl," Bobby said quietly, his own voice thick with tears. "Let's find somewhere private to talk."

Carolyn gripped his offered hand tightly and followed him like the lost child she was. Finally discovering a bench in a secluded corner near the coffee shop, they sat close to one another, fingers still laced. Then, as strange as it felt to Carolyn, they actually cried together, like a real brother and sister. All the years and distance that had separated them for so long completely vanished, as if it had never been.

"Here, baby girl," Bobby said at last, handing her a wad of tissue, "blow your nose."

Carolyn blew her nose obediently, never releasing her grip on his hand, and wiped her eyes. "Can you take me to Mommy's house now, Bobby? She needs me."

He cleared his throat and glanced over at Bob Lovell, who was standing nearby smoking a cigarette, looking miserable and uneasy. "I don't think that's really the best idea, Carolyn. It's very late and I'm sure she's already asleep. Why don't you and Bob stay with Wilma and me?"

Carolyn understood immediately; she knew what Bobby was saying. He was telling her in no uncertain terms that nothing had changed and she still wasn't welcome in her mommy's house. Not even now, with her beloved daddy gone. He was telling her that there was nothing she could do to make her mommy feel better, that the last person Mommy wanted to see was Carolyn. He was telling her that she was just as alone tonight as she had ever been.

Abruptly, all the pretty dreams that had kept her together on the airplane disappeared like the illusions they were.

The drive from Pittsburgh to White Oak and Bobby's house was quiet and solemn. As they traveled slowly through those familiar hills and down winding roads that were brightly illuminated by a full moon, Carolyn was alone in the backseat with her own thoughts and memories. Upon their arrival at Bobby's house, the two men carried the luggage inside while Bobby's wife, Wilma, enveloped Carolyn in a warm, maternal hug that made her feel safe—for the moment.

"I'm so sorry, sweetheart," she said softly. "I know how awful you feel. You let me know if you need anything. Anything at all."

Carolyn blinked away those embarrassing, ever-present tears and yawned. She was suddenly weak and trembling with fatigue. "Thank you, Wilma, but I'm fine."

"You look exhausted. Bob, please take Carolyn's bag to her room, will you?" Smiling, Wilma turned to Bob Lovell and offered her hand. "I'm so sorry, Mr. Lovell. We haven't been properly introduced. I'm Wilma Shaw. I hope you don't mind, but we have to put you on the sofa in the living room. Is that all right?"

"Oh, of course. Don't worry about me. I can sleep anywhere." Bob shook her hand with a shy grin. "I feel real bad for busting in on you folks this way…"

"Oh, don't be silly! We're so grateful that you came with Carolyn, Mr. Lovell. It was very good of you."

Not long after, when the house was finally dark and quiet, Carolyn lay on a twin bed in the spare bedroom and stared blindly toward the ceiling. She longed to sleep, but she couldn't. She longed to feel something, *anything*, but she didn't. Finally, when a single tear slipped out of the corner of her eye, inching its way into her hair, she welcomed it. It was the only sign she had that she was still living.

Terror and loneliness filled her world, just like the terror and loneliness she had felt so many years before, and—like back then—Carolyn had no idea how to fight it. She needed to find something sturdy that she could anchor herself to, but there was nothing there. Back then, she had focused on a Yellow Brick Road with her daddy welcoming her at the end of it, and that vision was all that had kept her strong. Now the Yellow Brick Road was empty…

And Carolyn could no longer see a reason to follow it.

George Shaw lay in repose in a very large, elegant viewing room at *Striffler's Funeral Home* in White Oak. Soothing music played in the background while lamplight illuminated the room, and elderly women ensconced themselves like queen bees in high-backed chairs for the duration of the viewing period. A long line of mourners filed slowly by the casket.

Oblivious to those solemn people moving past her, Carolyn stood rooted beside her daddy's casket and gazed down at him, trying to absorb and accept the knowledge that he was really gone. She couldn't take it in. She couldn't believe that this slender body no longer housed the warm and laughing spirit of the only person who had ever truly loved her.

She touched a black and white pin attached to the lapel of her daddy's coat. The words *Praise the Lord* were scripted in an elegant cursive.

Bobby moved closer and put his arm around her shoulder. "Dad was wearing that pin on his hospital gown the night he died," he told her quietly. "I insisted that Mom bury him in it. I thought he'd like that."

"I'm sure he would, Bobby."

"Sweetheart?" Mommy's voice was low and tense as she took Carolyn's hand. "I wish you would come with me, darling. Lots of people would like to see you."

Carolyn shook off her hand and fiercely gripped the edge of the coffin. "I can't leave him," she whispered. "He's my daddy...my poor dead daddy..."

Mommy shrugged and moved away, obviously unwilling to create a scene. Carolyn watched as the flawlessly groomed woman traversed the large viewing room, warmly greeting family, friends and acquaintances with welcoming hugs. How perfect she is! Carolyn thought in admiration. Even now, she's so, so perfect...

And then, abruptly, Carolyn found herself fighting back that strange, bitter resentment she had only felt a few times before. Her daddy had loved Betty Shaw with his whole heart, but this day she had scarcely spent a moment beside his coffin. She was too busy being perfect, attending to her guests, putting on a show...

On the other hand, Carolyn couldn't tear herself from his side. She was filled with a yawning, aching void more painful than any grief she had ever felt in her life. What did she care about anyone else in the room? She wanted to stay with her daddy.

She had *always* wanted to stay with him, and she couldn't bear the thought of leaving him now. No matter how cold he was to her touch, no matter how obvious it was that he was gone, she still needed to *feel* him. She still needed to stroke him and pat him and somehow remain in contact with him—for just the little time they had left to be together...

Suddenly, not far behind her, Carolyn heard a familiar voice—a diabolical, taunting, arrogant voice that stabbed into her memory like a bloody knife. Her heart turned over.

"Hello, Betty," she heard him say. "I'm very sorry about Pop."

She couldn't believe it, but he was here.

*Art was here.*

She went stiff and numb and ice-cold. She couldn't breathe, couldn't move, couldn't speak. Gripping the edge of the casket, she struggled to stand upright and fought vomit. She didn't know why, but someone was screaming…far in the distance…someone was screaming and screaming…

Dear God, who was screaming?

*Get him out! Get him out! Oh, please, God, get him out!*

Powerful hands gripped her shoulders and pulled her away from the casket. Bobby's firm voice broke through her hysteria just long enough for him to sweep her into his arms and carry her into another room. He murmured low in her ear, doing his best to soothe her even though she seemed beyond comfort. Managing to close the door behind him, he placed her gently on a velvet sofa and sat down beside her. He stroked the tousled hair out of her eyes, still trying to calm her, but Carolyn would have none of it.

Frenzied, she grabbed at his hands. "Make him leave, Bobby! He has no right to be here! Oh, Bobby, please make him leave!"

"Who needs to leave, Carolyn? Who are you talking about?"

"Art! Art is here, Bobby! Didn't you see him? Art shouldn't be here!"

"Why shouldn't he be here, Carolyn? He's Dad's son, remember?"

Carolyn shook her head frantically. She was panicked beyond all reason, beyond any relief. "You don't know him, Bobby… You can't know how he is! Oh, God, Bobby, please make him leave!"

Finally, seeming to realize that there was more going on here than he could even begin to understand, Bobby got to his feet.

"Okay, baby girl," he said gently, stroking her cheek, "you stay here. It'll be all right. I'll take care of it."

The next morning, July 2, 1973, dawned warm and sunny. George Shaw's funeral passed in a blur of loving eulogies and religious hymns, his body was laid to rest at the historical and prestigious Versailles Cemetery in McKeesport, and then it was over. With tears streaming down her cheeks and that painful lump still lodged in her throat, Carolyn glanced at the casket for the last time, then looked away. She reached for Mommy's gloved hand and was comforted by her answering squeeze.

"It's time to go, darling… Just a little bit longer now…" Carolyn bit her lip, nodded and moved closer, looking for protection from an outside world that seemed even more threatening than before. Although she was shattered to her core by the loss of the most important person to ever be part of her life, her heart also soared with elation at the tender reassurance in her mommy's voice. Surely that sweet comfort and support meant something! Perhaps her mommy had finally begun to remember all those years ago when she had loved her George, and adored her Carolyn, and had wanted them both to be part of her life...

Obviously George Shaw could no longer be with her, but Carolyn could. She couldn't take his place in every way, of course, but she could help. She could try to alleviate the loneliness her mommy would undoubtedly feel now. She could go places with her, and make her laugh, and do anything that her mommy wanted her to do.

Surely that's what would happen now...

Without knowing how she got there, Carolyn found herself standing in a parking lot beside a black limousine, still holding Mommy's hand and looking up into Bob Lovell's solemn face. He dropped an affectionate kiss on the top of her head.

"You take care of yourself, you hear?" His voice was thick and gravelly with repressed emotion. "And if you ever need anything, don't you hesitate to call. Don't you be a stranger, either. Clara's going to want to hear from you. You know how she is."

Carolyn couldn't speak. She could only nod.

He turned to Mommy. "Clara and I are both very sorry for your loss, Betty. Please keep in touch with us."

"You're not coming with us to Grandma Nellie's house?"

"No, I'm sorry, I can't. I have a flight out and my cab is here."

"Well, thank you so much for coming and for bringing Carolyn home. I appreciate it more than you know."

Overjoyed, Carolyn glanced up at her mommy. Maybe, just maybe, after all this time, after so much pain... It was almost too much to hope for. But Mommy *had* said it, hadn't she? Hadn't Carolyn heard her right?

*"Thank you for bringing Carolyn home..."*

The wake, a day-long affair held at Grandma Nellie Shaw's home, seemed to include all of White Oak. Carolyn concentrated hard on being the perfect daughter to her mommy, trying to answer her every need before Mommy even knew she had it. She saw to it that Mommy was comfortable in Grandpa Dew's easy chair. She saw to it that Mommy had enough ice in her drink. She saw to it that Mommy had her favorite foods on her plate, a pillow behind her back...

Carolyn didn't even notice who the other guests were. Exhausted and grief-stricken but running on nervous energy and pure adrenalin, she was determined to make herself indispensable to the woman who hadn't needed or wanted her for years. Nothing mattered more to her than that.

Finally, after what seemed an eternity, Mommy began to say her gracious good-byes to all the concerned friends and family gathered around her and made her way to the door. While she obviously enjoyed the attention, there was also a strange faraway look in her eyes, as if she wasn't truly with them any longer. Carolyn was unnerved by that expression.

Still, she was determined to remain beside her mommy, to somehow become vital and necessary to the woman's very existence. "May I go home with you for awhile? I'll be real quiet, I promise."

"I have a terrible headache, Carolyn, and I'm so tired…"

Carolyn fought simmering panic. It was happening again. "I'll help you, Mommy. Please let me come home with you!"

"I think Bobby's planning for you to stay with him…"

"Bobby's not ready to leave yet, Mommy. He's over there by the window, talking to Maureen. Don't you see him?"

Mommy finally gave in rather ungraciously. "Oh, all right, Carolyn. Come along. My head hurts too much to argue."

Carolyn heaved a sigh of relief and followed her mommy outside to a waiting limousine parked in the driveway. When the driver opened the door, they climbed in and settled back against the luxurious leather seats, both resting quietly for a moment. It had been an incredibly long day and Carolyn couldn't wait for it to be over.

"Excuse me, Betty, may I speak to you a moment?"

When that deep and familiar voice slammed into Carolyn's consciousness, her eyes flew open and her heart stopped.

"I haven't seen you at all, and I'd really like to visit with you before I leave. I have my car here and I'd be happy to take you home."

*Oh, my God, no…*

"That's very nice of you, Art," Mommy said quietly, "and I appreciate it, but I'm really tired."

"You know, Betty, it would mean a lot to me," Art continued as if Carolyn wasn't sitting there, glaring at him in hatred and warning. He reached into the limousine and took her mommy's arm. "After all, I just lost my father and I'm going home tomorrow."

"Oh, Art, I don't know. I'm awfully tired." She tried to pull her arm from his grasp, then gave up and shifted slightly in the seat, preparing to climb out. "Well, I guess it would be all right…"

Carolyn went nuts. Her panic was beyond hysterical. It was frenzied and frantic and completely out of control. She had to stop him. She grabbed her mommy and held on with every ounce of strength and determination she had. Her terror was so uncontainable that she shook from head to toe.

"Please don't go with him, Mommy! Please don't go!"

*He'll hurt you, Mommy! You don't know what he'll do to you… I know! He can kill you…*

"Carolyn, behave yourself! For God's sake, let go of me…"

"Mommy, no… Mommy, please!"

"Good grief, Carolyn, calm down!" Mommy's voice was frazzled as she tried to detach herself from Carolyn's persistent grip. "I'm sorry, Art. You can see how it is."

Art just stared at her for a long moment, then shrugged and turned away. Carolyn fought for breath as she watched him walk with a jaunty step toward his car—everything about him was arrogant and unconcerned. Lord, how she hated him! It was frightening how much she hated him…

But how she felt about him right at this moment didn't matter. All that mattered was that her mommy had, for once, listened to her, given in to her…

And because of it, Carolyn had saved her life.

Carolyn walked up to Mommy's bedroom and knocked on the door.

"Come in." The voice beyond was soft and muffled.

Carolyn took a deep breath, opened the door, and walked across the room carefully so as not to make any noise. Her mommy was curled up in her bed, almost in a fetal position, facing the wall. Carolyn knelt beside the bed and gazed for a long, silent moment at that still figure—it was obvious that her mommy wasn't going to show her face. Her back was as definite and as final as a granite wall.

Carolyn had never felt so lonely in her life.

"What do you want?"

Carolyn gulped. Her heart was thudding so hard in her chest that she could scarcely catch her breath, but she knew she had to speak her piece or die trying.

"Can I come live with you, Mommy?" she whispered.

Mommy's response was quick, but her voice was calm and quiet and steady. "No."

Tears welled in Carolyn's eyes and spilled down her cheeks. She stared at that unmoving back. "Mommy, please… I can take care of you. I can cook, and clean the house, and do stuff for you when you're too tired …"

"I want you gone. I can't make it any clearer than that, Carolyn. I want you out of this house and out of my life."

Carolyn shook her head slowly, in disbelief. "You can't mean that, Mommy…"

"Oh, I do mean it. I do. I never want to see your face again."

Only then did the panic hit. Carolyn was barely fifteen years old and she had just lost the most important person in her life, the only person who had ever really loved her. She needed something to hold on to and somebody who cared, *anybody...* All these years, George Shaw had been the buffer between his much-loved grandchild and this woman's irrational resentment, but there was no one to act as a buffer now. Now her rage could explode without anyone to stop it, and Carolyn knew it.

But it didn't matter. Heart and soul, Carolyn loved this woman and she could put up with anything as long as she was allowed to remain nearby. "Please don't send me away, Mommy! Oh, please... I don't have anywhere else to go..."

"Call Bobby. Call Clara. Call the devil." Mommy buried her face in the pillow so that her voice was muffled, but her final words were unmistakable. "Just get the hell away from me."

Life didn't make sense to Carolyn anymore—if it ever had. Carolyn's hysteria hadn't moved anyone. As always, Bobby Shaw had obeyed his mother, using his dead father's credit card to fly Carolyn back to the Lovell home in California, and he didn't seem to think there was anything unusual or ironic in that. The truth was, no one cared.

Now, back in her room at Clara and Bob's house, Carolyn had remained curled up in a ball on her bed, day in and day out for nearly a month, curtains pulled tightly closed against the brilliant summer sunshine, disinterested in her friends, lost in her misery and loneliness. She didn't eat. She couldn't sleep. She spoke to no one, and no one spoke to her.

As each day merged into night, Carolyn wandered back in time and examined her life, trying desperately to determine what she had done that was so terribly wrong. She wasn't wallowing in self-pity; she knew better than to do that. She just wanted to understand something that was incomprehensible to a fifteen-year-old girl who was suddenly and inexplicably alone.

"Carolyn?" Clara's worried voice came from outside the locked bedroom door. "Carolyn, are you awake?"

Carolyn tucked her knees more tightly beneath her chest and said nothing.

"I have some lunch out here for you, sugar. Won't you eat something?"

Carolyn closed her eyes. She didn't know for sure how long she had been in this room, or how long it had been since she had eaten anything, but she wasn't hungry at all. It was like her body had completely shut down, as if it understood that she was already dead inside. All that Carolyn wanted now was to die for real, and for good. Apparently her body intended to cooperate.

Clara's voice came again, this time stronger and more determined. "Carolyn! Carolyn, answer me!"

Carolyn didn't respond. Bob and Clara Lovell, as sweet and concerned as they were, didn't count in her overall scheme of things. She didn't know them well enough to call them *family*, and they didn't know her well enough to have a clue about who she truly was. They didn't know the secrets of Rose, or Texas, or angels that no one else could see—not in the way that George Shaw had. To them she was just a depressed and lonely child who would eventually get over the loss of her daddy. All they had to do was wait it out.

But Carolyn knew better. She no longer had a protector standing solidly between her and the outside world. Even more than her mommy, George Shaw had been her everything, her only incentive to survive the nightmare of Beaumont, Texas, the only reason she had fought to make it back home. George Shaw, and the Yellow Brick Road, had given her purpose. But that Yellow Brick Road wasn't going to help her now.

Clara hammered on the bedroom door. "Carolyn, I've had it with this nonsense, do you hear me? I've got a friend who works in the state hospital in northern California and I'm going to call her this minute, do you understand? Her name is Rose, and she's a nurse, and she'll be down here by tomorrow afternoon to take you back up there with her! All I have to do is ask! I can't do anything else for you, Carolyn, if you won't help yourself! Do you hear me?"

Carolyn's eyes were wide, shocked, staring fixedly at the wall. She hadn't comprehended anything at all—nothing except that hated name…

*Rose. Rose. Rose.*

Suddenly silent rage began to simmer and gurgle and bubble within her, then exploded with a fury that stunned her—simply because it was so unexpected. She didn't answer Clara, who was still hammering on her bedroom door, and she didn't make a move to leave her bed, but her mind was moving at a million miles per hour. If that woman honestly believed that she was going anywhere with someone named *Rose*, she was a lunatic and that's all there was to it.

Without any warning, Carolyn was thrown back into the survival mode with which she had once been so familiar. Her thoughts were crystal-clear, her goals were definite and precise, and she knew exactly what she was going to do.

"I'm getting the hell up out of here," she muttered to the empty bedroom, "and I'm never answering to anyone again."

It was time for her to forget everything she had known before. Somehow she would put the last fifteen years behind her and she would move forward on her own, the way she wanted to. No one would ever again control her, or her life. She would be in control of her own destiny. That was it, and that was all.

What on earth did she need adults for, anyway? Adults had screwed up her life without even thinking about it. They had preyed on her emotions, torn down her defenses, and broken her heart. They had moved her around like she was an old piece of furniture, and discarded her like she was a nasty bit of garbage.

She certainly couldn't do any more damage to herself than adults had done to her, could she? She knew she was young, but she was also smart, and attractive, and people liked her—no matter what Rose had told her over and over, or what her mommy had said. She *wasn't* useless, and she *wasn't* worthless, and she could be any damn thing she wanted to be.

Carolyn was finished listening to adults who didn't care about her, and trying to please people who didn't matter, and struggling to win an old woman's love who couldn't love anyone at all.

Carolyn Sue Shaw didn't need anybody. She could make it on her own.

# PART THREE

*Whatever is begun in anger ends in shame.*

**~Benjamin Franklin~**
**American statesman, writer and philosopher**
**(1706-1790)**

# CHAPTER THIRTEEN

Her 20th birthday celebration was over. Carolyn sat on the sofa, a plump throw pillow behind her back, stroking a purring black cat curled up in her lap. She gazed out the large picture window at the twinkling city lights beyond. Beside her, on a small end table, was a telephone that seemed to have a mind of its own—beckoning to her, whispering over and over, "Dial me...dial me...dial me..."

But Carolyn resisted the urge to pick up that receiver and place another call to her mommy in White Oak, Pennsylvania. She didn't know why she kept putting herself through this kind of pain and rejection, yet she continually did so—at least once a week. She had come such a long way since the days when she had been so dependent upon her mommy's opinion of her, yet she still felt the need, like a very young child, to go after—and receive—her approval.

Carolyn adjusted the pillow more comfortably behind her, scratched the cat's ears, and smiled as the purring grew louder.

"Oh, my sweet Pete," she whispered, "what would I have done without you?" A golden retriever lying on the other side of the living room lifted his head, looking slightly wounded. "And you, Chico, what would I have done without you?"

Chico rolled onto his back, pleased at her recognition, and Carolyn moved the pillow to a more comfortable spot behind her head. She closed her eyes and gave herself over to remembering.

She had come so far...so fast...

Whenever she looked back on the five years that had passed since her daddy's death in 1973, Carolyn didn't feel she had done too badly for herself. Folks had helped her as she went along, of course—Carolyn gave them that, plus her gratitude—but she had pretty much pulled strings and manipulated the system all on her own.

Clara Lovell's nurse-friend Rose had started it all, even though the poor lady never knew it. Within just a few hours of hearing that hated name, Carolyn had slipped out of the Lovell home through her bedroom window and never looked back.

The list of people that Carolyn had stayed with over the course of the next few years was so diverse it was almost bizarre. First she managed to find refuge with her school nurse, who eventually became her legal foster mom until she got pregnant for real. Then, for some reason, Carolyn ran away. She didn't remember why she had run; she only knew that she had and that she felt she had no choice. Then she lived for a little while with another teacher who, with his wife, already had six kids of his own. Carolyn liked this family a lot, but the state wouldn't allow them to take on any more children and she had to leave again.

The only people that Carolyn stayed in touch with in Escondido were her best friend Lisa McKenzie and her older brother, Michael. Although she didn't see them often, she did manage to talk with them on the telephone every once in awhile. Just hearing Lisa's laughter and Mike's deep voice helped Carolyn not to feel quite so different from the rest of the world.

Eventually and probably out of desperation, the state of California contacted Betty Shaw back in Pennsylvania, figuring that she would certainly want to help this mixed-up fifteen-year-old grandchild of hers, but that didn't work out, either. Carolyn could have told them not to waste their time or money, but they didn't ask her opinion so she didn't bother. She just hung around, waiting for the other shoe to drop.

Finally, Carolyn became a temporary ward of the state and the court sent her to an 85-acre ranch out near Alpine, California called *The Burrows Foster Home*. There were five girls at the ranch, including Carolyn, and she had really thought that she might do well out in the California mountains.

But she didn't last there very long, either; she couldn't remember why. She just knew that she had to get away from those vicious females almost as soon as she had arrived. They insisted on locking doors and turning out lights, there were nothing but stupid rules, and the girls were always blaming her for stuff she hadn't done.

The truth was, she was a nervous wreck. Some medical doctor near the home had even prescribed tranquilizers to help calm her down, but they made her robotic and zombie-like. She stopped taking them almost immediately. Finally, in a last-ditch effort to give Carolyn some roots, her old school counselor from Escondido, Allison Palerno, tried to get her admitted into a place called *The Oak Hills Ranch for Girls* or something like that. But this was about as dumb a spot to put a kid like Carolyn as anyone could have come up with because the girls ranged in age from nine to eighteen, and every one of them had been in trouble with someone, somewhere. Carolyn knew right off the bat that she would never stay there, no matter what Miss Palerno wanted.

Still, whenever Carolyn thought about Miss Palerno, it was always, *Poor Miss Palerno*. She had tried so hard to help and Carolyn loved her for it, but she was like every other adult who had tried to come into the mess that was Carolyn's life and fix it: she just made matters worse. She had even taken Carolyn to some shrink out in San Diego, hoping against hope that he might be able to help.

Yet after Carolyn had spent an hour in his office just barely touching on the details of her life, the psychiatrist had announced to Miss Palerno, "She's had a long-term, intimate, sexual relationship with George Shaw and we're going to have to help her work through it."

Carolyn's response had been a long, eloquent, dirty look. "You're out of your frickin' mind," she stated flatly, and that had been the end of her relationship with the psychiatric community on the west coast.

On the other hand, Carolyn had never quite known how she managed it—but California was seemingly unaware of Rose, Art, or any other member of the Lovell family. Consequently, they were never recognized by the court as viable blood relatives and no one ever went looking for them. While she thanked God for that, Carolyn was also pretty proud of herself. As far as she could see, she had actually managed to outwit an entire state government by keeping quiet about the most dangerous arm of her family tree, thus protecting herself from adults that she knew wouldn't hesitate to hurt her.

This proved to Carolyn, finally and irrevocably, that she could take far better care of herself than anyone else could. She could control her own destiny, especially if she didn't let anyone get too close. She had already figured out that as long as she knew the rules, there wasn't a game out there she couldn't play.

Then, just a few weeks before her sixteenth birthday, while enjoying a private dinner with Allison Palerno at a small local restaurant near the ranch, Carolyn had asked her social worker what she believed was an innocuous and simple question, nothing more than a conversation-starter.

But that question—and the answer—had changed her life.

"Last week one of the girls was talking about getting emancipated from the state of California, Miss Palerno. I was wondering how you do that."

"Get emancipated?"

"Yes, ma'am."

Miss Palerno had narrowed her dark eyes, looked at Carolyn speculatively, and took a dainty sip of her iced tea before she responded, "Well, in the first place, you have to be sixteen. Then you can only be emancipated if you're legally married—and you have to have a parent's permission. But don't even think about it, Carolyn. You're automatically free once you're eighteen. Don't be so impatient. You're almost there."

Carolyn had laughed and hastily assured the counselor, "Oh, I'm not going to do anything! I was just wondering."

She had immediately changed the subject to something much less volatile and hoped that Miss Palerno would forget all about it, which apparently she did. Then, very early the next morning, Carolyn had placed a long-distance call to Michael McKenzie's apartment in Escondido. While the phone was ringing, she prayed that Lisa would forgive her for asking this enormous favor of her brother…

"Hello?"

Carolyn's mouth went dry and her heart began to hammer. "Is that you, Michael?"

"Sure. Who's this?"

"Michael, this is Carolyn. Carolyn Shaw."

"Hey, Carolyn." As usual, Mike's deep voice was soothing and calm. He didn't sound in the least bit surprised to hear from her. "What's happening?"

Carolyn took a deep breath to steady her thudding heart. "Not much," she managed finally. "How are you?"

"I'm good. Is something wrong?"

Carolyn plunged in. "Michael, how old are you?"

"You know how old I am. I'm twenty-one. Why?"

He was going to think she was crazy, but she had no choice. "I just wanted to make sure."

"Carolyn, you're talking nuts. Make sure about what?"

"That you're old enough."

"Carolyn, what are you talking about? Old enough for what?"

She couldn't speak; the silence stretched on and on. What if he turned her down? What if she couldn't make him do what she wanted? What would happen to her then? No, he *had* to do it. He just had to!

Finally she just blurted it out. "Will you marry me, Michael? Just for a little while? Not very long, I promise…"

"Okay, that's it. You've lost it."

"Michael, please! Just listen to me and don't interrupt. I turn sixteen in three days. If you go with me up to Washington and we get Art's permission, we can get married and then I'm emancipated from California! Do you know what that means, Michael? It means I'd be free—and we only have to be married for a month, Michael! And then we could get a divorce and it would be all over with." There was dead silence on the other end. Terrified, Carolyn fought tears. "Michael? Michael, are you there?"

"Well…shoot. I haven't had a proposal in at least a week. When do we leave?"

Looking back on it now, Carolyn still couldn't believe how easy it had been. After she had turned sixteen on April 2, 1974, and Allison Palerno had agreed not to report her missing until after she had safely crossed the California/Oregon line, Carolyn and her impromptu fiancé had driven up to Olympia, Washington, to get Art Lovell's permission to marry.

This proved to be a little more difficult than Carolyn finding herself a husband, but not much. Carolyn's whispered threat that she would tell the authorities he had raped her three years earlier was so effective that he actually wound up getting the church across the street, hiring the preacher, *and* buying their wedding bands. His feverish participation wasn't enough to squelch her irresistible desire to see him squirm, but it was better than nothing.

By April 5, 1974, she was a married woman. For a very brief period, Carolyn had lived with Michael in his small house, grateful to him for giving her his name—but not grateful enough to give him much of anything in return. After all, she hadn't been interested in being a wife. All that had really mattered to Carolyn was that she finally possessed the most valuable piece of paper in the world, one that proclaimed her a free woman. And even more importantly than *that*, she had figured it out and pulled it off all by herself.

Regardless, Carolyn was still a kid and wanted to be like other kids. She still wanted to do the things they did; she still wanted to be *cool*. She learned to smoke, and smoked like a bad engine. She learned to drink, and developed a preference for Strawberry Hill, especially when she went to the beach with her friends. Using the memory of her mommy as a guide, she found she could cuss as fluently and with as much color as any sailor walking near the docks of San Diego.

The bottom line was, she'd had it with people jacking around with her, telling her where she could and couldn't live, and what she could and couldn't do. By God, she finally had her freedom and there wasn't a soul out there big enough to take it away from her...

Twenty-five days later, Carolyn and Michael McKenzie filed for divorce and that was the end of that. She left his house and moved in with a high school teacher-friend of hers named Betsy Mullins, hoping once again to establish for herself some kind of stability with an honest-to-God family. She might be emancipated and that was terrific, Betsy had reminded her, but she was still only sixteen, and sixteen-year-old kids didn't know what to do with that much freedom.

The problem was, Carolyn felt one hundred and sixteen, like she had lived a dozen lifetimes, and she didn't know any other kid who felt that way. Once again, no matter how much she smoked, drank, cussed, or tried to be like everyone else, she was still different. In addition to that, there were things going on in her head that terrified her, incomprehensible things, so she couldn't relax to save her life. She felt like she had to keep moving all the time, like she had to stay one step ahead of whatever it was that pursued her—but she didn't know what *it* was. She just knew that it was there, and it was dangerous. If she ever slowed down long enough for it to catch up, she had no doubt that it would engulf her and suffocate her and swallow her whole...

Then Robert Noonan, a good friend of Betsy's, had entered her life. For all Carolyn knew, he probably saved it.

Carolyn's earliest and most formative years had been spent in the warm embrace of a loving, nurturing family. It was from them that she had learned about God's love and compassion, and her daddy had often talked with her about the importance of having a church family—especially when things weren't going too well for her. So, when Robert Noonan had invited her to visit the North County Christian Church where he and his wife, Diana, were members, Carolyn had immediately and gratefully accepted.

She needed *something* in her life, she knew that much. She was functioning well enough to impress everyone watching her from the outside, but she wasn't happy. In fact, she couldn't even remember the last time she had been happy. Nowadays it seemed like she was always angry, confused, frightened. She was only sixteen and had no home, no family, no parents. Free or not, in Carolyn's mind she was still being shafted, shifted, and shuttled about. She was still a rolling stone with no place to land.

The only guidance Carolyn received, strangely enough, came from her daddy, who quite often visited her dreams and gave advice, left messages, and systematically messed up whatever illicit plans she might have been making. Carolyn didn't find these visits disconcerting in the least; rather, she welcomed and looked forward to them. They were all she had in her life that seemed to make sense.

The truth was, Carolyn was learning a very important lesson the hard way: freedom is fine, but people need to know what they're going to do with it. She didn't have a clue.

It was Vernon Gortner, the older pastor at North County Christian Church, who changed Carolyn's life, gave her confidence, and reminded her that in the eyes of God, no one is worthless. The very first time they met in the receiving line outside of the church, following services, Vernon had looked at her so intently with his piercing blue eyes that Carolyn thought maybe she had met him somewhere before. Then he had smiled, placed his hand gently on her shoulder, and invited her to have Sunday dinner with him and his family. There was something in his touch that had reminded her of her daddy, something that she trusted and immediately responded to.

By the end of that week, Carolyn had moved out of Betsy's house and into a comfortable home for girls attending college, subsidized and run by the North County Christian Church. For the first time in years, Carolyn felt that she belonged somewhere, she could actually accomplish something, and she was valuable to the people around her. She felt smart, attractive, and even talented. She played the organ during services, became involved with the youth group, and got her driver's license.

The women in the home became her family, her sisters, and included her in all their activities. The church board gradually took on the stabilizing responsibility of guardianship in her life, with Pastor Gortner's firm guidance at the helm. Carolyn blossomed beneath their loving tutelage and worked hard to make them proud of her. But the day finally came that she needed to strike out on her own.

At nineteen years old, Carolyn packed her black cat, Pete, her golden retriever, Chico, and her few belongings into a U-Haul trailer hitched to the back of her pride and joy—a gold 1970 Oldsmobile 98 convertible. Then, spreading out a map of the United States on her bedroom floor, she turned toward the wall and tossed a penny over her shoulder.

"Okay, Lord," she said aloud, "I promise wherever this penny lands, that's where I'm going."

When she turned back around and knelt down to look at the map more closely, Carolyn's eyes widened in disbelief. That penny had landed on the very state that she hated and feared more than anywhere else in the world: the state of Texas.

Even more unbelievably, the penny covered the city of Houston—only 88 miles east of Beaumont.

Carolyn had rolled out of California on August 16, 1977, the same day that Elvis Presley died. She drove over a thousand miles on east-bound Interstate 10, listening to nothing but Presley, Presley, and more Presley on the radio. She heard endless Presley love ballads, endless Presley early rock'n'roll sessions, and endless Presley fans sobbing into unseen microphones all over the United States.

When she finally arrived in Houston, she was sick of Elvis Presley and already detested this hot, humid, smelly, sprawling city that she had never seen before. She had five dollars in her pocket and no job. She had Pete and Chico in the back seat and no food for them or herself. But none of that mattered to Carolyn. She was free, even if she did have to sleep in her car, and she was going to make it on her own.

It wasn't easy. She exhausted herself by working in a sandwich shop during the day and as a cocktail waitress at night, but she was grateful for the long hours. Both jobs kept her busy, paying her enough to keep up the rent on a dank, dark, depressing apartment in the heart of the city, and she didn't have time to sleep.

Christmas that year was one of the worst that Carolyn could remember— almost as bad as the Christmases she had spent as a child in Beaumont, peeking through keyholes and watching other children opening their presents. She had no tree or decorations in her apartment, no heat, no lights, no friends who cared enough to stop by, and no food except for the tea and crackers that she generously shared with Pete and Chico.

Still, even though she had been frightened and lonely, when she prayed for God's help she had also prayed that He would never let her forget how bad this stage in her life really was. She didn't want it to be rose-tinted by the passage of time; she never wanted to think of this awful period as *the good old days*. She *wanted* to remember the poverty and the loneliness and the fear. She had looked at it as a learning experience, like it was just another one of God's tests to see how much she could take, and she was determined to pass it.

Pass it she did, and with flying colors. At least, on the surface...

By early 1978, Carolyn had landed a job singing telegrams all over the city. She made excellent money, worked hard, and played even harder. She moved into a lovely apartment on the rather fashionable Westheimer Dr., purchased some decent furniture and a new car, and finally considered herself legitimate. When she wasn't working, she juggled several boyfriends at the same time—each of whom seemed to think that she should marry *him* just as soon as possible.

But Carolyn had no intention of marrying again. Not quite twenty years old, she was finally living life exactly the way she wanted to. Her boyfriends were all different—some were wealthy and others were little more than cowpokes—but she called the shots and that's what mattered to her.

However, the one man she trusted above everyone else wasn't a boyfriend at all. He was her best friend, and his name was Larry Huebner.

Carolyn had met Larry through a man she frequently dated, and Larry barely made a ripple in her helter-skelter existence. She liked that; he was just *there*, never demanding anything from her. Nine years her senior and far more mature and responsible than she was, Larry had done everything he could to get her to slow down, to eat better and sleep more, but his passive, unemotional personality was no match for Carolyn's headstrong and willful nature. She did as she pleased, as fast and as hard as she could do it, and every once in awhile she remembered that he was around.

Larry hadn't seemed to mind. Apparently he agreed that there wasn't anything exciting about him, unless you counted that he had graduated from the University of Texas, was an up-and-coming engineer for a large oil company in Houston known as *LoVaca Gathering Company*, part of *Coastal States*, and had the potential to make a great deal of money. Other than that, Larry seemed to recognize that he wasn't the kind of man that a vivacious woman like Carolyn, determined to live life as fully and as close to the edge as she possibly could, would look at more than once. On the other hand, he was like a moth drawn helplessly to her light. He seemed to have an actual physical need to be where she was—perhaps so that he would be there when that light finally burned out.

Carolyn called him a Steady Eddie—sometimes affectionately, other times in exasperation. She was quite often offended because he seemed so unimpressed with the drama and constant crises that made up her daily existence, and finally even told him her life story just to see if she could get a rise out of him. He had lifted an eyebrow, told her he was sorry to hear it, and then asked if she wanted to go with him to get a hamburger.

Slender and balding with a reddish, rather unhealthy complexion, Larry held no sexual attraction for Carolyn, a fact that suited her just fine, and the role he played in her life was that of a trusted girlfriend. He drove her home when she drank too much. He listened, apparently enthralled, to her stories of dates and parties with other men. He even gave her fairly sound "boyfriend" advice when she asked for it. Placid where she was defiant, cool where she was fiery, Larry ultimately just seemed to be content as long as he was in the same room she was in, always sitting quietly in a corner somewhere in case she needed him. Carolyn knew that Larry loved her, maybe more than she had ever been loved before, and she was glad of it. But she couldn't love him back. At least, not the way he wanted and deserved to be loved. So they had stayed away from the subject and it had become like the eight hundred-pound gorilla sitting smack dab in the middle of the room: it was there and they knew it was there, but they just ignored it.

Now, opening her eyes and shifting the cat into a more comfortable position in her lap, Carolyn pulled herself back to the present and allowed her gaze to wander toward a vanilla-scented candle burning on a shelf beside the stereo. Next to the candle was a slender vase containing a single yellow rose. That petite and delicate rose was the basis for a huge dilemma.

Just a few weeks earlier, Carolyn had had a dream. Not a bad dream, not a nightmare, just a normal, ordinary, everyday kind of dream. And in this dream Carolyn had heard a deep, authoritative voice speaking over the background of what appeared to be the tall pine trees of east Texas.

"The next man who brings you yellow roses will be your husband," the voice said so clearly that Carolyn had been startled completely awake. She sat upright in the bed, big-eyed and shocked.

Carolyn wasn't *looking* for a husband. She didn't even *want* a husband. If the truth were known, as far as she was concerned husbands got in the way of a girl's freedom, and freedom was what was most important to Carolyn. But she recognized the voice in that dream. She had heard it a dozen times before.

She knew it to be the voice of God.

Once again Carolyn's wary gaze slid over to the rose. She glared at it angrily, hoping that it would disappear, but it didn't. It remained in that vase, soft yellow and diminutive and magnificent, seeming to stare right back at her. Of all the people in the world to have brought her this rose... Carolyn just couldn't believe it. She couldn't accept it. There were actually a couple of other men in her life that she might have been pleased to receive it from, but not Larry Huebner.

*God could not mean for her to marry Larry Huebner.*

Once more, still stroking the sleeping black cat, Carolyn eyed the telephone on the small end table beside her. Chico whimpered in his sleep as he dreamed some pleasant doggie-dream. It was a perfect, peaceful picture of warm domesticity, but Carolyn scarcely noticed it. She needed advice and she needed it badly.

Finally, Carolyn gave in. Like so many times in the past, her heart just couldn't listen to her brain, and her heart always ruled. She reached for the telephone, dialed, and waited as it rang…and rang…

Then, finally, that timorous, elderly voice. "Hello?"

All Carolyn could manage in response was a whisper. "Mommy? Is that you?"

Silence. A long silence. "How are you, Carolyn?"

"I'm great, Mommy! I'm doing really great! Are you okay?"

"I'm okay."

"I'm glad, Mommy."

More silence. Carolyn lit a cigarette, inhaled deeply. "I got a raise last week, Mommy, and I've only been there since February. They really like my voice…"

"Good."

"I was thinking, Mommy… Maybe you could fly down here and visit me for my birthday. I could pay for it."

"I'm too old to fly, Carolyn. Don't talk crazy."

"No, really, Mommy! I could pay for it…"

"I'm not flying anywhere, Carolyn."

"But I'm twenty years old today, Mommy—a girl doesn't turn twenty all the time! You could meet my friends and see my apartment. I could take you all over Houston—we'd have a ball! Come on, Mommy…"

"You don't have any friends I want to meet, Carolyn."

Carolyn exhaled a huge cloud of smoke. "What about Larry, Mommy?"

"What about him?"

"He gave me roses for my birthday"

"So?"

"I think he likes me a lot."

"You should marry him, then."

"Marry him?" Carolyn stubbed out her cigarette with shaking fingers. "You don't marry your best friend, Mommy."

"Well, you really don't need to worry about it, I guess. He wouldn't marry you anyway. He's got a reputation to protect. He's too smart to marry someone like you."

Carolyn closed her eyes, shook her head slowly, lit another cigarette and whispered, "Why do you do that, Mommy? Why do you *have* to hurt me?"

"I'm telling you the truth, that's all. Just the truth."

Tears stung. Carolyn bit her lip and said nothing.

Then, there was that bored voice again. "Stop trying to impress me. You'll never have a pot to piss in or a window to throw it out of. I'm going to bed."

There was a click in Carolyn's ear, then a dial tone. Carolyn hung up the telephone and angrily dashed the tears off her cheeks.

That was it. She was finished. If he would have her, and she knew he would, Carolyn would marry Larry Huebner.

# CHAPTER FOURTEEN

When the summer of 1978 blasted into Houston, no human being in his right mind wanted to be there. Like everyone else stuck outside on this humid Saturday afternoon, Carolyn and Larry were sweat-drenched and miserable. They finally crawled into their favorite coffee shop, where at least it was air conditioned.

After they were seated and the waitress had brought their iced tea, Carolyn lit a cigarette and tried to blow the smoke away from Larry. He hated the habit but, typically, he didn't complain. As the smoke swirled around his head, he just wiped the perspiration from his face, wrinkled his nose in distaste and leaned back in his chair.

He laced his fingers across his stomach. "What's on your mind, Carolyn?"

"Nothing. Why do you ask that?"

He chuckled. "I know you, and there's something on your mind."

Carolyn looked at him for a long moment, at first trying to get up her nerve, then losing it entirely. She shook her head and shrugged. "No...okay... Oh, what the hell. Can I ask you a question?"

He lifted an eyebrow and nodded, an oddly hooded expression suddenly clouding his rather plain face. Carolyn could almost see the wheels turning in his head. The man was a born negotiator and he always seemed to be one step ahead of everyone else. Still, she was positive that he wouldn't be ready for this.

She took a sip of her tea; the ice was wonderful. "You know, Larry, that's a beautiful house you bought. I like it."

"A statement, not a question, but I'll let it pass."

"Well, you know, Larry, you really do need someone to come in and fix up that house. I mean, it's dirty and you've got, like, no furniture..."

His left eyebrow shot upward again. "You want to be my maid?"

Carolyn stared down at the table and fiddled with a glass ashtray. She stubbed out her cigarette. "Of course not. Don't be ridiculous. Get me some more iced tea, will you?"

He motioned to the waitress for a refill, then reached across the table and gently took her hand. "Carolyn, are you all right? You don't look good."

She felt prickly all over and hot beads of nervous perspiration popped out across her upper lip. She could hardly catch her breath. For some reason, she was more frightened than she had ever been in her life, but she had no idea why.

Larry didn't question her again, but he didn't let go of her hand, either. When he finally spoke, his voice was casual. "This might not be the right time to bring it up, Carolyn," he began, "but then I've never been recognized for perfect timing…"

Carolyn's heartbeat was finally beginning to slow down from a sharp staccato to an unhurried thud and she looked at him with affectionate gratitude. She turned her hand palm-upward and laced her fingers with his, barely listening as his voice droned on. It was far more important that she pull herself together than that she say anything. Besides, it always took Larry forever to get to the point, so she had time.

"Anyway, I was thinking that you might kind of like to marry me," he finished. He might have been asking her to please pass the salt. "What do you think?"

Carolyn's wide, blue-gray eyes grew even wider as she looked at him in shocked disbelief. She wasn't sure she had heard him right. "You want me to marry you?"

"Well, you're too cute to be my maid." Only the thin sheen of sweat dotting his forehead gave away his nervousness. "So, what do you think? You want to get married?"

Just thirty minutes earlier that had been *all* Carolyn wanted—but that was thirty minutes earlier. Now, thank God, she had come to her senses. It wouldn't be fair to Larry to saddle him with a woman who didn't love him. He deserved far better than that. In fact, he deserved far better than Carolyn, period.

Then, unbidden and unwanted, Mommy's sarcasm sneered through her memory: *He wouldn't marry you anyway. He's got a reputation to protect. He's too smart to marry someone like you…*

"Carolyn, I know that I'm not the greatest looking guy and I'm sure not very exciting…but I love you and I'll take care of you, I promise."

Carolyn's eyes swam with tears and her chin quivered as she tried to summon up the nerve to do the right thing, but at the last minute her courage failed her. Instead she squeezed his hand and leaned in close to him. "I'd be proud to marry you, Larry," she said softly. "I'd be honored to be your wife."

*I'll be a good wife to him, I will. He'll never be sorry that he married me. I'll make him happy…*

Still, when his lips met hers in a brief, sort of acquaintance-friendly kiss, Carolyn's heart didn't even skip one beat. Her breath didn't catch in her throat. Her hands didn't tremble and her legs didn't grow weak. There was no thrill there, no fire…nothing. It was about as exciting as kissing a sponge.

Abruptly, she envisioned what she was certain would become a superficial and meaningless existence. She could see her days stretching far ahead of her—days without challenge, without goals, without hope. She could see herself traveling down a long and boring road toward the end of a life that was ultimately doomed to failure.

But it didn't matter. Carolyn would gladly sacrifice her youth, her fiery passion, her hard-won independence, and even her intelligence if she could gain the respect she craved from both her mommy and society. Especially her mommy. Marrying the highly regarded Larry Huebner, up-and-coming businessman who promised to one day be a pillar of the community, would give her that in spades.

The truth was: Carolyn would happily sacrifice her freedom just to prove a point.

Carolyn let herself into her apartment and patted Chico's head as he welcomed her home with youthful golden retriever enthusiasm. Right behind him, displaying classic feline disinterest, strolled Pete, tail high and purring loudly as he weaved in, out and all around Chico's legs. Carolyn locked the door and knelt on the floor, greeting both animals with warm affection.

"Hey, I'm getting married, you guys. What do you think about that?"

Chico licked her chin delicately—he wasn't a sloppy kisser—while Pete made himself comfortable in her lap. Carolyn fought sudden, inexplicable tears and tried to swallow the lump in her throat.

"We'll be all right," she whispered, scratching Chico's ears, "I promise I'll always take care of you."

Carolyn frowned. What on earth had made her say that? There was absolutely nothing scary about Larry Huebner. He was far too easygoing and ordinary to be scary. Even if he never did anything else in his life, he would always take good care of his family. She was sure of that. So why was she worried?

I'm not worried, she told herself firmly. I just feel...sort of...isolated. After all, she had no one to talk to except two loving animals that couldn't talk back. She had no one to share her Big News with—no family anyway. Just friends and acquaintances who would mainly be excited because her wedding meant another party.

Then, like the answer to a prayer she wasn't even conscious of praying, Carolyn envisioned a shadowy image that she hadn't thought of in years. In her mind's eye, she saw an older, immensely tall woman who had lived in a forest—a sweet-faced woman who had once been kind to her and tried to protect her from Rose. Even though Carolyn hadn't thought of her in a long, long time, her unexpected recollection of feisty Aunt Kat standing up to Rose and tucking a terrified, freshly-bathed little girl into a warm bed for the first time in months flooded her memory as clearly as if it had happened just yesterday.

Aunt Kat was family, and she had cared about Carolyn. If she was still alive, she was probably close by. Her house couldn't have been all that far from Houston.

What was her full name? Carolyn wracked her brain, trying to remember, but it just wouldn't come to her. It was foreign, French maybe...

Then, for some reason, Carolyn remembered that Aunt Kat had been married to Rose's uncle...or her brother...someone like that. What was Rose's last name? It was an interesting name...kind of pretty. What on earth was it? Belaire? No, that wasn't it. Mohair? McClaire?

*Mattair*! That was it, *Mattair*! Carolyn jumped to her feet, unceremoniously dumping a sleepy Pete out of her lap, and dashed into the living room, grabbing the phone book from beneath the telephone on the end table. Curling up on the sofa, Carolyn rifled through the pages with fingers that shook with so much excitement she could hardly hold the book open, and tried to find the *M*'s. It was an unusual name, there couldn't be many of them...

And there it was, all by itself: *Weston Mattair*.

Carolyn sank back into the sofa with a deep sigh, tears of joy filling her eyes. Perhaps she had family, after all. Perhaps there *was* someone who cared that she was going to be married, someone she could share that kind of big news with, someone in her family who might even want to be with her on her wedding day.

Carolyn grabbed a cigarette, lit it and dragged deeply before she picked up the receiver. What would she say if Aunt Kat actually answered the phone? The poor woman was much older now—she could have a stroke from the shock of hearing the voice of someone so far back in her past. Maybe Carolyn shouldn't call her after all. Maybe it was a selfish thing to do. Maybe it would be too painful...

No, Carolyn knew better than that. Aunt Katherine hadn't cared for Rose, she had made that clear enough many times. But she had definitely cared for the angry little girl who was malnourished and scared to death.

In fact, the more Carolyn thought about it, the worse she felt for not having remembered Aunt Kat when she had first arrived in Houston. She should have called her much sooner. It was inexcusable. On the other hand, maybe Aunt Kat wasn't well, or wouldn't remember...

Finally, before she could figure out a way to change her mind again, Carolyn dialed Aunt Kat's number and held her breath, waiting as the phone rang. After what seemed like eons, a breathless female voice answered, "Yes, hello?"

"Aunt Kat?"

There was a puzzled silence on the other end of the line. "Who is this?"

Carolyn cleared her throat nervously. "Aunt Kat, I don't know if you remember me or not... Aunt Kat, this is Carolyn. Carolyn Shaw."

"Oh, my goodness! Oh...really? Little Carolyn?"

Carolyn's eyes welled with tears again, but this time they were tears of gratitude. Her Aunt Katherine was actually glad to hear from her! There was no mistaking the happiness in her voice, no mistaking it at all.

Nearly overwhelmed with thankfulness, Carolyn whispered, "Yes, Aunt Kat, it's me."

"Where are you, child? Where are you calling from?"

"I'm in Houston, Aunt Kat. I have an apartment here."

"Oh, my goodness! In Houston! How long have you been in Houston?"

"Several months, but I just now found your number." Then, embarrassed, Carolyn had to admit with a chuckle, "I couldn't remember your last name until just this minute."

"Oh, that's all right, child. I can't remember my own last name half the time. We'll make up for it easy enough."

"I'm getting married, Aunt Kat, and I wanted to come out to see you."

"Married! Oh, my goodness! Well, you come right on out this second, you hear? Let me give you directions. Do you have something to write on? My house is sort of out in the boonies." Aunt Kat paused, then asked more carefully, "Do you remember my house, sweetheart?"

"I sure do, and it's a good memory for me. How do I get there?"

Carolyn's connection with Aunt Kat quickly developed into the most important relationship in her life, even more important than her relationship with Larry. For the first time in the ten years since she had been returned to her family in Pennsylvania, Carolyn had found someone who had *known her when*, someone who could, and would, validate without hesitation what had happened to her, someone who accepted her no matter what.

For the first time in all that time, Carolyn felt like she had come home.

Carolyn's initial visit back to Aunt Kat's rambling, run-down house just north of Houston off Highway 59 had brought home to her one important fact: regardless of whether or not two people shared blood (as Carolyn's daddy had called it), they could still be *family*. The fact that Katherine was only Carolyn's aunt by marriage didn't matter a whit to either Katherine or Carolyn. When Carolyn had parked in front of Aunt Kat's sagging front porch and got out of her car, the older woman had shot out of the house and swooped down on her, engulfing her in the most wonderful bear hug she had ever been given in her life. It was a welcome she would never forget.

Once more, just as when she had been a little girl, Carolyn was taken aback by Aunt Kat's height—nearly six feet of slender, statuesque beauty. Her short, dark hair was lightly laced with silver and there were fine lines around her eyes, but she was still lovely. Noticing that she was a little stooped now and moving cautiously, as if she was in pain, Carolyn was immediately concerned.

"Are you okay, Aunt Kat?" she asked, still breathless from the bone-crushing bear hug. "Are you hurt?"

"Oh, just some back problems, sweetheart. It comes with getting old. Don't you worry about me." Aunt Kat stood back, still holding Carolyn's shoulders, and analyzed her carefully. "Now, let me look at you. You're so pretty! I don't know who you look like. No one I know. Maybe on your daddy's side…"

"It doesn't matter, Aunt Kat. Where's Uncle Weston?"

"I just divorced that sorry piece of work, sweetheart. It's me now, out here all by my lonesome."

"Well, being alone hasn't hurt you, Aunt Kat. You look exactly like I remember you."

Katherine cocked her head to one side. "Really? You remember me?"

"Of course I do." Carolyn met her quizzical gaze head-on, then glanced away, slightly embarrassed. "Well…sort of. There's a lot I don't remember too well…" Her voice trailed away. "But you were good to me," she finished quickly, "and I remember that."

"Ah, bless your heart." Katherine had put her arm around Carolyn and gently walked her toward the house. "Let's go inside, sweetheart. It's way too hot to stand out here, and we have a lot to talk about…"

The relationship between the two women had deepened quickly, the same way that Carolyn would have loved for her connection with her mommy to have grown but knew it never would.

Aunt Kat's house soon became Carolyn's home away from home. When Larry gave Carolyn her beautiful engagement ring, a small diamond solitaire that would be set between two brushed gold bands and encircled with other, smaller diamonds, Aunt Kat was one of the first people Carolyn showed it to. When Carolyn began shopping for household items and decorations to beautify the house she would share with Larry, Aunt Kat was one of the people Carolyn called for advice.

Yet, even though she felt totally free to tell Aunt Kat just about anything, she still kept secrets…lots and lots of secrets.

Carolyn didn't talk about Larry, except what a good husband he was going to be and how she hoped she could make him happy. She didn't talk about love, or being in love, or loving the idea of love. She never mentioned those disconcerting blocks of missing time, or the chaos that so often seemed to reign in her head, or the frantic race that she always seemed to be running against the rest of the world.

As in the past, Carolyn only presented to Aunt Kat the happy, healthy face she thought the older woman wanted to see. Everything else she kept to herself. The truth was, she just didn't know any other way to be.

Then, one evening toward the end of June, Carolyn received a telephone call from White Oak, Pennsylvania, that was disturbing enough to push Aunt Kat all the way to the back of her mind.

Mommy's voice crackled through the phone. "I have some bad news," she said abruptly.

Carolyn rolled her eyes and flopped onto the sofa. *Of course you do. Why else would you call?*

"Well, hello to you, too, Mommy."

"Lightning struck the house during a storm the other night and a fire started up in Bobby's old room. All your stuff was lost. I thought you should know."

Carolyn was shocked into silence. All she could think about were her toys, her baby photos, her daddy's war medals safely stored in the top of her closet…

"Are you there? Say something. I don't have all day."

Carolyn could almost hear the toe of Mommy's shoe tapping impatiently against the kitchen floor. Tears welled and spilled over. "I'm here."

"Well, like I said, there's not much left."

Carolyn angrily wiped the tears off her cheeks with the back of her hand, then grabbed a Kleenex from a box beside the telephone and blew her nose with rude gusto. "I thought you said the fire was Bobby's room. Why was *my* stuff burned up?"

"Everything was wet and smelled terrible. We had to throw it all out."

*Like hell… What better time to toss out any reminders of me—or my daddy—than right after a fire? Who's going to question where anything is?*

"I'm even staying next door at Maureen's right now."

*So what? That's all you ever wanted to do anyway…*

"I'm flying home, Mommy." Carolyn's voice was firm. "I have some news of my own, anyway. I'm off the weekend of July fourth. Will that be all right?"

"You don't need to come."

"I know I don't *need* to come, Mommy, but I want to see what's left of my stuff."

The elderly woman's noncommittal response wounded Carolyn like a stinging slap across the face. "Well, come on, then. I guess I can't stop you."

At that moment something deep within Carolyn's heart turned hard and cold. This was not a woman who had loved without reservation. This was not a woman who had never been cruel to a child. This was not a woman deserving of a term of endearment like *Mommy*.

"Don't worry about picking me up at the airport, Mother," Carolyn said in a quiet voice that was sad and cold and resigned. "I'll get a cab."

Five years had passed since the last time Carolyn had been in White Oak, Pennsylvania, but nothing had really changed. The town was still modest, the people were still a little too self-righteous for her comfort, and Carolyn still felt like a greedy child with her nose pressed against a candy store window: always on the outside of small-town society looking in.

As she had in the past, Carolyn had almost immediately walked over to Grandma Rankin's cottage, not only because she wanted to visit the old lady, but because she wanted to find one place in the entire town where she felt welcome—and Grandma Rankin hadn't let her down. Giving a little squeal of excitement, the still-spry elderly woman had pushed herself out of the rocking chair on her porch, scampered to the steps, and then just stood there, all smiles and arms outstretched. Carolyn had dashed right into them and held on tight— once more the little girl looking for acceptance and love anywhere she could find it.

But Carolyn had found out soon enough that she was no longer that little girl. Far too much time had passed. Jimmy was gone now, Grandma Rankin told her proudly, off to college to study medicine. He was going to be a doctor, just like he had always wanted to be, so he studied all the time. No one saw him much anymore.

"I live in Houston now, Grandma," Carolyn confided, sitting beside her on the porch, "and I'm getting married in a couple of months."

"How wonderful, child!" Grandma Rankin patted Carolyn's hand. "What's his name?"

"Larry Huebner."

"Spell it."

Grinning, Carolyn spelled it slowly, then pronounced it correctly: *Heeb-ner.*

"Is that a German name?"

"Very German. Larry's father is Austrian, and his mother is Czechoslovakian. He's an only child, and his folks own a pretty farm in a small town not too far from Houston—in Wesley, Texas. Wesley is so little it's not even on the map. Anyway, their names are Eddie and Annie, and that whole area is filled with all his aunts and uncles and cousins. So, even though he's an only child, he still has a big family and I like that."

"Is he a nice man?"

"Oh, he is, Grandma! I think you'd like him a lot. He's an engineer and he works for a huge oil company. I think he'll be important one day."

Grandma Rankin's alert blue eyes immediately narrowed with speculation. Carolyn wished she could cut her own tongue out. "And that matters to you?"

"Well, not to me, but..." Her voice trailed away.

"It matters to Betty and Maureen. Am I right?"

"I guess so, Grandma..."

Whenever she was completely honest with herself, which wasn't very often these days, Carolyn had to wonder why White Oak's approval meant so much to her. It didn't make any sense. She was living in a huge city on her own, making her own way, buying her own stuff, not dependent on anyone except herself. How many women in this one-horse town could say the same? Not too many. Most of them were still staying at home, taking care of the children, being supported by and waiting on unappreciative husbands. Yet Carolyn had even purchased her own round-trip airline ticket and paid her own taxi costs, for crying out loud, and not many women around here could do that. She was an honest-to-God high roller compared to them.

But she *still* wasn't as good as they were and she never would be, no matter what she did. She knew it by the pitying, slightly disappointed way that Maureen and Mother looked at her. Whenever she was around those two absolutely perfect women, she always felt vulgar, loud, and socially inept. The last three days spent with them in Maureen's perfect little house had done nothing to make her feel any more competent or acceptable.

Now, thank goodness, it was almost time for her to go home. She honestly didn't care if she ever returned.

If her daddy had been alive, how different this visit would have been! When she had entered her childhood home and seen Bobby's burned-out bedroom, Daddy would have understood her tears and grief. He wouldn't have snorted rudely like Mother did. He would have taken her in his arms and held her for as long as it took for her tears to dry. He would have talked her through the loss of his war medals and her baby pictures. He would have understood.

He also would have been thrilled about her upcoming marriage to such a respectable, promising businessman. He would have given her the marital advice that she so desperately needed now, and he would have assured her that Larry Huebner was the luckiest man in the world—not the other way around. He would never in a million years have looked at her engagement ring the way her mother had, as if it had come out of a Cracker Jack box, and he certainly wouldn't have told her that she had better set the wedding date quick, before the guy found out the truth about her and changed his mind.

But her daddy was gone, and Mother had put up an impenetrable barrier to keep Carolyn out. In fact, Carolyn was convinced that that barrier was so important to her mother's sanity that she had personally destroyed every memento the fire hadn't consumed first.

*Well, it's just her and Maureen now, and that's all she's ever wanted...*

Carolyn squashed that familiar thought before it could become even more resentful. She was sick of thinking about it. As she made her way around Maureen's living room, looking at expensively framed family photos arranged on the walls, she couldn't help but notice that she wasn't in any of them. It was like she had never existed.

"That's a beautiful engagement ring, Carolyn," Uncle Artie said, touching her shoulder. He took her left hand, guided it toward the lamplight, and carefully examined the glittering solitaire diamond. "When's the big day?"

She looked at her daddy's younger brother with warm affection. "September 2nd."

"Right around the corner, huh?"

Carolyn nodded. Uncle Artie was just as handsome as her daddy had been, and there was something about the way his eyes crinkled up when he smiled that had always reminded her of him. He and George had been as tight as thieves through good times and bad, and Carolyn loved him for that.

"What do you want for a wedding present?"

"Oh, you don't have to give us anything, Uncle Artie. We're fine."

"Don't be silly. Every young couple just starting out needs a nice wedding present. What would you like?"

Carolyn looked directly into his snapping dark eyes and drew courage from their similarity to her daddy's. "Do you truly want to know?"

"Of course I do."

"Don't think I'm crazy, Uncle Artie, but... Oh, never mind. It's silly."

"Now, come on, Carolyn. You've really got me curious here. What is it?"

She took a deep breath and blurted, "I'd like for you to give me away. Since my daddy isn't here. It would be the best wedding present ever."

He didn't even hesitate. "Why didn't you say so? I'd be honored."

Carolyn nearly fainted. She grabbed his arm. "Really? You mean it?"

"Well, of course I mean it. Is your mother coming?"

Carolyn looked away from him then and shook her head. That familiar infuriating pain bubbled up in her throat again—it was a pain she couldn't stop, couldn't ignore, and couldn't ease. "She says she's too old to fly."

Uncle Artie took her into his arms as gently as if he had actually been her daddy, and for a moment Carolyn could almost imagine he was. The words he whispered to her sounded exactly like something her daddy would have said, and the determination in his voice was so familiar that her heart soared.

"Don't you worry about it for one minute, Carolyn. She'll be there, I promise. I'll see to it."

Uncle Artie was true to his word and flew Carolyn's mother down with him, with the promise they would continue on to Hawaii, a place she always wanted to visit. But whatever he had to promise, the end result was worth it. As long as they were in public, Betty Shaw was the perfect mother-of-the-bride, attentive and proud and devoted. Carolyn knew it was an act, but she enjoyed it anyway.

Now it was the night before the wedding and the rehearsal dinner was over. To Carolyn's relief, her mother and Uncle Artie left the restaurant for their motel in Brenham, just a few miles from Wesley Church where Carolyn and Larry would be married the next afternoon. Teresa Main, Larry's secretary and Carolyn's maid of honor, thanked them for the barbecue, said goodnight, and drove out of the parking lot in a hurry. Carolyn didn't really blame her. As far as she was concerned, rehearsal dinners and baby showers ranked right up there with root canals and ingrown toenails.

Now, standing outside of the restaurant, hand-in-hand and bathed in moonlight, Carolyn and Larry were alone for the first time in days. It was hard to believe that tomorrow evening, about this time, she would be Mrs. Larry Huebner and Larry's lovely two-story brick house in Memorial Park, located on Houston's west side, would be her new home.

To the dismay of her boss, Carolyn had quit her job singing telegrams and moved out of her apartment, Chico and Pete in tow, just two weeks earlier. And, right up until today, she had been fixing her new house with the housewifely dedication of Jane Wyatt in *Father Knows Best*, shopping until she was so exhausted she couldn't put one foot in front of the other. She sought perfection, making certain that the new bath towels coordinated with the new bath rugs, the new place mats matched the new pot holders, the new set of dishes went well with the new Formica-topped kitchen table, and so on and on and on.

She was nesting, an amused Aunt Kat called it, but Carolyn didn't see it that way. She was just trying—unsuccessfully—not to have a nervous breakdown.

Here she was, twenty years old and healthy, living with a man who had yet to do anything more than to kiss her goodnight. Carolyn had had her share of memorable sexual experiences, some far more memorable than others, and she knew how important that part of her life was to her. It was important. Very, very important.

The bottom line was, she was all charged up and nowhere to go. Larry Huebner certainly wasn't the man she was on fire for, but if she was going to spend the rest of her life with him, they had to start somewhere. They couldn't kindle the flame if they didn't find the heat…

But Larry wasn't interested. Not until after they were married, he said. He had too much respect for her. He had never been with a woman before and he wanted it to be perfect. He had been raised that way and he couldn't help it… Carolyn thought he could probably live that way for the rest of his life and never miss it.

She didn't know why, but she suddenly felt like she was going to jump out of her own skin and, as crazy as it sounded, she wasn't even sure whose skin she was actually in. It was a completely alien sensation, and it brought on a completely panicked response.

"Larry, I can't marry you."

"Okay."

Carolyn stared at him in disbelief. "That's all you're going to say? Okay? That's it?"

He shrugged. "What else do you want me to say? You can't marry me. Okay."

"Well, hell, I don't know…ask me why not!"

"Okay, why not?"

"Sweet Mary and Joseph, Larry!" Carolyn felt like she was losing her mind. His emotions were always the same, un-bumpy and monotonous, like the straight line reading of a dead man on a heart monitor. "Because I don't love you that way, that's why not! I mean, I love you, but I'm not *in love* with you."

He shrugged again and pushed a strand of wispy thin hair off his forehead. "I know that. It's okay."

"Good God, Larry! You're driving me crazy! I don't know what you're feeling! We need to set up some kind of a code. Jump up and down and foam at the mouth if you're upset, will you? Good grief, Larry, I'm trying to do the right thing here!"

"I don't need you to do the right thing. I love you. You'll learn to love me. It's no big deal."

No big deal…

What kind of man is this? What kind of man looks at the woman he loves and tells her it's no big deal if she doesn't love him back? What kind of man lives in the same house with the woman he's going to marry and never touches her…doesn't want to touch her…never even has to fight the desire to touch her? He's either the best man in the world…or he's stark raving mad…

*This is wrong. This isn't going to work. I'm fixing to make the biggest mistake I've ever made in my whole life...*

Carolyn wanted passion. She needed her life-partner to yearn for her, ache for her, desire her body and soul more than he wanted anything else in the world...

Larry seemed to read her mind. He took a step closer to Carolyn and tilted her chin upward so that she was forced to meet his eyes.

"Trust me," he told her softly, "you're all I want in this world. Trust me. I can wait."

# CHAPTER FIFTEEN

In spite of her misgivings, Carolyn married Larry Huebner at a tiny church in Wesley, Texas, on the afternoon of September 2, 1978. The wedding was lovely and the reception a kick, but like any good party it had to come to an end. Once it was over and the newlyweds had returned to their home, they sat on the edge of their bed and stared at one another.

*Now what?*

Every once in awhile a shout of laughter or an excited bark from Chico would erupt from the family room downstairs, breaking the silence and reminding them that they had a houseful of relatives, wedding night or not. As she gazed at Larry's pale face in the deepening shadows, Carolyn couldn't help but think that this ridiculous situation would have been almost funny had it not been so pathetic. The atmosphere in this bedroom should have been romantic and charged with sexual electricity, but there was no soft music, no candlelight, nothing to encourage a terrified young man. And his bride felt no eagerness or excitement. She didn't even feel any tenderness. She felt only apprehension and foreboding.

Now, without any shadow of a doubt, Carolyn knew she had just ruined her life.

She clenched her fists in her lap and cleared her throat. "Larry..."

Another burst of laughter erupted from downstairs.

Desperately, Larry grabbed Carolyn's hands. "We don't have to do anything tonight," he said in a strange and strangled voice, like he couldn't get enough air. His fingers were cold and clammy. "Too many people here, too much noise...I can't..."

Carolyn nodded quickly, weak with relief. It had been a long day and she honestly didn't have the will or the energy to break in a petrified twenty-nine-year-old virgin. Even though they were now husband and wife, the fact still remained that they were really only best friends and they would have to work—very, very hard—toward being anything more than that. She just wasn't up to the challenge tonight.

Standing up and yawning widely, Carolyn ran her fingers through her thick, curly hair, making a big production out of showing how exhausted she was. "That sounds fine to me, Larry, don't worry about it. I'm really beat to a pulp. Planning a wedding takes a lot out of a gal. I'm going to go take a shower, okay?"

"Are you sure? You don't mind?"

She dropped a quick kiss on the top of his balding head and nodded. "Sure I'm sure. Besides, we're leaving for New Braunfels tomorrow and that'll be a whole lot better than being here."

Larry looked almost sick with gratitude. "I feel bad about New Braunfels, Carolyn. It's not much of a honeymoon. It's only a few hours from here and we've only got a couple of days…"

"Larry, we've already talked about this. I love New Braunfels. Besides, we're taking the vacation time to go back to Pennsylvania for Christmas, remember?"

"I know, but…"

"Relax, Larry," she interrupted, touching his cheek. "We have the rest of our lives to figure this out."

He took her hand again and looked up at her imploringly. "I just want you to be happy, Carolyn. That's all in the world I want."

"Don't be silly, Larry. Of course I'm happy."

But, even as she reassured him, Carolyn was stunned to find herself infuriated by his pleading, puppy-dog eyes. Without any warning, his pain and weakness and duplicity filled her with roiling, boiling rage. By telling her that she would learn to love him and promising her a perfect wedding night, he had stolen her freedom. He had taken away everything that meant anything to her and replaced it with absolutely nothing.

Carolyn felt like a caged wild animal—and her husband was her keeper.

*Oh, sweet Jesus, just let me go… Stop looking at me like that… Don't beg, for God's sake, I can't stand it if you beg…*

And then she knew it, for certain: this would be her life, for the rest of her life.

Carolyn took a deep breath and forced herself to look at him with something other than the fury she was fighting to conceal. Sympathy, compassion, or maybe just friendship…anything but rage. She squeezed his hand and gently released it.

"Let me go now, Larry," she said calmly. "I need to take a shower."

He sagged and glanced away from her. He looked like a whipped dog.

Larry's hurt silence set the pattern for the way they spent their days. Just as he had done before they were married, he never argued as long as Carolyn allowed him to remain in her life—even if she was out of his reach. Consequently, within just a few weeks, Carolyn and Larry had fallen into a matrimonial arrangement more suited to an elderly, disabled couple planning their last days together than two young people eager to explore one another and begin traveling their duel road toward a fulfilling life that meant something to them both.

Instead, Larry worked long hours and lost himself in a bottle of Scotch on the evenings he came home at a normal time. Carolyn cleaned, decorated, and shopped in a frantic attempt to either alleviate or ignore altogether her boredom, frustration, and growing anger. They had no close friends as a couple, and no hobbies they could enjoy together. At night, when they climbed into their king-sized bed, Larry curled up on one side and Carolyn on the other, back-to-back, putting as much distance between them as they could. When he slept, Larry snored loudly enough to make the pictures go haywire all through the house, and Carolyn seldom slept at all.

As time progressed, the days and weeks running into one another in a blur of monotony and humdrum conformity, Carolyn grew so tense she knew she was going to explode. Her brain felt searing hot, like she was actually living inside a pressure cooker, and everywhere she went it was noisy. She could find no peace, no silence, anywhere.

Sometimes it even seemed to her that her mind was like an elevator filled with people, going up and down, up and down, faster and faster and faster, and all the people inside were talking at once...

As usual, Carolyn told no one. The more intense the stress became, the more she withdrew from Larry, her animals, and the insane life she found herself living. It was too much trouble to even get out of bed in the morning. But these difficulties weren't the kind she could discuss with anyone she knew—not even her beloved Aunt Kat—because she didn't understand her own reaction at all. Now she was so angry that she couldn't function. She could hardly breathe. Her brain didn't even work.

For the first time in years, Carolyn felt exactly like she had when she was a child and found herself trapped with people she didn't love and who didn't love her, like when she had been locked in a closet...and isolated...and unable to escape...

As Carolyn finished drying the last of the dinner dishes, Chico's playful barks and Pete's periodic kitty squeals came from the family room, punctuating a silence so malevolent it could have exploded. Carolyn turned away from the kitchen sink and stared at her husband, who was sitting at the table methodically draining another bottle of Scotch.

She'd had it, trying to talk to him like he was a normal human being. He wasn't normal. Nothing moved him. He didn't care about anything but his climb up the corporate ladder of LoVaca Gathering Company. If it was work-related, he responded. If it was Carolyn-related, he didn't.

Why in the world had he married her? She just couldn't figure it out. Even though she knew she had married him for all the wrong reasons, she had at least told him the truth. But he had lied to her. He didn't want her. She wasn't necessary to his life. He certainly didn't care about the hours she stayed home alone, unhappy and untouched and unfulfilled.

But before she could tell him how she felt, Carolyn was puzzled by a distant female voice, reeking with spite, that she had never heard before.

*"How do you think you're ever going to get it on with me if you sit around and drink all the time?"*

The blood drained from Larry's normally ruddy face and his eyes narrowed as he glared at Carolyn. After a long, silent moment, he deliberately picked up the bottle, poured himself another glass, and tossed it back.

*"Oh, that's real mature, Larry. That's gonna fix everything..."*

He cut her off. "What do you know about maturity? You don't do anything but sleep and shop." Then, pouring himself another drink, he added, "Shut that damn dog up!"

*"I will not. At least that damn dog does something!"*

Larry lurched from his chair and staggered toward her. His face was sweaty and pale; that lock of wispy thin hair fell over his forehead. His words slurred together.

"D'you wanna fight? Is that it? You wanna fight?"

Carolyn's heart slammed in her throat; she was so angry the entire kitchen seemed blood-red. That unfamiliar malicious voice shrieked through her head again.

*"Will that work, Larry? Will that get you stimulated? If it will, bring it on! Do you hear me? Bring it on! I want to do something! Anything! I don't give a damn what it is!"*

"Lord, you're a pain in the ass."

*"Well, I didn't used to be. You can thank yourself for that."*

Larry reached out and snatched her up so fast she didn't even see it coming, then jammed her up against the counter and shoved his face so close to hers that the putrid odor of alcohol on his breath was nauseating. She turned her head away and fought vomit. There was something familiar about this scene, about this smell...something diabolical and insidious and malignant... something she couldn't quite remember... Somewhere in the distance, a long, long way away, she could hear Chico's frenzied barking and Larry's bellowed oaths of rage, but the uproar didn't penetrate the fog of terror that abruptly blanketed her brain. It wasn't until he released her, grabbed the butcher knife off the countertop and shoved it down toward the frantic Chico that Carolyn realized his intention.

Screaming, she threw herself over her beloved dog. "You sick perverted freak—don't you hurt him!"

Then, even though she could hear a crazy woman screeching and cursing like a wild animal, she didn't know who the woman was and the words didn't register. They just floated away and disappeared completely.

*The child is small, young, and the Yellow Brick Road is back. She walks down it, but she doesn't know where she's going. She's heading toward a house she's never seen before... a forest that seems vaguely familiar... She enters it. The forest is dark and moist, enshrouded in a cold mist that dampens her cheeks and tickles her nose. The trees are tall with charred-black, naked branches reaching for a sky she can barely see...*

*The trees begin to change. Like rubber, they bend, lean, touch the ground. The branches wave, then morph into something that lives and breathes, something with visible bones and blood coursing through veins and a heartbeat thundering through the forest with the deep bass of a kettle drum...*

*The child is beyond terror as she dodges away from the clutching black fingers, weaving between the suddenly living trees. The trees begin to whisper and moan and laugh among themselves, filling the forest with all kinds of voices making all kinds of sounds—hoarse, demanding voices that ring and echo through the child's head...*

*A big-eyed, white-faced creature with huge teeth filed into sharp points leaps from a tree, confronts the child head-on, and raises a knife high in the air...*

*She begins to run. She runs as hard and as fast as she can, trying to escape from a forest that has abruptly become human and malevolent and evil. The ground, once firm and solid, becomes loose and squishy and begins to suck her feet downward toward the center of the earth, toward hell... She struggles to wrench herself loose but she can't. Like quicksand, the mucky soil swallows her ankles, her calves, her knees, her thighs—and then it gives way, turns her loose, liquefies into raging river of blood...*

Sweat-drenched and gasping for air, Carolyn shot upright in bed, clutching the sheets in terror. Moonlight streamed through the window on the other side of the bedroom, just as it always did. Beside her, Larry snored on, untroubled and unaware. But there had been nothing tranquil about Carolyn's sleep for the last few weeks—she could set her clock by the hideous nightmares that had awakened her between 3:00 and 3:15, every single morning since her terrible fight with Larry.

His abject apology the next afternoon hadn't helped, even though he had done everything but crawl to her bedside—and he probably would have done that had the growling Chico, lying next to the bed, permitted him to get that close to her. Still too traumatized to come downstairs, Carolyn had allowed him to sit beside her on the bed and, without even looking at him, listened to his tearful pleas for forgiveness.

Taking her hand in his, that now familiar hang-dog expression on his face, Larry promised to put down the Scotch; he could see what a problem it was becoming. He promised to spend more time at home with her; he could see she felt neglected and he was sure she was right. He even promised to visit a well-known urology clinic in Houston that might be able to help him solve what he now called *his problem*.

When she finally took pity on him and decided to put him out of his misery, she said only, "If you ever even *look* like you're going to hurt Chico or Pete or any other animal of mine, I'm gone. Do you hear me? I can't live this way. I *won't* live this way."

Carolyn had spent that entire day in bed, but the next afternoon she managed to join Larry on a short jaunt to a nearby shopping mall, where he bought her a beautiful Thomas organ and had it delivered to the house. Not long after that, he traded in her gold convertible on a gorgeous new Cadillac Coupe de Ville and proudly gave her the keys. He called it an early Christmas present so that their upcoming trip back to Pennsylvania would be more comfortable.

Yet, no matter how many *things* he bought her, nothing really helped. Finally Carolyn had to admit, at least to herself, that her problems might actually have little to do with Larry.

Memories she had thought were buried and forgotten had begun to re-surface, and she had no idea why. They assaulted her with a bloody vengeance, like a nightmare without end. There was no falling out of bed, no waking up, no gasping for air. There was nothing to protect her—she just lived the nightmare endlessly, over and over again. She heard the voices and felt the terror every hour of every day, and she didn't know how to make it stop.

Now, for some reason, she was reminded of the angels she had seen so often when she was little, but now the creatures in her nightmares weren't angels. They were vicious and horrible, an actual *physical* threat to her body and her sanity.

The angels she had seen before had been her friends. They had shielded her from hunger and pain and terror; she had always remembered them with loving gratitude. She had accepted them as a normal part of life—at least, a normal part of *her* life. And not only had she *seen* her angels, she had spoken with them and felt their presence and even shared meals with them. They had cradled her in the warmth of their protective embraces through cold days and lonely nights, and they had given her a reason to live.

Back then her angels had been her secret, and she had liked it that way.

Now she didn't know what to do. Her angels were no longer angels and they certainly weren't her friends anymore. The forest she had played in as a child now became a backdrop for a hideous nightmare she experienced almost every night, and the creatures she had once loved and trusted so much now seemed determined to consume her, body and soul...

She had to do something to save herself. She had to confront the memories. Ever since she had first arrived in Houston, she ignored the flat, ugly town of Beaumont only a couple of hours away because she was so afraid of it. But the close proximity of that source of her childhood pain and terror had never been far from her thoughts, and she now realized that she no longer had any choice. She had to meet that demonic town on her own terms or she would go completely mad.

Finally, one crisp and cloudless morning in mid-November, Carolyn saw Larry off to work and climbed into her new Cadillac. Then, adjusting the mirrors, she pulled away from her house and began the eighty-five-mile drive east to Beaumont. There she would look for the only person besides Aunt Kat who had been good to her back in those days: Rose's last husband, Beau LeBlanc.

When Carolyn entered the town, the first thing she was struck by was how heavily industrialized it was. Although she remembered clearly her first vision of the vast expanse of ocean outside the tiny window of the prison in which she had found herself, she hadn't realized that Beaumont was actually situated right on the mouth of the Neches River ship channel, very near the Gulf of Mexico. She also hadn't known back then that Beaumont was located only twenty-five miles west of the Louisiana/Texas border. The truth was, even though Beaumont was right smack dab in the heart of the rice-growing and timber-producing region of southeast Texas and Louisiana, what might have been a city's natural beauty was scarred by the over-abundance of petroleum refineries, petrochemical plants, steel mills, oil wells, and shipyards.

Trying to find *something* that looked familiar and failing miserably, Carolyn focused instead on picturing the handsome face of Beau LeBlanc. She couldn't help but grin at her recollection of the man who had given her a horny toad for a pet and defended her from as many of Rose's nasty moods as he could. When she was little, Carolyn had thought him malleable and weak just like every other man that Rose had ever set her sights on, but she had also recognized and appreciated his basic kindness to a hungry, frightened child. He could have ignored her like everyone else, even abused her had he had the inclination, but he never did.

Now she hoped to thank him.

Her grin faded and her heart began to thud uncomfortably as she realized that he might not have the same comforting memories of her as she had of him. Even though Aunt Kat had once assured her that Rose no longer lived in Texas, nor was she married to Beau, he might not welcome her with open arms, as Aunt Kat had. Worse yet, what if he still loved Rose and possibly blamed Carolyn for the break-up of his marriage?

She refused to surrender to all the bleak scenarios that her mind seemed to so easily concoct, and instead pulled into the parking lot of a small coffee shop she found near the ship channel. After refreshing her makeup in the rearview mirror and tousling her thick curls so that she would blend in more naturally with the casual clientele, Carolyn headed across the dusty parking lot in search of some breakfast and a pay phone.

Abruptly, Carolyn slowed her pace and looked around, heart pounding. There was something vaguely familiar about this place. The way seagulls screeched overhead. The way rickety stairs came down the side of the building from a second story above the café. The way the paint was peeling around the windows. When she pushed the door open, she was immediately assaulted by the mouth-watering aromas of fresh brewed coffee and hot pancakes. Carolyn stopped dead in her tracks, frowning.

She had been here before.

Carolyn automatically looked to her right, knowing exactly what she would see, and there it was: the pay phone attached to the wall. Straight ahead of her was the counter where she had been allowed to eat her first meal—as long as she acted deaf, dumb and backward. Fortunately, there was no sign of a fat, middle-aged man with dirty fingernails and rotted teeth. There was only a lanky young kid serving coffee.

Otherwise, everything was exactly the same.

A thick blanket of fog seemed to blur the room, obscuring Carolyn's vision and blocking reality. But when the mist lifted, she could see a white-faced little girl standing beside a lady who was so infuriated she could hardly talk. Terrified, the child struggled against diarrhea and nausea as she waited for the woman to hang up the telephone. In the background dishes clattered and customers chatted and country music played faintly on the radio…

Carolyn went queasy. She was light-headed and weak, drenched in sweat. She was going to throw up. Her stomach wrenched with violent cramps. She was starving and exhausted and her rear end burned… She could smell her own fear…

"Are you okay, Ma'am?"

With dizzying speed she slammed back into the present and stared at the young waiter, confused and unfocused. "What?"

"Are you okay? Can I get you something?"

*I gotta get out of here… I can't breathe… I gotta get out of here…*

"A phone book… You can get me a phone book."

Obviously worried, the young man smiled doubtfully. "Sure thing. Why don't you sit at the counter for a minute and I'll get you some water, how's that?"

She knew she was shaking and wild-eyed and scaring the kid silly, but she couldn't help it. She stepped away from him until her back was against the wall and shook her head. "No, not the counter… I'll wait right here. I'm fine. Really."

*Just get me the damn phone book…*

Before she knew it, the young man had returned, a tattered Beaumont directory in one hand and a glass of water in the other.

"Let's go to this booth back here, how's that?"

Carolyn followed him and slid into the booth he had suggested. When she managed to thank him for his help, he just smiled and moved away, obviously relieved to be rid of her. Sipping her water, she turned to the *L's* in the phone book. There, right at the top of the page, she spotted his name: *Beauregard LeBlanc.*

Carolyn stared at the phone number for several moments, still undecided about calling him, then took a determined, deep breath. Grabbing a dime from her wallet, she eased herself out of the booth and walked toward the pay phone.

Carolyn needn't have worried. Beau LeBlanc had laughed out loud when she had identified herself on the telephone, gave her immediate directions to his small frame house on the outskirts of Beaumont, and introduced her to his wife the moment she had arrived. Carolyn felt like she was his long-lost best friend.

Mrs. LeBlanc, a round, sweet-faced woman who smelled of talcum powder and baby shampoo, had enveloped Carolyn in a warm hug, planted a kiss on top of her head, marched her across the front porch and straight through the screened door. "You visit just as long as you want, you hear?"

"Yes, ma'am."

Now Carolyn sat across from Beau LeBlanc at his kitchen table and marveled at how easy it was to talk to him. His dark blond hair was streaked with white and his eyes were crinkled with laugh lines, but he was still the handsome and gentle man she recalled from so many years ago.

"So, you've gone and gotten yourself married, have you?"

"Yes, sir. Just a little over two months ago."

He grinned. "Well, you're looking kind of peaked there, little lady. Tell that husband of yours to let you get some sleep!"

Carolyn gave him an answering smile and nodded, tossing around in her mind for a quick change of subject. "Do you remember the horny toad you brought me to play with?" she asked suddenly. "I just wanted to thank you for that. It's why I came here today."

"Aw, don't, Carolyn. I didn't do half of what I should've done." Beau scowled and refused to meet her eyes. "I should've gotten you out of there. I should've gotten you away from her. But I didn't. So, don't thank me. I don't deserve it."

"You're wrong." Carolyn leaned forward intently, covering his hand with hers. "Nobody had been good to me for such a long time that I couldn't even remember how it felt to be human. I couldn't remember what it was like to be touched, or to get a present, or even to be able to play outside. But when you came, I got to do all that. You gave me hope, Beau. You gave me a reason to go on."

Staring at her hand covering his, Beau was silent for several moments. Carolyn knew he was trying to collect himself and didn't rush him.

"Do you know where your mother is?" he asked finally.

"My mother is Betty Shaw. She's up in White Oak, Pennsylvania."

"Oh. Well, Rose, then. Do you know where Rose is?"

"No, and I don't care."

Beau nodded, "I can understand that. Still, just in case you ever need to find her, she's in Florida. With my daughter."

Carolyn's heart stopped. *"Your daughter? She's alone with your daughter?"*

"It's all right. She's fine." He pulled his wallet from the back pocket of his jeans and flipped it open to a worn photograph of a young girl. Carolyn looked at it from a distance, but made no move to touch it.

*My half-sister... She's my half-sister...*

"Her name is Melissa."

Carolyn stood up so abruptly that she nearly knocked the chair over. "It's getting late. I need to be going."

Beau looked surprised. "Are you sure you can't stay for supper? We have plenty."

Carolyn planted a fierce smile on her face and grabbed her purse from beneath her chair. "No, thank you. I'd like to, really, but my husband will be looking for me."

Beau put his arm around Carolyn's shoulders and walked with her from the kitchen. As they stood at the front door, Carolyn's gaze was pulled, almost against her will, toward an ancient freezer at one end of the porch. When she looked at Beau, seeking confirmation, his expression told her that she was right and he understood.

Carolyn's heart jammed right up into her throat.

She moved toward the freezer as if she were in a trance. She knew it was an inanimate object, something that couldn't hurt her at all, but she glared at it just the same. She had been locked in that freezer along with spiders and spider webs. It had been dark and she couldn't breathe. She probably would have died in that freezer and no one would have known about it had Beau not come home early and jerked her out. The memory of that freezer, like the old washing machine, was a source of terror and pain for her. She had even seen it in her nightmares.

But when Carolyn reached out and touched that battered old freezer, it was an empowering moment, almost an epiphany. It was a moment in which she took control of her past and stood up to it. It was a moment in which she claimed her future and all the possibilities that might yet be waiting for her. It was a moment in which she shut down the memory of Rose and grieved for the child and said goodbye to the pain...

...or so she thought at the time.

# CHAPTER SIXTEEN

"Carolyn! Guess what! I've got news!"

Larry burst into the kitchen and dropped his briefcase on the table with a clatter. Drying her hands on her apron, Carolyn turned away from the sink and began taking dishes from the cabinet.

"Move your briefcase, Larry. Dinner's almost ready."

"Oh. Sorry." He grabbed it and placed it against the wall, then sat down at the table. "Don't you want to hear my news?"

Carolyn's head was throbbing and Larry's excitement wasn't helping. The truth was, she had never seen him this excited about *anything,* and that fact made her more than a little irritated. Filling two bowls with chicken and dumplings, she carried them to the table and set them down with a thump.

"What news?" She poured two iced teas and handed him one, then sat down. "Pass the salt, please."

"I had a meeting with Bill Greehey today."

"The salt, Larry. Pass me the salt."

Handing her the salt shaker, Larry looked so pleased with himself that Carolyn thought he was going to dance right out of his skin.

"Did you hear what I said?" he asked finally.

"You had a meeting with Bill Greehey today." Bill Greehey was a big boss at LoVaca, and Larry had meetings with him all the time. Carolyn couldn't see what the big deal was about this one. "What about it?"

Larry smeared a dinner roll with butter before he pronounced, "The LoVaca Gathering Company is now The Valero Energy Corporation."

Carolyn lifted one eyebrow and stared at him, waiting. Larry stared back at her.

"Yay," she said finally.

Larry chuckled. "Oh, what the heck… I got a big promotion today. Big. *Huge*. But it's not here."

Carolyn frowned. "What do you mean, it's not here? Where is it?"

"We're moving. To San Antonio."

"Just like that? We're moving?"

Larry nodded, "Just like that. We're moving. Pass the green beans, please."

"When?"

"Well, I need to be in my office by April, so we have a couple of months to get situated."

Now it was Carolyn's turn to give Larry a blank stare. Ordinarily she looked forward to moving—she didn't like to get too comfortable anywhere for too long—but she wanted it to be *her* idea. For Larry to just bounce into the kitchen and *tell* her they were moving was too much like her early years, when she had no control over her life.

"I'm not moving," she announced. "I'm not going anywhere."

"Carolyn, don't be a nut. You love San Antonio."

She wrinkled her nose in annoyance even as she thought: So what? That's not the point.

"And I won't have any more of these hour-long commutes just to go fifteen miles. I can get home for dinner earlier and I can spend more time at home."

"Well, it might work out…" she said, her voice trailing away uncertainly. Then, finally, she added, "I guess it'll be all right."

Larry gave her that boyish grin that always took the sting out of his sarcasm. "I'm so glad you agree, Carolyn. I'll tell Bill in the morning. Now, what do we have for dessert?"

That night, once Larry had gone to bed and she had taken a long, relaxing bath, Carolyn wrapped herself in her favorite red terrycloth bathrobe, put on huge fuzzy slippers, and made her way back downstairs. After fixing a cup of hot chocolate and hoping she could keep it down, she padded into the family room and curled up on the sofa. With Pete purring in her lap and Chico stretched out on the floor beside her, Carolyn stared blindly at the blank television screen.

She didn't sleep much anymore.

Carolyn wished she knew what in the world she was looking for. In every nightmare she had, she was looking for something. In every daydream she fell into, she was looking for something. She started projects and didn't finish them and used up far more energy than she possessed just because she was looking for something, but she had no idea what it was.

Even the trip to Beaumont three months earlier hadn't changed a thing as far as that was concerned. Although Carolyn had driven back to Houston believing that she had faced down her demons and won, that sense of loss and emptiness still remained with her every minute of every day. Apparently she hadn't won a single thing.

The nightmares still came every night, just like before, but now they had a new component. Now it seemed that every time Carolyn turned on the evening news, she heard that there was another kid missing from somewhere, stolen by someone. There was always some hysterical mother or father begging the police to help, pleading with the public to bring their missing child home. Then, at night, Carolyn's hideous dreams were filled with crying children and lost babies, all wandering alone through those living, breathing forests…

And even though the frequent news bulletins brought back such ghastly feelings—terror, physical pain, loneliness, even rage—Carolyn couldn't seem to find the actual memories that explained the emotions. It seemed the more time that passed, the less she could remember. And in order to explain to herself her loss of specific memories, she simply created stories to fit comfortably into those black, empty spaces in her mind.

The one thing Carolyn hadn't forgotten, though, was the promise she had made to God so many years before. She remembered quite clearly swearing to Him that if He could help her get home to Pennsylvania, she would one day help other lost children. She just didn't know how on earth she could do it. She wasn't well enough to help herself, much less anyone else.

Carolyn was so nervous these days that she could hardly eat and she almost never left the house. She was even going to see a psychotherapist now. Well, actually, she had only gone a few times so far and she wasn't even sure she would be going back, but it didn't really matter. She honestly didn't think he was interested in helping her, either. He seemed much more concerned about how she treated Larry than anything else, and Larry really wasn't Carolyn's concern.

Heck, Larry was fine. Larry had his job, his career, his precious newly-christened *Valero Energy Corporation*, and apparently that was enough for Larry. And now, tonight, he had come bouncing in the house to inform her that they were moving—and the devil with what Carolyn wanted. She had no life outside of Larry, right? Why should it matter to her where they lived? Houston, San Antonio, Timbuktu… It should all be the same to her…

Suddenly Pete meowed and nipped at her hand, bringing her up short—she had stopped petting his soft underbelly. Murmuring loving apologies, Carolyn stroked the cat back to sleep. Then, lighting a cigarette and blowing a smoke ring toward the ceiling, Carolyn allowed her mind to wander back to her exciting and romantic New Year's Eve…

She should have realized that spending 1979 with Larry wasn't going to be any different from spending 1978 with Larry. They had welcomed in the New Year together in their living room, but when it finally arrived, all they had done was seal 12:01 a.m. with the light, friendly kiss of two old buddies. When she had drawn away from him, Carolyn had been nearly overwhelmed with loneliness. And even though the misery in Larry's eyes told her that he was just as unhappy as she was, the shared emotion between husband and wife brought her no sense of connection.

Even after Carolyn decided to try a last-minute New Year's seduction, hastily slipping into a transparent black negligee and attempting to entice him with wine, some sexy Donna Summer music, and even a little hot-blooded, in-your-face dancing thrown in for good measure, Larry didn't really respond, physically or otherwise. As hard as it was for Carolyn to believe it, he just blushed, got up and went off to bed, leaving her alone and staring after him in utter incredulity. She had never felt so trashy and undesirable in her whole life.

As far as she was concerned, her emptiness was totally his fault. It couldn't be hers. Hadn't she done everything she could do?

Well, apparently not. Apparently now she was going to get to go to San Antonio and find them a house and get them all moved in...like she had the energy to do all that. And while she was killing herself trying to create a home for a man who didn't want to be in it, that man was going to be blissfully happy growing and developing his career...

It just wasn't fair. Here she was—smart as a whip, driven and energetic and just as ambitious as Larry. She was easily his equal. Yet, instead of being recognized for having done anything consequential in the world, she was stuck in this house, practically curled up in a fetal position, useless and hopeless, unheralded and unimportant to the rest of humanity...

That was Larry's fault, too, she thought now, completely wallowing in self-pity and thoroughly enjoying it. It sure must be nice to be him...

"Can't you sleep, honey?"

Larry's voice startled her and she jerked so hard that an indignant Pete jumped off her lap and Chico got to his feet immediately, moving closer to her. She yawned and shook her head.

"I never sleep. You know that."

"It's nearly 3:00 in the morning."

"Well, go back to bed. Don't let me stop you."

Ignoring the irritation in her voice, Larry scratched Chico's ears until the golden retriever finally relaxed and laid back down at Carolyn's feet. She stiffened when Larry sat beside her on the sofa and took her hand.

"I forgot to tell you something at dinner."

Carolyn tried to withdraw her hand, but his grip tightened on her fingers and she decided to leave it alone. "What?"

"I went to see the urologist yesterday. He said I have a prostate infection that I've probably had for years, and he gave me some antibiotics. I'm supposed to take them for quite awhile, but he thinks I'll be fine when I'm finished."

A rancor-filled voice that Carolyn sort of recognized from some other point in time spoke from somewhere inside her head: *Yeah, right... And I'm the Queen of Sheba... Whatever your problem is, stud man, antibiotics ain't gonna fix it...*

Shocked, Carolyn looked around her. Had she said that out loud? No, Larry looked the same and the animals were still sleeping, so apparently she had managed to keep that voice to herself. Relieved, she cleared her throat and said only, "No kidding."

Larry looked hurt. "Well, I thought you might be happy to hear that."

"I am. Real happy."

"I can tell."

"Go back to bed. I'm too tired to talk about this now."

Larry shook his head. "You know, Carolyn, I never meant to make you so unhappy," he said finally. "In fact, I thought I was the one person in this world who understood you and could make you happy—but I was wrong. So, when we get settled in San Antonio, if you're still so miserable, I think we should get a divorce." His voice quavered and cracked, but he managed to continue, "I'm not saying this because I don't love you, Carolyn. I'm saying it because I do."

She jerked her hand from his grasp and stared at him. "A divorce! We've only been married for five months, Larry. Don't be silly."

"Five months is long enough for me to know that I don't have what you need, Carolyn."

*Stud man, you don't have what any woman needs...*

Carolyn panicked. That hateful voice was going to say something out loud and then there would be hell to pay...

"Please go to bed, Larry, please! We can talk about this another time, okay? I... I don't feel well..."

The truth was, Carolyn could hear her mother's derisive laughter already. *"You couldn't keep that man for one year, you pitiful little whiner you..."*

Carolyn slapped her hands over her ears and fought tears. *Shut up...*

"Please, Larry! Go to bed!"

Looking more hurt than ever, he slowly got to his feet. "Maybe San Antonio will make all the difference, Carolyn. Maybe we'll be happy there."

She gritted her teeth, planted a determined smile on her face and nodded frantically, scared to death that she couldn't get him out of the room before that dangerous voice could be heard by someone other than her.

"I'm sure we will, Larry. I'm sure we'll be really, really happy there."

Carolyn and her Century 21 realtor, Marcy Tumlinson, cruised the King William Historical District in San Antonio for a couple of days without any luck, but Carolyn wouldn't give up. She wanted an old house, partly because she had always loved them and partly because her memories of the Rankin farmhouse were so comforting and warm that she wanted to duplicate them. Whatever the reason, she didn't intend to stop looking until she found exactly what she was looking for. She wasn't in any hurry, anyway, because she and Larry already had a buyer for their home in Houston, she was completely enjoying her solitary stay at the St. Anthony Hotel, and Carolyn knew that Larry didn't care where they ended up as long as it was convenient to Valero.

Finally, as a last resort, Carolyn and Marcy decided to check out one of the few remaining old neighborhoods near the downtown area. Turning on Elm Street, just off North New Braunfels Dr., they discovered a street that was more than just *old.* Rundown and depressing, it was populated by decrepit shanties and huge antebellum-style homes that had been converted into cheap apartments. Running visibly parallel to Elm Street was a walking trail on the outskirts of Fort Sam Houston, one of the oldest Army bases in the country.

None of that mattered to Carolyn when she suddenly spotted what she was positive would be *her* house—an old mansion exactly like one she had seen in a dream not a month earlier. She grabbed Marcy's arm in excitement.

"Oh, my gosh, this is it! This is my house!"

The realtor chuckled and turned off the engine. "Don't get too thrilled just yet, Carolyn. This house is old as the hills and it needs a lot of work." She looked over her shoulder nervously and shook her head. "The neighborhood isn't too great, either."

Carolyn gazed, mesmerized, at the mansion and immediately fell in love with its oddly-shaped windows, interesting towers, and the wide, welcoming front porch. The house looked like it actually had three stories, but she couldn't be sure and it didn't really matter. Unlike a bland tract home typically purchased by most young couples just starting out, this old place was obviously packed to the gables with history and personality. It might even be haunted. Carolyn had to have it.

"Tell me about it," she demanded.

Marcy glanced through the MLS listing information quickly. "Well, it says here that the house was built in 1890 and designed by Alfred Giles, a famous architect from that era. It was the staff house for the West Texas Military Academy – known today as TMI. And you'll like this: Douglas MacArthur himself lived here when his father was the commander at Fort Sam Houston. In fact, MacArthur actually graduated from TMI. Later on, if you wanted to go to the trouble, you could register this house as a historic landmark with the city of San Antonio."

Suddenly Carolyn heard her mother's words from a year or so earlier: *You'll never have a pot to piss in, Carolyn, or a window to throw it out of...* and it was all she could do not to bust out laughing. She leaned back with a sigh, clasped her hands in genuine pleasure, and whispered, "Oh, my mother would bust a gut if she saw this place..."

"Excuse me?"

Carolyn chuckled and opened the car door. "Come on, Marcy! Show me my house."

In July 1979, Carolyn and Larry finally moved into their "new" home. By the time they were actually able to hang their clothes in the closets, Carolyn had poured so much of her own heart into the house's refurbishment that it no longer looked like somebody's unloved child. Now it was beautifully painted both inside and out according to the historical era in which it had been built, every room was elegantly and tastefully furnished, and Carolyn felt like she had finally arrived.

She even called her mother the night they moved in, unable to keep from gloating. As proud of his new home as Carolyn was, Larry stood in the doorway to his wife's bedroom, listening with a mischievous grin on his face that let her know he completely understood.

Winking at him, Carolyn lit a cigarette and spoke into the phone. "Remember when you said I'd never have a pot to piss in or a window to throw it out of, Mother?" she asked after they had passed through all the normal chit-chat. "Well, I just thought I'd let you know: I have *three* pots to piss in and *thirty* windows to throw it out of—as a matter of fact, north, south, east and west windows! So, you were wrong, Mother. Have a nice night."

Hanging up the telephone, Carolyn threw back her head and laughed so hard that tears rolled down her cheeks. Man, did *that* feel good! For the first time in years, Carolyn finally had something her mother didn't have, or her sister, or her brother... She wasn't unworthy of a decent man, after all, and she wasn't living like a homeless bag lady on the streets of San Antonio. Her mother was wrong and Carolyn had finally drummed up enough nerve to let her know it.

"Pull yourself together," Larry interrupted suddenly. "I want to ask you a question. It's important."

Carolyn wiped her eyes and took a deep breath. "Okay. I'm okay. Shoot."

"What do you remember about your kidnapping, Carolyn?"

"What?"

"Your kidnapping, Carolyn. How did it happen?"

Why in the world was he asking that? Was she talking in her sleep more than usual? Her motor-mouth during slumber had been one of the main reasons she had asked Larry to let her have her own bedroom in the new house—that and his snoring, which was loud enough to awaken an entire cemetery...

Her frown deepened. "Why do you want to know that? I told you all about me a long time ago, remember? Not long after we met, I told you. I didn't lie about anything. Do you think I'm lying now?"

Larry shook his head. "No, no, of course not. Beau made it quite clear at dinner the weekend we went up to visit him and Sarah that it was all true. Shoot, he even gave us directions to the house that he and Rose lived in with you, and we actually drove out to see it, so I know that's true. I'm talking about the kidnapping itself. *What do you actually remember about the kidnapping itself?"*

Carolyn didn't like the way this felt. This was like one of those television cop show interrogations where every word she uttered might eventually be used against her. Yet Larry was her husband, her best friend, and she had always tried to be honest with him. He would be on her side if she talked straight with him now, wouldn't he?

"Please, Larry…come sit with me," she said finally, her voice shaking. "I haven't even thought about this in a long, long time. It's…it's hard for me."

He immediately sat beside her on the bed; he took her hand without a word. Grateful for his touch, she laced her fingers with his and gazed at their clasped hands. Right at that moment she felt connected with him in a warm, friendly way she hadn't felt since they had married.

"I don't remember much, Larry," she began softly, "and that's the truth. I remember a woman taking me out of my front yard and putting me in a car with a man I didn't know. At some point I remember getting on a Greyhound bus and the woman giving me an orange, but I don't remember when that was. Then I remember sort of waking up in a little room and being locked in and having a chain around my ankle and hearing the ocean outside. That's it. That's all I remember."

His fingers tightened around hers. "Did you know who the woman was?"

Carolyn shook her head. "She said she was my mother, but I didn't believe her. My mother is Betty Shaw and she lived with my daddy and my sister and my brother in White Oak, Pennsylvania. This woman was a lunatic and she couldn't be related to me."

Larry's voice was gentle. "But she *is* your mother, isn't she? You understand that now, don't you?"

"No."

"Carolyn, she is. You know that."

"She's not. *Betty Shaw is my mother*!"

He surrendered instantly. "Okay, okay. Then tell me this: how did this woman get you out of the front yard? How did she get you in the car? Who was the man with her?"

"I don't know," Carolyn whispered, her heart suddenly thudding uncomfortably in her throat. She swallowed hard. "What difference does this make? Why are you doing this to me…?"

"Where was Betty?" he persisted. "Where was George? Why did they let her take you?"

Carolyn stared at him, wide-eyed, and shook her head slowly. Tears trailed down her cheeks. "I don't know! And I don't understand why you're asking me!"

"I'm asking you because I want to know the truth, Carolyn. I want to know exactly what you remember."

"I've told you what I remember, Larry! I've told you the truth!"

This had gone far enough. Carolyn had told Larry everything she remembered and she wasn't going to let him get her all confused now. She had sorted everyone out in a way that made her comfortable and she wasn't going to change her story for Larry or anyone else. Her daddy had tried to explain it all to her a few times and she had refused to even try to comprehend what he was saying, so there was no way she was going to let Larry succeed at the same thing...

Suddenly Larry gathered her into his arms and held her close. "I'm sorry, baby," he murmured, "I'm so sorry..." He cradled her face in his hands and softly kissed the tears from her cheeks. "I won't ask again, baby, I promise. I believe you."

As he smoothed her hair away from her face, his lips were whisper-soft against her skin and Carolyn met him kiss for kiss, at first shyly, then with more urgency as her body—and his—finally began to awaken and respond. Slowly, almost timidly, she wrapped her arms around his neck and pulled him down with her into the thick mattress.

Then, as she felt his hands move over her body—caressing her at first with curiosity, then more insistently—Carolyn was finally able to give herself up to the passion and pleasure of teaching him how to love her.

# CHAPTER SEVENTEEN

The camera's flash went off and Carolyn relaxed against her pillow in her hospital bed, still smiling down at the angel-faced baby girl she held against her breast. Larry moved away from her, that perpetual, loopy grin he'd worn for the last two days still on his face, and eased himself into an overstuffed recliner in the corner. Welcoming the newborn and lining the walls of Carolyn's private room were sweet flower arrangements in adorable vases and pink cutesy balloons with curly streamers, most of them from Larry's colleagues at Valero.

"What's the baby's name, Ma'am?" a young hospital volunteer asked, waving a still-damp Polaroid photograph in the air before she finally handed it to Larry. "Here you go, sir. It's a great shot."

"Audra Nicole," Carolyn answered softly, "A beautiful name for a beautiful baby..." When she ran her finger lightly against the child's cheek, she was suddenly reminded of the velvety-soft petals of the African Violets Grandma Rankin had always placed in her kitchen window sill. Those ever-present tears of gratitude welled in her eyes once more, and again she thanked God for blessing her with this miracle infant.

Carolyn had never in a million years expected to discover she was pregnant. After all, it wasn't like she and Larry got together all that much—and, when they did, the experience usually wasn't very successful. But, like her daddy had often said, it only needed to work once...

As soon as Carolyn had accepted that she truly was going to have a baby, she quit smoking, cut out the junk food, stopped taking any medication that wasn't completely natural, and enjoyed a fairly easy pregnancy. The delivery, however, was very difficult. After nearly sixty hours of labor and then only with the assistance of forceps, their squalling little Audra Nicole finally entered the world on February 6, 1982.

Now, by this time tomorrow evening, the Huebner family, complete with their perfect new addition, would be heading back to their home on East Elm Street.

"Larry, ask the nurse to take the baby, will you? I need to get some sleep."

"Oh, I'll hold her..."

"I want to sleep, Larry, and I want you to go home."

"I'm leaving in just a minute, sweetheart. But I have something on my mind and I need to say it before I go."

Carolyn closed her eyes again. "Well, make it quick, Larry. My back is still killing me."

"Do you remember that doctor you went to last year? The one that said you were schizophrenic and put you on those terrible tranquilizers?"

Carolyn groaned. "Oh, Larry, why the hell can't this wait? Of course I remember him. The man was a lunatic. A… very…rich…lunatic."

"That's true, but be honest. You didn't give him much of a chance, did you?"

Carolyn closed her eyes and spoke through gritted teeth. "Larry, I saw him for fifteen minutes every other week for three months. That's all he wanted to see me for—just long enough for me to come in, get my meds, and pay my bill. I doubt if he even knew my name! We nearly went broke, and for what? For me to creep around that house like a frickin' zombie…"

"The only reason I brought it up is because you're going to need your rest once we get Audra home, and you don't sleep. You know that's true, Carolyn. You still have terrible night-mares, and they've gotten worse ever since that dentist put you under when you had your wisdom teeth pulled out last year. I hear you talking in your sleep almost every night, so I know you're not resting. Carolyn, I'm worried about you. We're going to have to find you some help, and I just want you to think about that."

Carolyn yawned and patted his hand again. "Okay, Larry. I'll think about that. Now will you go home?"

He chuckled, stood up and dropped a light kiss on the tip of her nose. "I'm going, I'm going. Call me if you need anything, okay?"

"I just need to sleep, Larry, that's all." She closed her eyes again, relishing the deep, cottony silence in her head. "I just need to sleep…"

*A little girl stands beside a coffin, an old lady on one side and a young man on the other. Who is the little girl? She's crying, crying…crying so hard she can't breathe. She's beyond consolation… She can't be comforted. The old woman is talking into the child's ear, hard and loud… Her voice trembles and is filled with hate… What is she saying? The little girl leans away from her, turns her head, but it doesn't matter. The woman keeps talking, keeps following the child …*

*"You killed your daddy! You killed your daddy! He wouldn't be dead if you had never come back… It's your fault… I hate you… You ruined my life…"*

*Who is the little girl? Why does the old lady keep saying that? She keeps saying that, over and over again…*

*The old lady's mouth keeps moving, but then her voice disappears… She looks like a fish out of water, gasping for air, struggling to breathe… But then her eyes widen and her face turns white and rubbery. Her mouth begins to melt, dissipate, liquefy, drip into her chin... Her head sags down into her neck, her skin begins to peel and chip like old paint... Her flesh falls away from her bones...*

*The little girl stares at her and screams and screams...*

"Miz Huebner, wake up! Miz Huebner... My goodness, Miz Huebner, please wake up!"

Jerking and flailing about in a frenzied attempt to drag herself out of the nightmare, Carolyn sucked in great, desperate gulps of air and fought to orient herself.

After just a minute, she realized that she was in a dimly lit hospital room with a worried nurse leaning over her bed. Carolyn didn't care that she was bathed in sweat and battling a knife-sharp pain in the small of her back; she was just grateful to know that she was alive. She wasn't standing with an old lady beside a coffin, after all, and no one was accusing her of killing anybody...

Carolyn leaned back against her pillows and closed her eyes once more, thankful for the cool, damp rag the nurse kept stroking against her face. She was so sick of this dream, this one horrible, constantly recurring dream that seemed to stay with her nearly every hour of every night. It hadn't even begun until she had been anesthetized for the surgery to remove her wisdom teeth well over a year ago, and it hadn't left her alone since then.

"Are you better now, dear?"

Carolyn nodded and blinked back tears. She was just so tired...

"Don't you worry about these bad dreams, Miz Huebner. They're not unusual right after you've had a baby, you know. Your hormones are all messed up is all."

Carolyn nodded again, too exhausted to argue. "Is it time to feed the baby?" she asked finally.

"She was asleep last time I was in the nursery, Miz Huebner, and I think you should let us feed her when she wakes up."

"No. Bring her to me."

"Are you sure? I really think you should rest..."

*She's my baby and you bring her to me! Don't you even think you can keep her from me!*

Carolyn's eyes flew open at the sound of that now-familiar voice shrieking in her head and she glanced anxiously toward the nurse, who was puttering around the room and didn't seem to have heard anything. Still, just to be sure, Carolyn cleared her throat, hoping to cover up whatever she might have said aloud.

"Will you please bring her to me now—if she's awake?" Carolyn asked finally, trying to sound respectful, even timid. "I just want to hold her for a little while."

The nurse didn't answer for a long time, making a big show of looking through Carolyn's medical chart, and emphasizing, at least in Carolyn's mind, that she was the one person who controlled Carolyn's right to mother her own child.

"Well...I guess so," she agreed finally. "But not for long, okay? I really need you to get some rest."

*Who the hell do you think you are? You get my baby in here to me and you get her in here now...*

Carolyn closed her eyes against the voice and swallowed her rising panic. Whatever or whoever this voice belonged to... she had to shut it up! It was going to get her into so much trouble...

Carolyn couldn't help but remember the demons her daddy used to warn her about, those evil spirits eternally battling God's angels for the souls of His own children, and she couldn't help but wonder if this voice was somehow related to such a spirit. After all, she had been visited by angels many times, *good* angels. Why wouldn't a wicked one try to join the crowd? It only made sense...

*Oh, wow. Now that's crazy. That's really crazy. You'd best be careful, little mama. If anyone finds out you're thinking like that, you'll lose everything... They'll even take this baby away from you...*

Carolyn closed her eyes, trying to block the voice and the threat that only she could hear, and waited impatiently for the nurse to return. This child completed her and would love her unconditionally. She would always want her mommy around, like Carolyn had always wanted her mother, but Carolyn would be different. She would be there. She would never turn her back on her child.

When Carolyn finally held the sleeping Audra Nicole in her arms once again, she gazed down at the baby's perfect little face. "You can always count on me, sweetheart," she vowed in a solemn whisper. "No one will ever hurt you like they did me. No one will ever take you away from me. I'll always be here for you."

Carolyn kissed the baby's soft, warm cheek and held her even more tightly, feeling at that moment a surge of maternal love so deep and pure that it brought tears of joy to her eyes. For the first time in her life, Carolyn Sue Huebner had a real purpose.

Now, finally, her life was *real*. Audra Nicole Huebner was real, her need for her mommy was real, and Carolyn was positive that this beautiful baby girl would change her environment, maybe even her entire existence. Everything bad in her life would disappear: there would be no more nightmares, no more unexplained voices, no more angry outbursts against her husband. Everything would be perfect. She would finally have the family she had always dreamed of.

Yes, God is good, Carolyn thought. He is very, very good.

Leola Seay (pronounced *Cee*), an elderly black woman with mountains of experience taking care of children, came into the Huebner household in April when Audra was only two months old, and promptly took over. Carolyn loved her on sight and affectionately nicknamed her *Ohler*. It would be much easier for Audra to say when she finally began talking. Over time, Leola became almost as much a nanny to Carolyn as she was to Audra.

As Larry steadily climbed the corporate ladder at Valero Energy Corporation, becoming more and more valuable to the company, Carolyn played the role of the dutiful, supportive wife. She presented a beautiful, healthy baby to her friends and lived in a lovely historical home that was the envy of just about everyone who knew them. She drove a luxury car and purchased anything she wanted on any number of credit cards. She had a nanny for her baby and a hairdresser that sometimes even came to her house so she wouldn't have to go out if she wasn't in the mood. Carolyn's life was as close to perfect as she had ever imagined it could be—at least, on the outside.

And the outside, her mother had shown her early on, was all that really mattered.

Still, as amazing as it seemed to her now, Carolyn had nearly lost everything when she and Larry had separated, and for what? A little excitement? Looking back on it, Carolyn realized that they had separated for no good reason that she could remember. She wasn't even sure how it had happened. Larry had just come in from work one day, she had told him to get the hell out, and he had gone. But not long after, when Carolyn had discovered she was pregnant, she had told Larry and he had returned home like nothing had ever happened. They hadn't even discussed it; they just fell back into their normal routines and life went on exactly as before.

The only change had been when Larry went to another urologist in San Antonio, seeking help for the prostate infection that still hadn't cleared up, and was put on a promising new sulfuric antibiotic. He and Carolyn both had high hopes that they might actually be able to build a somewhat normal relationship. But Larry had had an allergic reaction to the drug that was both disastrous and terrifying: his fever had skyrocketed and pus quite literally oozed from every pore on his body. A hysterical Carolyn had rushed him to the emergency room, frightened that she could have very nearly lost him.

That episode, as far as Carolyn was concerned, ended the whole question of sex within her marriage. It wasn't that important, she decided, not when you got right down to it. The bottom line was, nothing terrified her more than the thought that Larry might die and leave her, just as her daddy had. She even had nightmares about something horrible happening to him, nightmares so terrifying that she was determined to do everything possible to keep him blissfully happy and completely committed to her.

The truth was, it really wasn't all that difficult to keep Larry contented. All she had to do was listen to him talk about his job. It seemed that everything else in his life was secondary. She couldn't stimulate him sexually. He wasn't a religious man, so church attendance wasn't important. He handled the household finances and kept such a tight lid on that part of their life together that she didn't even know where they banked or how much money they had. His social contacts were either his colleagues at Valero or other members of the Optimist Club, so there wasn't much for Carolyn to do there, either. Ultimately, all she had to do was keep herself attractive in case she ran into someone Larry knew and make sure he got his dinner by 6:00 in the evening.

On the other hand, Carolyn's temper, always hot and inexplicable and impulsive, seemed to explode more often than it ever had before. Many times she lashed out at Larry so violently that afterwards she actually thought he would be better off if she just killed herself and let him move forward on his own. But then her instinctive sense of self-preservation would kick in before she could do anything permanent or stupid, and she would settle back down once more, trying desperately to smooth things over with her poor, befuddled husband.

Making matters just as bad as they possibly could be, Carolyn's internal life was also an inescapable nightmare—not only because it was loud and shocking and charged with vivid memories that she wasn't sure she actually remembered, but because she was forced to keep it to herself. She couldn't tell a soul about the voices she heard so often in her head, voices that sometimes whispered and other times bellowed like the roar of an oncoming train. And she couldn't tell a soul about those mysterious black holes of missing time that were becoming more and more frequent.

The one bright spot in Carolyn's life was Audra Nicole. She was an ideal baby, breast-feeding every four hours like clockwork and practically never crying. Still, although Carolyn loved to hold her and play with her, she also knew it wouldn't be long before she would be unable to carry on an intelligent conversation with anyone over the ripe old age of three. As hard as it was for her to admit it, little Audra Nicole, now affectionately nicknamed *The Dootie* by her parents, wasn't bringing perfection or a sense of serenity to her mother's chaotic life after all.

"I'm a pablum-brain," she told Leola one morning over coffee. "That's all I am. Just a dead-meat pablum-brain. I wasn't put on this earth to be Little Miss Suzie Homemaker, Ohler. I'm worth more than that."

"And just what's wrong with being a wife and mother, may I ask?" Leola demanded indignantly, clearing the empty cups and saucers off the table. "God made women to be wives and mothers…"

"Oh, Ohler, don't start with the God stuff! God gave me a perfectly good brain and I think He meant for me to use it! I don't think He meant for me to sit around here all day doing nothing, not making a difference in anybody's life. What kind of sense would that make? And I sure don't think He brought me through everything He brought me through…"

Carolyn's voice trailed away. Practically shell-shocked with disbelief because the solution was so obvious and simple, she gaped open-mouthed at Leola.

Leola gaped back. "What? What is it?"

Suddenly Carolyn was flooded with more excitement than she had ever felt in her entire life. "Listen, Ohler! Look at me! I've got this house. I've got the Dootie. I'm in this marriage, but it's not enough. You know it's not. I have to do something with my life! I need to take everything I've been through—every rejection, *everything*—and I need to pour it into something positive." Carolyn took a deep, trembling breath. "For children, Ohler. I need to do something positive for children. I promised God I would, and I will."

Leola frowned. "Are you sure, Carolyn?"

"I promised God that I would find other missing kids if He would just get me back home, Ohler, and I had forgotten it until just this minute! Well, not forgotten it, exactly, but the time was never right… Now the time is right, Ohler. It is! We're constantly hearing about kids disappearing and no one is doing a thing to find them. But, Ohler, I know how those kids feel! I know how scared they are, and I know how their families want them back. I'm smart enough to do this! All I need is some training to help me learn how to find them… I can do this, Ohler! I *need* to do this!" Restless, Carolyn jumped to her feet and began stalking around the kitchen like a caged animal. "I could start my own organization, Ohler, and I could make a *real* difference! What do you think?"

Leola's wrinkled face set in deep lines of disapproval. "I think you need to talk to Mr. Huebner."

"Well, of course I'll talk to Mr. Huebner! Will you stay with the Dootie, Ohler? I'll be gone a lot. I need a plan. I need a Board of Directors. I need training…"

"You need to slow down. Catch your breath. See what Mr. Huebner says."

Carolyn stopped pacing and looked at Leola, blue-gray eyes narrowed and sparking with fierce determination. "Mr. Huebner doesn't rule my life, Ohler. I've made up my mind—I'm going to do this. *I have to do this.* Larry will back me up. He won't try to stop me. He *wants* me to do something. He knows how bored I am…"

"Boredom isn't a good enough reason to take on the world, Carolyn. You'd best pray on this."

Carolyn softened suddenly and gave the elderly woman a quick hug. "It'll be all right, Ohler. You'll see. I'm *supposed* to do this. I've been praying on this for years."

Carolyn was right about Larry. He was very supportive. Of course, he really had no choice because he knew that once his wife had made up her mind to do something, there was no way he could stop her. So, as usual, he stood on the sidelines of Carolyn's life, quietly assisting her in any way he could, preparing for the inevitable day when she would explode into the collective consciousness of all those unsuspecting people in San Antonio, Texas.

By December 1982, Carolyn had incorporated her organization, calling it *Texas Child Search, Inc.* (TCS for short), and by January 1983 she had held her first Board of Directors meeting right in the dining room of her home on Elm Street. At this meeting Carolyn introduced a nineteen-page document entitled *Bylaws of Texas Child Search, Inc.* to her new Board members, which included a minister, a tax attorney, and even a family therapist, and also presented a corporate seal to them for their final approval, which she received. Officers were elected, a bank account was established, and the organization's nonprofit status forms were prepared for submission to the United States government. Carolyn was excited to find that the complexities of running her new organization finally appeased her boredom and brought her out into the world. The business itself was challenging and liberating and she loved everything about it.

As time went on, Carolyn began to realize exactly how much she could accomplish with the power she was accumulating just from allowing herself to be placed into the public eye. Unlike her husband, who was quietly efficient within his realm of important responsibility and who preferred to remain nearly invisible to everyone except his superiors, Carolyn found that she adored the limelight, thrived on being the center of attention, and saw no need to apologize for it. After all, a shy, retiring, unassuming woman could never bring awareness to the issue that Carolyn now saw as the most important work of her life, that of locating missing children, and she realized that no one could promote her or her message any better than she could.

The young Carolyn Huebner was aware that she was attractive, stylish, articulate, dramatic and passionate—all characteristics guaranteed to make her the latest darling of a media hungry for a new face and a new mission. She also understood that even if she didn't truly *believe* she possessed those qualities, she could certainly *act* the part—and that was most of the battle. Finally, she recognized that her personal story was what made her different from everyone else involved in the growing industry surrounding missing and abused children, and she was determined to exploit it.

The problem was, Carolyn couldn't remember much of her personal story. She knew that she had to find a means of glossing over the details that she couldn't recall, didn't know, or had no intention of discussing in public, and she had to do it so vaguely that a thorough reporter would find her story almost impossible to document, one way or the other. It was the only way that she could protect herself and her family, both in Texas and in Pennsylvania, and still accomplish everything that she hoped to accomplish.

It was during Carolyn's very first radio interview on a local station not long after she had established Texas Child Search that she introduced the story she knew would forever bond her to the hearts of the public.

"Many of us are wondering what got you interested in looking for missing children in the first place," the program host had begun rather diffidently. "After all, you don't seem the type…"

"What *type* should I be to take an interest in missing children? I'm just a human being. I'm a mother, a resident of San Antonio—and I was kidnapped myself back in 1963, when I was almost six years old. It's a natural progression of events for me to start an organization like Texas Child Search, wouldn't you say? I'm nothing special."

"*You were kidnapped?*" he repeated incredulously. "*At six years old?*"

Carolyn had remained cool, controlled, and expressionless. "Yes."

"Good Lord! Do you mind telling us what happened?"

"Well, I was playing with my brother on our front lawn back in Pennsylvania, and our mother could see us playing through the front window. Suddenly, out of nowhere, a car raced to the curb, squealed to a stop, and a man and a woman leaped out, scooped me up, and threw me into the backseat. I didn't see my family again for three years. All the time they had me, I kept promising God that if I got out of there alive, I'd help other children like me. It's that simple."

"You sound like it's no big deal, Carolyn, but it had to be extremely traumatic. How on earth did you get back home?"

"It's over," she had stated emphatically, "and it's been over for a long time. I don't dwell on it. I just intend to protect other children if I can. We've already established important working relationships with local and regional law enforcement agencies, and I plan to speak extensively everywhere I can to help raise public awareness regarding child abduction."

"Tell me, Carolyn, is this something you feel like you *have* to do?"

"Absolutely. I'm driven to do it. And what drives me is everything that's happened in my life. I got the idea for Texas Child Search, so I set it up, incorporated it, got good people behind me, and I went forward. The present and the future are all that matter to the lost children out there who need us to look for them. They don't care about my past and we shouldn't, either. Only the children are important. I'm not…"

And so what the media in San Antonio began to call *The Carolyn Huebner Legend* took root that night and seemed to flourish a little more every day after that. In spite of all her mother's dire predictions, the little girl from White Oak, Pennsylvania, had come a long way from a tiny room above a soda fountain in Beaumont, Texas. Now, not only was she married to an important man and the new mother of a beautiful baby girl, she was also president of her own missing children's organization—and she would be a household name before she was finished.

To Carolyn, it seemed that she was well on her way to fulfilling the promise she had made to God so many years ago. If she was successful, she could finally be proud of herself. If she was successful, she could finally put her past behind her. If she was successful, she could finally sleep through the night without nightmares or voices…

And, if she was successful, nothing else mattered.

# CHAPTER EIGHTEEN

By the time a one-eyed drifter named Henry Lee Lucas was arrested in the obscure little town of Montague, Texas, on June 11, 1983, Carolyn Huebner was well on her way to becoming a force in the movement to protect children from people like him.

Steely-eyed and unafraid, she worked with law enforcement and mental health professionals. Poised and passionate, she spoke to groups all over the state with as much fire as any politician out on the stump. An unapologetic operator, Carolyn took every opportunity to use the media in her efforts to publicize her crusade—but she also "walked the talk" by locating and returning several missing children to their families within the first year of her organization's existence.

Texas Child Search, Inc., functioned on private donations alone and worked within a $20,000 annual budget, so sometimes she was forced to use personal funds or beg friends for money to be sure that a child got home safely. In addition, she kept a packed bag in her closet just in case she had to leave town at a moment's notice. "We buy plane tickets with our money, not posters," she was fond of telling reporters. "Everything we do, we do for the children."

Blessed with an excellent memory for names, telephone numbers and addresses, and an amazing ability to organize those details, Carolyn began taking any kind of law enforcement course she could get into almost as soon as she had opened the doors. She learned how to fingerprint, document events with an eye toward court admissibility, and write reports acceptable to police officers. She studied interrogation techniques effective with young sexual abuse victims and joyfully accepted Aunt Kat's handmade gift of anatomically perfect dolls—one male and one female. She even began keeping a list of unidentified deceased people (mostly young girls) from around the country, just so she might be able to match them up with various active cases of missing kids she was working on. It wasn't long before she began papering her office walls with framed certificates of completed classroom hours, letters of recommendation from judges, lawyers and police officers, and awards of appreciation from just about everyone in-between.

But she couldn't have accomplished spit, Carolyn often declared, without the assistance of Retired Texas Ranger Jerome Preiss, who had joined her Board of Directors in early 1983. Old enough to be her grandfather, he was one of her greatest champions, willing to participate in anything she had a mind to go after—as long as it was legal.

Carolyn knew she could count on Jerome. She didn't understand why she had latched on to him so fervently, but she had. A legendary storyteller with a terrific sense of humor, his snapping dark eyes reminded her of her daddy, his wiry, tough strength made her feel protected, and his gentle, homespun wisdom helped keep her calm. She didn't know exactly what inner quality he possessed that she needed so desperately, but whatever it was he had it in abundance—and he offered it to her unselfishly, for no other reason than that he believed in her.

The bottom line was, Jerome loved all children—and all children loved Jerome. They weren't intimidated by the big gray Stetson hat he always wore, or the silver Texas Ranger badge he usually pinned to whatever shirt he was wearing, or the authoritative, bow-legged walk he had cultivated from his years on horseback while riding the Mexican border. In fact, these were all characteristics that children migrated toward and responded to, even if they knew he was going to come down hard on them for some act of bad behavior. It was as if they understood that he truly cared about every single child he came into contact with, and so they welcomed his correction.

Little Audra Nicole was no exception. The very first time he laid eyes on the child, he swept her up in his arms, nuzzled her cheek with his stubbly chin until she giggled, and said softly, "You're my little pretty, sweetheart, and I'll always be your PoPo, just like I am to my own grandbabies."

And so Retired Texas Ranger Jerome Preiss, known as *Geronimo* to his friends and colleagues, threw in with Texas Child Search, Inc., and became *PoPo* to the entire Huebner family.

As such, he was allowed to say just about anything to Carolyn—and he did. He worried about her penchant for picking up runaways she found on the back streets of San Antonio and bringing them home with her, and he didn't hesitate to tell her so. He was concerned because little Audra didn't seem to have anyone caring for her except the elderly Ohler, and he let Carolyn know it. Bothered by the fact that Larry and his wife obviously had no time for each other, PoPo—who had been married to his high school sweetheart since the early days of WWII—sternly recommended to Carolyn that she get her priorities straight.

Amazingly enough, Carolyn listened to him and even tried to take his advice. But more often than not she just went right on doing exactly as she pleased, falling further and further into the sordid netherworld of missing and exploited children.

But she couldn't stop.

She couldn't stop for Larry because his very presence only reminded her of how little they had together. She couldn't stop for Audra because the child's presence only reminded her of how little she had to offer. If she stopped, she would have had to face the chaos and emptiness that made up her private life, and she couldn't bear to do that.

She knew she was obsessed with the work, but she didn't care. She believed that the only way she could locate missing or abducted children was if she was obsessed with finding them—in a way that no one seemed to have been obsessed with finding her. If that meant she had to answer a phone call from a hysterical mother in the dead of night, or jump in an airplane at dawn to follow a lead that no one else would follow…well, so be it.

That's why Carolyn Huebner was returning kids to their families and no one else was, or so she thought. If people felt she was proud and arrogant, that was okay. If people believed she was brash and overbearing, she couldn't care less. If she made people nervous because she was all Attitude and it was either her way or the highway, that was just too damn bad. She was doing what she had set out to do, and she was fulfilling her promise to God.

But Carolyn's life wasn't all about running *from* pain and confusion. It was also about running *toward* the boundless joy she always felt when she successfully reunited a missing child with its family. Twice she had been privileged to witness the reunions because they had taken place in her own living room, and she had bawled like a baby. She wept for their happiness, and she wept because it was finally over, and she wept for herself because she remembered so clearly the day her mommy had come to get her and how it felt…

Then, on the morning of June 23, 1983, Carolyn's whole world changed. While reading the San Antonio Express and drinking a cup of coffee, her gaze was drawn to a headline at the top of page 9-A: *Self-proclaimed mass killer linked to 4 deaths.*

Frowning, she read further:

MONTAGUE (AP) – A former mental patient who claims to have killed 100 women has been drawing pictures in his jail cell of his alleged victims and already has been linked to four deaths in Texas, investigators said Wednesday.

Henry Lee Lucas, 46, of Stoneburg has been charged with murder in the death of an 80-year-old Ringgold woman, and last week led investigators to the body of a 15-year-old girl buried in Denton County.

At his arraignment in Montague on murder and weapons possession charges Tuesday, Lucas said he had killed as many as 100 women.

"I don't doubt him," Montague County Sheriff W. F. Conway said Wednesday.

Texas Ranger Phil Ryan said Wednesday that after his arrest June 11, Lucas started giving investigators the sketches and other information on possibly 60 different cases.

"He has given bits and pieces of information on different ones (alleged killings)," Ryan said. "I think that's exceeded 60, but we don't know if he is recalling one more than once. He may be recalling different bits and pieces about more than one."

Hale County Sheriff Charles Tue said Lucas admitted decapitating an unidentified young woman he picked up hitchhiking near Abilene. Hale County sheriff's deputies found the headless body in a ditch in February 1982.

Six weeks later, a head was found in the desert near Scottsdale, Ariz., that may have belonged to the corpse, Tue said.

"It is quite ironic, but he has the talent to draw," Tue said. "We've got some picture sketches he made from his jail cell."

Pathologists made a sketch of the dead woman, reconstructing her features from the skull, that is very similar to Lucas' drawing of his victim, Tue said.

Carolyn gulped down her now-tepid coffee, grabbed a notepad and began scribbling notes. Then, typically impetuous and reckless, Carolyn picked up the phone and dialed the operator. She wasn't sure exactly what she was after, or even why she was doing it, but she was absolutely positive that she had to get in the middle of this case. When the operator's husky voice finally responded, Carolyn took a shaky breath and asked, "May I please have the number for the sheriff's office in Montague, Texas?"

That evening, after the supper dishes had been done and Audra put to bed, Carolyn paused in the doorway of the dining room where Larry had mounds of Valero paperwork spread all over the table. His brow was furrowed as he studied a long column of numbers and drummed his fingers impatiently against the mahogany tabletop.

Carolyn cleared her throat. "Huebner, can I run something past you?"

He held up his hand and shook his head. "Wait just a minute."

"Larry, I need you. It's really important."

He gave an explosive sigh, leaned back in his chair and glared at her. "Carolyn, you go two weeks without speaking to me and now you can't wait five minutes…"

Carolyn ignored his sarcasm and sat across the table from him. "Have you heard about the arrest of a man named Henry Lee Lucas up in Montague County?"

Larry frowned, staring down at the column of numbers, shook his head and muttered absently, "Who's Henry Lee Lucas?"

"Well, I saw an article about him in the paper this morning. Apparently he's claiming that he's killed about a hundred people all over the country—mostly women and young girls—and he's drawing very good pictures of his victims for lawmen."

Larry frowned, cocking his balding head to one side in slightly more interest. "What's that got to do with you?"

"Not with me. With Child Search."

"I'm listening."

Pleased, Carolyn could see the wheels turning in his negotiator's brain and she knew she finally had his full attention. "I called the sheriff's office in Montague, Texas, this morning and talked to a Texas Ranger. I told him that TCS looks for missing people—primarily children—but that we are also trying to help law enforcement identify unknown deceased individuals. I said that I had read that this Lucas guy was drawing pictures of some of his victims and that I was interested in trying to match up our missing females with his possible victims… Specifically, I have nine missing girls and thirteen unidentified bodies that he might be able to help me with. Anyway, the Ranger and the sheriff told me to come on up."

Larry stared at her, pop-eyed in disbelief. "Are you looking to interview this wacko?"

She flushed angrily. "Larry, think about it! When am I going to get a better chance than this? The Ranger says that the man is singing like a canary and taking credit for every murder ever committed in every state in the country for the last ten years! And here I am with a list of dead or missing people seven pages long! What if this Lucas killed one of my girls and I didn't go try to find out? What kind of a person would I be?"

Larry held up his hand, clearly hoping to ward off the emotional onslaught Carolyn was preparing to launch, and shook his head. "Okay, okay! Where are they holding this guy, anyway?"

"Well, right now he's in Montague."

"Where on earth is Montague?"

"It's a little town about seventy-five miles north of Fort Worth—I could drive there in five or six hours, tops. I wouldn't need to stay there very long, a day or two at most, and Ohler could stay with Audra while I'm gone. What do you think, Huebner?"

Larry yawned. "I don't like it a bit…but…what the devil. I'll see you when you get back."

Carolyn pushed her chair away from the dining table and stood up, now more determined than ever to find a way to compare notes with this alleged serial killer. Larry just wasn't a risk-taker and she understood that, but she also knew that taking risks was the name of the game in her field. All she cared about was learning if Henry Lee Lucas could supply answers for her grieving families.

Later that evening, when Carolyn discussed her plan on the telephone with PoPo, the former Ranger's advice was simple. "When you get up there, Kid," he said, "be real careful. You know what they say about small Texas towns. Just get in, ask your questions, and get the heck out."

By the time Carolyn pulled into the parking lot of the Montague County Jail in the early afternoon of June 28, she had already checked into a small motel in Nocona, about eight miles north of Montague, and stopped at the Nocona Police Depart-ment to meet with an officer who wanted her to show Lucas a file.

"This girl was murdered in Lubbock back in 1975," the lawman had explained, "but her parents heard about this guy and wanted us to ask him about her. They brought it up to us a couple of days ago. I thought you might be able to help us out."

"Of course," Carolyn agreed instantly, glancing down at the file cover. A photograph of a lovely young woman with long platinum hair was stapled to the front, and the name *Deborah Sue Williamson* was printed right beneath it. She was so stunning that Carolyn was sure no man would ever forget her, even if he'd only seen her once. "She's beautiful."

"You bet she is, and her folks are really good people. Just all busted up, y'know? I'd like to help 'em out."

Carolyn nodded again. "I know. I'll do my best."

Now, sitting across a table from the alleged serial killer in a tiny glass-partitioned room in the back office area of the Montague County jail, Carolyn noted that Lucas' hands were cuffed in front of him instead of behind his back, and he wore street clothes instead of a jail uniform. This, she discovered, was so that he could chain-smoke and constantly drink coffee, addictions that the lawmen catered to, and his casual clothing apparently helped him feel more comfortable when he "visited" with investigators.

Carolyn was intrigued by the common feeling around Montague that the man with wavy black hair and a glass eye might be one of the worst mass murderers of the 20th Century, but apparently he was—or at least that's what he wanted everyone to believe.

And Carolyn believed it. She didn't think she had ever been so frightened in her life, even though a Texas Ranger was in the room with her and Lucas himself seemed hesitant and even slightly nervous. She didn't know the details of this man's life, or the particulars of the many crimes he was so nonchalantly confessing to, but she knew *evil* when she came upon it—and evil was sitting right across the table from her.

Carolyn opened her briefcase and pulled out a stack of files, hoping that no one noticed her trembling fingers. Clearing her throat, she looked straight at Lucas, meeting his curious gaze head-on, and gave him a friendly smile. She had to be fearless, she knew, or it was all over.

Predators smell fear. They feed on it. She wouldn't allow him to feed on hers.

"My name is Carolyn Huebner," she began softly, shuffling her files so that she could get through them as quickly and easily as possible. "I have an organization in San Antonio called Texas Child Search, and I have a few pictures here of some missing girls. I'd like to show you a picture and you tell me whatever you can—if you know her, or about her, or if you've ever seen her before. You just take your time, okay?"

Lucas nodded, dragged deeply on his non-filter cigarette, and blew the smoke toward the Ranger seated protectively behind her. "Okay."

Carolyn moved a photograph across the table. "Now, this isn't a very good picture," she said in a businesslike voice, "but you might recognize her. Her name is Annette. She's very pretty. She has long blonde hair."

After a substantial pause during which Carolyn held her breath, Lucas shook his head and stubbed out his cigarette in the already-full ashtray beside his empty coffee mug. "Nope, haven't seen her."

"Okay, that's good." Carolyn shuffled through her files again, grateful to have something to do with her hands. "You ever been down around the Texas coast?"

"Oh, yeah. Corpus Christi and all like that."

"You remember what years you were there?"

"Let's see…1981, May of '81. I've been in Houston, Pasadena, all back through there. Hey, Phil, you think I could get another cup of coffee?"

"Sure thing, Henry. You need anything else?"

Lucas shook his head, obviously pleased that this brawny lawman was going to wait on him, and answered, "Naw, I'm fine. Thanks."

Carolyn nearly swallowed her tongue when the Ranger left her alone in the room, but she forged ahead and kept her voice steady. "Okay, what about this little girl? Her name is Charlotte."

"Yeah, I picked her up and—this is one of the girls I been tryin' to convince the cops is dead in the San Antonio area."

"Do you remember when?"

"Sure. That was in…uh…1970."

Carolyn went weak with relief. "In 1970, this girl was only two years old."

Lucas gave her a snaggle-toothed grin. "Well, she's lucky, ain't she?"

The Ranger that Lucas had so familiarly called *Phil* returned, unlocked the door and pushed it open. "Here's your coffee, Henry." He set the steaming mug down on the table and took a step backward. "You got enough cigarettes?"

"Yeah, I'm good. Thanks."

"I'll be right outside, Miz Huebner," the Ranger said, rubbing his eyes and yawning. "I need some air. You gonna be all right?"

Carolyn nodded, acting as if she couldn't care less, but those wicked little butterflies fluttered around in the pit of her stomach again. Finally, she pushed the photo of the lovely Deborah Sue Williamson across the table and watched him carefully.

"How about this girl?"

Lucas didn't hesitate. "Nope. Never seen her."

Carolyn would have loved to have gotten a different response from Lucas, but she was sure that he was telling the truth. She spent another couple of hours or so with him, going through the motions of pushing photos across the table, writing down notes and reactions—his and hers—but she didn't really think he had all that much to offer. In her opinion, Henry Lee Lucas was a small-time drifter out to gamble everything he had, which wasn't much, in exchange for free cigarettes, all the hot coffee he could drink, and fifteen lousy minutes of fame. But she also knew beyond any shadow of a doubt that he was a cold-blooded killer.

When Carolyn finally stepped out of Lucas' room and into a conference area filled with rough-talking Texas lawmen, the air was heavy with cigarette smoke and unasked questions. Carefully placing her briefcase on the table, she looked around the room and held out a hand that still trembled uncontrollably.

"Gentlemen," she announced, "I haven't had a smoke in three years, but right now I'd smoke rolled horse manure. Do any of you have a cigarette you'd be kind enough to offer a lady?"

The dog-and-pony show that Lucas had been so happily directing when Carolyn first met him in June, 1983 escalated into a surreal three-ring circus by the middle of 1984 – and Carolyn occupied a front row seat.

Even though an irate Montague County judge had issued a gag order before Carolyn ever met with Lucas, nothing seemed to stay quiet for long. Just a few months after Carolyn had interviewed him, Lucas was brought on a murder warrant to Georgetown in Williamson County, a lovely area north of Austin, Texas. By the end of 1983, homicide investigators from all over the United States were calling the Williamson County jail, hoping to link the drifter to unsolved murders in their own jurisdictions.

In an effort to handle what looked to be a developing feeding frenzy, the Texas Department of Public Safety, which oversees the Texas Rangers, formed a task force. Headed up by experienced Ranger Sgt. Bobby Prince and including another Ranger as well as the sheriff of Williamson County, Jim Boutwell, the task force's full-time job was to try to coordinate the hundreds of inquiries streaming in from around the country with all the open investigations they had been made aware of. Also assisting the task force on an as-needed basis were two members of the DPS Crime Analysis section in Austin, other crime labs around the country, the aircraft division—and Carolyn Huebner herself.

Carolyn would never have become involved with the task force if the lawmen hadn't claimed to need her help so much. The truth was, all she really wanted to do was move on with her life and forget she had ever met Henry Lee Lucas. But when Jim Boutwell had asked her to sit in on the interrogations taking place in Georgetown because Lucas seemed to be more relaxed when she was nearby, Carolyn couldn't turn the sheriff down. They were all law enforcement and they were all bound to help one another. If the task force needed her, she had no choice but to be there.

Yet the entire situation was ludicrous as far as she was concerned. After all, seated at the center of this hoopla was a street-smart operator who had never been the center of anything in his entire life, and he ate it up. The victim of extreme abuse and abject poverty as a youngster, Lucas was now receiving three squares a day, all the cigarettes he could smoke, and enjoying frequent rides in comfortable vehicles over all the back roads and interstates of Texas. These favors were designed to stimulate his memory so that he could describe for officials more easily where and how he might have committed his murders, but Carolyn believed that Lucas was smart enough to keep manipulating the eager lawmen so they would continue to cater to him.

Who, she often wondered, was playing whom?

Henry Lee Lucas had declared that he had killed at least 350 people during a murder spree lasting from 1975 until 1983, but his confessions didn't stand up under Carolyn's close scrutiny—or the close scrutiny of a few others. The more meticulously she examined the times and locations of all the murders he claimed to have committed, the more convinced she became that it was physically impossible for him to have done them all.

Regardless of all these discrepancies, however, Carolyn knew she had to keep her mouth shut. She was working with law enforcement, she was as much law enforcement as they were, and she couldn't publicly question their evidence or their cases. It was too dangerous, not only for her but for the future of Texas Child Search. She had way too much to lose—and so did her kids.

Consequently, when Carolyn wasn't running back and forth between Georgetown and San Antonio trying to make life easier for the lawmen babysitting Henry Lee Lucas, she tried to forget the truth of what she believed was happening up there. In order to fill whatever free time she had left, Carolyn gave speeches, granted interviews, and continued working closely with parents, looking for their missing children. She also took more law enforcement courses—including a two-day seminar on the sexual exploitation of children at Sam Houston State University in Huntsville, Texas.

It was late afternoon when Carolyn returned from Huntsville and parked her late-model gray Buick in the driveway. Keeping the motor running and the heater on, she lit a cigarette and remained in the driver's seat for a few moments, gathering her thoughts and enjoying the cocoon-like privacy of the plush interior.

Things were going to get hectic real soon. It was just a few weeks until Christmas, so she would be extremely busy shopping and doing all the other traditional stuff she always did, but at least she could take a break from Henry Lee Lucas...

"Carolyn!"

Startled, Carolyn jerked, racked her knee against the steering wheel, and swore. She glared at Leola, who stood, shivering, knocking on the window. Carolyn lowered it.

"What are you doing out here, Ohler? Get in the house—I'll be there in a few minutes! Good grief!"

"There's a lady on the phone and she wants to talk to you now. It sounds important."

Carolyn frowned and shook her head. "Ohler, what's the matter with you? Take a message."

"Well, I would, but she said she'd hold on when I told her I thought I heard you in the driveway. So she's holding on."

"Damn." Carolyn turned off the engine, dropped the keys in her purse, and opened the car door. There went her five minutes alone with her thoughts. "Did she say what's so important?"

"Well, she said she's the president of some children's organization here and she heard that you could interview molested kids. She's working with a little boy and his mother, and she says they need your help. Really bad. He's only three. I thought you'd want to talk to her."

Carolyn closed the car door and locked it. She would have to get her luggage later. "Come on, Ohler, let's get you in the house. Did she give you her name?"

"Yeah, she did," Leola nodded. "Her name is Ronni. Ronni Hoessli."

# PART FOUR

*Everyone carries around his own monsters.*

**~Richard Pryor, Comedian~**

**(1940 - 2005)**

# CHAPTER NINETEEN

After Carolyn Huebner and I had finished our conversation on the telephone, I picked up the newspaper article that had given me the idea to call her in the first place and looked more closely at a rather grainy photograph of an attractive young woman. I re-read the headline and skimmed through the more important details of the story: *Troubled Kids Have a Friend, President of Child Search Organization Comes to the Rescue.*

Carolyn Huebner, founder and president of Texas Child Search, Inc., is attuned to the plight of runaways and lost children...

...Huebner works closely with law enforce-ment officials, following every lead possible to find lost children...

...She talks with the friends of missing youngsters, uses police computers, fingerprints and—in the case of murdered children—compares dental records in her diligent detective work.

...The San Antonio based Child Search organization handled 28 missing child cases last year. And, Huebner helped solve 20 of those cases...

...That's not a bad clearance rate, considering that, nationally, of the 2.5 million children reported missing each year, about 500,000 never are found...

...Huebner attributes her success to being able to understand the emotional trauma exper-ienced by missing children and their parents...

Carolyn Huebner was kidnapped at age six...

I looked even more closely at the photograph in the center of the page. The woman who squinted against the sunlight was obviously intense and committed. She was also very young to have accomplished so much.

Our conversation had lasted at least thirty minutes and she had been so knowledgeable that I was thoroughly impressed, especially when she told me about her recent certification in interviewing and videotaping sexually abused children, which was why I needed her help. I scribbled her phone number onto a card in my rolodex so I wouldn't lose it and carefully placed the newspaper clipping in a drawer.

Carolyn Huebner might well be exactly what I was looking for.

I knew I was in no position to be picky. Francesca Kellerman and her three-year-old son, Troy, desperately needed someone who worked closely with and was highly respected by law enforcement. If that part of the article was correct, then Carolyn Huebner might be the *outsider* that could help us make our case.

And we had been looking for just such an outsider for several months—since the spring of 1984, to be exact, when my then-nine-year-old daughter, Michaela, had awakened my husband and me early one morning to whisper that our next-door neighbor—her best friend's father and a retired military man whom we trusted implicitly—had been molesting her since she was six years old.

It never occurred to us not to believe her accusations. Her childish descriptions of sexual activities were too dead-on to be fantasies and we turned our case over to the authorities immediately. Yet, even though this man ultimately copped a plea and went to prison for a brief period, I knew that justice hadn't been done.

Many times afterward I claimed that if I had it to do over again, I would have shot this scumbag myself, dumped his useless body into the San Antonio River, and gone home to enjoy my first good night's sleep in years—instead of putting my little girl through a legal system as cold and dispassionate as ours.

It wasn't true, of course. Intellectually, I knew that vigilante justice was never the answer, but it always made me feel better to say it.

Because we were a law-abiding family, we learned the hard way how to maneuver around the pitfalls and landmines of our various criminal and civil procedures. The experience was so brutal that, by the time it was over with, we wanted to share our painfully-gained knowledge with everyone we came into contact with, whether they wanted to learn about it or not.

Within a few months, my husband, Kevin, and I had started our own chapter of a statewide organization known as MAAM, which had been created a few years earlier by a woman in Corpus Christi to help the families of sexually abused children. The word spread quickly that we were a couple that would not only walk strangers through a nearly incomprehensible maze of legal technicalities, but we would discuss it publicly as well.

From the moment the word got out that there was a local organization dedicated to fighting for the rights of children instead of perpetrators, our phone never stopped ringing.

It was our own private form of therapy, and it was effective.

Then one morning in late December, 1984, Francesca Kellerman called me about her three-year-old son, Troy. Although the little boy was very bright and extremely verbal for his age, he had apparently not given a "good" videotaped interview to a caseworker concerning his alleged molestation by his father. The Department of Human Resources had closed the case based on a lack of evidence, and, as far as the social worker was concerned, it was over.

But it wasn't over for Francesca. She was an intelligent, professional woman frightened out of her wits because DHR ordered her to give her beautiful little boy to his father every other weekend, regardless of the child's accusations and her own unshakable belief that he was telling the absolute truth. As his behavior became more bizarre and uncontrollable, Francesca's determination to protect him intensified as well.

Finally, hearing of our organization through a newspaper article and having utilized the last of her resources, she called me. As always, I tried to listen and commiserate, but I figured there was nothing I could do. But by the time she was finished with her story, I was so infuriated by the system's injustice and lack of concern for this little boy that I knew I had to take it just as far as I could.

I also knew that there was nothing I could do by myself. I realized that the time had come for us to unearth someone *outside* the system, someone who could identify with young victims even more than I could, someone who wouldn't be intimidated by law enforcement, and someone whose word would be respected by authorities.

If the newspaper article I had read was anywhere close to the truth, I knew we needed someone like Carolyn Huebner.

Francesca Kellerman, her son Troy, and I finally met Carolyn at her house in early February, 1985. The Huebner home was magnificent: two stories with towers and oddly-shaped windows and a long front porch. Several alley cats perching on the porch railing and lounging on patio furniture added a homey if slightly comical touch to the scene.

The front door opened and a smiling young woman walked down the porch steps toward us. As we shook hands all around, she spoke in a languid Texas drawl that seemed much more pronounced than when I had spoken with her on the telephone.

"Howdy! I'm Carolyn Huebner. Y'all must be Ronni and Francesca."

"That's us," I responded with a grin. Gesturing down at a little boy standing silently between his mother and me, I added, "And this handsome guy is Troy."

Carolyn Huebner immediately dropped to her knees so that she was eye-level with the child and offered him her hand. "Hi, there, Troy—I'm Carolyn Huebner. You can call me *Carolyn* if you want to. Would you like to come inside and see some really neat stuff I have for little kids?"

Troy glanced up at his mother for permission. When Francesca nodded and Carolyn had gotten to her feet, he trustingly tucked his hand into Carolyn's and walked with her to the house. She spoke over her shoulder to us as we brought up the rear. "Hurry up, y'all! It's cold out here and I have coffee on."

By the time we had all reached the front door, I was trying to figure out a way to extinguish my cigarette before I went inside, but Carolyn shook her head.

"Don't worry about it. I smoke like a train myself and so does Detective Roberts, so you're safe. Come on in."

When I stepped into the wide entrance foyer, I saw an impeccable glassed-in parlor on one side and a rather mussed but comfortable family room on the other. The ceilings were at least ten feet high. But more than anything else, my admiring gaze was immediately drawn straight ahead to a full-length, full-bodied oil portrait of a flirtatious younger Carolyn dressed in an evening gown, red-gold curls piled high on her head, looking over one shoulder.

Francesca didn't seem to notice. She moved closer to Carolyn and whispered nervously, "You mentioned a Detective Roberts?"

Carolyn nodded, glancing down at Troy, and answered in a low voice, "When Ronni told me that your ex-husband lives in Terrell Hills, I called the Chief of Police there—he's a friend of mine—and asked if he would send a nice investigator out here to keep us company. He's just going to sit in the living room and watch TV with you ladies while Troy and I check out my dolls."

"I don't play with dolls!" Troy objected, jerking his hand away from her grasp and glaring up at her. "I'm a boy!"

She nodded slowly and seriously, as if she were giving grave consideration to his objection. "I know," she said finally, "and you're a really big boy, too. But these are very *special* dolls, and I only show them to very special children. You sure you don't want to see them?"

Troy's innocent cobalt-blue eyes grew suspicious. "What's so special about 'em?"

Immediately understanding his mistrust, Francesca squatted in front of him and stroked his cheek. "You can go with her, Troy. It's okay. I'll be in that room right over there and you just holler real loud if you need me."

I looked at Carolyn curiously, wondering just how far she would go in insisting that he leave his mother, the only security he had, and accompany this strange woman into a room he had never seen before. The social workers I had observed in the past would simply have taken his hand and marched him off, whether he liked it or not…

But not Carolyn Huebner. When the little boy's lower lip trembled and his eyes filled with tears, she touched his white-blond hair. "Never mind, Troy," she told him softly, "you don't have to come with me. This is a safe place for children and you never have to do anything here that you don't want to do."

There was something in her voice that nearly broke my heart, something that I couldn't hope to identify—but whatever it was, it brought a lump to my own throat. Then, as her cool, detached professionalism seemed to dissipate right before our eyes, I began to understand what made Carolyn Huebner so unique.

Without any warning and without caring in the slightest bit about her audience, her voice actually seemed to change, become a little higher-pitched. Her posture shifted; in some imperceptible way, she seemed to carry herself a little differently. Even her face altered, became softer, a little more childlike... It was uncanny, eerie, and completely inexplicable.

Somehow, Carolyn Huebner had climbed into the mind of a tormented three-year-old boy. Without any problem at all and in a way I had never seen before, she seemed to have *become* this child.

Troy accepted her transfiguration without question.

As if he completely understood her and simply didn't want her to be distressed, he took her hand and said softly, "I'm okay now. Can we go see your dolls?"

Little Troy Kellerman's videotape was powerful.

In it, when Carolyn had casually shown him a jar of Vaseline mixed in with a few other common household items like baby powder and hand lotion, he grabbed the container out of her hand and threw it across the room. He then proceeded to describe his father's sexual abuse by graphically—and accurately— demonstrating sodomy and oral penetration on her anatomically-correct dolls.

Carolyn was thrilled to tears when the child's videotaped testimony proved so strong that an obviously disgusted civil judge ordered that this father never again be allowed to visit his son unsupervised.

On the other hand, even though they did agree to press criminal charges against the father, prosecutors refused to accept that same powerful videotape as evidence because it had been made by someone *outside* of the Department of Human Resources. To add insult to injury, they also claimed that Carolyn wasn't properly trained (even though she probably had at least a dozen hours more training than any of their investigators), and, they said, she had obviously coached the little boy because his tape was too good for his age...

Anyway, there it was. Although it hurt for her to admit it, there was nothing more she could do. All that really mattered right now was that little Troy Kellerman was protected—at least for the time being.

Besides, Carolyn was once more involved in another crisis all her own.

Storm clouds were gathering two hundred miles to the north, seething and churning around the McLennan County Courthouse in Waco, and it wasn't going to be long before all hell broke loose.

Now, nervously chewing a thumbnail, Carolyn sat at her desk in her office and peered around a stack of files at PoPo. Seated across from her in a comfortable easy chair, he held a subpoena in his hand and stared at it as if he couldn't quite believe what he was seeing. Frowning, he even adjusted his reading glasses more firmly on his nose—just to be sure. Finally he shook his head and dropped the paper on the desk.

"When did you get this?"

"A couple of days ago."

PoPo removed his glasses from the bridge of his nose and carefully placed them into his shirt pocket. Carolyn could tell by his furrowed brow, squinty eyes and tightened lips that he was thinking…hard…

He looked up suddenly. "Anything else you want to tell me, Kid?"

Carolyn bit her lip. "Well, I got a phone call the other night. Somebody said that I'd better keep my mouth shut or I'd be suckin' up water in the San Antonio River—the hard way. Then they hung up."

"Okay, first you get a subpoena from the attorney general himself and now you're gettin' death threats. You want to tell me why?"

Carolyn waved a cloud of smoke away from her face and rubbed her bleary eyes. She was so exhausted she couldn't even think anymore, but it didn't take a brain surgeon to figure this one out.

"Attorney General Jim Mattox has opened an investigation on the Rangers and Henry Lucas in Waco. This subpoena is for me to go up there and testify about what I know."

PoPo rubbed his stubbly chin and chuckled. "Hot damn. You got a nervous Ranger somewhere. Someone's afraid you're gonna testify about them closin' cases on Lucas. I told you not to give that interview in the Dallas papers, Carolyn."

Carolyn kept chewing on her lip and nodded. How had she gotten herself into this mess, anyway? All she wanted to do was find out whether or not Lucas had killed any of her girls. All she wanted to do was the right thing.

Carolyn lifted her head and looked directly at PoPo. "I'm scared someone's going to hurt my Dootie…"

"Aw, calm down, Kid. Ain't nothin' gonna happen to your Dootie. After all, these are Texas Rangers and they don't hurt babies. Get Ohler to take her home with her 'til this dies down if it'll make you feel better. By the way, how does Larry feel about all this?"

Carolyn snorted and shook her head. "He's not talking to me anymore. He says I got myself into it, so I can just get myself out of it."

When PoPo finally got to his feet, he looked every inch the take-no-prisoners Texas Ranger he had been in his heyday. He gave an unconcerned yawn designed to calm her down, but it didn't work. She was scared silly and she couldn't hide it.

"You ain't got much choice, Kid," he said, sliding his cigarettes into his shirt pocket as he prepared to leave, "and sometimes that's the best place to be. No choices. So you take that subpoena and you do what they want."

"But what about me, PoPo? Someone doesn't want me to talk…"

PoPo stroked the Texas Ranger badge he had pinned to his vest and didn't say anything for a long time. Finally, he met her gaze with eyes that were as hard as gunmetal. "Don't you worry, Kid. I still know people up there and I ain't too old to make a phone call or two. Them Rangers up there now…they're just young fellers that got in over their heads. There ain't one Ranger up there that wants to mess with this old man."

Carolyn leaned her head back against the passenger's side headrest and closed her eyes. She couldn't remember the last time she'd had a good night's sleep, so she was infinitely grateful to the attorney general for sending one of his own men down from Austin to take her back up to Waco. Interstate 35 North was incredibly dull for hundreds of miles and she hated driving it under the best of circumstances, which these definitely weren't.

Yawning, Carolyn let her mind wander back through these last few weeks. They had been some of the most difficult of her life and she had gone through them alone. PoPo had done everything he could, and Ohler had taken Dootie home with her, but Larry hadn't been any help at all…

Even while she was receiving threatening telephone calls, Larry didn't want to hear about them. Even after two gunshots had exploded near the living room window, Larry shrugged it off. And even though her nightmares had returned full force to rip her screaming from sleep, Larry didn't have one minute's comfort to offer her. Even when she begged him to come with her to Waco, even when she wept and told him how much she needed him, Larry hadn't even looked at her. In fact, it seemed that he had developed a way of looking *through* her these days—like she was invisible, like she didn't even breathe the same air he did, like nothing she had to say could possibly be interesting, or important, or even relevant to him. She almost wished he would start yelling at her again, just so she could be sure that he knew she was there… Now, to cap it all off, he was sending her up to Waco by herself, as if there wasn't even the smallest possibility that she might meet up with someone who wanted to hurt her… What kind of husband was that?

"Here we are, Miz Huebner," her driver said, unceremoniously interrupting her thoughts and jerking her back to the present. Carolyn sat up straight and looked around, trying to get her bearings as he pulled into the back parking lot of a small hotel.

They were in downtown Waco, near the courthouse, and if she had been afraid before, she was terrified now. Her driver seemed nice enough, but she didn't know him from Adam. What was to keep him from turning her over to whomever it was that wanted her dead? She had to have been crazy to let PoPo talk her into doing this! She should have kept running…she was good at running…she could have outrun a stupid subpoena…

The driver reached across the seat to rest his hand on her shoulder. He gave it a gentle, understanding squeeze. "You're safe here, Miz Huebner, I promise. You can trust us."

Her eyes swam with tears as she looked at him, but she managed a nod. She had never felt so alone in her life.

Carolyn had been home for two whole days, but she didn't think anyone had noticed. Audra screamed all the time, Larry dashed out the front door to get to work just as early as he could, and even Ohler went about her business with a set, disapproving expression on her normally sweet face.

Carolyn gulped in a deep breath and sank beneath the bath water, luxuriating in its dark silence and aromatic warmth. Honestly, she thought, after everything I've just been through, is it really asking too much for one quiet evening at home? After all, no one else is interested in Lucas, or Waco…no one except PoPo…

Ah, sweet PoPo—where would she be without him? He was the only person who seemed to give a flip about what had happened to her up there in the McLennan County courthouse. She hadn't heard a peep from Larry until he had come in that night hollering for his supper like it was any other night, but PoPo had called her the minute he thought it was time for her to be home.

As soon as she had picked up the phone, without even a greeting, he had asked, "You okay, Kid?"

"I'm fine, PoPo."

"So, how'd it go up in Waco?"

"It was pretty awful, PoPo—but I survived."

"I never doubted that you would, Kid. Tell me about it."

Carolyn sipped at her iced tea and took a deep breath. "Well, a guy named Pete Cleary came down from Austin to pick me up and he drove me back up to Waco. He was a really nice guy, PoPo. You would've liked him. Anyway, once we got there, another guy—he was from the DA's office, I think—met us at the hotel, and they set up shop outside my room. Late that night I got a phone call. This man said, "You testify, you're dead," and then he hung up. That's it. Scared the bejesus out of me. I didn't sleep all night."

PoPo gave a long whistle. "Go on."

"The next morning, when it was time to leave, the guys took me to the courthouse and—you're not gonna believe this, PoPo!—I had to go up the fire escape so no one could see me. It was the only way I could get to the Grand Jury room on the fourth floor. It was the most bizarre…"

"Aw, c'mon, Carolyn… This is the old man you're talkin' to!"

"No, really, PoPo! It's true! And then, when I sat down at this long table to start answering the DA's questions, a phone rings behind me, and I hear someone say, 'Who is this?' Later on I find out that a man called right into the Grand Jury room and all he said was, 'She's dead.' That's it. Just, 'She's dead.'"

PoPo whistled again. "Nothin' else? No idea who he was?"

Managing to hide the fear she still felt, Carolyn squeaked out a tentative chuckle. "I guess they saw me go up the fire escape after all…"

But the former Ranger wasn't even faintly amused. "I don't need to tell you—I'm not crazy about this, Kid."

"Oh, I'm all right, PoPo. I'm just real tired."

"Where's Larry? Does he know you're home?"

"No, I haven't heard from him."

"Well, call him, Kid! He'd want to know you're safe."

"Why, PoPo? He doesn't care…"

Another piercing wail came from downstairs, shocking Carolyn straight up and out of the tub. She grabbed a towel and hastily dried herself, then wrapped it around her head. Slipping into her favorite white terrycloth robe, Carolyn threw open the bathroom door and yelled downstairs.

"Damn it all, Larry, can't you shut her up?"

Is everyone else's family like this? She wondered absently. Audra's piercing shrieks stabbed right into her eardrums, actually making her eyes hurt and her teeth ache. What was it about Larry that he couldn't control his own child? He was so used to negotiating *everything*, constantly making deals with *someone*, that he just couldn't accept the obvious impossibility of negotiating with a three-year-old. Especially *this* three-year-old. She was so intelligent and manipulative that he was like silly putty in her tiny hands. He didn't stand a chance and she would win every damn time, but he never seemed to learn his lesson. It was like he thought every single night that this time it's going to be different…

Carolyn had tried numerous times to talk to Larry about his apparent inability to communicate with a little girl as perceptive as Audra, but he always became too defensive for them to discuss it.

"Who do you think you are to tell me how to raise my own child?" he would demand, glaring at her with such visible dislike that she would take a nervous step backward. "Good God, Carolyn, an alley cat is a better mother than you are…"

Carolyn just didn't know what she could do to make anyone happy in this family. She was failing miserably just like her mother had always said she would, and there wasn't a thing she could do to stop it.

"I've told you to get in bed ten times, Audra Nicole," Larry shouted from the kitchen, "and I'm not going to tell you again! I'm counting, one, two, three…"

Carolyn desperately squeezed her fists against her temples as hard as she could; there was clamoring inside her brain unlike anything she had ever experienced before. Screaming, moaning, laughing…chaotic commotion…louder and louder…

"Oh, for God's sake, Larry!" Carolyn hollered, des-perately trying to drown out the uproar in her head, "Don't start that countin' crap again! All you're teachin' her to do is frickin' count!"

Shaking with rage and frustration, Carolyn stomped down the stairs and into her office. Turning on the light and slamming the door behind her so hard that the certificates on the wall went crooked, she threw herself into the swivel chair behind her desk and grabbed her cigarettes and lighter from beside the telephone.

For the first time Carolyn noticed that the answering machine was blinking a message alert, but before she pressed the button to listen, she lit a cigarette and took a deep drag. Beyond the office door she heard Larry finally successfully ushering Audra up the stairs to her bedroom. Carolyn heaved a sigh of relief, pressed the *play* button on the answering machine, and leaned back in her chair to listen. The female caller's unfamiliar voice was husky and thick, as if she had been crying. Frowning, immediately putting her own problems to the side and grateful to have something else to think about, Carolyn turned up the volume.

"Hi, Carolyn, it's Ronni. Sorry I missed you. I just wanted to let you know that my father died last week and I'm in the process of closing down MAAM. I have Francesca Kellerman's full file here and I need to know if you want it or if I should give it back to Francesca. Please give me a call as soon as you can…"

A lump formed in Carolyn's throat and her own eyes filled with tears; her fingers shook as she turned off the answering machine. The grief she heard in the woman's voice was all too familiar, and she remembered that emptiness like it was yesterday. Dropping her cigarettes and lighter into her bathrobe pocket, Carolyn stood up and walked slowly toward the door. She would arrange to get the Kellerman file back as soon as she could. After all, she had gotten Francesca a new lawyer—Ricardo Calderone, a terrific family law attorney who sat on her Board of Directors—and she had asked Dan Marshall, a psychologist who also worked with Child Search, to see Troy at a reduced rate if possible. So Carolyn definitely wanted to stay current on the Kellerman case; she had too much invested to just give it up. She would call Ronni back tomorrow and maybe they could visit. She turned off the light and closed the office door behind her.

Larry had apparently gone on to bed—the television was silent and the house was dark. Carolyn made her way up the stairs, grateful for the momentary hushed stillness. As she did every night, she stopped in the doorway of Audra's bedroom to check on her. As it was every night, the room was bathed in the soft lavender glow of a Cinderella nightlight.

But the Dootie's bed was empty.

Carolyn grinned and shook her head. She knew where Audra had gone. She was in her mommy's room and sleeping in her mommy's bed until Carolyn finally left the office and came up to carry her back into her own room. Bless her little heart...

As much as it pained her to admit it, Carolyn knew that Larry was right about one thing: she needed to spend more time with her little girl—more *quality* time. She needed to stop screaming and dig up a little patience from somewhere. Every once in awhile, when she could stop long enough to pay attention and listen to her own voice, Carolyn vaguely realized how much she sounded like her own mother—the shrieks, the curses, the accusations...

Well, I can't do anything about it right now, Carolyn thought wearily, tiptoeing down the hall to her bedroom. She was too tired and all she was up for tonight was moving Audra back to her own bed. But tomorrow Carolyn would give Ohler the day off and she and Dootie would do something neat together. Maybe they could go to the mall, or the zoo...

Carolyn peered into the shadows of her dimly lit bedroom and her smile froze. There was no sign of Dootie anywhere. For the first time in her life, she didn't know where her baby was. Her mouth went dry. Heart pounding, stark terror welled up in her throat and she ran to Larry's room.

Carolyn threw open his door and turned on the light.

Her panicked words died on her lips. Gawking in disbelief, she took in the scene before her. It was a scene she had never even imagined...a scene right out of her nightmares...

Naked, moaning, Larry writhed on top of the sheets, frantically masturbating. Not two feet away...her head near his knees...lay his little girl, curled up beside him. Carolyn gasped, walked into the room and wrenched Audra off the bed. Holding the child tightly in her arms she backed away, so shocked she couldn't think of anything except to get her baby out of this room, away from this man…

Eyes bulging with terror, Larry jerked straight up in the bed. Pasty-faced and panting and pathetic, he babbled and pleaded and cajoled. Tears streamed down his cheeks. But his words were gibberish to Carolyn. His mouth moved slowly, as if he were underwater; all she could hear was the thudding echo of her own heartbeat pounding in her head.

Carolyn whispered soothingly to Audra and backed away toward the bedroom door. But then, when Larry edged toward the side of the bed, her vision turned blood-red with rage. She came to a dead halt and stood rooted to the floor.

Larry froze. "Huebner, it's not what you think… I'd never…"

Her eyes narrowed and her hatred was so palpable she could taste it. "Shut your filthy mouth before I kill you."

"Huebner, please…listen to me…"

Then, as she looked at him sitting so stunned and forlorn in his bed, she realized that he looked like every child molester she had ever seen before. He was a sniveling, whining, putrid piece of crap…

He was Troy Kellerman's father.

He was Michaela Hoessli's next door neighbor.

He was a pervert. He was Art Lovell. And he was back.

# CHAPTER TWENTY

"Dan? Dan, it's Carolyn. I hate to call you so late, but I have an emergency…" Dan Marshall, one of the psychologists who worked closely with Texas Child Search, was accustomed to Carolyn's late night calls. "It's okay, Carolyn," he interrupted, yawning. "How can I help?"

Carolyn's voice shook as she fought tears. "Dan," she whispered, "this is personal—I need you to swear you won't say a word to anyone."

"You know I won't."

"Please, Dan. Promise me."

Now he sounded wide awake, alert. "I promise, Carolyn. What is it?"

"Dan, I just found Audra in Larry's bed and he was… masturbating…" The nausea was rising again; she could taste it in the back of her throat. "Dan, I don't…"

"With her there?"

"Right next to him."

"I'm on my way." The phone clicked in her ear.

Carolyn hung up. "Oh, thank you, God," she whispered, "thank you…"

Kneeling down beside the bed, Carolyn tucked a lightweight blanket around Audra's slender shoulders and blinked hard against the tears. As she gazed down at her baby girl, stroking the silky blond hair away from her face, her heart twisted. Audra Nicole looked exactly like Carolyn at three years old; the resemblance was uncanny. Suddenly her fear was overwhelming.

*Sweet Jesus, I want to protect her! I don't want her life to be like mine! She's so little, and I don't want her to be alone…*

"Mommy?" Audra's baby voice was sleepy.

"What is it, Dootie?"

"Mommy, are you still mad at Daddy?"

Carolyn struggled to maintain a calm, controlled demeanor. Her training had prepared her well—intellectually, at least—to talk to anybody's child about a possible sexual assault, but it hadn't prepared her *emotionally* to talk to her own…

Audra was her baby. Larry was Audra's daddy. This happened in other families, not in hers. She was more experienced, more perceptive and intuitive than other women. She would recognize that she was living in the same house with a pervert, where maybe another woman wouldn't. He *couldn't* be a real threat, could he? She would know…wouldn't she?

"What do you think, Dootie? Should I be mad at Daddy?"

Audra yawned; her wide blue eyes fluttered closed. "He was just washing his hands, Mommy," she murmured. "That's all."

Carolyn stroked the child's velvet-soft cheek with an icy finger and took a deep breath. "Did he touch you, Audra? Did he touch you like we've talked about?"

Audra shook her head and burrowed deeper into the pillow. "He was just...washing his hands..."

The little girl's voice trailed away; her breathing became deep and even. When Carolyn heard the doorbell ring, she got to her feet and left her bedroom, closing the door softly behind her. As she hurried downstairs to let Dan Marshall in, she noticed that Larry's light was still on, and she knew he was lying in that bed just waiting for her to come barreling into his room and blow his brains out. She could visualize his face, all sweaty and colorless and mottled with fear, and that mental image pleased her. He needed to be afraid...

Carolyn opened the front door and pulled the psychologist inside. "Thank you so much for coming, Dan! I hated to ask, but I didn't know what else to do..."

Dan Marshall was a tall, wide-shouldered man with power built into every muscle, and his attitude was always one that didn't tolerate any nonsense. But tonight he seemed even more determined and businesslike than usual. "Are you okay?" he asked immediately.

Those damn tears welled again, but she fought them and nodded. "I'm okay."

"Where's Audra?"

"Asleep in my room."

"Did you talk to her? Did he touch her?"

"She doesn't understand. She says he was washing his hands."

Dan let out an explosive sigh of relief. "Good! Where's Larry?"

"In his room."

He nodded and headed for the stairs. "If you have any guns in the house, break them down and hide them. I don't want Larry to get his hands on them. I'm going up."

Carolyn had no weapons in the house, at least not that Larry was aware of, but she just nodded and followed close behind him. He obviously knew what he was doing, and she needed someone around who could think straight.

Dan knocked on Larry's door and waited for a full five minutes. When Larry finally responded, he was fully dressed and far more composed. "Hello, Dan."

"Larry, may I come in? We need to talk."

Larry opened the door wider, stood aside as Dan entered his bedroom, and closed the door firmly in Carolyn's face. It wasn't long before he came out of his bedroom, carrying his briefcase in one hand and an overnight bag in the other.

Carolyn stood silently in her doorway, watching him through blurry, tear-swollen eyes, and felt as though she were floating above them all in some kind of bizarre out-of-body experience. It was like she was a stranger to herself, as if even her searing emotions didn't belong to her…

Larry stopped in front of her, set his bags down, and touched her shoulder. When Carolyn grimaced in disgust and shrugged away from him, he shook his head and picked up his bags.

"I'll be at the Riviera near my office," he said quietly, "if you want to talk."

"The only person I want to talk to is my lawyer. I suggest you do the same."

"Well, if you change your mind…"

"I won't."

"It was a bad judgment call, Huebner, that's all. Remember, I love you."

Those were the last words he spoke to her. As he made his way slowly down the stairs, Larry's shoulders were slumped and his body seemed almost bent, as if he were a very sick, very old man. Carolyn watched him without an ounce of pity; she felt only hatred and rage.

*I love you, Huebner…*

How could he say that and actually think he meant it? What he had called *bad judgment* was nothing less than a brutal betrayal of trust—and no one knew more about *that* than Carolyn did. What he apparently believed she should be able to shrug off and walk away from was, in fact, an act that had ripped through her spirit, crucified her soul, and annihilated any faith she would ever have in him again.

She could no longer trust her own husband, and she didn't know how she could live with him without that.

In just two days, Carolyn had done everything she was trained to do. She interviewed Audra with her anatomically-correct dolls, which made the little girl feel very important because her mommy was doing with her the same thing she did with all the other children that came to her house, but it didn't change her story in any way. Carolyn took her to her pediatrician to be absolutely certain there had been no penetration and was almost sick with relief to discover that Dootie was perfectly intact.

Even Dan Marshall was satisfied with Audra's answers because they were given in such open, childish terms that he was convinced she wasn't concealing or embellishing anything. But that didn't keep him from giving Carolyn a stern warning.

"If Larry comes back here to live," he said, "always remember this: even though Larry wasn't touching Audra, her presence alone sexually stimulated him in a completely unnatural way. You have no idea where it might lead from here."

Carolyn knew his warning was dead-on and it scared her to death. But she had other, more practical issues to think about.

Carolyn's years of instability and poverty had taught her the importance of being able to provide her child with a roof over her head, plenty of food on the table—and a father that came home at 6:00 every night. This father had a lot of warts, Carolyn conceded, but what father didn't? At least he gave them what they needed financially and freed Carolyn to do what she felt she *had* to do, which was search for missing children.

By the end of the week, and at her request, Larry returned. As soon as he walked into the house, Carolyn made a monumental attempt to act as if everything was normal. But she couldn't even look at her husband without experiencing an overwhelming sense of revulsion, and he couldn't meet her eyes without looking miserably embarrassed. Only Audra acted as she always had—an overwrought, totally demanding, tiny tyrant. Yet now, instead of being firm with her, Larry negotiated a little harder and gave in a little more, as if he would do just about anything in the world to please her, satisfy her mother, and maintain the status quo.

Carolyn tried to ignore the situation—not because she didn't care, but because she didn't know what to do. She realized that she had to keep what she had begun to think of as *the incident* a secret. She also knew that she could never talk to anyone about it—except perhaps Dan Marshall—because Larry would be ruined if she did. And if Larry was ruined, so was Carolyn. Her child deserved far better than that.

So, once more, like so many times before, she was alone with a secret.

"Pray, child," Ohler would advise whenever Carolyn brought up the shambles that was her family life. "Just open yourself up and God will lead you."

But Carolyn didn't feel right about praying. She had turned her back on God for so long that she was positive He wasn't interested in hearing about her problems now. He had lots more important things to worry about than Carolyn Huebner's screwed-up life. On the other hand, she could still hear her daddy's soothing voice in the back of her memory, reminding her that God would always be with her, no matter what…

There was nothing she yearned for more than the peace she had found without any effort at all when she was alone and frightened as a child, but somehow that peace had vanished. She could still remember those beautiful angels who had embraced her and remained with her in that closet. She could still envision Jesus Himself standing above the cornfield on the outskirts of White Oak, Pennsylvania, His hands stretched out and touching the stalks of corn. She could still see them all, as clearly as if they had visited her in her prison only yesterday instead of more than twenty years ago.

Now Carolyn was in a prison again, but this time it was one of her own making. This time the angels didn't come, and this time she didn't know how to find them.

Still, Carolyn knew who could help her, and she knew that all she had to do was ask. It was Ohler who had all the answers now, and it was Ohler who had had them in the past. Carolyn recognized and appreciated that this stooped little old lady was a Godsend, not only because of her love and ability to efficiently care for the precocious Audra, but because of the strong and unabashed relationship she shared with God.

Carolyn now especially looked forward to what she called *Leola's little praise moments*—moments in which Leola, puttering around the house and tending to her chores, would suddenly and without warning burst into song, joyously singing an old hymn that Carolyn had grown up with. Or she might say softly, spontaneously, "Oh, thank you, Lord!" These delightful little moments never failed to remind Carolyn of Grandma Rankin, taking her back to her childhood and the contented hours she had spent on the front porch of the old farmhouse, or inside the huge Assembly of God church she had attended with her family as a very young child in White Oak, Pennsylvania.

Yet, while Leola had a peace of spirit that Carolyn longed to share—a peace of spirit that actually seemed to *emanate* from the old woman's lined face and bent posture—Carolyn knew that she had been too busy before and was still moving way too fast now to share in the quiet serenity that made up Ohler's spiritual world.

Regardless, Carolyn sometimes found the time to take Audra and join Leola at her small, red brick church in the heart of downtown San Antonio. There they were warmly welcomed by an all-black congregation that certainly seemed to understand what God's love was all about and rejoice in it. Carolyn inevitably left the services feeling buoyed with inner happiness and determined to change her lifestyle to make a little more room for the Lord. After all, He had been so good to her...

Yet, no matter how good her intentions, Carolyn always seemed to find herself immersed in either her work, her problems, or both—with God once more relegated to the background of her existence, unseen, unfelt and unappreciated. The real truth was, Carolyn had lost control of her life. No matter how perfect everything looked on the outside, the Huebner family was fighting for its very survival.

And no one was struggling more than Carolyn.

Nighttime was the worst. If she was in her office and she heard Larry go upstairs, she automatically left her desk, ran to her door—and listened. If it was too quiet for too long, Carolyn made a mad dash up the stairs and headed straight for Audra's bedroom...just to check...just to be sure. Living in constant emotional turmoil, she feared for the safety of her child, was outraged that she had to be afraid at all, and bitterly resented the cold fact that she had no way out. She felt like a rock climber fighting to scale a steep mountainside, protected from certain death by nothing more than a thin line of rope: one misstep could easily be her last.

As usual, Carolyn's only real peace came from her work. Once Larry was gone for the day and Audra was safely established in Ohler's loving care, Carolyn carried her coffee and cigarettes to her office. She always closed her door behind her and took a deep breath before settling in for the day. It was quiet in here; she could think and she could do what she did best. She could go outside of herself and deal with other people's problems. It was the only way she knew to survive.

Not long after I had left that nearly hysterical message for Carolyn about the death of my father, I came to my senses. Instead of shutting our organization down completely, I chose to turn it over to one of our members, a very competent woman and a good friend of mine, who then merged it with another group that monitored child sexual assault cases in court.

Moving away from our organization not only freed me up to spend more time with my little girl, but to return to my true passion as well, which had always been writing. Still, it was clear that I wasn't going to be allowed to step away from actual involvement in child abuse cases all that easily.

Even though Carolyn and I had originally worked together to protect just this one child, the Francesca/Troy Kellerman sexual assault case had exploded through the Terrell Hills and San Antonio communities like a fast-moving malignancy, beginning with the tortured outcry of that beautiful three-year-old boy, then growing to include the heart-stopping allegations of his thirteen-year-old stepbrother, then finally involving four other young boys in the neighborhood—and a video camera. It was the kind of case that sucked the blood out of everyone who came into contact with it.

Because Carolyn had produced and retained in her possession the videotape in which Troy Kellerman had accused his father of "checking my butt with his pee-pee," she had an emotional commitment to the protection of this beautiful little boy. And because she had begun to appear on radio talk shows to expose the turtle-slow pace of the legal system in San Antonio, at least as it related to child abuse, and using an anonymous Troy Kellerman as a primary example, she had begun to thoroughly aggravate those within Sam Millsap's office, our current district attorney.

Although I had never had reason to return to Carolyn's home after the day she had videotaped Troy Kellerman, we had spoken on the telephone frequently, trying to work out a strategy that might protect the little boy, and laughing whenever we came up with a solution that would have been quite effective but probably wasn't completely legal. We, like everyone else in the sordid, depressing field of child abuse, had relied on our sense of the ridiculous and our ability to curse fluently in order to keep our sanity. But we hadn't become personal friends, choosing instead to keep our relationship on a completely professional level.

It was autumn before Carolyn finally returned my phone call. She didn't apologize about her delay in calling me back, and she didn't mention the death of my father. In fact, she seemed unaware that any significant time at all had passed since we had last spoken.

But I knew a lot of time had passed—so much time, in fact, that I seldom talked with Francesca anymore, I was hardly current in local child abuse cases, and I had no intention of changing any of that. So, when I answered the phone and heard Carolyn's businesslike voice, I was more than a little wary.

But she didn't seem to notice my cool and rather distant attitude. She was completely fixated on what she wanted to say. "Do you still have the Kellerman file?" she asked abruptly.

I frowned, a little confused and more than slightly irritated. "Just a copy of it—I gave the original to the lady who took over MAAM. She's working with Francesca now, I'm not. Why?"

"Well, do you think you could bring it to me? I've just been subpoenaed by Sam Millsap—that's the DA…"

"I know who Sam Millsap is."

"Well, some folks don't. Anyway, I'm supposed to appear at the 226th District Court on September 3rd. Apparently they've finally set a date to take Troy Kellerman's father to court and they may want me to testify—without the video, of course. I'm on standby. But your file added to mine might really help me out."

Shocked, I held out the receiver and stared at it. What's with this woman? I wondered. She doesn't return a phone call for weeks, acts like she just talked to me yesterday, and insults my intelligence right out of the chute. She knows I've lost my father and closed down my organization, yet she thinks nothing of asking me to drive twenty miles to take a file to her house that I offered to give her a long time ago…back when it was convenient for me…

If she wants it so badly, why the devil can't she come pick it up herself?

But the craziest part of it all was that she sounded like we had never worked together for one minute on the Troy Kellerman case, like we had never laughed together, or discussed strategy together... It was as if I had imagined it all.

I swallowed my irritation. Finally, after a few seconds, I managed to give a fairly civil response. "I've got some stuff to do tomorrow morning. I guess I could bring it out to you then. I can't leave today. I'm working."

"Tomorrow morning's fine," she answered brusquely. "I'll see you then."

And she hung up.

I stared at the phone for another long moment, then gently replaced it in the cradle and shook my head. Either I've been out of this field so long that I've forgotten how goofy we all were, I thought, slightly amused, or this woman doesn't even remember her own name...much less mine...

"Let's go to the kitchen and get some coffee. Then we can go in my office and talk."

Once again I stood in the wide foyer of Carolyn's antebellum home and gazed up at the full-length portrait that had so gripped my imagination the first time I had seen it. Flanked on either side by potted greenery, the portrait reminded me of an old plantation where the Lady of the House—always perfectly coiffed and sweet-faced and indomitable—looked down from her elevated place on a wall and watched out over her domain.

Since this portrait was the focal point of the entire entrance, I wondered if it was indicative of Carolyn's personality. Did everything actually revolve around her, as it seemed to imply? Was she the center of everything that happened in this house?

I pulled myself away from the portrait, which by now seemed almost hypnotic. Handing her the Kellerman file before I forgot I was carrying it, I followed her through an elegant dining room into a large, comfortable kitchen that obviously catered to the family. A toddler's drawings were attached to an enormous refrigerator; little notes were stacked beside a coffee pot and a telephone on a long counter, and a big window over the sink looked out into a rather ragged backyard. It was a room I felt right at home in.

Carolyn set the file on the counter and took two mugs out of the cabinet. "Cream or sugar?" she asked.

"Both, thanks. I'll fix mine."

Carrying my cup of steaming coffee, I followed Carolyn back to her office, which was located off the family room, and stood in the doorway. It was painted in a soft mint green and had a small, feminine bathroom attached. It contained an enormous cherry wood desk stacked high with files, manila envelopes, letters and photographs, a matching armoire filled with more files, tape recorders, video equipment and two anatomically perfect dolls, a separate stand-alone file cabinet, an enormous copy machine, and two easy chairs in front of the desk.

One wall—the one that Carolyn faced from her desk chair—was riveting. The undeniably nosy writer in me was fascinated by all the awards and certificates that this young woman had received in a comparatively short period of time. But right smack in the center of it all, itself perfectly framed, was one of the eeriest photographs I've ever seen.

In the August 1984 issue of *Life Magazine* a profile shot of a smiling Carolyn with murderer Henry Lee Lucas accompanied a general article on serial killers. She stood in front of a map of the United States, and Lucas himself appeared to look at Carolyn with an admiring, snaggle-toothed grin on his face. I stared at the photo, chilled, and glanced over my shoulder at her.

"This is that Lucas guy, isn't it?"

She had seated herself behind her desk and lit a cigarette. I suddenly felt uneasy, like she was appraising me and waiting for my reaction to her wall of triumphs, but she just grinned. "Yep. That's Henry."

I turned back to the photo and knew just from looking at it that she wasn't a born-and-bred Texan—no matter how much she wanted to sound like one. Her curly, light brown hair was piled high on her head in the style worn by many southern women, but her complexion was too flawless for her to have ever spent any significant time out in the hot Texas sun. Creamy smooth and alabaster pale, there wasn't a freckle or a blemish on it. Her blue-gray eyes were wide, thickly lashed and fiercely intelligent, her broad smile natural and unforced, and the beginning of a little double chin made her seem all too human.

To me, she appeared more like one of those fresh-faced Englishwomen you always see in the movies with the perfect skin and big eyes, rather than the 'rough-talkin'-Texas-broad-hangin'-out-with-cops' that she seemed to want to be.

It was a really creepy picture, I thought, but it *was* in *Life Magazine*, after all…

I continued prowling around the office, not because I'm nosy (which I am) but because she just had so much interesting stuff on the walls. I stopped before a small Polaroid photograph hanging, almost hidden, beside the armoire and looked at it more closely. It was a picture of a casually dressed Carolyn standing beside a rather plump, balding, middle-aged man.

"Who's this?"

"Larry. My husband."

She answered my question with about the same amount of affection she would have shown if she had said, *my garbage man*. It unnerved me because I loved to show off my husband, and I loved to talk about him. Kevin was, in fact, the neatest guy I knew.

But Carolyn apparently didn't feel that way about Larry. "He looks like a bowling ball with ears, doesn't he?" she asked, snorting with a sort of chilly disgust that I couldn't quite understand. After all, he couldn't help it if he was balding. "I bought him a really expensive toupee last year," she continued, "but he flat refuses to wear it. So, he looks more like my father than my husband and he's only nine years older than me."

I looked at the photo more closely and stifled a chuckle. He *did* bear a rather comical resemblance to a bowling ball with ears.

"He has a nice smile," I offered finally, for lack of anything better to say. "What does he do?"

"He's the chief negotiator for Valero Energy Corporation. He's gone a lot...thank God."

Okay, I thought, now completely uncomfortable, that's enough. I'm not going any further with this...

I dropped into one of the easy chairs in front of her desk. "Where are you from, Carolyn? You told me once, but I can't remember."

"White Oak, Pennsylvania, not too far from Pittsburgh." She leaned back in her plush leather swivel chair and fixed her gaze on me. "My daddy's gone now, but my mommy still lives there. How 'bout you?"

Her use of the endearment *mommy* kind of threw me—it didn't fit that controlled image—but I shrugged it off. We all have special names for those we love.

"I was born in Tucson, Arizona," I said aloud, "but I don't claim anywhere really. My father was in the Air Force, so we moved every two years until he finally retired here in San Antonio when I was thirteen. I've lived here ever since."

Abruptly, Carolyn changed the subject. "So you're not workin' with kids anymore, huh?"

I shook my head. "No, I'm just writing. Or, I should say, learning to. I needed to be home with my family. Especially my daughter. She needs me."

"Yeah, I can appreciate that. You're lucky to have a family you want to be home with."

I kept quiet; the bitterness in her voice warned me away from saying anything. "Don't you have a little girl?" I asked finally.

"Yeah, Audra. She's three. We call her *Dootie*."

"Where is she?"

"Upstairs with Ohler."

"Ohler?"

"Leola, her nanny."

Wow, a nanny! I thought enviously. I've never even known anyone who had a nanny…

Of course, once I thought about it, I realized I had never *wanted* a nanny for my daughter. And we never needed one. We had two sets of grandparents living within ten miles of us, aunts, uncles, and cousins living nearby, and friends all over the place. We wouldn't have had room for a nanny.

"Well, she's awfully quiet for a three-year-old. I haven't heard a peep out of her."

"She knows better."

I ducked my head to hide the astonishment that exploded all over my face. There was something in Carolyn's voice that I just didn't like, something hard and cold. She seemed to recognize that her words had offended me.

"I don't want her to be so bonded to me that she can't function on her own," she explained seriously. "That's just not healthy. I want her to be so secure in herself that she doesn't need me or my approval to get along in life."

I stared at her. Good grief, I thought, that baby's only three years old! If she doesn't bond to you, she's going to bond to *somebody*…

An angry-red flush splotched Carolyn's neck as she looked away from me. "She's better off with Ohler than with me, anyway. I'm way too busy right now."

I took a deep breath and nodded, looking at the scattered files and tall stacks of paperwork piled up all over her desk. "I can see that."

"You can't imagine, Ronni. There's just so much going on that I'm overwhelmed. Half the time I don't even know where to start." She took a deep breath, then plunged in. "We've been trying to establish a search and rescue team since late last year, but I think we're going to have to give up on that. It's just too much. We're trying to set up a joint effort with the National Child Safety Council to produce a directory for law enforcement of all the unidentified deceased juveniles around the country. It's a huge undertaking. I have speeches to give, and missing children to find, and more ideas than I know what to do with. What I really need is a wife. Someone to keep me organized and free me up to do what I do best—look for missing kids." She finally paused for breath, grinned, and pushed her hair away from her face. "You wanna be my wife?"

I shook my head and snorted. "Not hardly. I'm already a wife—and not a very good one. Besides, I don't know a damn thing about missing kids, or finding them."

Carolyn's face grew serious, her eyes narrowed. "You don't *have* to know anything about missing kids. That's *my* job. Look, Ronni! You know how to handle the media, you've run your own organization, you've written and given speeches—God, do you know what a huge help *that* would be?" Her voice cracked with excitement. She all but bounced out of her chair. "Hot damn, you know how to talk on the phone, don't you? And you know how to get the details out of a victim and put a case together—look how well you did with Francesca's! I'm tellin' you, we'd be great together, Ronni! It'd be scary, what we could accomplish!"

I grabbed my purse and car keys, stood up and stared at her in utter disbelief. "You're out of your mind," I stated bluntly. "The last thing I want to do is crawl back in that sewer, Carolyn. I gave already."

"Ronni, come on…think about it…"

"There's nothing to think about, Carolyn. I'm done. I don't have any more to give."

After a long, silent moment, she slowly nodded her understanding, but she couldn't hide her disappointment. "I don't blame you, Ronni. Who in his right mind wants to spend a single minute in the company of the perverts I get to see everyday?"

Not me, I thought, absolutely not me. I didn't want to go back into the field of child abuse or missing children or anything in-between. I wanted to write, and be with my husband, and raise my little girl. I wanted to be *normal*, whatever the devil that was. In fact, I actually wanted to rediscover what it felt like to be bored…

Carolyn Huebner's world was obviously anything but boring. She and I were kindred spirits under the skin, and I recognized it. We were both motivated by anger and a fierce desire to change the world. We were also utterly convinced that we were strong enough, smart enough, and brave enough to do it.

Even before I left Carolyn's house that evening, I knew that at some point in time we were going to unite forces. I could feel it in my bones; it was meant to be. I just didn't know when.

It was going to happen because Carolyn was right. Alone we were flailing against the wind. Together we could make a difference.

# CHAPTER TWENTY-ONE

"PoPo, this is Ronni Hoessli, my chief assistant."

I laughed and offered my hand to the tall, gangly man who blew into the kitchen while lighting a cigarette and removing a large cowboy hat at the same time. After getting himself organized, his calloused fingers closed over mine as he gave me a hearty handshake. "Well, howdy do, little lady! I'm right proud to meet you!"

I couldn't help but grin at his enthusiasm. "Just to clarify, Mr. Preiss, I'm Carolyn's *only* assistant—which is why I'm the chief. Anyway, I'm happy to meet you, too."

"Well, I'm just glad you decided to join us, little lady. The Kid needs help. And if you're gonna work around here, you'd best call me *PoPo* like everyone else in this family does."

I smiled and nodded, looked up at his dark, sun-weathered face, and instantly fell in love. He didn't release my hand right away but held it for a little while, as if I were the most important person in the room, and there was something warm and comforting about that. His gaze was steady and intelligent, but his black eyes snapped with laughter and good humor. I understood immediately why Carolyn adored him.

"You got coffee, Kid?"

"You know I do, PoPo. Sit down and take a load off."

Dropping his hat on the table, PoPo pulled out a chair, turned it sideways, and sat down, stretching his long legs straight out in front of him. "It's cold outside, even if it *is* April! I must be gettin' old." He chuckled and winked at me. "Hell's afire, who do I think I'm kiddin'? I *am* gettin' old!"

"Don't be silly, PoPo. You'll never get old." Carolyn poured steaming hot coffee into three matching mugs, handed me one, and carried the other two to the table. Sitting at an end where she could easily see us both, she added, "Grab that big ash tray by the phone, Ronni. PoPo smokes more than the two of us put together."

I stared at her, then picked up the ash tray and slid it to the center of the table.

Most of the time the words *please, thank you,* and *do you mind* just weren't in this woman's vocabulary, a fact that irritated me beyond description. I hadn't been bossed around so much since I was two years old, and this had been going on since I had first begun working in her house several months earlier. I now felt that I was nothing more than her whipping girl—someone she could give orders to, create imaginary crises with, and use to build up her own ego. In fact, just a few nights earlier I had decided that I could no longer participate in the farce that was Carolyn's life.

In truth, Carolyn Huebner wasn't the woman I had first thought she was. Instead of being determined, persistent, com-passionate, and a friend to missing children everywhere, she was actually little more than a whirlwind of unfocused tornadic activity. While her fight for kids was genuine, it was more than a crusade or even a way of life. It was an obsession, a way for her to feel important and prove she was valuable to society. She was hungry for the limelight, so eager for publicity that every move she made seemed geared toward gaining it. She needed attention and affirmation like an alcoholic needs booze, and I didn't understand why.

As a consequence, the beautiful portrait in the foyer had taken on new meaning for me: I had begun to see it as a lie. With her hair piled up and princess-like gold tendrils trailing down her back, Carolyn appeared elegant and old-fashioned, sweet and feminine and classy. Yet now I had begun to realize that this was just another example of the surface "Carolyn" that was put on display for others to see and admire; the sweetness didn't have much root in reality.

In fact, as time passed, I was shocked to discover that she was loud and obnoxious, foul-mouthed and rude, superior and condescending—a publicity hound who showed an amazing lack of empathy toward anyone who didn't agree with her. Her emotions were uncontrollable, impulsive, extreme, and over-whelmingly embarrassing if you happened to be in the same room with her when they exploded. Unfortunately, I never knew when that was going to happen.

I learned that Carolyn's anger could escalate into rage with little or no provocation. Hostility could become total antagonism. If you didn't agree with just a portion of what she said, then you didn't agree with her at all. If you didn't stand with her on any one thing, then you had deserted her completely. Every emotion that Carolyn felt was over the top and off the charts. She didn't know how to be just a little bit sad; instead, she was in the depths of depression and despair. She didn't know how to be just a little bit irritated; instead, she was livid with rage or murderously infuriated. Every emotion was magnified a million times over for her. The intensity of her personality was so draining that it was virtually impossible to be around her for very long.

She also seemed incapable of being happy. If everything in her life was running smoothly, she sabotaged it. If she didn't have a crisis to manage, she created one. It was as if she didn't feel *worthy* of happiness, or peace of mind, or even simple contentment.

Looking back on it, it's a wonder that Carolyn and I ever became friends at all. I didn't make a habit of socializing with people that weren't good for me—and she wasn't. But there was something lost and vulnerable in Carolyn that she just couldn't conceal beneath that prickly exterior of defiance and bravado. I didn't know what it was or where it had originated. I just knew that it was something she was trying desperately to hide.

So, if I could ease that tortured part of her, I wanted to try. And every once in awhile I found that I could help in some tangible way, like when the flattened knuckles on her right hand hurt her and she couldn't write legibly, or when her legs ached and she needed someone to keep her mind off the pain. I never asked why her knuckles appeared squashed or her gait sometimes became stumbling and awkward; I didn't think it was any of my business. In fact, I never asked her anything at all and she seemed to appreciate that.

When the day finally came that she chose to volunteer an explanation, I was stunned by the story that she told. Even during my two years of working with abused children and their families, I had never heard anything like it.

"The woman that took me—her name was Rose—used to run my fingers through the wringer on an old washing machine out on her back porch," Carolyn related in a distant, nonchalant voice, as if everyone had this experience when they were little. She looked at her right hand ruefully. "This one's worse than the other one, but at least I can still use it. And I had to learn how to walk all over again when I finally got to go back home to my folks because I didn't eat right and I didn't get any exercise for three whole years. So, now my legs hurt sometimes and I walk funny. And I have a back problem that first showed up after I had Audra. But it passes."

"Wasn't anyone kind to you back then, Carolyn? Didn't anyone try to help you?"

"My Aunt Kat did—and I still visit her—but no one else, really. Don't worry about it, Ronni. It's over now. It's no big deal."

Still, while it appeared that Carolyn didn't want to talk about the kidnapping, everyone else did. People seemed obsessed with it, thrilled by it, eager to learn every detail they could—and Carolyn, an eloquent and powerful speaker, tried not to let them down. Her audiences apparently didn't notice how careful she was when she answered their questions or how smoothly she avoided giving away too many particulars. But I noticed, and her evasion bothered me.

I thought that perhaps that was why she seemed to feel it necessary to lash out at everyone around her who cared about her—her little girl, her nanny, even her closest colleagues. Yet the real recipient of her wrath, even her hatred, was her husband. And I didn't understand that.

I would never forget the first time I met Larry, right after the New Year, 1986. He had come home from work earlier than expected, surprising both Carolyn and me in the office, but she had scarcely even glanced up from her desk. I, on the other hand, stood immediately and walked toward him, my hand outstretched.

"Hi, I'm Ronni," I had told him, a little embarrassed by the way his wife ignored him. "I'm glad to finally meet you."

When his fingers closed around mine, I was surprised—and a little put off—by how icy they were and how limp his handshake was. Like any good Texan who puts a lot of stock in the strength and firmness of a man's grip, I pulled my hand away as quickly as I could and tried to give him the once-over without him noticing.

This was a man who didn't want to stand out in a crowd, for whatever reason, and it was a cinch that no one would have looked at him twice. Everything about him appeared to be the same color so that somehow, especially when compared with Carolyn's stylistic flair, he seemed to be neutral and drab. His rumpled business suit was brown, his tie was brown, and his thinning hair was brown. Only his round face had any color at all, and it was an unhealthy rosy-red that seemed to perpetually glisten with sweat.

As time went on, I had to remind myself that Larry Huebner was a very important executive at Valero Energy Corporation. He was a top negotiator for them, and a man didn't climb that high if he wasn't intelligent, eloquent, and stubborn as hell. He had to be utterly convinced of the rightness of his company's position and fiercely confident in his ability to articulate it. I knew instinctively that Larry Huebner, no matter what face he presented to all of us, was not a weak man, nor could he be easily manipulated.

Carolyn seemed to believe that she was stronger and smarter than her husband, more respected and appreciated by everyone around her than he was, and always acted as if she had the answers and he was too stupid to even know the questions. It seemed to me that this was a very dangerous attitude to have toward one's own mate, but it didn't seem to bother Larry in the slightest. He just took whatever she dished out, as if he was grateful that she had noticed him at all, and then moved on.

It was the saddest, most unequal relationship I had ever seen in my life.

My own husband refused to socialize with them, claiming that all he ever wanted to do when he was with them was to cold-cock Carolyn so that Larry could finally say something without her interrupting or putting him down. I knew better than to try to change his mind. Kevin was an easy-going guy who loved to have a good time, but there was nothing he hated more than a woman who treated her husband like horse manure—especially in public. He just lost all patience and became nearly irrational, so I didn't want him around them, anyway. Consequently, the only time the four of us went anywhere together was when the occasion was something I couldn't talk my way out of.

I had only worked with Carolyn for a few months when I realized that I had made the biggest mistake of my life by coming here and trying to help. Carolyn needed more than I could give her, and I wasn't qualified to take on the problems she had. I also knew that she couldn't outrun the demons that tortured her every single day of her life.

It was a race she couldn't win. Sometimes she seemed determined to take on the world, like she was some kind of super hero, barking orders to individuals who could sink her and Texas Child Search in a heartbeat, while at other times she was timid and shy and almost childlike in her desire to be taken care of. She could make enemies out of friends and not even know how it had happened. But, still, she kept trying. She tried so hard that sometimes she actually lost entire blocks of time, a disconcerting phenomenon that often made me wonder if I wasn't the one going nuts. Yet if I asked her about it, she just gave me a blank stare and changed the subject.

But instead of seeking help, Carolyn's bizarre solution to all this craziness was to keep taking on more and more cases, creating a living environment so heart-wrenching and nerve-wracking that no human being could have survived in it for long and still remained sane. She hardly ever slept. She contacted law enforcement all over the country with torrents of brilliant ideas that seldom went anywhere, spent hours on the telephone, gave speeches and interviews to anyone who asked, even drove around town looking for runaways and stray kids.

Even so, she couldn't seem to find one spare moment for her own child, beautiful little Audra who remained upstairs in the care of sweet old Leola, and she didn't seem to realize how strange this appeared to those of us on the outside looking in. If the child materialized at the office door asking for a moment of her mother's precious time or wanting to show her something she had made, Carolyn thought nothing of screaming at her like a fishwife and scaring the little girl half to death.

"Get out of here!" she shrieked, glaring at Audra until the child paled, backed out of the office and turned tail toward the stairs. "Can't you see I'm busy?"

As far as Carolyn was concerned, she was a terrific mother because she kept an immaculate home and had a hot meal on the table every evening. She didn't seem to realize that her daughter needed much more than that, or that the affection she gave without hesitation to other people's children was affection she usually withheld from her own.

On the other hand, she was far too protective of Audra, especially where Larry was concerned. Although she couldn't make time for the little girl herself, she didn't appear to want Larry involved with her, either. If Carolyn had to go out of town, she nearly always asked Leola to take Audra home with her instead of leaving her with her father, and that seemed pretty insulting to me. But, as usual, Larry didn't argue with his wife—at least not in public.

To be in that house was to be part and parcel of an endless cycle of hostility. Every time Carolyn displayed that vicious streak of cruelty toward either her daughter or her husband, I couldn't help but wonder if it was indicative of her own upbringing—even though she told me at least once a day how perfect and wonderful her own mother had been.

But I knew better than that. I had overheard several long-distance conversations between the two women that had actually hurt my heart to listen to. Even though Carolyn sent her mother money every month and bought her lovely gifts for no reason at all, she always seemed to be begging for some kind of approval from her mother, some little bit of affection, some tiny smidgeon of love… I had even found Carolyn sobbing like a baby in her office one morning after she had hung up the phone with the woman she had so many times called *the perfect mother…*

"Ronni! Are you listening to us? What do you think?"

Carolyn's strident voice pierced my thoughts and slammed me back into the present. "What do I think about what?"

"I said I'm going to go public and endorse Fred Rodriguez for District Attorney. I'll do it as a private citizen, of course—not as a representative of Texas Child Search—but I firmly believe that we gotta get Sam Millsap out of there. The man is useless as tits on a boar hog—we'd be better off with the devil himself as DA than Sam Millsap!"

"There's nothing private about you, Carolyn," I chuckled, pulling out a chair and joining them at the table. "What's the big deal about Millsap, anyway? One politician's the same as another."

She stared at me, her blue-gray eyes widening in disbelief. "What do you mean, what's the big deal?" she demanded angrily. "Have you forgotten that Millsap's prosecutors didn't even object when little Troy Kellerman had to climb on the stand, face his daddy, and that creep hollered out, "Hi, Troy!" They didn't ask for a mistrial or anything! That baby froze right in front of everyone and the judge had to throw the whole damn case out of court! What kind of District Attorney allows a child to go through something like that? Especially with the kind of evidence we had! Do you honestly think the Troy Kellerman case is the only case he's let go down the toilet?

"Be careful what you say, Kid!" PoPo interrupted sternly. "You have a Board of Directors to answer to, and they won't like you givin' political views in their name."

"I said I'd do it as a private citizen."

"Calm down, Kid," PoPo interjected soothingly. "Your job is to find missin' kids, not to take on the Good Ol' Boy Establishment of San Antone, Texas. You'd best stay outa this fight."

But Carolyn remained in the thick of it, just as I knew she would. She went on television and radio programs, interviewed with print reporters, and spoke before every group she could think of about the failures of Sam Millsap's office, especially in the field of child abuse. She didn't tell any lies and she spouted off statistics and she told stories like no one else could tell them. She was a one-woman wrecking crew on a mission and there was nothing anyone could do to stop her.

It was time for me to move on.

When I told Carolyn that I just couldn't work with her anymore, I gave her every excuse I could think of: I lived too far away, the traffic was too congested, my daughter needed me too much, my husband missed me, and I wanted to write. I really believed that our friendship had a better chance of surviving our very different personalities if we had some distance between us, and I really hoped that perhaps together we could still have an impact on our city if I moved out of her sphere of influence. To her credit, she was sympathetic and understanding and wished me the best.

I wished her the best, too, but deep inside I knew that she was a train wreck just waiting to happen. I also knew that I didn't want to be around when it did. In other words, the only thing I didn't tell her when I left was the truth.

Once I was safe in my own home and away from Texas Child Search, my relationship with Carolyn changed entirely. I returned to writing, and was actually able to remain focused on the goals that I had had for years. For the first time in months, I felt as if *I* was controlling my destiny, not Carolyn. For the first time in months, I got out of bed in the morning with a sense of purpose, a schedule that allowed me to do all that I wanted to do, and a set of goals that were exciting to me. For the first time in months, I wasn't confusing my identity with that of anyone else.Once again I was getting my life back.

And then, in June 1986, incumbent Sam Millsap lost his race for District Attorney to newcomer Fred Rodriguez. When Carolyn Huebner, in her typical grandiose fashion, took credit for his defeat, both publicly and privately, she added one more powerful name to an ever-growing list of people that would be more than happy to pay her back when the opportunity came.

In November, Carolyn called to tell me that she and Larry had separated and he had moved into a guest apartment belonging to one of her board members. From now on, she said, everything was going to be perfect on Elm Street...

I wasn't sure I had heard her correctly. "What are you talking about, everything's gonna be perfect?" I blurted out finally. "No one else is crazy enough to put up with you, Carolyn!"

Carolyn snorted. "No one needs to put up with me for very long. I just want to get nailed to the sheets once in awhile, that's all—no questions asked." Chuckling softly, she added, "And Larry sure ain't the guy to do *that*! But there're lots of guys out there that will."

I shook my head, confused. There was that west Texas accent again, and that shrill tone in her voice, and a blatant, in-your-face sexuality that I hadn't noticed before. Talking with Carolyn was becoming just a little awkward these days because half the time I wasn't even sure who I was talking to...

"Besides," she drawled, "we're gettin' along a lot better now since we ain't livin' together. We always did. We're great buddies, y'know? We gotta just leave it at that."

"What about Audra?" I asked finally.

"Aw, you know Audra." Carolyn snorted again. "She don't give a flip about Larry. Treats him like crap anyways. She'll be nicer to him if she don't see him so much."

"Well, I guess he'll see her on weekends..."

"At my house," Carolyn interrupted quickly. "He can see her on weekends at my house—if I'm at home. Otherwise he'll have to see her at Leola's place."

I was suddenly exhausted. This woman didn't recognize reality even when it stared her right in the face. "Carolyn, that's crazy. You know you can't dictate visitation. Larry's gonna have her on weekends and holidays just like everybody else. Besides, he's got the money, not you. He's going to get a real good attorney and you're not going to call the shots like you have up until now."

"I sure as hell am." Her voice was low and determined. "He ain't gonna hurt me no more, and he sure ain't gonna hurt my Dootie. He knows I can stop him. And I will."

This conversation was so creepy that I could actually feel the hair lift on the back of my neck. I was finished with the whole discussion. "Carolyn, I need to hang up now. We'll talk later, okay?"

"You think I'm nuts."

"Don't be silly."

"You do. You think I'm nuts."

"Whatever you say. I'm hanging up now."

"There's stuff you don't know that's happened in my house, Ronni," Carolyn whispered suddenly. "Stuff between Larry and Audra...just once...over a year ago..."

Something icy and fierce gripped my heart like a vise; it was all I could do to breathe. I had been here before—too many times to count—and I didn't want to come back here again. I couldn't believe what I was hearing.

Still, suddenly, I could see answers where there hadn't been any before. Suddenly I could understand Larry's need to appease his wife and even his child—it was a common enough practice when there was a question of sexual abuse involved. Suddenly I could appreciate Carolyn's disrespect and hostility toward him—any woman worth her salt would have behaved the same way. But what I couldn't comprehend for the life of me was why she had stayed with him for all this time.

"Can you tell me what happened, Carolyn?" I asked finally.

As she related the story to me, I was intrigued by how cold and distant she sounded, like it had happened to someone else—and to someone else's child. She had apparently even managed to give it a label: *the incident between Larry and Audra.* It was hard for me to understand any of this because every time I had to tell my daughter's experience to anyone, my voice still shook and tears still streamed down my cheeks and it was still all I could do not to throw up. But apparently Carolyn could catalogue her life in such a way that nothing could touch her if she didn't want it to.

I had to ask the question. "Why did you stay with him, Carolyn?"

"Well, where else was I gonna go? If I left him, I would've had to close down Child Search—and Child Search was all I had…"

Suddenly, without any warning, her ability to compartmentalize so thoroughly made me angrier than I had ever been before in my life. More times than I could count, I had listened to her trash other women for staying with men that abused their children—where was the difference? Why was it acceptable for her to remain with a man who thought that masturbating in front of his daughter was nothing more than *bad judgment,* for God's sake? Just because of Texas Child Search? How could she have ever, *ever* left that little girl alone with him for even five minutes? What made her any better than anyone else?

I tried to control my rage. "What's so different now?" I asked quietly.

"Fred Rodriguez wants me to interview for a position as a child advocate in the Family Violence Unit," Carolyn interrupted, her voice squeaking with excitement. She was apparently unaware of how angry I was—or, if she knew, she didn't care. "If I get it, I'm closing down Child Search." She paused, then added, "Unless you want it."

"No. Absolutely not."

"That's what I thought," she chuckled. "So, anyway, I'll have an income…"

I shook my head in disbelief. "You're kidding, right?"

"Of course I'm not kidding! I'll be making my own money and I won't have to be worrying about Larry and Audra all the time. It'll be perfect, Ronni. I'll be working *inside* the system instead of always being on the outside looking in, like some little kid with her nose squashed up against a window…"

"Be careful," I warned. "Rodriguez is no different than any other politician—he can turn on you in a heartbeat. You're nothing to him."

"You're wrong, Ronni. He cares about kids, he really does. And I'll have so much more clout working *in* his office than *outside* of it."

Once I realized that she truly believed what she was saying, my anger disappeared as quickly as it had come. Nothing else mattered except that I had to make her see reason. Taking a deep breath, I plunged in. "Carolyn, you have power right now because *you don't answer to anyone.* You're a loose cannon out here and they can't control you. But once you go to work in there, Carolyn, they own you. You know that."

"You're wrong, Ronni," she persisted. "They'll listen to me! And to you, too. They'll listen to you because I'll be in there, *making* them listen…"

I could see it coming. Just as she had so many times before, Carolyn was going to take on all the problems of the world and try to solve them. I had never felt such a terrible sense of impending catastrophe, such an appalling premonition of loss and ruin…

In her usual out-of-control manner, Carolyn Huebner was careening down a murky path toward her destiny and there was nothing I could do to stop her.

# CHAPTER TWENTY-TWO

1987 promised to be a kick-ass year for pedophiles, child killers and kiddie porn entrepreneurs in the big city. Or at least that's how it seemed to Carolyn, who was looking at the latest stack of files threatening to topple over on her desk in the Bexar County Family Violence Unit.

Although she had originally been hired to work as an advocate/liaison between the unit and outside attorneys, victims, and sometimes the courthouse staff itself, Carolyn had begun to function more as a jack-of-all-trades—mainly, she thought, because her overall law enforcement experience was so wide-ranging. In addition to her liaison duties, she was now performing what amounted to investigation review, making certain that every individual and all documents related to a case were accounted for and in order. She also prepared children to testify in court by taking them to the very courtroom in which their cases would be heard. However, although her workload was diverse and somewhat satisfying, it wasn't sufficiently time-consuming.

Not surprisingly, Carolyn had discovered early on that her boss, Joel Fischer, couldn't keep her busy enough. The two prosecuting attorneys that she had been assigned to assist, Caitlin Fowler (who had become one of her new best friends) and Blake Thurmond, couldn't keep her occupied, either. Within just a couple of weeks, she was helping all the lawyers in the Family Violence Unit with their cases, making the rounds at the courthouse to keep up with the local gossip, and visiting the Sheriff's Office just to find out what was going on in the county.

Now, sitting at her desk, Carolyn clasped her hands behind her head and tried to mentally recap how she had come to be here. As usual, everything had gone down so fast that she wasn't quite sure how it had happened. She was just grateful that it had...

After Carolyn had been interviewed by Bexar County's newly elected District Attorney, Fred Rodriguez, he had invited her to suggest some changes that she thought might make the Family Violence Unit more effective. Thrilled that he had actually *requested* her input, she hadn't wasted any time. With the help of one of her board members, Carolyn had outlined her ideas, submitted them almost immediately, and then held her breath. She had never wanted a job as desperately as she wanted this one.

In early December 1986 Carolyn had invited Larry to lunch and they spent hours talking about their hopes and goals for the New Year. Their conversation had been so strange, more like best girlfriends chatting over coffee than a separated husband and wife, but that was what Carolyn had most missed about Larry. When things were comfortable between them, Mr. and Mrs. Huebner could be like two little old ladies gossiping together on the front porch.

"Wouldn't it be great if I got this job?" she had asked, giving a little bounce of excitement in her chair at the kitchen table. "Just think…l'il ol' me! In the DA's office!"

"Have you found anyone to take over Child Search?" Larry asked. "You know… just in case?"

"Well, I mentioned it to Ronni, but she doesn't want it. I don't blame her, but I don't know anyone else I could turn it over to."

"Maybe we should just cross that bridge when we come to it, okay? Let's see if you get that job first."

Perhaps *because* they were no longer living together as man and wife, they had actually managed to return to being best friends. Carolyn found herself looking forward to hearing from him in the evenings and often thought of how much he would have enjoyed this concert or that trip had they been together. She had even stopped seeing other men, at least for the most part, and once again she told Larry nearly everything, just as she had done in the earliest days of their relationship. And when she finally received a firm job offer in mid-December, she and Larry were both thrilled beyond words.

By the second day of the New Year, Carolyn had gone to work in the Family Violence Unit. Even though she had always enjoyed the luxury of her home-office, she was delighted with her windowless little space in the Bexar County courthouse. Since no one in law enforcement ever worked in extravagant surroundings, Carolyn liked the fact that she had only a desk and two uncomfortable chairs, a computer, a set of inexpensive bookshelves, and one lonely file cabinet. The set-up actually made her feel like she belonged.

This was the place where she was ultimately going to make a huge difference in her community, she was sure of it. This was the place where everything she had gone through in her life was going to pay off.

At about the same time and in a supreme effort to make everything look normal to everyone else, Carolyn invited Larry to move back home. People appeared to think that was best for her family—especially her mother. Betty Shaw seemed determined to let her know during every phone conversation that she wasn't surprised Carolyn couldn't keep her husband happy. Consequently, since Larry's co-workers were pleased and her board members were thrilled, Carolyn was sure she was doing the right thing.

The only person in the group who disagreed with Carolyn's decision was Ronni. In fact, she more than disagreed. Her voice had sounded cold, distant, and almost angry when Carolyn told her that Larry had come back, but that was all right. Carolyn understood. After all, only Ronni and Dan Marshall knew the truth about *the incident between Larry and Audra.* No one else had a clue. Ronni was just concerned about Audra's safety. And while Carolyn had tried several times to reassure her, it was clear that Ronni remained unconvinced.

But Carolyn wasn't worried. Larry knew that he wouldn't live to see another sunrise if he ever did anything so stupid again. Audra would be just fine.

She had to be.

The bottom line was, Carolyn had to depend on other people to worry about Audra. Her job in the DA's office was far too important for her not to give it her full attention, even though it didn't require nearly as much physical energy as she had hoped it would. In fact, she was actually thinking that she could continue heading up Texas Child Search if she handled her schedule carefully. She had never required much sleep and she really hated having too much time on her hands...

Without warning Carolyn's office door, which she had left ajar, swung open. Her boss, a swarthy-faced man with salt-and-pepper hair and a huge handlebar mustache, stood in the doorway holding several files in his arms. "Excuse me," Joel Fischer said apologetically, "but do you have a minute?"

"Sure. Come on in."

"Thanks." He dumped his files on top of Carolyn's desk beside her computer and absently moved a silver-framed photograph of Audra away from the increasingly high stack of paperwork. "I've got a real problem, Carolyn."

"Can I help?"

He rubbed his impressive mustache thoughtfully and looked away from her. "Maybe. I hope so. When you were working with Child Search, how many missing kids do you think you saw the files for?"

"I don't know—hundreds, I'd guess."

"Do you still have the files?"

"Sure. Some of them are packed away, but I have them."

"If I gave you pictures of kids to look at, do you think you might recognize one of them from your Child Search days?"

"It's possible." Cocking an eyebrow, Carolyn looked pointedly at the new files. "What's this about?"

"Have you been following the Ray Moberg case at all?"

"Just what I've heard on the news...that his stepdaughter is missing." Carolyn paused, then added gently, "Mr. Fischer, don't you want to sit down?"

"No, thanks, I'm fine. Debbie Moberg disappeared on January 9th right out of her mother's house, but she's no runaway. She's dead and I know in my gut that Moberg killed her. But we don't know where she is and he's not telling us. It's hard to prosecute without a body. It can be done, but it's hard. If we got something else on him, it would be a lot easier—he might even start singing for his supper. He raped his daughter—she's eight years old—and she's willing to testify against him, but you know how those cases go. They're never a sure thing."

Carolyn frowned, waiting for him to get to his point, but he remained quiet. Finally, a little uneasy, she decided to prod him. "Sir, I'm not following you..."

Fischer drummed his fingers on top of one of his files. "The cops got these photos from Moberg's house. Although we might not be able to get him for the murder of his stepdaughter or even the rape of his child, we can still get him for kiddie porn or aggravated sexual assault or indecency..."

"That sounds like a good plan, Sir...but I'm *still* not following you. What do you need *me* to do?"

"Moberg is in a lot of these pictures with these kids and we don't know who they are." Fischer looked sick to his stomach, but he managed to continue, "We can still get him, even without a child's verbal testimony, but it would be a lot easier if we knew who at least one of them was. Besides, these are just babies and we need to find them. They need help. I thought you might take a look at the pictures for us, Carolyn. I thought maybe you could ID a kid or two. I know it's a long shot, but it might pay off."

Carolyn's breath caught in her throat, but she didn't let on. Instead, she shrugged and nodded like it was nothing. "Sure. I can do that."

"I'm warning you—they're graphic as hell..."

Carolyn met his worried gaze head-on. "It won't be the first time I've seen nasty pictures of creeps with kids, Mr. Fischer. Do you have any idea how many victims there are?"

"I've counted close to a hundred."

Carolyn closed her eyes and gave a long, soft whistle. "Sweet Jesus..."

"I'm afraid that Jesus doesn't have anything to do with this, Carolyn. Moberg is the devil incarnate and I want him. Hell, we *all* want him. Can you help?"

"You know I'll do everything I can."

"Well, just do your best. I don't expect any more than that."

Once Fischer had left her office and closed the door behind him, Carolyn reached for a single file with an ice-cold hand—but she couldn't make herself touch it. All she could do was stare at that stack of paperwork and shake her head. The poetic irony didn't escape her. You thought you were going to get out of the sewer, she told herself, slightly amused. You thought the DA's office would be easier...

As Carolyn flipped on her desk lamp and pulled the files toward her, she was forced to accept the fact that once again she had been wrong. It wouldn't be easier. It wouldn't be easier at all.

Fifteen years earlier, as a terrified child imprisoned in a cheap motel room, Carolyn had looked into the smoldering eyes of Art Lovell and recognized the face of evil. Years later, while working in Texas Child Search, she had come to believe that she had seen all the wickedness that human beings could commit upon each other. She was positive that she could no longer be surprised, or shocked, or even disgusted.

After all, she once sat across from Henry Lee Lucas in a north Texas jail and listened to him describe how he had murdered young girls and raped kids and had sex with dead women and animals. She had accompanied grieving parents to their local morgues and held them in her arms as they tried to identify the often decomposing bodies of their murdered children. She had gone after child molesters in day care centers, and pederasts in Boy Scout troops, and parents that sold their kids to the highest bidders. For the longest time, she had been sure that she had seen it all.

But now, as Carolyn spent countless hours scrutinizing the Polaroid photographs of Ray Moberg sexually attacking little girls barely out of diapers, she knew that she hadn't even skimmed the surface. In picture after picture, as she carefully studied victim after victim, she struggled against the visual reality of vaginal invasion and oral assault and anal penetration of toddlers. She did everything she could to disregard the blood and mucous and seminal fluid…but the stomach-churning stack of photographs just seemed to go on and on and on.

Still, Carolyn assured herself, she had seen so many pictures like these over the years that Moberg's physical acts of brutality against the children weren't really registering in her psyche at all. She forced herself to look at each image just long enough for it to seep deeply into her subconscious, then compartmentalized what she saw. This way, no matter how vicious the photos were, they couldn't actually *touch* her. It was a methodical system that had always worked before.

Yet something different was happening this time. This time the images that burned themselves into her mind and into her memory were images of the little girls' *faces*—not their genitals. She dreamed about them when she went to sleep at night and she saw them first thing in the morning. She felt their terror and tasted their tears when she held her own child in her arms. Every time she went through the pictures, bile and nausea burned the back of her throat but she kept going through them, over and over and over, until she had finally accomplished her mission.

Within just a couple of days Carolyn had recognized and identified two of the children from cases that she had worked in Child Search a few years earlier and that made it all worth it. Or so she thought.

Carolyn couldn't tell that it mattered much to the Family Violence Unit, not in the long run. In fact, it seemed to her that, with every day that passed, the attorneys became more and more patronizing, gave her busy work that anyone with a grade school education could handle, and kept her away from cases that had any real substance.

It just didn't make sense to Carolyn. Why had they bothered to hire her if they didn't want to draw on her unique experience? Why had District Attorney Fred Rodriguez himself bothered to tell her that he admired her spirit and drive if he had no intention of encouraging his prosecutors to use it?

Sometimes she felt like she had burned most all of her bridges when she had decided to go to work in the DA's office. She didn't talk to Ronni as often as she had before because Ronni was writing all the time now; besides, they didn't seem to have nearly as much in common as they had during the Child Search days. She seldom saw PoPo or any of her other board members, and Larry was working even more hours with Valero now than he had before their separation. She visited with a couple of the attorneys in the unit every once in awhile and her boss seemed to like her, but...

"Hey, Carolyn, wait up!"

Startled, Carolyn halted and stood uncertainly on the courthouse steps, shading her eyes from the afternoon sun and squinting toward the familiar but disembodied voice. She didn't wave and head back up the steps until she recognized her old friend and former board member, Ricardo Calderone.

"Hey, there, Rick, how are you?"

"I'm good, Carolyn, real good. Everything okay with you?"

Carolyn shifted her briefcase from one hand to the other and gave him a big hug. She hadn't seen him in months—ever since they had last met on the Troy Kellerman case—but he was still the same Ricardo: tall and husky with thick, wavy, blue-black hair and a great grin that exposed shockingly white teeth. She hugged him again.

"I'm terrific, thanks. I thought you'd come around the DA's office to see me once in awhile. You must be busy."

"You got that right. Say, Carolyn, can I talk to you a minute?"

Carolyn felt around in her purse for her cigarettes, then caught herself and stopped. Sick and tired of the chronic bronchial infections she had been suffering for the last few years, she had quit smoking after she had gone to work in the unit. "Sure. What's going on?"

"Let's go over here in the shade, okay? It's a little more...private."

Frowning, Carolyn followed him to a concrete bench beneath an ancient oak tree and sat down. She knew better than to push or hurry Rick; he would say what he had to say in his own good time. Yet she could tell by his thundercloud expression that something had him more than a little irritated.

"Come on, Rick," she said finally, "what's going on?"

"Actually, that's what I'd like to know. What's going on in the DA's office, Carolyn? Since when does Joel Fischer not return an attorney's phone calls?"

"What're you talking about?"

"I'm talking about Harold Best."

"Okay. Who the hell is Harold Best?"

"Are you serious? You've never heard of him? Everyone's heard of Harold Best."

Carolyn sighed and shook her head. "Okay, I'm an idiot. I haven't."

"Well, all you need to know is that he's a very rich, very powerful man in this city, and I'm representing his wife in her battle to keep custody of their little girl. Or, rather, I'm trying to. We have evidence—good, hard, medical evidence—that he has sexually abused his daughter quite significantly…"

"How old is she?" Carolyn interrupted quickly.

"She'll be four in a couple of weeks."

"Four!"

Rick held up his hand. "Please, Carolyn, let me finish. I don't have much time. Anyway, the police filed the case against him a couple of months ago and the DA's office—which was then being run by Millsap—should have taken it before a Grand Jury for indictment before Fred Rodriguez even took over. But nobody has."

"Maybe it got lost in the shuffle."

"Sure it did," he responded sarcastically. "Anyway, whatever the reason, the case hasn't seen the light of day and I haven't seen a damn thing about it anywhere. In other words, Harold Best, who's being represented by a top-notch defense attorney, has disappeared from the radar completely."

Carolyn frowned. "Why is he being represented by a defense attorney if no one's filed any charges?"

"Covering his ass, probably. But he wants full custody of his daughter, and he's retained Ray-Don Leonard to help him get it."

Carolyn whistled in appreciation. "He can afford Ray-Don Leonard?"

"He can. He's also very good friends with our illustrious sheriff, and he's spent a couple of summer vacations with the head of Commissioner's Court—who recently got him a position on the Coliseum Board. None of this means a damn thing except that he knows people, and that can hurt us. A lot. For all I know, it already has. Our custody hearing would go so much better if we had our indictment, but we're running out of time—and I can't get Joel Fischer to call me back."

Suddenly annoyed, Carolyn ran her fingers through her short, curly hair and met Rick's angry gaze with a fiery one of her own. "So, what do you want *me* to do about it? Fischer's my boss, for God's sake! I can't tell him whose phone calls to return!"

"I don't want you to *do* anything, Carolyn," he said in the same unruffled manner he had always used when she got too heated up. "I just want to know what the delay is, that's all. I thought maybe you could find out for me."

Tears of frustration burned behind Carolyn's eyelids; she was grateful for her dark sunglasses because she didn't know why on earth she always seemed so ready to cry. All she knew was that she needed to get away from Ricardo Calderone just as soon as she could. To her mind, this conversation only emphasized how helpless she really was.

She took a deep breath and fought for calm. "I'm sorry, Rick. I didn't mean to jump on you. But the thing is, if the case was in our office I'd know it. It would have come across my desk. Trust me on this, Rick—the file isn't there."

"Please, Carolyn… I'm begging you…"

Everywhere she looked, someone wanted something from her…

Finally Carolyn stood up. "I'll check it out," she promised, picking up her purse and briefcase. "Give me a day or two and I'll call you."

"Thank you, Carolyn," Rick responded fervently, obviously relieved. "My client is getting panicked—and, honestly, so am I. This little girl is in a lot of danger. If her father gets custody of her, she's done for…"

Carolyn didn't even answer. She just walked away from him, feeling more disturbed and isolated than ever as she headed back to her office. Rick was right to be concerned, she thought, because she had never known there to be any connection between a criminal sexual abuse case and a civil custody matter. In her experience, the two had always been completely separate. If there was solid evidence against this man, he should have been indicted. It didn't matter who he was, and it didn't matter how much money and power he had…

Carolyn picked up her pace. There *has* to be a reason for this situation, she assured herself, now taking the courthouse steps two at a time. It *has* to be an oversight on Rick's part. Surely Fred Rodriguez or Joel Fischer wouldn't engage in cover-ups that might jeopardize the safety of children.

By the time Carolyn reached her office and closed the door firmly behind her, she was wheezing and out of breath. Most everyone was still at lunch and even the phones were silent, so the normally bustling unit was actually quiet. Turning on her computer monitor, Carolyn typed in the alleged perp's name with shaking fingers: *Best, Harold.*

There it was, right on her screen: the case had been logged in on the computer on December 6, 1986, by a Lt. Robert Martinez, SAPD. The accused: Harold Joseph Best, owner of Best Bedding and Accessories, Inc. The victim: his daughter Kelly Lynn Best, three years old. It was just as Rick had said.

So, where was the case file? Why hadn't she seen it? If the police had had enough evidence to present to the DA's office that long ago, this Harold Best should have been indicted within two weeks—three at the outside. But here it was, already February, and there was no sign of any activity at all.

Carolyn quickly jotted down the case number on a slip of paper and dropped it into her handbag, then shut down her computer and left her office. For the first time since she had begun working in the unit, she actually felt the need to protect herself—but she wasn't sure from whom. She closed the door firmly behind her.

Carolyn wasted no time getting to the all-important Central Filing office located in the center of the courthouse; she stepped up to a small window. Taking the slip of paper with the *Harold Best* case number from her bag, she pushed it across a counter. A young woman seated at an old metal desk stood up, shoved the last bite of a MacDonald's hamburger into her mouth, and wiped her hands on a napkin.

"Yes, ma'am?"

"I'm sorry to interrupt your lunch," Carolyn said with a smile, "but I'm an advocate with the DA's office and we can't find this case file. Can you see if it's here?"

"Let me check." The clerk took the slip of paper, looked at the number, and headed toward the rear of the file-stuffed room. After several minutes she returned to the window, shaking her head. "I'm sorry. It's been checked out."

"Are you sure?" Carolyn frowned. "Maybe you could look again..."

"I've already looked twice, ma'am. It's been checked out."

"Okay, thanks."

Carolyn hurried back to her office. This is good, she assured herself, fighting her rising panic. The list of places where the file might be had narrowed considerably. It had to be in the hands of some investigator—there were three, after all—or in the possession of an assigned prosecutor. In fact, they might even now be in the process of preparing the case to go before the Grand Jury...

Carolyn breathed a sigh of relief. The more she thought about it, the better she felt. Now that she knew for certain the case file had been checked out, probably by someone in her unit, it shouldn't be any big deal to find it.

Letting herself back into her office, Carolyn dropped her purse onto her desk and stared blindly at her blank computer screen. In less than a half-hour, she thought, just about everyone would be returning from lunch and she could begin asking around. Then, almost immediately, she changed her mind. She would work this alone. She knew that she needed to be very careful whenever she worked *inside* the system; asking too many questions could sometimes alert the wrong people.

Carolyn crossed the hallway and entered Caitlin Fowler's office, which was wide open, as usual. Her good friend's desk was covered with information about Ray Moberg, the horrific case to which she had unfortunately been assigned, and a few scattered phone messages, but nothing else. Carolyn moved on to the office of the other attorney she had been hired to assist, Blake Thurmond, but it was impeccably neat, as always, and there wasn't a single loose file lying around anywhere.

Finally, more out of a hopeful last-ditch effort than any kind of true hunch, Carolyn walked down the hall to Joel Fischer's office. She stood there for just a moment, then looked around uncertainly and knocked on the door. If he answered, she would have to come up with some reason for wanting to see him. If he didn't, she would just let herself in. After all, she was only hunting down a case file that she should have seen weeks ago. She wasn't breaking any laws...

There was no response.

Taking a deep breath, Carolyn opened the door and walked inside, gazing around the office with almost clinical detachment. There were family photos on top of a file cabinet, diplomas and certifications on the wall behind his desk, and a set of red-and-gold law books in his bookcase. His *In Box* contained phone messages and a few unopened letters; his *Out Box* was empty. There was nothing unusual. Then, just as she was turning to leave, she spotted a few manila folders resting haphazardly near the back of his desk.

Not even caring that the door was open and Fischer was due back from lunch any moment, Carolyn rifled through the files, checking the labels on the computer-printed tabs. Two names were familiar to her; one was that of a wealthy Texas banker and the other a prominent real estate developer, but neither were important to Carolyn. It was the last file that caught her notice, the file labeled *Best, Harold*.

Carolyn didn't even open it; she didn't care. It obviously wasn't meant for her eyes, and that was okay with her. All that mattered to her was that now she could call Rick Caldarone and tell him to calm down. Everything was going to be fine.

Joel Fischer, Carolyn's own boss, was personally going to give this case his full attention.

On Saturday morning Carolyn got up early, took her shower, wrapped herself in a warm, fluffy bathrobe, and padded downstairs for her first cup of coffee. She could hear Audra's high-pitched baby-laughter bursting from the kitchen as she responded to something a teasing Leola said, but the warm sounds of domesticity and family didn't soothe Carolyn's ragged nerves. She was too tired to enjoy much of anything. Ever since she had seen that stack of Moberg photos, she hadn't had a decent night's sleep.

If there was anything Carolyn wished she could do, she wished she could talk to Larry about her work in the DA's office—but she knew she couldn't. For one thing, he was far too busy with his own job, which was a good thing since he was the primary breadwinner for the family. He also traveled a lot, frequently flying off with other executives in Valero's plush Lear jet to some part of the country where he would negotiate another important transaction for his company. Although Carolyn missed him when he was away, it wasn't any big deal. She missed him like she missed the comfort of a well-broken-in pair of shoes.

Nowadays, whenever Larry let her know he was leaving town again, Carolyn played the good wife role to the hilt. Smiling and cheerful, she saw to it that his bags were packed and he had everything he needed, but they kissed and hugged good-bye at the front door like casual acquaintances. The truth is, Carolyn often thought ruefully, we probably both breathe a huge sigh of relief every time he has to leave home.

Now he was gone again, and Carolyn had the weekend to herself. Yawning, she made her way into the kitchen, waved sleepily at Audra and Leola, and aimed for the gurgling coffee pot at the back of the cluttered counter. Fumbling through cookbooks and pill bottles, she pushed aside a single paper plate dotted with names and phone numbers and finally found her favorite mug. She poured herself some steaming black coffee and rubbed her eyes.

"I thought I'd straighten this kitchen today," Leola said in a bright, energetic voice that made Carolyn want to slap her. "That counter's a mess. Is there anything up there that's important?"

"Good grief, Ohler—I don't know! Leave it alone. I'll take care of it." Carolyn made her way to the kitchen table and sat down. "Has Larry called this morning?"

"Nope. Were you thinking he would?"

Carolyn snorted. "Not hardly. I was just asking."

That was a joke. When she and Larry had first gotten back together, they had promised each other to give their relationship everything they had, but their promises had turned up empty, like all the others. Perhaps they had grown so far apart that they could no longer even *see* each other, much less connect on any level, but the fact was that Carolyn and Larry—the two former best friends who had once been able to talk about practically anything—just didn't talk much anymore.

"Are you two fighting again?" Leola asked in a voice so soft that Audra, who was playing with some building blocks in a corner, didn't hear.

"Of course not, Ohler. It takes too much energy to fight."

Leola's shrewd black eyes narrowed. "You should talk to him about your work, Carolyn. He could help you."

Carolyn snorted again and shook her head. "He can't help me, Ohler. I wish he could, but he can't."

There was a very subtle reason that she refused to discuss her work with Larry, although she was ashamed to admit it to anyone. It was all she could do to admit it to herself. But the truth was, she was terrified that she might say something wrong, something that would trigger him to engage in some perverted sexual act with his own daughter. Intellectually she knew that the odds of that happening were slim-to-none, but emotionally she wasn't certain at all.

"Carolyn, do you want this?"

Startled from her thoughts, Carolyn splashed hot coffee on the table and swore under her breath. She glanced at the ragged-edged paper plate that Leola was holding in the air. "What's that?"

"It's your own special filing system, I guess. You want me to throw it out?"

"No, there might be something important on it." Carolyn winked and added in an ominously low voice, "A secret code…or a hidden treasure…or the name of a CIA agent… You never know."

"All right, all right!" Chuckling, Leola turned back to the counter. "I'll just put it here by the phone."

"Thanks, Ohler."

Rubbing her temples, Carolyn downed the last of her coffee and looked over at her daughter, who was still playing quietly in the corner. She was such a beautiful child, Carolyn thought, invaded by a sudden deep and inexplicable sadness. Audra, cozily wrapped up in her favorite Winnie the Pooh jammies, was tiny and slender, blonde with wide blue-gray eyes, an uncanny replica of her mother at the same age. Carolyn's throat thickened with tears. She had to do better. She had to give more…

Carolyn ducked her head to hide her tears. "Come here, Dootie," she said softly, holding her arms out, "come here and give your mama a hug."

# CHAPTER TWENTY-THREE

"Excuse me, Carolyn. Can you come in here a minute?"

Sighing, Carolyn looked at the aging man everyone called 'the last string investigator' and tried to tuck the stack of files she was lugging to her office more firmly beneath her chin. Wiley Arnold should have retired at least five years earlier and no one had an inkling why he was still working in the DA's office, but he was. At least no one gave him anything important to do and Carolyn was grateful for that. She was getting tired of running after people and cleaning up their messes.

"Can't it wait, Wiley? I've got tons of work to do..."

"No," he interrupted brusquely, "it can't wait. I need to show you something."

"Oh, c'mon, Wiley, give me a break..."

"*Now*, Carolyn. I need to show you something *now*."

"Okay, okay. Let me put this stuff up and I'll be right back."

"Thanks. Hurry up, will you?"

Damn it all to hell, Carolyn thought furiously, stalking into her office and dropping the folders on her desk, what's got the old fool so upset this time? It wasn't like she didn't have enough to do! The United States Customs Department had just asked the DA's office to allow her to work in child pornography undercover stings for them periodically, which her boss had enthusiastically permitted, so she was now waiting for instructions from them. She was also trying to close down Texas Child Search without losing everything she had built, and she was running after everyone in the unit trying to clean up their messes... Sometimes she felt like a cornered rat racing back and forth in one of those perennial mazes without escape; she just knew she wouldn't be able to stop until she dropped dead of exhaustion.

Carolyn felt suddenly guilty. It wasn't like Wiley bothered her very often, and he was a really sweet old guy, so she supposed she could give him thirty minutes of her precious time.

Still waiting for her in the hallway, his nut-brown face taut with nervous intensity, Wiley gripped her forearm with iron fingers, pulled her into his office, and closed the door softly behind him. Walking to his desk, he picked up a legal-sized file resting beside his computer and handed it to Carolyn with a dramatic flourish.

"I thought you might want to see this."

She read the computer-printed name tab on the folder and her heart sank. This wasn't good. In fact, she couldn't think of anything worse. "How did you get this?"

"How do you think I got it? Joel gave it to me."

Carolyn frowned. That could only mean one thing, and she didn't like it. "Joel did? When?"

"The end of February."

Carolyn's heart gave a painful thud. "He gave you the Harold Best file at the end of February?"

"Yeah. I've had it about a week." Wiley gave a self-mocking grin and shrugged his slender shoulders. "You don't need to tell me what that means, Carolyn—I know. The cases that they want to forget about end up in this office. I don't give a damn about that. What I'm worried about is this kid."

I'm worried, too, Carolyn thought, but she said nothing. This case seemed to be following her around like a black shadow, haunting her. Every time she thought she had seen or heard the last of it, she ran into it again—but evidently she was the only one who did. No one else seemed to be bothered by it at all.

Yet toward the middle of February, right before Joel had apparently turned the Best file over to Wiley, an obviously agitated Rick Caldarone had phoned her again and asked her to check the computer one more time for an update on the case. Everything was taking way too long, he said, and something was seriously stinking in Denmark. This time Carolyn found that the status report read, *Investigation Complete – Awaiting Indictment, February 17, 1987.* She had breathed a huge sigh of relief.

But Rick hadn't been impressed. In fact, his voice had dripped with angry sarcasm. "Well, that's just great. Maybe you could tell me just when the hell this guy is gonna be arrested."

"Once he's indicted, they'll pick him up. You know the drill, Rick. These things take time."

"If you have money and power, they apparently take *lots* of time. Anyone else would be *under* the jail by now."

"Excuse me, Carolyn." Wiley's voice interrupted her thoughts and brought her abruptly back to the present. "Please look at that file, will you?"

Carolyn sat down at Wiley's desk and began going through the folder. The more she went through it, the more she learned that she hadn't known before. An excellent videotape had been made by a DHS social worker with little Kelly Lynn at the end of 1986, and as soon as he had learned that SAPD was filing charges against him, Harold Best had rushed straight over to his daughter's pediatrician to see what medical proof was available. Carolyn perused page after page of written statements and testimonials, report after report of physical evidence citing vaginal tearing, bruising, and penetration by unnamed objects, and she couldn't understand why none of this data had ever been presented to the Grand Jury. It just didn't make any sense.

Suddenly Carolyn's mouth went dry and the room began to spin. Perspiration popped out on her forehead and slid down the back of her neck. For a moment she couldn't even breathe as she stared in disbelief at the small photograph in front of her. A naked blonde toddler no more than three years old lay spread-eagled beneath a glass coffee table, her blue-gray eyes wide and provocative as she gazed deeply, searchingly, into the camera...*Audra...Audra, oh my God, Audra. Who took this picture of my Dootie?*

Carolyn fought a losing battle for orientation and balance. Her brain felt thick, coagulated, soggy—like oily leftover gravy. She couldn't hear herself think. There was a deep, gravelly voice railing somewhere in the background of her mind, but she couldn't understand him. He was angry, vicious...but she couldn't decipher his words...

*Oh, my God... Dootie... my Dootie ...*

Carolyn forced herself to look at the photograph again just to be sure she wasn't losing her mind. She wasn't. She knew she wasn't. The resemblance between Kelly Best and Audra Huebner was so strong, so uncanny, that only a blind person would miss it. It was surreal, unbelievable. Then, right before her eyes, the child's features began to melt and liquefy, slowly, like dripping candle wax—and her pale, haunted face became Carolyn's. The shadowed blue-gray eyes and stringy blonde hair and stubborn little chin were part and parcel of the child locked in that closet twenty-two years earlier...

Far, far away, she heard the whining, plaintive, reed-thin voice of Audra...or someone...young... Who was it...?

Slowly, breathlessly, as if she were swimming upward through Jello, Carolyn wrestled her way back to herself, the present, and the calm reality of Wiley's office. She took a deep breath and tried to push the voice—no, *all* the voices now scrambling to be heard—down into the secret hiding places where they had always lived. Then, very gradually and one by one, they began to dissipate and float off until they disappeared completely. For just a single fleeting moment, Carolyn allowed herself to luxuriate in pillow-soft silence.

Finally, managing a tremulous smile, she closed the folder and looked closely at Wiley, amazed that he seemed to have noticed nothing unusual in her behavior. For the first time since she had come to work here, she was glad that he was so lousy at his job.

"Can I make a copy of this?" She was amazed at the coolness in her own voice. It didn't even tremble.

"I've already done it." Wiley pulled out the bottom drawer of his desk and removed a file folder. "Here you go. But remember: you never got it from me."

"Of course not. You're a good man, Wiley. Thank you."

Wiley flushed with embarrassment, then cleared his throat and tried to sound big-guy tough. "Not a problem. These cases can get you right in the gut. But, listen, Carolyn, I want to show you something else. It's important."

"What's that?"

Wiley fished through a stack of paperwork beside his *In Box,* pulled out a single sheet of violet-hued stationery, and passed it across his desk to Carolyn. Her mouth fell open in astonishment as she read it. In a few sentences reminding Fred Rodriguez just how much assistance he and Mr. Best had given to his campaign, Best's attorney Ray-Don Leonard then finished his letter by asking that the District Attorney give him time to *straighten out this misunderstanding himself.* Carolyn had never seen anything so blatant in her life.

Folding the letter, she handed it back to Wiley and rubbed her fingers against her skirt. Her hand suddenly felt dirty. "Did Joel give you this, too?"

"Naturally. Now, listen. If you were to check the computer today for an update on the Harold Best case, Carolyn, you'd find that the status has been changed back to *Investigation Pending.* So, someone in this office is following orders. I don't know who, but someone, and it's not up to me to find out. It's not up to you, either."

"Then why did you give me this file?"

Wiley shrugged. "You're the only one who cares. I'm thinking that you're smart enough to figure out a way to protect this little girl, even if no one else wants to. But you need to be careful, Carolyn. I know Ray-Don Leonard and I know Harold Best. I've done side work for both of them. They're dangerous."

She frowned. "Investigative side work, you mean?"

"That's right."

"Good God. Does Joel know that, too?"

"I told him about it when he gave me this case, but he said it didn't matter. I think he's either wrong or he doesn't give a damn. I think it matters a lot. I think it's a conflict of interest that would get this case thrown out of court...if it ever gets that far."

"And that's the key, isn't it, Wiley?" Carolyn eased herself to her feet and tried to hide how shaky her legs still were. "Apparently someone doesn't intend for it to ever get that far."

"Ronni? I don't know if you remember me or not, but this is Lupe Caldarone, Rick's wife…"

"Of course I remember you," I interrupted warmly, leaning back in my swivel chair to ease my aching shoulder muscles and closing my eyes against the green glare of my word processing screen. The sentences were beginning to blur together. "We met at a Child Search board meeting last year, didn't we?"

"We did. I hate to bother you like this…"

"You're not bothering me at all," I interrupted again. I yawned and rubbed the back of my neck. "I'm glad to get a break. How can I help you?"

"I don't know if you can, Ronni, but I can't think of anyone else."

"Well, that certainly sounds mysterious. Try me."

"Rick is handling the divorce of a woman who has a four-year-old daughter. She discovered that her little girl was being sexually abused by her natural father, beginning back in 1985, but she never reported it to anyone because her husband is a very wealthy and politically influential man here in San Antonio and she was afraid to…"

"The mother *knew* this but she never reported it?"

"Not until November of 1986. I know what you're thinking, Ronni, I do. I don't understand it, either, but there it is."

"Lupe, the truth is, I don't get involved in this stuff anymore," I said firmly. "I've had to get out of it just to keep my own sanity. I'm really sorry, but…"

"Please, Ronni. You don't need to get involved. I just wanted to know if I could give your telephone number to our client. She's so upset and she doesn't know what to do, or how to handle her child, and I thought you might be able to talk with her if she needed to talk."

Against my better judgment, I gave in and permitted Lupe Caldarone to give my number to this unknown woman. And for the next few weeks I held my breath. Gradually I began to relax and even managed to go back to writing an article I had promised to have finished by the end of the month. I played with my family. I cleaned my house. I did normal things that normal women did, and I no longer jumped when the telephone rang. In short, I forgot all about her…

Until the morning of April 2, 1987.

This time when the phone rang, it interrupted my train of thought and I answered it abruptly, almost rudely, still glaring in frustration at my screen. The damn paragraph I was working on just wasn't right…

"Hello!"

"Is this Ronni?" A woman's unfamiliar voice was soft with uncertainty.

I frowned, still staring at the screen. What in the world was wrong with this paragraph? The transition was off, that was it... Just one sentence was haywire...

"Yes, it is."

"Ronni, you don't know me," the woman continued, "but my name is Glenda Best. My attorney's wife, Lupe Caldarone, gave me your number..."

I slammed back into reality with a painful thud. "Who?"

"I'm sorry. This isn't a good time. Maybe I should call later..."

I was so embarrassed I could hardly speak. "No, no – it's fine, Glenda! The phone just startled me, that's all. How can I help you?"

When Glenda launched into her story, all that really registered in my mind at that time was how frightened she was – of everything. She was afraid of her soon-to-be-ex-husband. She was afraid of his attorneys. She was afraid of the judges, the doctors, the social workers. She was even afraid of the friends that she and Harold Best had once shared; she was afraid of their position, their money, their power. This overwhelming fear was something that I had felt before in incest families, and it was the one thing that I could *not* relate to, even though I was also the mother of a sexually abused child. Yet I also knew that I didn't have the right to judge this woman. After all, I hadn't walked a single inch in her shoes.

But the one thing I could do, and did do, was *listen*. The more I listened, the more appalled I became. And the more appalled I became, the more difficult it was to keep my anger in check...

Finally I just couldn't take it anymore; I completely forgot my determination to remain uninvolved. Just as I had three years earlier, as president of my own organization, I thought of the child that no one was fighting for—no one except this mother who had taken her sweet time getting to this place. "I have a friend in the DA's office, Glenda. I'm going to see if she can tell me anything."

"Do you really?" She went almost breathless with excitement. "Rick says that Harold has the DA in the palm of his hand. Do you honestly think your friend could help?"

"Don't get your hopes up, Glenda. I don't know. But I know she'll check it out for me, if nothing else."

"Okay. I understand. But please tell her that our custody case goes to court on April 28th and if we don't get an indictment before then, I don't think we can win. Will you tell her that?"

"I'll tell her."

"What's your friend's name, Ronni?"

I was silent for a long moment. Even though that was more information than I was willing to give, I also realized that the three of us might soon be playing a very dangerous game. Glenda needed to be reassured about the accuracy of my information.

"Let's just call her *my little bird in the DA's office*, okay?"

"Little Bird it is, then. Thank you, Ronni. Thank you so much. I'll never forget this."

I was suddenly exhausted. "You're welcome, Glenda. Give me your number, and I'll call you back."

Carolyn gazed in disgust at a new legal-sized box that a Customs agent had just carried into her office and placed on her desk. She spoke softly into the telephone.

"Thanks for remembering my birthday, Ronni. Nobody else did."

"Nobody? Not even Larry?"

"Well, yeah... Larry sent flowers from Houston. He'll be there until Friday."

Just then Carolyn's intercom buzzed and a secretary's throaty voice interrupted. "Agent Roth wants you to call him as soon as possible, Carolyn. He says not to look in that box until he talks to you. Did you get that?"

"I got it, Lisa. Ronni, I'm sorry, but I've gotta go."

"Sure. Oh, wait, Carolyn—I nearly forgot! Listen, I just spent the last hour talking to one of Rick's clients. I wondered if you could check something out for me."

"Don't say anymore. We're talking about...um...*Father Knows Best*...right?"

"Father... Knows... Best... oh, right! That's right."

"Later, Ronni. I can't talk here."

"Gotcha. I'll wait for your call. 'Bye now."

Carolyn hung up the telephone slowly. She was sick to death of Harold Best and his cronies down at the courthouse. He was making her life—and that of Rick Caldarone—absolutely miserable. Everywhere they turned, he stopped them. Everyone they spoke to backed up, turned around, and played stupid. Every time they thought they might have made some headway, they ran into a brick wall and knocked themselves out. Joel had even told Rick during an accidental meeting at a local gas station that the DA's office was waiting to see what would happen at the civil hearing before they moved ahead on a criminal level. A dirty case just didn't get much more transparent than that.

There was no doubt in Carolyn's mind that Harold Best was being protected by her own department. Consequently, her involvement—and now Ronni's—was a waste of time. How many times had they talked about how kids had no voice in the United States simply because they weren't old enough to vote and they had no money to contribute to political parties? Countless times...

Still, Carolyn could tell by the hopeful note in Ronni's voice on the phone this afternoon that she actually believed there might be something that Carolyn *could* do. But why on earth would she think that? It was just as clear as a Texas sunrise: This little girl, this Kelly Lynn Best, was going to become yet another victim—not only of a rich and powerful pedophile—but of a legal system that just didn't give a damn.

Poor Rick, Carolyn thought helplessly. She had never seen him so torn up. She had called him immediately after her meeting with Wiley Arnold, and she had been afraid he was going to have a heart attack when she told him how the case was being stalled. Furiously, Rick had called Joel right away, but of course that phone call—like all his other ones—wouldn't be returned. Joel, Carolyn had discovered, was tossing those messages into the trash.

Now, in desperation, Carolyn turned her attention back to the large box on her desk. This was a case she could do something about. She didn't want to touch it, but she had no choice. Finally, adjusting the container so that she could see the name scrawled in black marker on the label, she winced when she read it: *Gallardo, Gary.*

Customs had been watching this guy for months and they had apparently pulled off a successful bust today. Now she had to call Agent Stephen Roth, a guy that was about as friendly as a scorpion, and find out what he needed from her. No matter what his preliminary instructions had been, she just had to take a look in that box. Just a peek, she told herself, nothing serious...

Lifting the lid slightly and peering inside, Carolyn caught her breath. There were hundreds of photos, hundreds and hundreds of photos—and she didn't have to look at a single one of them to know what they were. She knew. And she knew, without even asking, what it was that Agent Roth wanted her to do.

Carolyn closed her eyes, swallowed hard, and put the lid back on the box. It wasn't just any box. It was a Pandora's Box, and all the evil in one man's soul would soon be released – if not upon the world, then certainly upon the fragile psyche of an angry and frustrated woman.

The box labeled *Gallardo, Gary* contained 619 gut-wrenching pictures of naked children, and Carolyn went through every single one of them. Using a magnifying glass in an attempt to locate identifying marks on kids she might not otherwise recognize, she carefully studied children in all kinds of sexual positions with adults, other children, and even animals. She was advancing a cause much more important than the state of her own mental health, she told herself, and she was strong enough to do this. After all, no one else could. No one else had any idea who these children were. She didn't, either, but she had a better chance of spotting one or two, just as she had in the Ray Moberg case. The number of actual little victims was astronomical and unknown, but it didn't matter. The Customs folks believed in her. They *needed* her to do this for them. The children *needed* her...

And so, day after horrific day, hour after hour after hour, Carolyn poured over various-sized photographs of children being victimized and brutalized and terrorized within an inch of their sanity and their lives. And every day the work took another bite out of her soul.

She couldn't get away from it. She couldn't talk to anyone about it. Ronni was wrapped up in the Harold Best fiasco, and Larry was the last person she would even *mention* it to. Her house offered no respite because it felt cold and empty, more like a mausoleum than a home, and even the normal demands of her own child grated on her ragged nerves. Then, inexplicably and for the first time in years, the ugly memory of Art Lovell and all that he had meant in her life returned full force.

The nightmares came back with a vengeance and, with them, the voices. Some of them were voices she hadn't heard in a long, long time; others she had never heard before. They talked over her and through her and even inside of her. It was an onslaught of noise and Carolyn couldn't get away from it.

Carolyn knew that she was running closer and closer to burnout; the precipice loomed straight ahead and she was going right over the edge.

Sitting in front of Rick Caldarone's desk, I opened the Harold Best file, preparing to go through the multitudinous pages of medical information, court transcripts, and police reports just to be certain there wasn't anything here that I didn't know, but Rick's voice stopped me. "Hold up a minute. I nearly forgot. I have something you need to see."

My heart gave an extra thud before it settled into a regular pounding rhythm that was actually kind of frightening. If I left right now, I could get the hell out of this mess before it was too late—but I knew I wasn't going anywhere. This was something I was going to see all the way through, no matter what.

Rick pushed a large envelope toward me and its label made my heart sink: *Photos/Kelly Lynn Best/11X14*. I had worked with Carolyn, and in my own organization, long enough to know the filth and sadness that those photos would inevitably depict. I took a deep breath and steeled myself as I opened the envelope.

Although the naked little girl gazing sensuously up through a glass coffee table was breathtakingly beautiful, that wasn't what caught and held my attention. And even though she was obviously posed and clearly frightened, I wasn't focused on that, either. All I could see was that she bore an eerie resemblance to little Audra Huebner. It was a similarity so striking that I actually had to look twice to be sure I wasn't seeing double.

But I managed to keep my shock to myself and asked, "Do you know where this picture was taken?"

"In Best's living room back in 1985, right after he and his wife separated," Rick answered instantly. "She found several pictures of Kelly hidden in the bottom drawer of Harold's desk in his study at their house, but this was the only one that really jumped out at her as maybe being in the 'kiddie porn' category. There were also a couple of magazines in that drawer with pictures of kids that are in a vault here in the office. But she didn't confront him with any of it until sometime in 1986."

"What made her finally report the abuse to the police?" I asked curiously. That was something I had wanted to know from the beginning, but I hadn't felt comfortable asking. Now, since I was deliberately getting in so deep, I was determined to find out.

"Kelly didn't actually tell her mother what he was doing to her when she stayed with him until the end of 1986. She was just three years old. Glenda called DHS right away and they told her what to do. Kelly gave a very coherent statement to the police like they instructed, and then she did a good videotape with a social worker using dolls right afterward, so that immediately put Best on the defensive. Anyway, we got a court order stating that he couldn't be alone with her anymore, so she was safe—at least for the time being. At almost that exact same time, Best took out a six-month loan against one of his companies for $35,000 and gave it to Ray-Don Leonard as a retainer. She knew then that she was in for a fight."

"Have you seen the video, Rick?"

"I have."

"Is it that good?"

"It's very good. She's a really smart, well-spoken kid for three years old. By the way, Ronni, you know that she just turned four this February, right?"

I nodded and thought how strange it was that little Audra Huebner had had a birthday in February as well. She was almost exactly one year older.

"Has Joel Fischer seen this video?"

"Yes. He saw it in December of 1986 with a prosecuting attorney named Anna Kensington. She was with the 187th district court at that time, but she's no longer there."

"Figures," I muttered.

"And now Fischer claims he's never seen it. But I've talked to Miss Kensington and she swears that she was sitting right beside him when they watched it."

I whistled under my breath and turned my attention to the thick file still resting unopened on the desk in front of me. Opening it, I quickly skimmed a psychologist's report about Kelly and her allegedly too-dependent relationship with her mother and then looked at the author's name more carefully: *John Carroll, Ph.D.*

I didn't remember Glenda mentioning that this well-known San Antonio doctor had interviewed her daughter, but maybe she had... At any rate, the name rang a personal bell for me and I tried to scour my memory for cases I had specifically worked in which he was involved, but I couldn't place it. Regardless, I knew that he was a very important man in the medical community and that he was often hired by wealthy fathers seeking custody of their kids. Many of us in the child abuse field had no respect for him at all because we knew that he would say anything for a price.

"Some people I've worked with call John Carroll a pimp or a hired gun," I said, closing the file, "but I just call him a whore. He's dangerous."

"That's why we want this indictment to come down before the custody hearing is held on April 28th. If he's indicted, it won't matter what John Carroll or anybody else says. The judge will be forced to make sure that Kelly is protected from him until the criminal trial is over."

"But if he's *not* indicted, then Harold Best could actually win full custody, couldn't he?"

"That's right. And I believe someone in the DA's office is trying to pull that off."

"They've seen all this evidence?"

"All of it. But Joel Fischer apparently has no intention of doing anything with it except keep it under wraps for as long as he can. He's throwing away my messages and he's given the case to an incompetent investigator that's getting ready to retire. Carolyn told me all that."

"Well, she would know."

I leaned back in the plush leather chair and closed my eyes. I needed to gather my thoughts. Carolyn and I had been acting together every step of the way on this case, like two trapeze artists operating perfectly in sync, but she hadn't told me that she was also working so closely with Rick. To me, that was odd. Carolyn usually told me everything.

"Let's get on the same page here, Rick," I said at last. "Is there anything else Carolyn has told you that I need to know?"

He was silent for quite awhile as he considered my question. Finally he shook his head. "I don't think so. There's only one thing that really matters. The

DA's office has decided *not* to move on this case and that decision puts Kelly in direct danger. We have to find some way to change their minds."

When the light bulb suddenly went off in my head, I could have slapped myself for being so blind.

"What if I went to the press? I mean, what if I wrote a letter to Bobby Edmonds, that reporter with the Express-News? He's a good friend of Carolyn's. I'm sure he'd be interested in all this political intrigue swirling around the courthouse and jeopardizing the safety of a little girl. As a writer, I know I would be. And, since we have two, maybe three weeks until the actual custody hearing, we still have two, maybe three opportunities for a prosecutor to present all this incriminating evidence to the Grand Jury. They meet every week, so if we can pique Edmonds' interest and get him to start asking questions just a few days from now, then Mr. Rodriguez still has plenty of time to do the right thing."

At first Rick looked uncertain and even a little nervous, but the longer he thought about it the more excited he seemed to become. Finally, drumming his fingers vehemently on his desk, he gave an enthusiastic nod.

"It might work at that, Ronni! But we've only got a couple of weeks before the hearing, so you'll need to move fast. When can you get it done?"

"Is tomorrow morning soon enough?"

"Carolyn will need to approve it before you send it so we can be sure the facts are right—we can't make any mistakes. And then I'd like to read it, too, if you don't mind. In fact, it might be best if we mail it from my office, Return Receipt Requested. What do you think?"

"Sounds good to me."

"Well, it sounds *great* to me! If Rodriguez doesn't give this case to the Grand Jury before Edmonds starts writing headlines about influence peddling in his office, it'll be too late. He'll lose his reelection and we'll lose this case."

Suddenly I felt compelled to remind them who and what this was all about. To me, it wasn't about Fred Rodriguez or his reelection campaign. It wasn't about Glenda Best or Harold Best or Ricardo Caldarone. It wasn't even about corruption in the DA's office.

As far as I was concerned, this case was about protecting a child.

# CHAPTER TWENTY-FOUR

"I hope you don't mind me dropping in like this."

Laughing and shaking her head, Carolyn pulled me inside. "Of course not! When did it start raining? Oh, it's great to see you! Where have you been?"

Frowning, I looked at her more closely. The foyer was dimly lit, as usual, but the deep purple shadows beneath Carolyn's eyes were the result of sleeplessness, not bad lighting. "At Rick's office. Are you all right? You don't look good."

"Sure I am!" Her voice was too loud and too enthusiastic as she cozily tucked her hand in the crook of my arm, leading me toward the kitchen. "I'm making some hot tea. Do you want some?"

I didn't like the way this felt at all, but I couldn't put my finger on what was wrong. "Let me call Kevin first, okay? It's getting late and he'll worry."

"*That* must be nice."

"What?"

"Having a husband that worries about you." The copper teapot began to whistle, but Carolyn didn't remove it from the stove. She just stood and stared at it. "I love that sound," she whispered. "It reminds me of my mother... and my kitchen back home..."

Then, catching herself, she giggled in embarrassment and jerked the teapot off the burner.

The sudden silence was eerie.

Just to give her a moment to collect herself, I turned my back on her, leaned against the kitchen counter, and reached for the telephone. Pulling it toward me, I knocked over an empty pill bottle and sent a grimy paper plate flying to the floor. I knelt to pick it up, then looked at it more closely and frowned. On one side Carolyn had written several names, titles, offices, and telephone numbers; on the other side she had written just one—a full name and a complete address.

"Who's Johnny Bartlett?" I asked curiously.

Carolyn shrugged and reached for two coffee cups hanging from her mug tree by the sink. "I don't know. Why?"

"It says *Johnny Bartlett, Gretna Louisiana* on this paper plate. Who is Johnny Bartlett and where the hell is Gretna, Louisiana?"

Frowning, Carolyn shrugged again and took the plate out of my hand. "Never heard of 'em." She stared at what was obviously her handwriting for quite awhile, then shook her head. "I hate it when that happens," she muttered. Suddenly she snapped her fingers. "I know who he is! Don't you remember,

Ronni, about a year ago, when this retired cop called us here in the office and gave us all this bullshit about how he could get rid of anybody for a price? It was after I took that kiddie porn over to the FBI..."

"What kiddie porn?"

"All those dirty pictures that one of the Fox Photo employees found when she was developing film for a customer. She turned them over to Child Search, don't you remember? And we decided to give them to Paul Hastings, my friend in the FBI. Then, about a week later, this Johnny Bartlett fool called and told us to call him if we ever needed—well, you know—his services." She laughed and winked at me. "I meant to put his information in my file with the Grand Wizard of the KKK, but I forgot."

I stared at her. "The Grand Wizard... Good grief, Carolyn! Are you serious?"

"Of course I'm serious. I told you about him...you just don't remember. He offered his services back when I first started Child Search—and he offered 'em free. Nice guy, huh? I got lots of offers like that." She chuckled and returned to preparing our tea. "But it's like I've said before: If I was gonna kill somebody, I'd just kill 'em—all by myself. I know how to do it. And the odds of gettin' away with it are a whole lot better if you work alone than if you hire someone, because then no one else knows. Hell's bells, Ronni—you know how it is! Nine times out of ten, hit men are just tryin' to set you up." She winked at me again as she carried our coffee mugs to the table. "Now, you go on, honey. You'd better call Kevin before it gets any later."

I nodded and phoned my house, watching her out of the corner of my eye. Her nasal Texas drawl—which only seemed to occur when she was stressed out—had returned full force. When Kevin answered and I assured him that I was fine, I wished there was some way I could talk to him in code. I needed to let him know that there was something bizarre going on with Carolyn, but I couldn't say a word. I had to wait. Hanging up and returning to the kitchen table, I pulled out a chair and slumped in it, suddenly almost unbearably weary. Staring hard at my mug of steaming spiced tea, I tried to think of a way to say what I had come here to say...

Finally, Carolyn broke the silence. "What's wrong, Ronni? Somethin's on your mind."

All I could do was take a deep breath and plunge in. "I want to write a letter to Bobby Edmonds about the Harold Best case and how Fred Rodriguez is refusing to prosecute it. Rick agrees that it's a good idea. What do you think?"

Carolyn's face went white. Her expression of pure terror told me that not only did she disagree—she thought we were completely out of our minds. Tears welled and spilled down her cheeks. She shook her head frantically and grabbed my hand with a grip like steel.

"No! No, no… Oh, my God… Oh, please, no…" She was babbling, almost incoherent with panic. "Ronni, you can't do that to me! Please, Ronni, don't do that…my job… It'll cost me my job…"

I tried to pull my hand away. "Carolyn, calm down! What on earth is wrong with you? It'll be my letter to Edmonds, not yours! We'll even mail it from Rick's office! I'm not *asking* your permission about this, Carolyn. I'm *telling* you: it's what I'm going to do. I just want you to know about it. We're out of options here and there's a little girl's entire life at stake. Have you forgotten that?"

She didn't answer. Instead, her chair scraped against the linoleum as she jumped up and began prowling the kitchen like an angry, caged animal. Finally, after several moments, she seemed to come to some kind of a decision. She glared at me. "Of course I haven't forgotten it!" she exclaimed. "How could I forget it? Rick won't let me forget it… *You* won't let me forget it… But you're not facing facts here, Ronni. We can't win. Don't you understand that? Do I have to spell it out for you? *There…is…no…way…we…can…win.*"

Stunned silent, I stared at her and shook my head incredulously.

"What?" she demanded. "What?"

"I can't believe what I'm hearing," I answered finally. "I can't believe that *you*, the great Carolyn Huebner, are willing to sacrifice a child for the sake of a job in a crooked DA's office!"

As Carolyn's eyes widened in shock, I could have kicked myself. That was so uncalled for, I thought, mortified. That was so unfair… "I'm sorry, Carolyn! God, I'm so sorry! I didn't mean that, honest I didn't!"

She shook her head and held up her hand to halt my apology. "No, you're right, Ronni. You're absolutely right. I've just been thinking of myself. I've been so upset because I couldn't really help Rick—and that's never happened before. I've always been able to help. It's always been like I could *will* things to happen, Ronni, but I can't this time…" Her voice trailed away uncertainly. "This time it's just bigger than I am…"

As she stood holding on to the edge of the counter, white-knuckled and somehow alone, I was completely unnerved by a vulnerable, please-help-me expression on her face that I had never seen before. Her formidable determination, which had so often irritated me, was gone. Now she seemed terrified and confused, like a child suddenly ripped away from her mother. For a moment I actually believed that I had glimpsed the frightened little girl snatched right out of her front yard so many years earlier…

Then, as if I had imagined it all, Carolyn appeared to come back to herself. Rubbing her hands together briskly, she was once again coherent and efficient and all business. I was relieved to recognize her.

"Before we write our letter to Bobby," she said in the no-nonsense voice that I was so familiar with, "I think we should write one to Fred. We should tell him everything and give him a chance to check it out—just in case he doesn't know what's going on. And we should warn him that we're going to the media if he doesn't do the right thing. What do you think?"

I snorted. "Fred Rodriguez doesn't know what's going on in his own office? You're kidding, right?"

"I owe it to him, Ronni, and you owe it to me. Even if you think he's scum, you can give *me* that much, can't you?"

Chastened and slightly ashamed, I nodded. "You're right. I'm sorry."

After all, I thought, who was I to tell her what to do or how to do it? Everything important in Carolyn's life was riding on this decision, and I understood that. The least I could do was to offer her my friendship and support.

"I'll call you in the morning and read the rough draft to you, okay? Then, once we're happy with it, you can take it to Rick and he can mail it to Fred from his office. Our names won't be anywhere on it. You should be fine."

She nodded silently, a faraway look in her eyes, as if she was no longer in the same room with me. I couldn't help but wonder where she was, what she was thinking.

"Carolyn," I asked suddenly, "would you like to talk to Larry about this before we do it? He might see something that we're not seeing."

She shook her head and avoided my eyes. "No. Larry wouldn't understand. I've always tried to keep him and Dootie out of my work, and I don't want to change now. He's too busy, anyway. Besides, we're trying to sort of rebuild our relationship—for whatever that's worth. I'm even thinking about taking him to New Orleans for a second honeymoon. I haven't decided yet, but I'm thinking about it."

"Well, that would be really nice. I'm sure he'd enjoy that."

Once again, what Carolyn had always called *the Larry and Audra incident* knocked at the door of my memory. I tried to turn it away and disregard it as completely as Carolyn seemed to do, but I couldn't. On the other hand, it was none of my business. If she could take him to one of the oldest, most romantic cities in the country and kindle in him a passion that had apparently never been there before, more power to her. She was a bigger woman than me. I wouldn't even be able to *live* with him, much less let him…

I stood up. "I really need to get going. I hate to drive in the rain, you know?"

Carolyn grabbed my arm and held on. "Wait. I want to say something. I know how you feel about Larry, and I understand. I do. But maybe it's something *I* did, you know? Or something I didn't do. I've just this minute decided, Ronni. I'm going to close down Child Search completely and I might even quit my job. I could just be a wife and a mother... I've never really done that, you know? I'm thinking that if I get him away from here, if we could just go somewhere and be alone, this would all be over and we would be good together..."

I patted her hand maternally and moved away from her. Sometimes she could change her mind as rapidly as the shapes and colors in a child's kaleidoscope, and the mercurial personality alterations I was witnessing more and more often confused me so much that I truly didn't want to be around her. Sometimes just being in her presence could make me doubt my own sanity.

Yet these weren't sentiments that I could express; she would never have understood. "You don't owe me any explanations, Carolyn," I said aloud. "We're very different women, you and I. Your marriage is your marriage. It's not mine. Now, I have to get home. Call Kevin for me, will you, please?"

Her explosion of words seemed to be finished; her nervous energy seemed to be calmed. She gave me a sweet, tremulous smile, nodded, and held up her hand in a gentle good-bye. Once more she wore an expression I had never seen before. As I left her house and walked toward my car, my head lowered against the rain, I couldn't erase the haunting memory of it from my mind.

There was something final about that quiet smile, something indescribably peaceful—as if she had come to a decision that she was deliberately keeping from me. And, as I drove carefully down dark, slick streets toward home, I tried not to think of Carolyn, or her Dootie, or her ridiculous "second honeymoon." All of that was beyond my comprehension.

Instead, I focused on the letter I was going to write to Fred Rodriguez first thing in the morning.

It didn't work. We mailed our letter anonymously in early April, Return Receipt Requested, and asked that an answer be sent back to Attorney Rick Caldarone. For two weeks, we sat back and waited hopefully for some kind of response, but all we received was a receipt from the DA's office signed by someone whose signature none of us recognized.

"Well, that's it, I guess," I told Carolyn during a late-night telephone conversation just a week before the Best custody battle was due to begin. "It's all over. We can't even go to Bobby Edmonds now. It's too late for him to do anything."

I swallowed the lump in my throat and blinked back tears. Everything we had done was futile, a complete waste of time. I should have done what I wanted to do in the first place: I should have gone straight to the press and the hell with Fred Rodriguez or anybody else. Instead I had done what I had sworn I wouldn't do. I had taken my eye off the ball. I had forgotten who—and what—this case was all about.

"You blame me, don't you?" Carolyn asked softly.

"Of course not."

"Yes, you do. I can hear it in your voice. But I've done something, Ronni, and Rick is really excited about it. You want to know what it is?"

I shook my head wearily. Carolyn's determined enthusiasm was often exhausting, but still it could sweep me along like a damned tsunami. As usual, I was compelled to hear her out, just in case...

"Sure, Carolyn. Tell me what you did."

She chuckled, low in her throat. "You're gonna love this, Ronni. I took those pictures—the ones of Kelly—to Paul Hastings in the FBI. Rick and I think that Kelly's civil rights are being violated by the DA's refusal to prosecute this case—and you know what?"

I sighed. "What?"

"Paul agrees. And he's promised to look into it."

I snapped to in disbelief, fighting against hope. "The FBI is going to look into it? Honestly?"

"Honestly."

"Oh, my God..." I caught my breath in excitement. "This is great, Carolyn! This could work! If the FBI gets involved, it doesn't matter what happens anywhere else! They could stop this whole nasty setup in its tracks, couldn't they?"

She sounded smug. "They sure could. Paul promises that we'll hear back from him in just a few days at the very most. And I know him, Ronni. He's a good guy. We can trust him."

I had no reason to doubt her. She had worked with law enforcement for years and I knew that many of them actually owed her. Look at what she had risked to help Attorney General Jim Mattox just a few years earlier: she had actually testified against crooked criminal investigators that were determined to use Henry Lee Lucas to close their cases. Look at what she had sacrificed emotionally just recently to help the U.S. Customs Department: she had spent hours pouring over indescribably horrific pornographic photos of babies so that Gary Gallardo would be sentenced to more than five minutes in prison. Look at what she had done to help prosecutors in her own unit try to stop a sick, murderous pedophile like Ray Moberg...

Carolyn Huebner had given everything she had to law enforcement. Now, I thought, surely they would give something back to her...

Carolyn slowly hung up the telephone in her office, shocked to her core. For the first time in ages, she couldn't think of a single thing more to do. As hard as it was for her to admit, she had actually run out of ideas. The one man she had truly counted on, her so-called friend FBI agent Paul Hastings, had never called her back, and Rick hadn't heard a word from him, either. It was as if everyone in the entire world had disappeared, leaving Carolyn alone to fight for a helpless child that no one else cared about.

Now, at least according to Ronni, the game was finally up.

Thunder crashed, then reverberated through the dimly lit office, followed by a white-brilliant strike of lightning. Driving rain pounded against the roof. To Carolyn it seemed that it had been pouring for weeks, but she didn't mind. This rare monsoon season seemed appropriate, complementing her relentlessly dark mood. The blazing sunshine and warm breezes so typical of San Antonio's springtime would have been a slap in Carolyn's face simply because she was so miserable—and so unaccustomed to losing.

But she had lost this time. They had all lost. Tears slowly trickled down her cheeks; the overwhelming sense of helplessness grew until she could hardly breathe. Just because she needed something to do, she pulled her legal-sized notepad more closely to the lamplight and stared down at it, praying that her nearly incoherent scribbling might give her a fresher perspective. It didn't.

Carolyn would never forget Ronni's words if she lived to be a hundred years old.

"Rick and Glenda agreed to a settlement this morning," her friend had said softly, her own voice thick with anger and tears. "Apparently they didn't feel they had any choice."

Carolyn couldn't believe her ears. "Why?"

"Well—and I'm sure this will surprise you—our esteemed child psychologist, Dr. John Carroll, changed his mind at the last minute and said he was going to advise the court that Harold Best was the better parent. Because of the good doctor's high standing in the community, Glenda didn't feel she could risk going up against him after all. In other words, Carolyn, she just fell apart and Rick let her do it."

"You know better than that, Ronni. Rick's her lawyer and he has to do what she wants. He's not going to fight if she won't let him. What was the final agreement?"

"Best will get weekend visitations with Kelly beginning in a few months and day-long unsupervised visitations beginning immediately. He's going into some kind of therapy for perverts and Glenda says she has to be satisfied with that."

Carolyn's mouth went dry. *Unsupervised visits*! "There's money involved," she stated. "Women don't do something this dangerous for nothing. How much money?"

"Nine hundred dollars a month in child support and a substantial cash settlement based on her getting out of her house within thirty days. But that's not all there is to it."

Carolyn's heart dropped. She couldn't believe it. "There's more?"

"You bet there's more. When I talked to Glenda tonight, she was nearly hysterical. But what I gathered was that Harold Best's current wife—I didn't catch her name—is Dr. John Carroll's office manager. How about that for a conflict of interest? Anyway, Glenda said she couldn't go any further with her case because there wasn't any way that her files would be confidential. She also said that Harold had threatened to testify against her if she didn't agree to an out-of-court settlement. So, since her personal files might as well be public, and the good doctor has turned against her, and The Pervert obviously now feels powerful enough to threaten her with the loss of her daughter, she just cratered..."

Another blast of thunder wrenched Carolyn back to the present. Heart pounding, she pushed her notepad away. There were no answers there. The appalling scenario remained the same: if Fred Rodriguez had just done his job and indicted the creep back when he was supposed to, Harold Best could never have won any kind of custody of his daughter. But now, because the District Attorney was in bed with the Good Old Boys of Bexar County, a four-year-old child would be handed over to the man who had already been freely using her little body for his own pleasure...

A man who was a malicious sadist like Art Lovell... A child who was an isolated little girl like Carolyn Sue Shaw...

Ever since the beginning, Carolyn had been determined to protect every child that came into her sphere of influence and she had done her very best. She had fought to keep them all from ever knowing the terror and helplessness she had felt for so many years, and she had done a remarkable job.

But now she had failed, and a little girl was going to suffer exactly as she had.

The phone rang and I jerked up the receiver. I knew who it was. "Hello?"

"Ronni?" The barely controlled hysteria in Glenda Best's voice was unmistakable. "Is that you, Ronni?"

"What's wrong?"

"We signed the final papers this afternoon, Ronni," Glenda gulped, "and I didn't realize... I mean, I didn't under-stand what was happening when I agreed... Oh, my God, Ronni, what have I done?"

*You've signed your kid over to a pervert for $900 a month,* I told her silently, biting back my fury. *What do you think you've done?*

"Ronni, say something! Tell me what to do!"

"There's nothing you can do, Glenda. The damage is done."

"I have to start giving her to him next Saturday! They're going to be alone together!"

*Lady, you're so sharp you scare me. That's what 'unsupervised' usually means.*

"All you can do is let him know that you're on to him, Glenda," I said aloud. "Let him know that you're going to check every inch of her from the minute he brings her home, and remind him that she talks to you..."

"He'll just tell me that he's got friends and for me not to even think that I can coach her because no one's going to believe me..."

I sighed and closed my eyes. How in the world had I been drawn into the web of this woman's whining neuroses in the first place? I had never met anyone so afraid of another human being in my entire life. I didn't even know what Harold Best looked like, but he had to be an ugly, intimidating monster if she was willing to offer up her child just to keep him happy...

"Glenda, you need to calm down," I said finally. "What's done is done, and you've done it. Now you have to try to protect her—you know, warn him off, stay in touch with your lawyer, take her to her pediatrician periodically—until she's old enough to refuse to go with him."

"That's ten years from now, Ronni," she whispered.

"Yes. It is."

There was a long silence and I knew what she was thinking. For the first time since she had signed those papers, she was actually visualizing the next decade of her life. She was watching herself as she gave her defenseless little girl to Harold Best weekend after weekend, knowing that she hadn't had the courage to stop him...

Of course, I reminded myself, Fred Rodriguez hadn't had the courage, either. No one in the entire DA's office had had the courage—except Carolyn and that ineffective little investigator, Wiley Arnold. Those two would have taken on everyone if they could have. Even the FBI had appeared impotent in the face of this man's power, so it wasn't fair to blame just Glenda. It was a cold and uncaring legal system that had let down little Kelly Lynn Best, handing her over to the man that was going to leave his nasty imprint on the rest of her life.

"I want him dead, Ronni."

I didn't even blink. Hers was a common statement, one that I had made many times myself, and I understood that the desire for revenge was a normal and empowering human emotion, something that simply had to be worked through. It wasn't anything to get upset about.

"Did you hear what I said?"

"I heard you."

"I mean it, Ronni. I want him dead. This is never going to end unless he's dead. He's going to destroy my child."

*Really. You should've thought of that before…*

"Are you there, Ronni? Can you help me?"

"No, I can't—but I know someone who might."

I was sure that Carolyn could talk her down. No one was more eloquent and empathetic with disturbed women than Carolyn. I had watched her do it more times than I could count, and I felt confident that I was placing Glenda in good hands.

But to be honest, I didn't really care whether I was or not. Passing her on to someone else was nothing more than desperate self-preservation on my part. As I gave her Carolyn's number, all I could really think about was getting off the phone and away from her. I was finished with this miserable woman, her pathetic materialism, and her inability to accept what she had done to her own child. As far as I was concerned, I had had my last nightmare about her and her wretched family.

By turning Glenda Best over to Carolyn's loving and efficient guidance, I honestly believed that I was taking my life back. But nothing could have been further from the truth. In actuality, I might as well have given it away.

# CHAPTER TWENTY-FIVE

Carolyn stared at the name, address and phone number written on the back of the dirty old paper plate before she dropped it back on the kitchen counter. *Johnny Bartlett, Gretna, Louisiana...* No, she couldn't do it. No matter how much Glenda Best begged for her help, she just couldn't do it.

But when she imagined Harold Best with his hands all over that beautiful child, she remembered her own hopelessness when she had been imprisoned in Beaumont and couldn't help but wonder how many people had kept silent about little Carolyn Sue Shaw because they were afraid to get involved. How many people had looked beyond her bruises way back then, and made excuses for her obvious malnutrition, and ultimately convinced themselves that what they were seeing with their own eyes wasn't real?

She just couldn't be one of those people. She couldn't be a partner in turning a child over to scum like Harold Best and then forgetting about it like it didn't matter. She had been on the receiving end of that kind of terror for too many years. She had to stop it if she could, no matter what happened.

So it was that late one afternoon on May 13th, Carolyn finally broke down and called Johnny Bartlett—the "hit man" in Gretna, Louisiana who had offered Texas Child Search his services nearly a year earlier. With just a little quiver of nervousness in her voice, she told him that she had a job for him if he was still interested.

"Hell, yeah, I'm interested," he said in a thick gravelly voice that made her want to clear her own throat. "I had surgery awhile back and work's slow. I need the money."

"Well, maybe you're not in any condition to do this job..."

"I can do any job you've got for me, little lady. What's this all about?"

Carolyn told him the details of the Harold Best case and was encouraged by every expletive he muttered. It was clear that he understood her anger and appreciated her desire for justice. She felt as if they were on the same wavelength, like they were both peace officers who had simply taken a different fork in the same road.

"So, you can see why Mrs. Best feels she has no choice in this matter, can't you?" Carolyn finished finally.

"Sure I can. That's why I do what I do. Folks can get their justice and I can make a livin'. It's a good trade-off. How long ago did she call you?"

"Just a few days ago. Do you want her phone number?"

"No."

"Well, then, I can give her your name and phone number so she can call you."

"No. You're my contact. I don't deal with anyone else. You'll handle the money transfers—everything."

"Oh, no… Wait a minute… I can't be in the middle of this, Mr. Bartlett! I have a family, a good job… My husband is an important man…" Carolyn's voice cracked with panic. "I'm only making this call for Glenda Best—just to put you two in touch with each other because she asked me to…"

"Listen, I really want to help all of you, but I have to protect myself. You're a smart lady. You can understand what I'm sayin'. Hell, I'll even drop my price down to $10,000—I usually get $20,000—but I'm only doin' it because it's you askin' me to and because it's for a kid…"

Carolyn's head was throbbing; she just couldn't seem to think straight. Her voice—one that she just barely recognized—seemed to come from a long way off.

"This ain't what I intended, Mr. Bartlett," she said firmly. "Fact is, I don't want no parts of it."

Her answer didn't seem to bother him a bit. "Sure, little lady, I know what you mean. It's a big decision. You sleep on it."

Carolyn hung up the telephone slowly. This was not a man she wanted to play games with; he knew his business and he was serious about it. He was dangerous, and he sure wasn't going to be intimidated by the likes of her.

On the other hand, he would finish off Harold Best without even blinking and little Kelly Lynn would be safe. Nothing was more important than that. Johnny Bartlett was right. She needed to sleep on it.

The next morning it hit her. Ronni's original idea of contacting Bobby Edmonds was still a good plan. The media could still light a fire under the appropriate people and save a little girl's life. It wasn't too late for that. Carolyn poured herself a cup of coffee, dialed Bobby's number at work, and waited impatiently for him to answer. When he finally did, she went weak with relief. Now she could fix it. Now she could make everything all right.

"Bobby? It's me, Carolyn."

"Hey, Carolyn! How are you? How do you like this weather?"

She had no time for small talk. She had to make up for a million lost opportunities. "I hate it. When can we get together, Bobby? I think I have something for you."

Like any talented journalist, Bobby Edmonds could smell a good story twenty miles away—and Carolyn had never let him down. She always spun the best yarns, gave the best quotes, and provided the most bang for the buck of any source he had. She knew that this was the only reason Bobby ignored the torrential downpour going on outside and agreed to leave his office to meet her at an old coffee shop not too far from her home.

Spotting Bobby's red Toyota with the dented right fender parked near the restaurant's entrance, Carolyn quickly pulled her late-model Buick Park Avenue into the slot beside it and shut off the engine. Since the deluge seemed to have finally slowed to a drizzle, at least for the moment, she didn't even bother to grab her umbrella out of the back seat. She rushed out of her car and pushed her way into the nearly empty restaurant before the rain could begin again.

As Carolyn stood in the lobby looking for him, she shook the moisture from her hair. Finally, spotting him in a back booth, she took a moment to study him a little more carefully. Bobby Edmonds was actually a very attractive young man, she thought, surprised she had never really noticed that before. His hair seemed darker and a little wavier than usual, probably because it was still wet, and a stubbly five-o'clock-shadow outlined his jaw even though it was mid-morning. Finally, as if he felt her gaze on him, he looked up and waved.

Carolyn waved back and hurried toward him. Sliding into the booth across from him, she pulled notes out of her handbag and organized them on the table in front of her. Finally, fighting for some small feeling of control, she looked up and met Bobby's worried gaze.

"Are you all right, Carolyn?"

She didn't answer him right away. Instead she tried to decide which move would be the right one: to tell the truth, or make up a lie. She chose the truth.

"No. I'm not."

"What's the matter?"

She shook her head and held up her hand, looking away from him. She had to get a grip on herself. She had to control this meeting or there was no telling what would happen...

"The DA's office is corrupt, Bobby," she said finally, "and I have to stop it. A little girl's life depends on it. She needs me and I can't help her. There are other cases that aren't going anywhere, either, but the case I'm talking to you about is a deadly one."

He cocked an eyebrow. "I'm listening."

Carolyn took a deep breath and then dove in. She started at the very beginning of the story and tried hard not to leave out any details, but she could see by the glassy-eyed expression gradually spreading across his face that he didn't understand what she was saying. She wasn't making sense; he couldn't keep up with her... She knew that she was babbling like an idiot, she could hear it far away...somewhere beyond her own ears... Finally she just stopped talking and stared at him.

As if he was embarrassed for her, Bobby shook his head and looked down at his notes. "What's this guy's name?" he muttered finally.

"I can't tell you that."

"Okay. What's the kid's name? What's the mother's name? Who are we talking about?"

"I can't tell you that, either."

Bobby carefully placed his pen on top of his notepad. "Carolyn, you've been in this business with me for a long time and you know I can't do anything with this. You've made serious accusations against your entire unit, but you can't back any of it up. You haven't given me a single name that I can run with or a single judge I can talk to or even a single courtroom I can start digging in… Carolyn, are you crying? Aw, come on, don't cry!"

She could feel the tears streaming down her cheeks; she could taste them on her lips. She could hardly breathe in and out beyond the boulder-sized lump in her throat.

"I'm human, okay?" she blurted finally. "Why is it always all right for everyone to cry except me?"

Bobby reached across the table and gripped her hand. "You're right," he soothed softly. "You just go ahead and cry…"

Carolyn tried to focus on him, but in her mind's eye she couldn't see anything except little Kelly Lynn Best, blonde and naked and spread-eagled beneath a glass coffee table, a dead-ringer for Audra and baby Carolyn herself. Then, as if she were standing right there watching them, she could see a crowd of leering, middle-aged men slowly circling the little girl, moving closer and closer, smirking, breathing heavily, glistening with sweat and heat and desire…

*You sick perverts… Not again… You're not doing it again…*

Carolyn jerked her hand away from Bobby's grasp and sat straight up, fighting panic. She recognized the voice as the same one she used to hear so often but hadn't heard in a long time. And instinctively she recognized it as the voice that would claim her very soul if she didn't silence it now…

"What the hell are you doin'?"

Larry looked up from the book of bedtime stories he was reading to Audra and shrugged. "What does it look like I'm doing?"

"Get off her bed. You ain't got no bus'ness bein' on her bed."

"Carolyn, for God's sake…what's the matter with you?"

She knotted her fingers together in front of her to hide their trembling, and took several deep breaths. There was a sharp pain in her chest and a strange, filmy cloud filtered her vision. She closed her eyes.

"I'm goin' to bed and I want you out of this room. Right now."

For once, Larry didn't argue and he didn't try to negotiate with anyone. Very casually, as if he had all the time in the world, he got to his feet, tucked his daughter beneath her soft pink comforter, and dropped a light kiss on her forehead. "Good-night, Dootie," he said softly. "We'll see you in the morning."

Carolyn turned on her heel and left the bedroom without a single word to either of them. It was too dangerous for her to speak; she had no clue what she would say or who she would sound like. The voices were back, and they were loud, and someone was berating, threatening, menacing... Behind them all was the high-pitched wail of a terrified child.

Once again the house was huge and dark and silent. In her room, Carolyn's bed was wide and deep...and empty. Shivering, she climbed into it, snuggled deep down into the mattress and pulled the blankets up to her chin, praying for rest, praying for quiet, praying for peace. She was safe here in this dark vacant space, somewhere deep in the center of the world.

But she wasn't. She wasn't safe at all.

Somehow she had moved from her cozy bedroom to an enormous ice cold gymnasium, and there were tiny blonde-haired baby girls piled everywhere stretched all across a floor that opened up and widened like a river. Hundreds and hundreds of tiny blonde-haired baby girls screamed out Carolyn's name and begged for help, over and over and over... but she couldn't move. Somehow she was bound at the wrists and tied to the bed; she couldn't help at all. She could only watch in horror, terrified and powerless...

Then the men walked into the room, all kinds of men, and none of them had faces. Faceless, nameless men lowered themselves over the tiny blonde-haired baby girls, and, with massive erect penises, ripped into their little bodies until their blood erupted and splattered and filled the room to overflowing like the rising waters on the *Titanic*.

Then, as Carolyn struggled to sit up and fight her way to help the children, she saw the sea of dead babies riding waves of blood between her and the tiny blonde-haired baby girls—babies that she would have to move aside or step on or walk across if she wanted to save anyone, including herself...

Carolyn bolted upright in bed, sweat-drenched, heart slamming in her throat, and fought back the scream that hovered just outside her consciousness. It had happened again...this dream...a dream so powerful she was afraid to sleep, yet even more afraid to awaken...just in case it was real. But it wasn't real. She just needed to make it stop.

Grabbing a notepad on her bedside table and locating the Gretna, Louisiana, number, Carolyn reached for the telephone and dialed. After just a few rings, a thick gravelly voice barked, "What the hell… You know what time it is?"

Carolyn caught her breath, terrified, but she had to do it. She knew she had to do it. All those babies…all those tiny blonde-haired babies…

"Mr. Bartlett," she whispered, shaking like a leaf in a wind storm, "please help me. I need to talk to you about that job…"

"I'm taking Larry down to New Orleans for a second honeymoon this weekend." Carolyn told Ronni proudly. "I'm paying for the whole thing myself."

"You decided to go, huh? That's great. Where are you guys staying?"

"At the Hilton, down near the French Quarter. And we're going to take a day-long cruise on the *Creole Queen*, too. It's all part of a special Memorial Day weekend package that the Hilton's offering called *A Dream Weekend*. Sexy name, huh? Lots of Dixieland Jazz at Pete Fountain's place and a champagne brunch…" Carolyn gave a wistful chuckle. "I've always wanted to do that. Our marriage counselor suggested that we get away together and I couldn't think of anything better than this."

"You're going to a marriage counselor? I didn't know that."

"Yeah, well…for whatever that's worth. I don't care much for her—I think she's a waste of money—but Larry likes her."

"She could be right, you know. You might just want to give her the benefit of the doubt."

"Well, actually, I'm a little worried about something, Ronni…"

"What's that?"

"Well, you know…Larry isn't the bravest guy on the block. In fact, he's really pretty wimpy. And there's lots of street crime down there in New Orleans. I just hope that if someone comes after me, he doesn't turn tail and run."

"That's crazy, Carolyn. Why on earth would you worry about that? You know the rules of the street. Just stay in well-lit, well-populated areas and you'll be fine."

"Well, to tell you the truth, I was thinking that maybe you and Kevin would like to come with us. Kevin's a big, strong guy. It would be great to have him around…you know. Just in case."

"You want us to go with you on your honeymoon?" Ronni's burst of derisive laughter ended in an unfeminine snort. "I think that's going just a little too far. You need to learn how to…you know…do it…by yourselves. Besides, Kevin and I are going fishing this weekend."

"Oh, come on, you can go fishing any time! And it would be my treat!"

"No, thanks, Carolyn. You go on down to New Orleans with your husband and have a ball. It'll be good for you to get away…"

When Carolyn hung up the telephone, she felt strangely bereft, like she had just lost her anchor. Something was wrong… She knew something was wrong, but she didn't know what it was. There was a threat looming in the murky recesses of her mind, an intense, dangerous, menacing threat that she could *feel* with every fiber of her being but didn't understand.

Finally, frightened, exhausted and lonely beyond anything she had ever felt before in her life, Carolyn instinctively dialed her mother's telephone number. Just as she had so many years earlier, she called the woman who had once been her savior and her protector, perhaps the only reason she had ever survived at all.

"Mommy?" Carolyn hadn't called her mother *Mommy* in years, but she suddenly felt the need just to say the word. *Mommy*. It was such a soothing word; it brought with it a sense of security. "How are you, Mommy?"

"Well, I'm kind of busy right now, Carolyn. Is this important?"

Not a single *how are you…how's the baby…* Not even a *hello…*

Carolyn fought the tears that suddenly threatened to take her voice away. "No, no, it's not important." She cleared her throat and stared blindly out her kitchen window. "I just wanted to tell you…I love you, Mommy. I just wanted you to know…"

"Oh. Okay. Well, like I said, I'm a little busy now."

"It's all right, Mommy. I know how it is. It was good to talk to you."

The responding *click* of her mother hanging up the telephone reverberated through Carolyn's head with all the finality of a lethal gunshot. She was alone with her nightmares and her voices, and there was no one anywhere that could help her.

Once again, like so many times before, she was alone. She couldn't talk to anyone. There was no one in her life that could even begin to understand…except the voices. They talked with her. They comforted her. They even instructed and led her. They were all out of the box now, but she was no longer afraid of them. In fact, these days she looked for them. They kept her from feeling so alone. They lived for her, made decisions for her, protected her.

And, once more, like so many times before, they came forward to keep her secrets.

# PART FIVE

*I cry to thee, O Lord;*
*I say, Thou art my refuge,*
*Give heed to my cry;*
*For I am brought very low!*

*Deliver me from my persecutors;*
*For they are too strong for me!*

**Psalms 142:5-6**

# CHAPTER TWENTY-SIX

"Ronni, are you there? Ronni, this is Larry. Please pick up if you're there."

I hit the *playback* button on the answering machine, frowned, and looked at my husband. Larry Huebner's voice repeated, "Please pick up if you're there," but this time I heard a slight quaver that I hadn't noticed earlier.

"Kevin, what time is it?"

He glanced at his watch. "Nearly 8:00 in the morning. Why?"

"Well, if you and I had gone to New Orleans for a second honeymoon like Larry and Carolyn did, would you be calling *her* at this hour?"

Kevin grinned and gave me a lewd wink, then yawned. "No, but I'm not Larry Huebner. Besides, Carolyn called begging us to go with them just a few days ago, remember? I think that's pretty crazy." He yawned again. "Well, you'd better call him back and find out what he wants. I'm gonna take a shower and then I'm going to bed. You guys can figure out how to save the world."

I played the message once more and shook my head in confusion. Carolyn might be crazy, but her husband wasn't. In fact, he was the calmest guy I'd ever seen. No matter what emotion he was feeling, no one else ever knew it. We even had a standard joke around our house when it came to Larry Huebner: *If you're mad, stomp your foot twice so we can tell...*

"Ronni, are you there? Ronni, this is Larry. Please pick up if you're there..." Yes, there it was. Larry's voice was shaking. "Okay. It's Saturday, May 24th at 7:10 in the morning. Something's happened here, Ronni. Call me back at the New Orleans Hilton—Room 2420. Tell the operator that you're returning my call—otherwise they won't put you through. They'll think you're media. Please, Ronni. It's urgent."

I scribbled down the phone number he left, trying to second-guess what might have happened, but nothing made any sense. Leave it to Carolyn to find the media, I thought, slightly irritated as I dialed. It's like no matter where she goes or what she does, she's going to find some silly reporter. But Larry was used to that. He wouldn't care. It would take a lot more than that to upset him...

"Hello? Room 2420, please. This is Ronni Hoessli in San Antonio, Texas. I'm returning Larry Huebner's call. Can you put me through?"

"One moment, please. I'll have to clear it with Mr. Huebner."

*Good grief! What in the world is going on?* I rubbed my eyes wearily. See what happens when you leave? I asked myself. The whole stupid world falls apart...

"Ronni, thank God you called!"

"What is it? What's happened?"

"Where've you been?" Larry's voice cracked; he sounded shell-shocked.

"What do you mean, where've I been? Kevin and I have been fishing all night up at Canyon Lake and we just got home if it's any of your business, which it isn't..."

"What made you decide to go there?" he demanded.

"Good grief, Larry! What's wrong with you?"

"I'm sorry." He took a ragged breath; his voice was thick with tears. "Lord, I'm so sorry."

"Larry, let's start over, okay?" I settled on the floor Indian-style, lit a cigarette, and prepared for a long conversation. I obviously wasn't getting to bed any time soon. "What happened?"

"Carolyn tried to have me killed last night."

I chuckled. "Try again. That's not funny."

His voice was hard, cold. "I agree. It's definitely not funny."

I stared blindly at my cigarette burning in the ash tray and couldn't think of a single thing to say. I could feel it in my bones: he was telling the truth.

I started to tremble. "Talk to me, Larry," I said quietly. "Tell me everything that happened."

"I don't know exactly." I heard him take a deep breath and knew it was taking every ounce of energy he had to tell me his story. "Carolyn had been real proud of this trip, Ronni. She called it a 'second honeymoon' and she planned it all herself. Then, while we were on the plane, she told me that it was a combination business/pleasure trip and that she had to meet some cop about a missing kid when we got to the hotel. I was a little irate about that, but I wasn't surprised.

"Anyway, when we landed last night about 6:00, we rented a car and went to the New Orleans Hilton Towers Hotel. Almost as soon as we got to our room, Carolyn got a telephone call—I guess from this guy. She told him that she would see him shortly. Then she told me to go down to the coffee shop and wait for her, so I did. Then, about 7:30, a couple of FBI agents walked up to me and asked if I was Larry Huebner. Of course I said I was and they told me that my wife had hired a hit man to murder me. They said I was in danger and that I needed to stay in the coffee shop until they gave me the all clear. So I did." He cleared his throat nervously. "That's about it."

My God, he wasn't kidding. This had really happened. My right temple began to throb.

"Have they arrested her? Is she in jail?"

"Yes."

"Has she talked to the FBI?"

"They say she did, but only because she thought they were going to let her see me. As soon as she realized they weren't going to allow that, she shut up. So I don't know how much she actually told them."

"Did she have an attorney with her?"

"No."

"And she talked anyway?"

"Yes."

That was crazy. Carolyn knew better than that. "Have you seen her since then? Have they let you talk to her?"

"No."

"Do you *want* to see her?"

"I don't know."

I finally ran out of questions, but it didn't matter. I couldn't think anymore anyway. My brain had stopped working. It was like everything was moving in slow motion—my blood, my heart, everything.

"Ronni, can I ask you something?"

"Sure."

"When did you and Kevin decide to go to Canyon Lake?"

"A couple of weeks ago. Why?"

He didn't say anything for a long time, but I didn't rush him. Larry wasn't the kind of guy you could rush. Still, when he finally spoke, I couldn't believe what I was hearing.

"You weren't in on this with her, were you, Ronni?"

"Of course I wasn't! Why would you even ask me that?"

He sighed. "Why wouldn't I? Carolyn doesn't make a move that you don't know about. And then, when this happened and I tried to call you, you weren't home. It didn't... well, it just felt...wrong to me. I needed to know." His voice broke. "I don't know who I can trust now, Ronni. It just happened last night and this place is already crawling with media. Nobody is who they seem to be. The hit man was some kind of an FBI informant—thank God. My own wife says she wants us to put our marriage back together but then she takes me down here to kill me... Oh, jeez, Ronni, you're right. I shouldn't have asked you that."

My eyes filled with tears and for a moment I really thought my heart would break. The truth about what Carolyn had done to this poor man was finally beginning to sink in. But then, on the heels of the pain came rage. I had never been so angry in my life. Still, I kept this emotional meltdown to myself. Larry Huebner wasn't the kind of man who would understand emotional meltdowns.

"Larry," I said aloud, "I need to tell you something. It's important."

I could actually hear him swallow. Hard. "What?"

"Larry, she can't call me here. I can't talk to her. And you know she's going to call—just as soon as they tell her she can."

"I know, Ronni." He sounded relieved that I hadn't told him anything more momentous than that. "I don't know when I'm going to talk to her myself. But, if I do, I'll tell her to lay off, okay?"

A lump the size of Gibraltar seemed to be lodged in the back of my throat and I was suddenly freezing to death. Exhaustion was finally setting in. "Thank you, Larry. When are you coming home?"

"Well, we were supposed to take a day-long cruise on the *Creole Queen* tomorrow and I'm going to go ahead and take it. She's paid for it, after all, and I need to think. My plane ticket back to San Antonio is for Monday afternoon and I'm going to keep that flight. I have to meet a guy at work on Tuesday morning. Besides, I can't even see an attorney until then, either here or there, so there's no point in hanging out down here. Also, I have to get Audra squared away—I guess with Ohler or my folks."

I was amazed. His wife had just been arrested for trying to have him murdered and he was already working out his week. You had to admire a guy like that...

"Ronni, do you think you and Kevin could pick me up at the airport? I really need to talk to you. Maybe we could all go to dinner..."

"What time are you due in?"

"I'm flying in on Continental, landing at 5:20 on Monday evening. Do you think you guys can meet me?" His voice broke again. "I really don't want... I just don't want to be alone right now, Ronni. The truth is, I don't know who my friends are."

I bit back tears and looked up to see Kevin standing in the doorway, a questioning expression on his face. "Don't worry about a thing, Larry," I said softly. "Everything's going to be all right. We'll pick you up Monday evening and we'll go to dinner."

"The bottom line is this, Ronni, and you know it's true: If Carolyn had truly wanted me dead, I'd be dead. Period. End of discussion."

Larry stabbed a fork into a slab of lasagna dripping with cheese and tomato sauce and shoveled it into his mouth. Whatever else had been going on with him, I thought in astonishment, it sure hadn't affected his appetite. I picked at my spaghetti, not in the least bit hungry, and finally gave up. I couldn't eat a bite.

"Have you seen her yet?" Kevin asked, pushing his empty salad plate away and tackling his own lasagna with gusto.

"No, and I don't want to. I just can't deal with all her theatrics right now."

"I can imagine," Kevin muttered. "I've never been able to deal with them." I shot him a dirty look before I turned my attention back to Larry. "I don't understand how this could have happened without any of us knowing *anything*. It just doesn't make any sense."

"Ronni, it's not unusual for *me* not to know anything." Larry carefully placed his fork on his plate and looked at me intently. "Carolyn deliberately kept me out of her life. She said it was because she wanted to protect me and Audra from her work—and the crazies she sometimes came into contact with—but I never believed that. I knew the truth. Carolyn was never interested in me unless she needed something. Then I was her best friend. Like now...you just wait. Within the next week or so, I'm going to be her knight in shining armor. I'm going to be the love of her life. That's what'll happen. It always does."

I didn't answer; I wasn't in any mood to argue. Besides, I couldn't get beyond one vitally important fact: This man—even though he probably had every right to whine about Carolyn's neglect—was the same man who had betrayed his wife's trust by masturbating in the presence of his little girl. To me, that one sordid episode trumped everything else. And, as a consequence of that single action, Larry Huebner was not a man I could ever respect.

I shook my head, trying for the umpteenth time to remove that disgusting image from my mind, and changed the subject. "Does she have a lawyer yet?"

"No. They'll give her a public defender until we can find someone."

"Larry, why do they think she did this? What motive have they come up with?"

Scraping the last of his lasagna off his plate, Larry seemed—to me, at least—to be buying time. When he finally spoke, I noticed that his hand was shaking as he wiped tomato sauce from his mouth with a cloth napkin. The streak of red against white looked like blood.

"You have to understand something, Ronni. When the FBI agents found me in the coffee shop and told me that Carolyn was under arrest for hiring a hit man to kill me, I just went nuts. Well, not where they could tell, but... Anyway, they asked me if Carolyn had said anything to me about money recently, or maybe about life insurance, and I snapped to the fact that she had mentioned life insurance on the plane. I mean, she had asked me if I thought we had enough...you know, in case the plane crashed..."

"So?"

"Well, I mentioned that to the FBI—the fact that she had brought it up..."

"And they said she must have wanted you dead for the insurance, right?" I interrupted in disgust. "Jeez, Larry, you just handed them the motive. They didn't even have to work for it."

"I know." His eyes filled. "It was stupid of me..."

"No, no—that's not what I meant. What I meant was, Carolyn and I used to laugh at how unimaginative FBI agents were. Any time they can't figure out a motive, they just stick money in there somewhere. It can be a dime or a million dollars, it doesn't matter."

"Carolyn didn't need money, Ronni," Larry said seriously. "She had credit cards everywhere, she had her own bank account, and I never refused her anything. I guess she could have killed me for lots of reasons, but money wouldn't have been one of them."

"But money's the one they're going to use. What else did you tell them?"

"There wasn't anything else I could tell them. I don't know anything else. But they told *me* a few things. They told me that she had paid this hit man with Child Search travelers checks…"

I nearly fell out of my chair. The words just exploded from my lips. "Are you out of your mind? What are you talking about?"

"You heard me. She paid him with $500 worth of Texas Child Search travelers checks, $50 denominations. They also said something about the title to a piece of property we own up at Lake Conroe—she was going to hand that over to him to keep as collateral until the insurance money came in, usually within thirty days. But that's crazy, Ronni. The title is in my name—it was mine before we were married—and she doesn't even know where it is. Oh, and then…get this: they also said that she was supposed to bring a picture of me to give to this guy, but she didn't bring that, either."

I frowned, puzzled. "That's way too many stupid mistakes and Carolyn wouldn't have made one of them. She didn't do this."

"It's on tape, Ronni. They've got it all on tape."

I stared at him in disbelief. "Are you sure? Have you heard it?"

He nodded, looking away from me, and his chin quivered. "A little. I could only listen to a little. But it was her voice."

"Well, then, she didn't *mean* to do this. Larry, did you know that she called us just a couple of days before you left for New Orleans and absolutely begged us to go with you? She said she'd even pay for everybody. Did you know anything about that?"

"Of course not. That's nuts. Why would she want you guys to come with us on a second honeymoon?"

"Well, she said something about street crime. But if she knew you were going to get knocked off, why would she want Kevin and me right smack in the middle of it? Why would she want to risk us? Carolyn spends all of her time trying to protect her friends, not hurt them. I'm telling you, this just doesn't make any sense at all."

Larry actually managed to chuckle. "You think? Well, it gets better. Every single phone call she made to this guy she made from our private telephone, so it's all right there in our phone bills. She left a paper trail everywhere, and it won't take a rocket scientist to follow it."

All I could do was shake my head. "Paper trail or not, Carolyn would never take a dime from Texas Child Search for any reason other than to look for a missing kid, period. As far as she was concerned, that wasn't her money and she felt very strongly about that." My mind was racing now. "Even when she was talking recently about closing down Child Search, she was determined to do it right. She called one of her old instructors out in California—I can't remember his name now... I think it was Jim something or other—to see if his organization could take over the assets of Texas Child Search." I shook my head again. "No, Larry. Even if she wanted you dead as a doornail, she would never have touched that money. And she certainly wouldn't have done it in a way that virtually *guaranteed* she'd get caught. Travelers checks, for crying out loud..."

Kevin chimed in for the first time. "Unless she wanted to."

"Wanted to what?"

"Get caught."

"What are you talking about?" I demanded. "Why in the world would she want to get caught?"

"Heck if I know. But I don't see any other explanation for someone as sharp as she is to be making so many stupid mistakes, do you?"

I sank back in my chair and looked at him, stunned. In a bizarre sort of way, what he said made perfect sense. Suddenly I thought of an old song...or was it an old movie? I couldn't quite remember, but it was called *Stop the World! I Wanna Get Off!* ... or something like that...

And suddenly I could see Carolyn Huebner, out in front, playing the lead.

After all, for the last few years nothing about Carolyn had made much sense. What had it been like to live in her head? I was sure that if I had been her, I would have done anything and everything I could to make it all stop...

But I hadn't done anything to help. All I had done was try to get as far away from her as I could. I had watched while she had made important commitments to her closest friends and then forgotten about them. I had kept my mouth shut when she had gone on wild shopping sprees, purchasing items she didn't want and couldn't remember buying. I hadn't told anyone when she had spent hundreds of dollars on clothing she wouldn't be caught dead wearing, and boasted about sexual rendezvous she had had with men she didn't remember...

Even when she had called me on the telephone dozens of times, sobbing as if her heart would break and crying out, "I just can't do this anymore, Ronni! I just can't do this anymore!" I, like everyone else, hadn't listened.

She was, after all, the strongest woman I knew, the most determined and persistent... Other people might break down and crack up, but Carolyn Huebner wasn't among them.

I caught myself and refused to give in to my natural inclination to feel sorry for the woman I had once believed I understood. She had tried to kill her husband, and there was no way I could understand that. It was beyond me.

"What are you going to do now, Larry?"

"What do you mean?"

"I mean, what are you going to do? Are you going to get a divorce?"

Larry shook his head and averted his gaze, chewing on his bottom lip thoughtfully for quite a long time. I didn't rush him. Even though I didn't know him well, I knew he would give me an answer when he was good and ready.

But I was wrong. Instead, he answered my question with a couple of his own. "What do you think I should do? What would you do if you were me?"

"Oh, Lord, Larry—that's not fair. I don't know…"

"Well, I know what I'd do," Kevin interrupted brusquely. "I'd get a divorce and take my kid as far away as I could. She's crazy."

Even though Larry nodded his understanding of Kevin's position, it was clear that he didn't agree. "Carolyn has been through stuff that you don't know anything about," he said softly, "and don't take that personally, Kevin. I'm sure the way you feel is the way everyone is going to feel by the end of the week. But the point is, no one knows her better than I do. She's my wife, my best friend, the mother of my child, and she didn't mean to kill me. I know that just as sure as I'm sitting here tonight." He paused and gave us an uncertain smile. "I'm going to back her up every step of the way, and I hope you'll stand with me while I do it. It won't be easy because the media is going to go after her with all guns blazing—they're already smelling blood. I'm going to need all the friends I can get. And, Ronni, you can't desert Carolyn now. Please don't do that."

I looked at Kevin, and he looked at me, and we both looked at Larry as if he had completely lost his mind. Yet, even while my husband shook his head in total bewilderment, I understood. Larry owed her his allegiance and he knew it. It was as simple as that.

Finally, after a long moment, I nodded. "Okay, Larry. We'll play it any way you want to. Have you talked to PoPo yet?"

"I talked to him right after I talked to you the first time. He's baffled, just like the rest of us. But he asked an interesting question, Ronni—one that you might be able to answer."

"What's that?"

"Do you know when, where and how Carolyn got the name of that hit man?"

My mouth dropped. "Oh, my God…What is his name?"

Larry shrugged. "Johnny something-or-other, I think. I don't remember. But I think he actually was from Louisiana."

Immediately, like a mirror image in my mind's eye, I saw that ragged-out paper plate on Carolyn's kitchen counter. On one side of that plate she had written several names, titles, offices, and telephone numbers. On the other side she had written just one—a full name and a complete address.

An icy chill settled over me; by the time I answered, I couldn't stop shaking. "I'd bet just about anything that his name is Johnny Bartlett, he's a retired cop, and he lives in Gretna, Louisiana. He called us about a week after Carolyn turned some kiddie porn over to a friend of hers in the FBI. He said he would do anybody for a price, and she and I laughed about it. She wrote his name and stuff on this paper plate and forgot about it."

"How long ago was that?" Larry asked.

"Oh, gosh. About a year ago, I guess. It's been a long time."

"Huh!" Kevin grunted. "Doesn't that seem a little fishy to you? She gives some dirty pictures of kids to the FBI and a week later an FBI-informant-so-called-hit-man calls her out of the blue and offers to do anybody she wants. Just seems a little weird to me."

Larry's eyes narrowed as he looked at me more closely. "How is it that you remember it so well now?"

"I saw the paper plate again on your kitchen counter just a couple of months ago and I asked her about it. The main reason I remember it is because I'd never heard of Gretna, Louisiana. And the main reason I remember his name is because she said she had meant to file it with the Grand Wizard of the KKK and forgot. That got us on the subject of hit men...and so...I remember it."

"What do you mean, it got you on the subject of hit men?"

I shrugged. "She just gave me her standard lecture on how stupid it is to hire hit men because then...more than one person knows..." My voice trailed away incredulously. Tears welled, spilled over, streamed down my cheeks. I couldn't even breathe.

Larry nodded slowly and reached across the table to pat my hand.

Chaos reigned inside her head, like she was in an overcrowded elevator with everyone talking at once, and the elevator zoomed up and down, up and down, faster than the speed of sound...

Suddenly an unfamiliar voice shrieked a threat from beyond the edges of her consciousness. "I'm gonna kill you, bitch, you hear me? I'm gonna kill you!"

For a moment Carolyn didn't know whether the voice was real or not, but she couldn't take any chances. She looked frantically around a large, shadowy room lined with cots, but there was nowhere she could hide. Finally, out of desperation, Carolyn propelled herself backward until she was squashed against an icy cement wall, her bloodshot eyes wide with terror. "What d'ya think about that, white girl? You ready to die?"

Fighting tears, Carolyn shook her head and pressed her body even harder against the concrete wall, praying to become invisible just as she had so many years earlier. But this time it didn't work.

"Jolie, you touch that girl and your ass is mine."

Before Carolyn could locate her savior, powerful fingers gripped her forearms, hauled her to her feet, and pulled her toward the rear of the room. "Honey," a rich contralto voice said in her ear, "you better come with me before Jolie kills you."

Carolyn didn't argue but clung to the woman's hand until they reached a few empty cots. "Sit down right here and stay. This be your place now. I'm Chandra Greene."

Trembling with relief, Carolyn could barely manage a whispered *thank you* as she sank down onto the makeshift bed. Her legs were so weak they wouldn't hold her upright any longer.

"And this here is Esmerelda Jones," the woman continued. "She's the only other fed in here—just you and her."

Carolyn frowned. "Fed?"

"Federal prisoner—she's in on a drug charge. We all call her *Mother* just 'cause she's so damn old."

Mother sat down beside Carolyn and took her hand. "Well, I ain't as old as all that—but I'm sure as hell old enough to know better than to be in here. And don't piss off Chandra. She's in here on account of she had a gun and crazy folks ain't s'posed to have guns."

Carolyn stared at her and said nothing.

Mother frowned and cocked her head to one side. "You ain't got a clue about where you are, do you, child?"

Carolyn shook her head.

"You're in Orleans Parish Prison, honey. It's just a county jail for real, but ain't nowhere worse in the whole damn country. We're lucky. We're in a part that folks call *The Clinic*, but it's the nut ward for sure. You know why you're here?"

Carolyn's eyes welled with tears. "No," she whispered.

Mother patted her shoulder awkwardly. "Aw, don't worry 'bout that. Most the rest of us don't know why we're in here, neither. I 'spect it'll come to you soon enough. Were you drinkin'?"

Carolyn shook her head again.

"How 'bout dope? Did you do some dope?"

"No."

"Hustlin' on Bourbon Street?"

Carolyn stared down at her hands so hard that her fingers actually blurred before her eyes. *Bourbon Street. Bourbon Street. What was it about Bourbon Street?*

"You weren't hustlin' down French Quarter way, were you? Naw, I don't b'lieve that...not a nice white lady like you..."

*The French Quarter. Bourbon Street...*

Suddenly Carolyn was more terrified than she had ever been in her entire life. She had obviously done something awful, something bad enough to warrant her being thrown in jail, yet she had absolutely no idea what it was. But that was all over now. Whatever she had done had to do with the French Quarter and Bourbon Street...

Even though she was terrified, Carolyn understood instinctively that these women could smell her fear, and fear made her vulnerable. She had been here before—not in this prison, perhaps, but in another one just as dangerous— and she had to prove to everyone around her that she wasn't a total lunatic. She needed to stand up, prove she was in charge... As she rose to her feet, Carolyn suddenly noticed that the back of her left knee was throbbing. Twisting around and trying to reach behind her to touch the affected area, pain shot through her upper abdomen, right beneath her breasts. She stifled a gasp.

"What's wrong, child?" Mother asked gently. "Are you hurt?"

Carolyn shook her head. "I don't...I don't know."

"Come into the light. Let's take a look."

Carolyn took a step backward. "No, no...I'm fine. I'm all right. Really."

Mother chuckled. "I ain't one of those, child. Come on. Let's take a look."

Carolyn stopped arguing and obediently lifted her shirt—an orange shapeless thing she hadn't noticed she was wearing before. She caught her breath in disbelief. There was an enormous blue-black and purple bruise nearly covering the middle of her belly, and she was so certain there was another behind her knee that she didn't even bother to look.

"Hold out your arms," Chandra ordered angrily, speaking for the first time. "Let me see your arms."

Once again Carolyn obeyed. Clear bruises about the size of handprints smudged the tender inner flesh of her upper arms, but she had no idea who had grabbed her or where she had been when it happened.

"Who got you, girl?" Chandra whispered. "What in hell did you do?"

Carolyn bit back the tears and shook her head. Like so many other times in her life, she couldn't remember. She hadn't the faintest idea...

Then, slowly, a series of moving pictures arose out of the mist that seemed to enshroud her confused and addled brain. At first they appeared like a progression of dim and unfocused photographs, but very slowly they began to sharpen and become more vivid. Carolyn was nauseated and terrified by the memory, but she had to follow it through...

*She's meeting a man in a hotel room. He's fat and rough, with greasy silver hair, and the word "Alaska" is tattooed on his forearm. She asks him if he's from there, but he doesn't answer. He just stares at her and motions for her to sit at a table where there are two chairs and an overflowing ash tray. He isn't nice and she feels a deep, stomach-churning fear that actually brings bile to the back of her throat. The man speaks to her.*

*"You bring a picture of hubby?"*

*She shakes her head vehemently... No, no, I don't have one, she tells him tearfully... I didn't bring one... Her voice cracks with panic and now she's shaking so hard her teeth chatter.*

*"How about the deed to the land?"*

*She shakes her head again. "I don't...I couldn't find..." Then, in an effort to appease him, she says something about travelers checks...*

*Furious, the man leaps to his feet and points to the door. She opens it and scurries down the hallway. Even though she longs to hide, she's too frightened of the man to displease him. So she rushes into her own hotel room, grabs some checks from an inside pocket of her briefcase, and returns to the man. She knocks on his door and when he answers it, she moves past him as if she doesn't even see him. But she does see him because she hands him the travelers checks... His grin seems to mock her. She turns away and leaves the room.*

*As soon she steps back into the hall, several strangers claiming to be FBI agents surround her and cuff her hands behind her back. She doesn't cry out or beg for mercy. She doesn't fight or offer excuses.*

*She only says, very softly, "Thank you..."*

# CHAPTER TWENTY-SEVEN

Larry called me a couple of weekends after Carolyn's arrest, having just returned from his first trip back down to New Orleans. He sounded exhausted and frazzled, but also hopeful.

"Can you and Kevin come over this afternoon, Ronni? I have something really important to ask you." He paused and added, "In fact, it's more than important. It's urgent."

"We'll be there," I answered instantly. Even though I was still upset with Carolyn, I had given in and accepted a phone call from her just a few days after our dinner with Larry. But I hadn't talked to her since then and I was aching to hear all the details. "What time do you want us?"

"As soon as you can. PoPo's coming, too. I just need to be sure that we're all on the same page. We can't negotiate if we're not—and we have some serious negotiating to do."

*That's* why he sounds hopeful, I thought. Larry was big on everyone being on the same page—after all, he was the Great Negotiator—and I certainly wasn't going to argue with him.

On the other hand, Kevin didn't want anything to do with any of it. "Look," he said even more ungraciously than usual, "I've got better things to do with my time than deal with that crazy woman's problems..."

I let the tears well and spill down my cheeks. "Please, Kevin," I begged, "you know how the media is—they're following me everywhere and it's going to be worse at Larry's house! Kevin, I won't even be able to get out of the car without you..."

Well, that was stretching it a little, but not by much. We had all begun living with our phones off the hook or answering only by pre-established coded rings between friends. I was forced to take Michaela to school and pick her up via back roads, and I was constantly interrupted while I ran my errands by someone saying, "Excuse me, but do you mind answering a few questions..."

I couldn't believe the whole crazy situation. Even though national newspapers, tabloids, and television reporters were joyfully embroiled in a bloody feeding frenzy, most of the articles ended up being just rehashed stories stolen from somewhere or someone else. But what truly astonished me was how print and television media across the country appeared determined to destroy this woman and her legacy. She seemed to be everywhere. And instead of using any one of a hundred lovely available photographs, they *had* to use her mug shot, which was one of the most frightening pictures I'd ever seen in my life.

Kevin's voice, now more gentle, pulled me back to the problem at hand.

"Look, baby, you're the one who's bound and determined to hang tough with all this, not me, so you go on and go. Just leave me out of it."

But of course I talked him into coming with me.

By the time we arrived, PoPo's antique Cadillac was already parked in front of Carolyn's house. And, as I had expected, two men who were obviously reporters loitered beside the fence. They headed toward us as we climbed out of the car.

"Excuse me…"

Scowling, Kevin was beside me before I could even respond. He held up his hand. "It's Sunday. Don't you have somewhere else to be?"

He ushered me up the porch steps and rang the bell. Cracking the front door just slightly, Larry reached out and pulled me inside.

"Hi, you guys—thanks for coming," he said breathlessly, closing the door behind us. "Can you believe those jerks? I haven't had a minute's peace since this happened. Come on into the kitchen—PoPo's already here."

I had never seen Larry so nervous and agitated; it was actually kind of scary. Consequently, after we had greeted PoPo with warm hugs and joined him at the kitchen table, I took a moment to observe Larry a little more carefully.

Carolyn's husband had never looked particularly healthy to me. He was too soft from years of sitting at a desk and his complexion was always mottled. But now he looked even more unwell. Now his eyes were bloodshot and purple-ringed with exhaustion, his thinning hair looked as if he hadn't washed it in days, and his hands trembled like an old drunk after a bad night. My heart broke for him.

Former Texas Ranger Jerome Preiss, on the other hand, looked like he always did: tall, angular, weather-beaten and incredibly bow-legged. And even though I knew that he loved with all his heart the young woman he called *The Kid*, he was as cool and composed as ever. To me, he was like the proverbial port in a storm; no one could calm me as completely as PoPo could.

I immediately felt more in control. "Okay, Larry," I said, "what's so important?"

Larry placed a legal-sized manila folder on the table in front of him. "Well, several things. First of all, as you probably heard on the news, Carolyn was indicted last week on two separate counts of "solicitation to murder." She'll plead Not Guilty, of course. That's standard." He removed a piece of paper labeled *United States of America Versus Carolyn Sue Huebner* from the folder and held it up. The matter-of-fact heading sent cold chills down my spine. "One count was for the interstate use of a telephone, believe it or not, and the other was for the actual solicitation itself." He paused and looked around the table. "The next thing is, I finally talked to Carolyn on the phone."

I sat up straighter. "When?"

"On June 3rd, the day before the indictment was handed down."

"How did she sound?" PoPo asked. "Is she all right?"

Larry shook his head. "I don't think so. Emotionally she's all over the place. One minute she's crying and telling me how much she needs me, and then the next minute she's cussing me out and bossing me like I'm the one who tried to kill *her* instead of the other way around. She's trying to run the show, as usual." He pulled several sheets of paper covered with Carolyn's rather childish handwriting from his folder. "Her attorney gave me these letters yesterday. I thought you might want to read them. It seems she's found God."

Kevin chuckled and spoke for the first time. "Well, that's no big surprise. Everyone finds God in jail."

PoPo grinned and said nothing, but I shot him a dirty look and muttered, "Your cynicism is showing, my love..." Then, after skimming all the letters and finding that they said pretty much what Larry had predicted they would say—she loved him, she was sorry, she needed his support now more than ever, and God definitely wasn't going to abandon either one of them—I had to ask the question that had been uppermost in my mind from the beginning.

"Did she tell you *anything*, Larry? These letters are all about *her*...what *she* wants, how *she* feels... But I want to know what happened!"

Larry looked at me for a long moment and didn't answer. There was something in his eyes that made me squirm, but I didn't rush him. Finally he pushed several pieces of paper stapled together across the table. "This is the FBI's version of Carolyn's statement. I just got it yesterday as well. Read the second paragraph on page two."

As I began reading, my stomach lurched and seemed to plunge straight to my feet. I felt like I was tumbling down a pitch-black elevator shaft at a million miles per hour.

Federal Bureau of Investigation
Page 2
5/23/87

...Mrs. HUEBNER said she then telephonically called JOHNNY BARTLETT in Gretna, Louisiana, and told BARTLETT that she had somebody who needed his assistance and had a problem which she needed taken care of. She stated that JOHNNY BARTLETT understood through her remarks that she was calling him to arrange a murder contract for this wife and friend of her's (sic), the victim being this wife's husband. CAROLYN stated she asked JOHNNY how much this contract would cost, and it was eventually agreed on that the contract would be for $10,000.00.

BARTLETT stated to her that this would be his minimum price. She stated that once the price was agreed upon, she gave BARTLETT the wife's first name as "GLENDA," and told BARTLETT that GLENDA wanted her husband murdered. She indicated to BARTLETT that GLENDA had photographic evidence of her husband sexually abusing his daughter...

I placed the papers back on the table, met Larry's eyes incredulously, and heard a woman's hysterical voice shriek through my memory.

*"I want him dead! This is never going to end unless he's dead! He's going to destroy my child!"*

I was nearly overwhelmed with shock and disbelief. Oh, dear Lord, I thought, this is all *my* fault! If I had never told Glenda Best to call *the little bird in the DA's office*, Carolyn would never have contacted Johnny Bartlett. But because I had had such a desperate need to rid myself of Glenda Best and all her problems, I had passed her on to Carolyn, believing her to be much stronger than me and far more capable of handling this pathetic, devastated woman than I was...

I had never been so wrong in my life.

"What do you know about this, Ronni?" Larry asked quietly.

There was no point in not telling the truth. Besides, I had nothing to hide. So, blinking back tears and taking a deep breath, I launched into the convoluted story of Harold Best, his ex-wife, and the little girl who looked so much like Audra. Every once in awhile PoPo would interrupt with an astute legal question about Fred Rodriguez, the corruption in the DA's office, or Rick Caldarone, but for the next hour or so I did most of the talking.

Finally, running out of words, I looked around the table at the three silent men staring at me and asked softly, "Is this my fault? Did I cause this?"

Larry and PoPo both shook their heads, but Kevin was the first to explode. "No way! Don't you start blaming yourself! Carolyn would be the first to tell you..."

"You didn't dial that phone, kiddo," PoPo interrupted sternly. "You just did what you guys always did—you worked together on a case that happened to go south. The big difference is, you gave it up when you realized you couldn't win, and she didn't. As Carolyn would say, Ronni, that's it and that's all."

"Well, actually, there's a little more to it than that," Larry said. "Carolyn has an attorney now, and I think you guys will like him. His name is George Simno and I talked to him Saturday morning—after Carolyn was released on that $5,000 personal recognizance bond Friday afternoon. She was finally removed from the county jail Friday night and taken to Marion Manor, which is a halfway house run by nuns or something like that. George says she's sick and needs a doctor for strep throat. Since two different shrinks testified that she wasn't a threat to the community or to me, a magistrate named Alma Chasez released her and said that jail wasn't the place for her, anyway…"

"Hold up a minute," I interrupted. "What shrinks? Where did they come from?"

"Well, one of them is a Dr. Eugene Usdin, a forensic psychiatrist that heads up the Oschner Clinic down there. He's apparently a really important guy. Anyway, George tells me he's going to get copies of every medical report ever done on Carolyn so he can prove that this breakdown—if that's what it was—was predictable and might have even been prevented…"

"What are you talking about?" I demanded. "How many shrinks have seen her? How many reports have been done?"

"Listen, Ronni," PoPo interjected gently, "Carolyn has seen psychotherapists, hypnotherapists, psychologists, counselors and psychiatrists for years. The problem was that she never stayed with anyone long enough to get any real help, and no one had the guts to stand up to her. So, I think what happened in the past was that when things got too nasty in therapy, she just quit and said she was fine as frog's hair. But she ain't fine. She ain't been fine for a long, long time."

"She never told me any of that, PoPo. Why wouldn't she tell me that? Good grief, she's told me everything else!"

"Oh, I doubt that, kiddo. Fact is, she probably don't *know* everything else."

I frowned. "What do you mean?"

PoPo shook his head. "I've said too much already. Go on with your story, Larry. You were tellin' us about this magistrate that said Carolyn shouldn't be in jail…"

"Right. Well, she also said that she didn't understand what the government was doing in Carolyn's life to start with, or something like that—which was the question you asked in the very beginning, PoPo, when you wanted to know where Carolyn had gotten Johnny Bartlett's name in the first place.

"Anyway, now George tells me that the federal prosecutors have been pushing Carolyn to give them the name of the woman—this Glenda Best. If she'll give up the woman, they'll make a deal. But Carolyn won't do it."

I responded without even thinking, "Of course she won't."

Larry looked startled. "Well, why not? What could it hurt? There's no proof. It's just Carolyn's word against hers…"

I stared at him in disbelief. "Larry, you're smarter than that! If Carolyn tells them Glenda's name, they'll go after Glenda as a co-conspirator in a "solicitation to murder" scheme. Shoot, they might even come after *me* for telling Glenda to call Carolyn in the first place—not that that would ultimately hold any water. But if all that happened and Glenda Best ended up in prison—or was even just *accused* of conspiracy—then what would become of that little girl?"

Larry frowned. It was clear that he honestly didn't understand. "She'd end up with her father?"

"That's right. And do you think for one minute that Carolyn would ever allow that?" I shook my head and answered my own question. "No way. Absolutely no way. She may be as crazy as a loon, I don't know. But I do know this: she'd stay in prison for the rest of her life before she'd let anything else happen to that little girl."

Nobody said a word; the heavy silence stretched for what seemed like eons. Finally Larry broke the stillness with a single statement.

"Well, I guess that's it then."

"What do you mean, *that's it?*"

"If she's not willing to bargain with the only ace she's got, then she's going to have to throw herself on the mercy of the court and pray for the best."

I couldn't believe my ears. For the first time since Carolyn's arrest, anger at Larry began to simmer deep within me. Not only did he fail to recognize how his own perverse actions in front of his little girl might have contributed to his wife's fragile state of mind (a subject I wasn't free to raise in front of PoPo), but he was also unable to see an abused child and her mother as anything more important than bargaining chips.

So much for the Great Negotiator, I thought furiously. At that moment, what I perceived as Larry Huebner's selfish lack of empathy was more than I could even comprehend.

"There's something else, Ronni."

I glared at him, but he seemed completely oblivious to my anger.

"The magistrate said that Carolyn could come back to San Antonio if she had a place to stay. I don't want her in my house—you can understand why—but I don't want her to have to stay down there in New Orleans, either. Audra needs her mother and I need to understand what happened. On the other hand, my own attorney advises me to keep my distance until I'm sure she's...well, you know...not a threat to me."

"You have an attorney?" For some reason I was surprised to hear that, but then I realized it was probably an excellent move on Larry's part.

"He's just walking me through all the legalities of this and advising me when I need it. I *am* the victim here, after all." I don't know what it was that made me realize that Larry was thoroughly enjoying his new-found power over his suddenly vulnerable wife, but there was something in his voice that I had never heard before—something arrogant and even self-righteous. On the one hand I couldn't blame him; the poor man had been under her thumb for years. On the other hand it infuriated me that he seemed so unaware of the part he might have played in this tragedy...

"Well, you certainly don't owe *me* an explanation if you want to get a lawyer, Larry. Has he spoken with this George Simno?"

"Not yet. I'm just not quite ready to deal with Carolyn—or her attorney, for that matter. But since the magistrate says she can come back if we find her somewhere to go..." Larry's voice trailed away and he looked directly at me.

But it was Kevin who spoke up and stunned us all. "She can stay with us."

I couldn't do anything but stare at him in shocked disbelief.

"It's what you want, isn't it?" he asked softly.

As I nodded, my eyes filled with tears of gratitude and I reached for his hand. I was positive that we had to do this simply because terrible things could happen if Carolyn went home to Larry too soon. I was sure she would be safe if she stayed with us. Or, at least, she'd be *safer*...

How strange that it was always *Carolyn's* security I was concerned about and not Larry's...

I poured Carolyn a glass of white wine and prepared to flip on the tape recorder. "Are you sure you want to do this now?" I asked. "We have plenty of time..."

Carolyn shook her head and leaned forward intently. "No, we don't. My trial will probably start in a couple of months and I want all this on tape before then. I mean it when I say that I want you to write a book about my life, Ronni. I didn't go through all this for no reason, I know I didn't. So, I want to tell you about myself..."

But I knew she couldn't. The last several days that she had been with us had shown me that. She couldn't tell me what she didn't know.

Still, actually sharing living space with Carolyn had alerted me to issues I had never realized she had. I found that I had to leave the closet light on in the bedroom because she couldn't be alone in the dark. We had to leave doors ajar because she panicked if she thought she was closed in. If a telephone call wasn't immediately returned or someone was too busy to speak with her, Carolyn instantly regressed and became a spoiled rotten, verbally abusive 10-year-old. Her personality changed so frequently and with such rapidity that my own head was constantly spinning.

PoPo had been right. She may have been treated by every mental health expert in the country, but no one could have helped her. She was simply too good at hiding and keeping secrets—not only from others but from herself. At least now, if for no other reason than that it had been mandated by Magistrate Chasez, she was seeing highly respected forensic psychiatrist Dr. William Reid, who was trying to help her understand what had happened.

Yet, while she seemed to have bonded with him very well during the brief period that I was what the legal system called her *third-party custodian*, I was pretty sure that she wouldn't continue to see him if the judge lifted her order. And while this realization disturbed me, it also helped ease my overwhelming sense of guilt. Whatever Carolyn had done, she had done on her own—and for her own reasons.

"Okay." I settled myself across the dining table from her, poured my own glass of wine, turned on the recorder, and began speaking. "This is Ronni Hoessli, June 17, 1987, and this is the start of a series of interviews with Carolyn Sue Huebner. Right now I'm going to read the beginning of a transcript given to me by Carolyn that will be used by her attorney, George Simno, in her upcoming trial."

I proceeded then to read the rather dull basics of anyone's life—name, rank and serial number—and didn't become interested until I stumbled onto the following paragraphs containing Carolyn's words, verbatim:

"The Shaws lived in McKeesport, Pennsylvania, thirty miles from Pittsburg. When Arthur Lovell contacted his father, George Shaw, he said he had this baby girl and could he bring me up there. George agreed, and I went to live with the Shaws when I was approximately nine months old. At that point in time, the name *Carolyn Sue Shaw* was given to me.

"Life was normal. My paternal grandparents were known to me as *Mommy and Daddy*, Bob and Maureen were *my big brother and big sister*, and I was never told any different...

"I remember that there was a lot of stress in the house when I was about five and Mom was very protective of me. I remember not being able to play outside much, and once I was down in the cellar with Mom. I remember she crawled across the kitchen floor another time to get animal crackers and I remember Maureen and her boyfriend looking in the woods once for something. I never knew what they were looking for, but we couldn't come out of the cellar until they found it.

"Then I was in the hospital and I had a very private room. My doctor was Dr. Taxel and he was also very protective of me. I don't know why I was in the hospital, but I was never alone. My room had lots of toys, just like at home. One afternoon some woman came in, grabbed me, and started screaming at me. I screamed and Dr. Taxel came in and actually tackled her and threw her out. I was taken then from the hospital to another place I can't remember and then they took me home. All I remember after that is that one minute I was in my house, it seems like, and then I was in this car with a man and a woman..."

I flipped off the recorder and stared at Carolyn. "This doesn't make any sense, honey," I said carefully. I pushed the transcript across the table. "Read this to yourself and then try to explain it to me, okay?"

Carolyn read the transcript—several times, I suppose, because it seemed to take her forever—and then she finally looked at me with a strangely defeated expression on her face. She shook her head slowly, tears welling in her eyes.

"I've been running from this for a long time," she whispered, "but I don't know any more than what's written right here. Honestly. I don't. Ronni, I've spent my whole life trying to put the pieces together, but they just don't fit anywhere. They don't."

I reached across the table and grabbed her hand. "Then you need to find out, Carolyn. You need to fill in all these blank spaces in your life. You also need to prove that this so-called *Huebner Legend* isn't fiction and you need to stop these vicious reporters dead in their tracks." I squeezed her hand. "But more important than anything else, Carolyn, *you* need to find out who you really are."

Finally, in mid-June, with Larry's magnanimous permission and Magistrate Alma Chasez' blessing, Carolyn left Ronni's house and returned to her own home, hoping for a little peace and privacy. It wasn't to be. She couldn't leave her house without being swarmed by screeching media, the telephone never stopped ringing, and notes pleading for interviews constantly fell through her mail slot.

In addition, Audra had become even more tyrannical during the time Carolyn had been gone, and Larry seemed to have morphed into a pompous, self-righteous autocrat who took great pleasure in making her miserable. Of course, he was gone most of the time (working long hours, he said, to pay their astronomical legal and medical bills) so she didn't have to deal with him too often, but just thinking about him made her angry. Besides, she thought, if he was so worried about the legal bills, why on earth had he gotten his own attorney? It wasn't like she *meant* to kill him, for crying out loud! Even Ronni hadn't seemed to understand that, feeling the need to remind her at least a half-dozen times that Larry would be dead if Johnny Bartlett had been a *real* hit man... Good grief, didn't they realize she knew that?

There seemed to be only one person in Carolyn's life right now who wasn't judgmental, didn't think she was crazy, and never asked any questions—and that person was Ohler. The sweet old lady never changed. She still wore that perpetually peaceful smile on her face, she still had her soft little praise moments, and she still burst into wonderful gospel songs whenever the spirit moved her.

She was the one individual that Carolyn could completely depend on. She also seemed to be the only person that Audra would listen to…

Carolyn was grateful that the Dootie was close to Ohler simply because she was so angry all the time that she knew she wasn't any good for her little girl. Maybe it was because her therapy was difficult and seemed to bring the worst out in her. She was having hideous night terrors again. She heard voices arguing in her head all the time. She saw flashes of light and memory that seemed free of time and space. Whatever the reason, Carolyn knew she was in no shape to take care of a rebellious six-year-old.

Perhaps the worst part of it all was the way in which Art Lovell had somehow returned to torture her every waking moment. When she woke up in the morning, she saw his face. When she went to sleep at night, she heard his voice. Sometimes she even thought she smelled the odor of his body when she tossed and turned in her bed. Then, just when she realized that she was alone and he was nothing more than a fiendish, satanic memory, she was filled with so much rage that she was sure she would explode into a million bloody pieces of flesh and bone.

Finally, out of sheer desperation, Carolyn sat down at the huge cherry wood desk in her office, set up her tape recorder and connected it to her telephone, just like in the old days. She dialed the operator.

"Information," a husky voice said in her ear. "How may I help you?"

Carolyn took a deep breath and said softly, "Olympia, Washington, please… Do you have a listing for Arthur Lovell?"

When a man answered the telephone, Carolyn nearly hung up. She recognized that voice—she had heard it in every nightmare she'd had in the last two months. But she also knew that she had to confront this reality now if she was ever to begin healing…

"Hello? Hello?"

"Art?"

"Yeah."

"This is Carolyn."

He didn't skip a beat. It was like she called him every other night. "What can I do for you?"

"I want to talk to you."

"Okay."

*Okay? That's it? Just…okay?*

"Are you somewhere that you can talk to me privately?"

"Yeah, I'm fine. What's up?"

*This man was a damn psychopath.*

"I just wanted to talk to you. I had some things on my mind and wanted to talk about it."

"That's the best thing to do," he agreed, suddenly enthusiastic. "That's the Lord's way—communicate!"

Carolyn nearly gagged. "Oh…you're a Christian now?"

"I certainly am. I don't believe in anything else."

*How convenient…*

"Well," Carolyn said abruptly, "what's been bothering me lately is what happened in Portland, Oregon, between you and me."

There was such a long pause that for a moment she was afraid he had hung up the phone, but finally he cleared his throat and answered, "That was a different person. You're not talking to the same person anymore."

She ignored him. "I just want to know why it happened."

"Well, that other person was sick, I guess. The devil had him."

"Did you know that what you were doing to me was wrong?"

"I don't think so. The doctor said I was a mixed-up person."

"So you've been to a doctor for this?"

"You bet! But the Lord helped me more than anybody."

*The Lord, huh? That's a good one…*

"How come you never came to me? How come you never told me you were sorry for what you did?"

"I told you I was sorry for all the misery I caused you the last time we talked and I truly am. There's nothing I can do to make it go away. All I can do is pray you can deal with it because I was able to deal with it, and…uh…"

*When was the last time we talked, you scummy piece of garbage? You never told me anything… You never said you were sorry…*

"That was sexual assault, Art," she blurted, fighting the rage.

"It was worse than that. But, Carolyn, you gotta let it all die. That's what the man told me. It's like a bad dream."

"Well, I'm still living this nightmare, Art."

"I feel for you."

It was all she could do not to throw the phone through the wall. She had to distance herself from this man and the power he still had over her…

"Don't you think you should have done something?" she asked quietly.

"Carolyn, if there was anything I could do to replace your…"

"Virginity?"

"Your trashed childhood, I would. Don't you think it's bothered me all these years?"

"No," Carolyn snorted, "I didn't know it bothered you. I didn't know you had a conscience at all because you never came to me."

"Carolyn, if it was possible, I would have. All I could do was to live the rest of my life correctly, and with the Lord's help and the help of a few others I've managed…"

"You've managed. Well, let me ask you this: the fact that I was your natural child made no difference to you, did it?"

"All I can tell you is—Rose is the one that's at fault."

Carolyn's mouth dropped. "It's Rose's fault?"

"To a degree—Rose and my mother's. That's the understanding I got."

"You don't want to accept any of the blame for that night in Portland?"

"A person's mixed up from childhood on. I didn't know right from wrong in that area because I was never taught."

"You didn't know that a grown man shouldn't have sex with a thirteen-year-old girl?"

"I told you I was sick, and if you don't think it's a sickness, you go check on it…"

"Oh, I know what the sickness is," Carolyn interrupted angrily. "It's called *pedophilia*. It's a sexual perversion where children are the preferred sexual object. I know all about it."

"That isn't what motivated your abuse."

"Oh, really? What motivated my abuse?"

"My disturbed childhood."

Carolyn was stunned into a one-word response. "Oh."

"It's different."

"You mean you're not willing to accept any of the blame *at all*?"

"I was deprived of having you as a child. Having you as *my* child. The whole situation deprived me. And I—this is what the doctor said—I didn't learn to love you as a child, as a father would, and I was trying to make up for it and showed it to you in the way I knew…"

*Oh, God, I've heard that one before, too.*

"Having sex with me was the way to show me that you cared?"

"It was the wrong type of affection…"

*No kidding…*

"And I remember the conversation, too," Carolyn interrupted. "I remember what you told me you were going to do. You were going to take me to Reno. Remember that?"

"Yeah, I…well, it's like a blur…like a bad dream…"

"How convenient for you to forget when I'm still living it."

"No, I didn't forget. It's just a bad dream, and it's trashed me, and I've been to the brink of just getting it over with…"

*Aw, you're breakin' my heart!*

"Well," Carolyn said, her voice dripping with sarcasm, "here I got a whore for a mother..."

"I apologize for that."

Carolyn ignored him. "... and I got some sailor that can't keep his pecker in check for a father..."

"Carolyn. Listen. There's not a day that goes by that I don't think about you and hope you're well and doing good and that the Lord's on your side. Not a day."

"Well, maybe the Lord's on my side, but I'm not well and I'm not doing very good. I'm facing the biggest battle of my life. I'm sick of the crap. I'm sick of the nightmares. I'm sick of feeling nasty."

"It wasn't your fault."

That statement stunned her; a huge lump suddenly swelled in her throat and she had to fight back tears. The last thing she wanted to do was to let him hear her cry. "That's right," she managed finally. "It wasn't my fault."

"Listen, I have to go. If I can help you, give me a call, okay?"

"Sure. Sure I will."

*That'll be a cold day in hell...*

Carolyn hung up the telephone and took the audiocassette tape out of the recorder. Even though the tears now flowed unchecked down her cheeks, she felt validated and strangely free for the first time in years.

She had met the Beast on her own terms, she had called the shots, and she held the proof in her hands.

# CHAPTER TWENTY-EIGHT

Like everyone else who has ever looked at prison as a very real possibility, Carolyn was willing to do whatever it took to stay out of it. If they wanted her to get out of her line of work, that was fine. If they wanted her to go into therapy, she was okay with that. She went to church with Ohler, played with Audra as much as she could, and tried to keep up with the mundane daily chores of running a large house. She had even gone into her psychiatrist's hospital for several days not long after she had taped her conversation with Art…

It didn't mean anything, of course. It was just for a rest. The media was so obnoxious that she couldn't even grocery shop until midnight, so Dr. Reid's Colonial Hills looked like an elegant place to get a little peace and privacy. It really hadn't been any big deal.

Of course, she *had* gone a little nuts in the crowded ward lobby the night she saw the cops parade Ray Moberg across the television screen in handcuffs, having finally admitted to murdering his stepdaughter and raping his little girl. As clearly as if it were yesterday instead of several months earlier, Carolyn envisioned her boss, Joel Fischer, carrying hundreds of photographs belonging to that monster into her office…graphic, hideous pictures of children being forced to do graphic, hideous things…

Carolyn had lost it right there in the lobby. Suddenly, to her, all the male patients wandering around in their hospital outfits and needing a shave were…of course…child molesters. She was embarrassed when she looked back on it and recalled that Dr. Reid had to explain to her that all the men needed shaves because they were in a mental ward and it wasn't like anyone handed out razors…

But that had been her only real breakdown and she had come back home in just six days, refreshed and more in control.

As long as she could stay home, Carolyn was positive she could get well. She had always done everything else she had ever set her mind on doing, so why couldn't she do that? As long as she didn't go to prison, as long as they didn't lock her up, she would pull through this.

Yesterday she had been sure of it.

Today was a different story.

Today she was sitting across the kitchen table from Larry and staring at him in wide-eyed disbelief. Today she was so angry and frightened that she couldn't even think straight.

Carolyn had believed that once she got back home, everything would go back to normal. It was *her* home, after all; surely she could rule her own environment. In an attempt to tighten that control, she had babied and pampered Larry ever since she had returned so he could learn to trust her again. And Larry was eating it up, growing more and more pompous every day, acting as if he now had the right to expect this kind of Miss Suzie Homemaker treatment...

But it galled and infuriated Carolyn beyond even her well-known ability to express herself. She was sharing living space with a man who had betrayed his daughter's innocence and didn't even seem to realize it, who couldn't make love to his own wife—and probably didn't want to anyway, and who had threatened her physically and even gone after her beloved golden retriever Chico with a knife... Did he think she had forgotten that? Well, she hadn't forgotten that. She would *never* forget that.

And now he was asking her to cop a plea just to save his sorry ass. He was supposed to be her best friend! He was supposed to love and protect and take care of her! Well, that was crap. He had betrayed her trust, as far as Carolyn was concerned, just like everyone else she had ever allowed to get next to her.

Otherwise, why would he ask her to do this? She had a great case—he knew that! When he talked to the press, that was all he talked about...how she had burned out in her work, how she got her past and present confused, how he understood why she might have broken under the strain of all these terrible cases...

In fact, to everyone on the outside looking in, Larry Huebner's battle for his wife's freedom was the most vivid and pure example of true love they had ever seen. He was indeed the proverbial Knight in Shining Armor Riding in on his White Steed to Rescue the Damsel in Distress.

It was a new position for Larry, and he liked it—especially since most of the articles presented Carolyn like some kind of a demented she-devil with the morals of an alley cat, the ambition of an unethical politician on his way up, and the ego of a publicity-crazed rock star. Her husband obviously had the patience of Job, reporters said, quoting her so-called friends. He was a saint and she didn't deserve him.

But now he had changed his mind, deciding to dump her like a worthless hunk of road-kill, and it was a cinch the press wouldn't blame him for that. She couldn't win, and he couldn't lose.

A strange humming noise droned through her head. "Why, Larry?" she whispered. "Why are you doing this to me?"

He wouldn't look at her. "You don't seem to understand, Carolyn," he said finally. "I have more than just you to think about. I have to take care of all of us."

"I'm not stupid. I know that."

Now he met her gaze, but his own eyes narrowed. He said nothing.

She shook her head. The buzzing noise increased; she coughed and cleared her throat to drown it out.

"Carolyn, if the…incident…with Audra…comes out, I have no job. There's no way that Valero will keep me on. I won't be able to get another job anywhere—my reputation will be completely ruined. We'll lose everything and probably end up back on the farm with my parents."

Carolyn stared at him, wordless. The thought of losing her home was even more terrifying than the idea of going to prison.

"But that's not all," he continued. "You know that George is going to find Rose and bring her into the courtroom. Have you thought about that? And he'll put your mother on the stand, too. So, there they'll be—Betty Shaw and Rose Lovell. That's a pair, isn't it? Plus, he'll probably drag Art out of the woodwork, too… What a feast for the press, huh? Just think what *that* will do to your little girl…"

Carolyn's eyes filled; she couldn't even breathe. Behind the strange humming in her head, Larry's voice seemed to pulsate louder, softer, louder, softer—in and out of her consciousness. The validity of his words just barely pierced a nearly impenetrable wall as strong as gunmetal wrapping itself around her brain.

"And there's something else that I'm sure you haven't thought of. What about this child you're fighting so hard to protect? That whole story is gonna come out, Carolyn, and there won't be anything you can do to stop it. Not only that, but you could actually get Ronni into trouble. Not just Glenda Best and her little girl, but Ronni…"

Trembling, Carolyn held up her hand, warding off his barrage of words, and shook her head so fiercely her teeth rattled. Why wouldn't he just shut up?

"I'll make you a deal, though," Larry continued casually, as if he hadn't just ripped a jagged crater through her world. "If it comes right down to it, I promise that I'll write a letter to the judge—a very confidential letter—telling him about my situation with Audra and how it might have contributed to all this. Between that and everything else you and George have done, I'm positive you won't get any jail time. Plus, I'll publicly plead with the judge to let you come home with me—he can mandate therapy, of course—and…"

*Oh, you're lovin' this, aren't you?*

When that voice finally exploded through the constant buzzing in her head like some earth-shaking climax, Carolyn bit down hard on her bottom lip to keep the words inside.

"I'm not telling you this just for my benefit, Carolyn," Larry continued in a soothing, patronizing tone of voice that made her livid. "You think that I'm the only one who's going to be hurt if the truth about the Audra situation comes out, but what about you? What about your own dirty laundry? You go to trial,

Huebner, and all that comes out. All of it. So you need to do this for all of us…including yourself."

*Man, you just don't know when to frickin' shut up, do you? Who are you to tell me what I need to do…*

"And you know that if the court doesn't order you to go into treatment, you won't go. We've seen that, haven't we? And…"

Now Carolyn looked straight at him, and spoke above that voice yammering senselessly in her head. "Wow, you've thought this all through, haven't you? You've got this all figured out."

"I know I'm right. If you plead Guilty, it stops right here…"

"And I could go to prison, Larry. For a long time. I guess that's okay with you?"

He sighed. "If you cop a plea, Carolyn, then we know exactly what they're going to charge you with: they're going to charge you with two counts and that's it. The federal prosecutor John Volz has already said so. But if you force this to go to trial, they're going to charge you with the maximum—one count per phone call *plus* the actual solicitation—and you could get as much as thirty-five years. They could also fine us $250,000 *per phone call*, which could be well over a million dollars! Now, you might be willing to take your chances with that, but I'm not. Trust me, Carolyn. I know what I'm doing…"

*Yeah, buddy, you're saving your ass, that's what you're doing…*

"You might want to keep something else in mind, Carolyn."

"What?"

He played his final trump with a face set in stone. "I'm not going to go broke or jeopardize Audra's lifestyle to pay an attorney thousands of dollars to defend *you* for trying to kill *me*. Think about it. I may be a lot of things, but I'm not stupid. I know where to draw the line and I'm drawing it right here."

Backing away, Carolyn stared at him. She had always thought that she ran the show in her own home, that Larry was far too weak to stand up to her, but she couldn't have been more wrong. Like an egocentric child, she had underestimated him and fallen prey to her own hype: she was strong…she was smart… she was fearless. Unfortunately she was learning the hard way that Larry Huebner owned her—and he had always owned her. Because he held the purse strings, she had no choice but to keep her mouth shut. She had no choice but to do what he told her to do.

Carolyn felt like a cornered rabbit dashing back and forth through a maze, unable to find an escape, until finally she had to accept the truth: *there was no way out.* She had no choice but to throw herself on the mercy of the court.

There was so much static behind Ronni's voice as she gave a careful, measured response to Carolyn's announcement that Carolyn couldn't help but wonder if her phone was tapped. "When I talked to you just a couple of days ago, you told me you were going to trial because George was convinced you could beat this. Now you tell me you're going to plead out. What's happened between then and now?"

Carolyn winced, but she managed a steady enough answer. "I haven't got any choice. I've just told George and PoPo, and now I'm telling you. I'm sure it's the right thing to do. All that matters to me now is that you and PoPo come with us to New Orleans for the sentencing. Will you do that? PoPo said he would."

"Of course," Ronni answered automatically. "What did George say?"

"Well, he wasn't happy, of course, but he says I can change my mind right up until I actually go to court to formally enter my plea, so I guess that option stays open. Besides, Larry says he's absolutely positive that I'm going to get probation with mandatory therapy, so why go through the nightmare of a trial? Think about what will come out…think about who can get hurt… No, Ronni, this is the right thing to do. I'm sure of it."

"Well, whatever you decide, I'm behind you all the way. And if this is what Larry wants, that's fine, too. He certainly has a right to say what he wants."

"He says he'll write a confidential letter to the judge about the incident with Audra if worse comes to worse. I think that might help."

"Wow. A confidential letter to a judge. That's big of him."

Carolyn quickly changed the subject to one safer. "I've decided to see if they'll let me go up to White Oak to visit my mother before I'm sentenced."

"What on earth for?"

"All the files…you know…about Rose and what happened back then." Just thinking about it made Carolyn's heart thud with both excitement and raw terror. "I've talked to George about it and he thinks it's a terrific idea. He says there's not a chance in hell that the judge will send me to prison if we can put all those pieces together. And it's like you said, too—I need to find out what happened."

"Will they let you go?"

"George says he'll go to Magistrate Chasez and get an amended order from her so I can leave. If worse comes to worse, he can come with me."

"Is Larry going?"

Carolyn snorted, "Are you kidding? He says he has to work and he doesn't have the time right now. But I don't want him to come, anyway. I'm better off alone."

"Does your mom have the files you need?"

"I doubt it. She probably threw them out with the garbage years ago. But I think my daddy said that his attorney was a woman named McKee—first lady lawyer in McKeesport or something like that. Anyway, once George gives me the go-ahead, I'm going to find her office and see if she still has anything there about me."

"I can't believe the press hasn't gotten their hands on any of this, Carolyn," Ronni mused in a low voice. "Doesn't that seem funny to you?"

"Not really. I never gave out any information that they could use to bother my family up there. For them to dig all that up would have been work and it's been easier for them to just make me out like I'm a crazy liar." Carolyn gave a self-mocking chuckle. "Besides, I didn't want anybody to realize how much I didn't know about myself. I mean, that's pretty embarrassing—not knowing who you are."

"Well, I don't know why. Lots of people don't."

That's true, Carolyn thought, but they have normal reasons for it…like they were adopted and the birth mother is hiding out somewhere. They're not like me. They don't have little patches of memory bouncing around where none of it makes any sense… Carolyn took a deep breath. There was *one* fact that she knew, though, and she owed it to Ronni to tell her the truth. Still, when she spoke, Carolyn's voice was little more than a whisper. "I have something else to tell you."

What she was going to do now was so hard. It took trust and pure nerve—neither of which she had in abundance these days—but she needed for Ronni to know the whole truth. Especially now.

"I'm listening."

Carolyn closed her eyes and wiped her sweating palms on her jeans. Why was this so hard? Ronni was her best friend and she would understand this. She had lived with it herself…

She had to just jump in and get it over with. "Art raped me when I was thirteen years old," she blurted, "and I confronted him a few days ago and I got it all on tape. I've even transcribed it—the whole conversation. I'm taking the tape up to White Oak and I'm going to tell my mother and I'm going to play it for her if she doesn't believe me."

"Art is your birth father, right?"

"Yes."

Carolyn's heart pounded as if she had just run a 20-mile marathon. It was all over now. But Ronni's voice was matter-of-fact, like she had just listened to Carolyn recite her grocery list.

"Well, I knew that. I didn't know it was Art, but I knew it was someone. Don't you feel better now?"

Carolyn sagged in relief. "You knew it?" she asked incredulously.

"Sure. Michaela and I figured it out a long time ago. I watched you work with little Troy Kellerman and I knew it, way back then. And I've seen you with Michaela. You're well-trained, Carolyn, but it takes a lot more than that to really *connect* with a sexually abused child the way you do."

"Well, why didn't you say anything?" Carolyn demanded indignantly.

Ronni laughed out loud. "What was I supposed to say? *Excuse me, did someone diddle you when you were a kid*? No. You had to get up the courage to say it out loud. Now you've done that. It's a huge step, Carolyn, and I'm proud of you."

Carolyn was silent, fighting tears. It meant so much to her to know that someone was proud of her.

"Really?" she whispered. "Are you really proud of me?"

"I really am. Now, you take that tape and you *make* your mom listen. You *make* her believe you." Ronni's voice finally broke. "Trust me, Carolyn. Once she gives you that, you can start getting well."

Carolyn couldn't believe that Magistrate Alma Chasez down in New Orleans actually trusted her enough to allow her to travel all the way to White Oak, Pennsylvania on her own, but she did. Carolyn was more grateful to that judge than she could ever express because she desperately needed to see her mother one more time before those iron doors slammed shut behind her—something she felt in her gut was going to happen. To Carolyn, Betty Shaw was still her mother. Carolyn still adored her, still needed her approval, still yearned to hear her say just once, *It's okay, Carolyn. I believe you...*

Now Carolyn carefully placed a tape recorder on her mother's dining table and removed a cassette tape from her handbag. She sat down.

"Mother, I called Lois McKee's office last week to see if she still had my files from when I was little, and I found out that she had just passed away. But a man there said I could come get whatever she had if you would come with me and sign a release so he could give them to me. Will you do that?"

"Sure."

"Mother, I have something to tell you."

Betty Shaw looked at Carolyn for a long, silent moment before she shook her head slowly. "Carolyn, why does everything have to be so dramatic with you?"

Carolyn didn't answer.

Mother pushed herself away from the dining table. "Would you like some tea before you get started with whatever this big drama is going to be?"

"That would be nice, thanks."

Heart pounding, Carolyn watched her mother move slowly toward the kitchen. She was still tiny and slim, forever the graceful ballerina, but she seemed to have aged substantially during the several years that had passed between this afternoon and the last time Carolyn had seen her. Audra had been an infant then and Mother had been a real pistol, but now she seemed surprisingly mellow, almost subdued. Carolyn couldn't help but wonder if she was well.

When Mother returned to the dining room carrying two cups of steaming hot tea, she had a forced smile on her face—like she was going to be a good hostess if it killed her—but Carolyn hardly noticed. Instead she accepted the tea with a preoccupied nod, a muttered "thank you," and wondered how to start this painful conversation.

Mother sat down, lit a cigarette, and started it for her. "What's going on, Carolyn?"

"Before I tell you this, I need you to understand something, Mother. I'm telling you this because I need you to know it, not because I expect you to do anything about it."

"Okay."

"Mommy..." The pet name slipped out before Carolyn could stop it. A fog of terror suddenly enveloped her entire body. What if it was all for nothing? What if she called the little girl a liar...again...like always...

"Mommy..." Her voice sounded funny to her own ears, crackling and childlike, as if it was coming from miles away instead of from her own throat. "Art raped me, Mommy."

The silence was heavy, sweltering, filled with skepticism. "When?"

"When Daddy sent me back to Washington the second time."

"Why are you saying that? Why do you always make up such horrible things?"

The terror lifted as quickly as it had come and suddenly Carolyn could see clearly. She met her mother's disdainful eyes with a fierce expression of determination in her own. "I have it on tape, Mother."

"You have *what* on tape?"

"I called Art about a month ago and confronted him. He admitted it, Mother, and I have it on tape."

"Let me hear it."

Carolyn dropped the cassette into the recorder and looked at her mother. "Are you sure?"

"Oh, for God's sake, I'm not a child! I *have* to hear it." She took a fierce drag on her cigarette. "I won't believe it until I hear it."

That did it. Carolyn could show no mercy. She flipped on the recorder and turned up the volume...

As the conversation droned on, filled with Carolyn's accusations and Art

Lovell's excuses, she watched her mother as if from a great distance and wondered why she couldn't seem to feel anything. As the minutes passed, the elderly woman slumped down in her chair, slowly, like a rag doll, until her head rested on her arms and her cigarette steadily burned out. She suddenly appeared old, defeated, and filled with as much pain as she had inflicted upon the little girl who once begged for her love.

Carolyn turned off the recorder and slowly moved to her mother's side, then dropped to her knees. She placed a tentative hand on the elderly woman's shoulder and whispered, "I'm so sorry, Mommy. I tried to warn you. I didn't want you to hear that..."

As Betty Shaw lifted her head, Carolyn was shocked to see that she was crying. And when the elderly woman took her in her arms, held her close, and whispered, "Oh, God, look what I've done," Carolyn couldn't hold back her own tears.

No matter what happened now, even if she went to prison for the next thirty-five years, no one could ever take the beauty of this healing moment away from her. It was one memory she would treasure forever.

Still, even as she was finally given the opportunity to weep with her mother, she didn't feel like a grown woman seeking support from her family during one of the most trying periods of her life. Instead she felt just like that terrified little girl trying desperately to find her way back home.

Her brow furrowed in confusion, Carolyn sat cross-legged on the floor in the living room, surrounded by legal documents dated nearly thirty years earlier. Wrapped in a terrycloth bathrobe, her still-lovely face glistening with cold cream, her mother was curled up on the sofa, smoking one of a hundred cigarettes and watching warily as Carolyn skimmed through the yellowing pages of her life.

"Mother, can I read you some stuff they're printing in the newspapers about me? It might help you understand what I need to know...and why..."

"Read me whatever you want."

"Okay." Carolyn shuffled through an oversized manila envelope until she found a single news clipping. "This one came out right after I was arrested: 'Although much has been written about Mrs. Huebner, she remains a mysterious figure about whom there is scant public record. The kidnapping incident in Pennsylvania never has been confirmed, despite attempts by reporters for various publications who have searched police and court documents...' "

Carolyn's voice trailed away for a long moment and she busied herself with putting the clippings away in the envelope. Finally she looked at her mother. "That's pretty typical stuff. All of a sudden, no one believes me. In my hometown, they call this *The Huebner Legend*, and if I don't prove that I didn't make it all up, I might go to prison. I know you've never wanted to talk about it, Mother, and I've tried very hard to protect you, but now…"

"I know, Carolyn, and it's all right." Stubbing out her cigarette, she immediately lit another. "See if you can follow along with your copies, okay?" She held up one set of legal papers, with the flourishing title of In the Orphans' Court of Allegheny County Petition for Adoption of Carolyn Sue Lovell written across the top. "Let's start at the beginning. These are your legal adoption papers. They're very clear on important points, so follow along carefully. George Shaw was your grandfather and I am your step-grandmother—see that? George's son, Arthur Dean Lovell, brought you to this house in 1959 when you were about ten months old. He asked us to keep you until he could get on his feet because his wife and your birth mother, Rose Mattair Lovell, had abandoned him and behaved like such a slut that he couldn't live with her anymore. Then he left.

"We took you to the doctor and found that you were suffering from malnutrition and neglect, so we just decided right then to make you our own. On September 6, 1962, we legally adopted you and you became Carolyn Sue Shaw. Your mother…"

"*You're* my mother," Carolyn interrupted automatically.

Mother held up her hand and nodded. "Okay. *Rose* was nowhere to be found and we knew only that she had been born in Florida. We had no address for her and she had never contacted us.

"We thought that was the end of it. It certainly should have been. But just a few months later, we find out that Rose had shown up out of nowhere and appealed the adoption to the Court of Common Pleas of Allegheny County, Pennsylvania. It was also at this juncture that we learned that Art had actually *stolen* you from Rose rather than face the possibility that he would lose custody of you—and we felt really badly about that. So we told Rose that we would turn you over to her, but not until you became acquainted with her and we could see that there would be some maternal bonding there." Mother paused and waved a thick cloud of cigarette smoke away from her face. "Are you following this?"

Carolyn nodded, completely absorbed. "Go on."

"Okay…well…Rose came to McKeesport and talked with us. She even met you. Do you remember that?"

"No."

"Well, she did. Anyway, she was constantly contradicting herself, so we knew she was lying just about every time she opened her mouth, and I got more and more nervous about you being with her. I just didn't trust her at all. We even hired a detective to go to her house in Beaumont and find out how she lived. That was the only reason she admitted that she had an illegitimate daughter by a married man—and he was paying for all this legal crap. If it hadn't been for him, I guess, none of this would have happened.

"Anyway, she didn't have much interest in you the whole time she lived in McKeesport and you never did take to her. She got another married boyfriend while she was here—even though she'd only been here about a month—and finally we just decided we weren't giving you back to her, period. I spent hours hiding you from her—it was just crazy. We'd hide down in the basement while she banged on the front door…"

"And one time someone crawled across the kitchen floor to get me animal crackers because I was hungry…right?"

Mother nodded, a softly reminiscent smile on her face. "That was me. Another time Bobby stuck you in the drier to hide you, and once we even had to put you in the hospital for several days because your nerves were shot. Rose showed up and your doctor actually threw her out of your room. It was a terrible time, but we were in a fight that I understood. We all understood it… Carolyn, are you all right?"

Carolyn was more than all right. She was thrilled because those inexplicable flashes of memory had finally been explained and validated. She wasn't crazy. It had all really happened.

She bit back tears of pure joy. "I'm fine. Go on."

"Anyway, finally, we had a full hearing in front of a wonderful judge and he actually listened to everyone—including you—before he decided that it was in your best interest for us to keep you. I think he was the only intelligent person involved in this whole mess.

"But Rose wasn't finished. By now I think she was just thoroughly pissed off, you know? Anyway, a couple of weeks later, she filed an appeal to the Superior Court of Pennsylvania—and this time it was granted, reversing the lower court's decision. In fact, not only was it upheld, but George and I were blasted for not looking harder for Rose and a number of other reasons, none of which made much sense to me. But if you read the closing paragraphs of the Superior Court decision, you'll see that the real issue to those guys was that you *belonged* with your birth mother, no matter *what* she was and no matter how long you had been with us or how happy you were. They ignored all the evidence, not to mention your fragile mental health by that time, and just handed you over to Rose like what *you* needed didn't matter a hill of beans.

"Well, of course, we appealed that decision all the way to the Pennsylvania Supreme Court, but they refused to hear our case at all and that was the end of it. So we had to have another hearing to see how to transfer you from our care to hers, and one of the judges that been on our side called Rose into his chambers. He asked her if she had anybody in Texas and she said she didn't, so he told her, 'Well, this is the way I feel about this. I feel really bad for this little girl and these people who have raised her. She's about ready to go to school next year, and I'd like her to go to school with kids she's been playing with. And if you can manage it, I'd like you to stay in this territory.' And she agreed like it was nothing.

"Well, she had a couple of rooms in Duquesne, just across the river from McKeesport, and she asked if she could come get you so you could spend the night at her apartment. The judge agreed and she came and got you that afternoon.

"So, the next morning when we got up, I noticed that there was some nerve medicine here that we had been giving you because all the court stuff had you so upset, and it was still here on the counter. George said he'd take it to you before he went to work and he left.

"A little while later I'm washing windows, and I see George practically staggering back up the sidewalk. Even though I opened the door and asked what was wrong, I already knew the answer. I knew you were gone. I could tell by the look on his face.

"After that, your daddy lost his mind. I don't know any other way to put it. He went to bed and he wouldn't get up until his brother, your Uncle Artie, finally busted in and threatened to beat him to death if he didn't get back to work. His heart was broken.

"Anyway, Rose wouldn't let us have anything to do with you. If we sent a toy for you, we had to send one for the other kid. We even sent your dog down to you, thinking that you'd feel better if you had something from up here…"

Carolyn shook her head, totally confused. "You knew where I was?"

"To begin with, sure. Later on, no. We eventually lost track of you."

"I never got any toys—and I sure never got a dog… At least, I don't think…" Carolyn's voice trailed away. "Why didn't you come get me?" she demanded suddenly. "Everywhere I went I looked for you! I just kept waiting and waiting…"

"Carolyn, think about it," Mother answered patiently. "We didn't have any more money, and Rose had legal custody of you. She stole you from us and broke a verbal agreement with a judge, but once she had you with her in Texas there wasn't a thing we could do.

"Then, almost three years to the day after you first disappeared, I got a phone call from Rose and she says, 'I have to talk and don't you say anything until I'm done. Carolyn—we just can't control her down here and she's caused so much trouble and the school psychologist has talked to her and they say we'd better send her back to the people she loves or she'll be nothing.' And then she tells me, 'You'll have to come and get her.' That's all she said."

"I never saw a school psychologist. We moved around all the time. I never even went to school! At least, I don't think I did…"

"I figured that out soon enough. Anyway, when I brought you back from Texas, I told your daddy that if everything I'd heard down there was true, you needed a psychiatrist. You were also way too skinny—the doc said you looked like a concentration camp victim—and you moved like an old lady. George promised to get you all the help he could, but he didn't. He got into religion pretty heavy after you disappeared and his answer to everything was prayer. He never got you to a doctor and wouldn't hear of me trying to get you one, either.

"So, the final result was that I lost everything, Carolyn. I lost your dad, and we lost his business, and..." Her voice broke. "And...I guess you lost everything, too."

*Yes, but so much pain could have been avoided if someone had just told me the truth...and if someone had just listened to me...*

Carolyn recognized that her mother's whitewashed version of the truth wasn't *exactly* the way it had happened. She remembered that her daddy had attended the parent-teacher meetings without her mother, that *someone* had found a tutor for her, a counselor, and even a special instructor to teach her to walk all over again. Carolyn was sure that her mother hadn't done all that. She had been too disinterested, almost from the beginning...

Still, the bottom line was that little Carolyn Sue Shaw was just an unimportant statistic to a panel of black-robed men that wouldn't remember her name if it was thrown at them today. It hadn't mattered to them what she wanted or needed as a little girl—it had only mattered that she and her family acquiesce to their egos, experts and edicts. Consequently, she was just another child victim of the system—like little Troy Kellerman, or Kelly Best.

It was history repeating itself, over and over and over again.

Still, even though it had taken twenty-three years, she finally knew the truth. She finally knew who she was; all the pieces in her life were beginning to fit.

It was, at least, a first step...

# CHAPTER TWENTY-NINE

Carolyn had only one week before her sentencing hearing took place on September 9th down in New Orleans, and she knew it was going to be her last week of freedom. No one else seemed to believe this as much as she did, but Carolyn could feel it in her gut. Still, she managed to put on a good face. Even now Larry, Ronni, PoPo and Carolyn were all sitting around her dining table going through a mountain of legal documents, medical reports, letters of support for George Simno to submit to the presiding judge, and anything else they could find that might be helpful.

It wasn't going to work. That had been very clear to her when she had gone back down to New Orleans, right after her return from Pennsylvania, to formally enter her Guilty plea before Judge A. J. McNamara, who was sitting in for her sentencing for judge Morey Sear. That right there had seemed like a bad omen to Carolyn: the judge that George wanted was at home, sick with the flu.

The formal hearing itself had been a nightmare, too, especially when the judge had said, "Do you understand, Mrs. Huebner, that if you give up your right to a trial, and if you plead guilty and I accept your plea, you would give your rights up, all of the rights that I've mentioned, and the Court will enter a judgment of guilty based on your plea and later sentence you based on that finding of guilty based on your plea? Do you understand that?"

The hardest thing that Carolyn ever had to do was to answer, "I do."

But she did...she understood, all right. Even though Larry had told the judge directly that he did not fear for his life, Carolyn knew that she had given up all her rights and now she had nothing left. Her fate was in the hands of strangers, and all she could do was pray for just a little bit of compassion.

Carolyn leaned back in her chair and rubbed her eyes. She was exhausted, but she couldn't think of anything else she could do to prepare for this upcoming hearing. Last weekend she had taken Audra and Ronni's daughter, Michaela, up to the Pedernales River for a picnic being held by Ohler's church— just in case she didn't get another opportunity to spend so much precious time with people she loved. She had begged Larry to come along and even told him that she felt in her heart she was going to go to prison, but he had looked at her like she was crazy and shook his head.

"There's no way that's going to happen, Huebner," he had declared. "I'm going to make a public declaration of support on the stand and no one's going to have the nerve to go against what the wronged husband wants. But, in the meantime, I have to work so I can go to New Orleans with you. Don't you worry about a thing. You go on and have a good time. We'll have another picnic later…"

How can such a smart man be so stupid? she wondered now. He honestly thinks that all he has to do is tell the feds to jump and they're going to ask how high… Poor deluded idiot. He's in for such a shock… They don't give a damn what he wants… This is all about winning to them. They don't care what happens to me…or him…

Carolyn felt this way even though her attorney, during negotiations with the federal prosecutors, had gotten them to agree that they wouldn't ask for any prison time in exchange for Carolyn's Guilty plea. In fact, their promise to "stand silent" was made during a telephonic conference call with Carolyn, Larry, George and Dr. Reid, so there were plenty of witnesses, but Carolyn just didn't feel right about it.

She knew who the feds were, and she didn't trust them.

"Hey, did you guys see this?" Ronni's voice squeaked with excited disbelief as she pushed a beautifully handwritten letter across the table. "I just found this in your mom's stuff… Carolyn, did you know this was in here?"

Carolyn picked up the letter dated November 28, 1968, and stared at it, unable to believe her eyes. Picking her way through the misspelled words and bad sentence structure, she managed to read the first real validation of her childhood on paper that she had ever seen:

" 'Dear Betty and  George, I'm writing this letter trying to make peace with the world & people.

" 'I know that it has been sometime since I wrote but it wasn't possible. I haven't felt up to it. I have been under mental strain and I'm now in the hosipatal taking treatment to recover. The doctor said it would be at least three week here then treatment outside.

" 'Carolyn probably never mention me are asked have you heard from me. Betty the doctor has told me to accept the fact that Carolyn wants to live with George & you and her being a child that even though she has been hurt by me it wasn't because I didn't love her but sick mentally and couldn't control myself. I only pray that someday she will forgive and come to love me as her mother.

" 'I'm sending her something for Xmas. I hope I'll be out of the hospital in time to mail it before Xmas come.

" 'Will close for now. Answer if you see that you want to. As Ever, Rose' "

Carolyn looked at Ronni, who was wearing a large, imbecilic grin and bouncing in her chair like an overactive two-year-old. Carolyn shook her head. "Can you believe this?" she asked in disgust. "Art says what he did wasn't *his* fault… Rose says what she did wasn't *her* fault… The doctors all say that these pitiful people can't control themselves, so I guess it's *my* fault. They didn't know what *they* were doing, but I'm going to prison because *I* did..."

"You're not going to prison," Larry said firmly, closing a legal-sized file and setting it off to the side. "Give me that letter so it doesn't get lost."

"Okay, Kid, listen to this," PoPo interrupted. "This is from your Aunt Kat to the judge and I bet you'll find it real interestin'. Ready?"

Carolyn shrugged, "Sure."

"Okay. Here's what she says:

" '...The crime for which she is accused is so totally out of character of her. I have known Carolyn for a large part of her lifetime, since she was about six years old. I was married to her biological mother's uncle for 18 years.

" 'My husband's niece, Carolyns (sic) biological mother, was one Rosie Jane Mattair, who started out as a young girl making her living off men. She met and married a serviceman in California, because, at the time, wives received allotments. She became pregnant and from all indications, continued her escapades even then. As I understand it, when the baby, Carolyn was born she would leave her alone and continue with her previous lifestyle. Her husband reportedly came home one evening and found the baby alone in the apt., unattended. At this time she was about 3 months old. He took the baby, went AWOL from the service, and fled to Pennsylvania, where his parents lived. He adopted this child to his Mom and Dad, by telling the Court her Mother was dead, so I was told at that time. Carolyn was raised by these people, as her parents, until she was about 6 yrs. old.

" 'Rosie Jane visited us over the next 5 or 6 yrs. and never mentioned the baby. Then after all this time had passed, she came wanting advice from her uncle about how to get her baby back. Her uncle was full of advice on how best to do this. I tried to tell her the child would not know who she was, and it would be cruel to take her from her family. Her uncle told her to go to the city where they lived, set up residence, and try to get her through court, but if this failed, to take the child and get back to Texas any way she could. She got the court to give her visitation rights, and was finally awarded custody with the stipulation she stay in Pennsylvania, so I was told. But she took her uncle's advice and fled to Tex. immediately after custody was awarded. She wound up at my house with a very frightened little girl who had been taken by someone who told her 'I'm your Mother.' She only spent one night with us and left. She would come back and visit every few weeks, but the child was always very quiet, frightened, and withdrawn. She eventually became very friendly with me because I was good to her and offered her love. She would tell me things like Rose would not feed her, would lock her in a closet, beat her and other things for punishment because she wanted her family...' "

PoPo's voice trailed away and he was quiet for a few minutes, but Carolyn could see that tiny muscle working in his jaw like it always did when he was angry or upset. While she waited patiently for him to speak, Carolyn remembered with affection the statuesque beauty that had been her loving Aunt Kat...

"Why is it that folks never come out with these stories 'til it's too late?" PoPo asked finally. He pulled a crumpled pack of cigarettes from his shirt pocket, took one out, and lit it. "Just think," he continued, waving away the smoke, "if outsiders—or even family members—would just get involved when the kids are little, maybe the kids wouldn't grow up and land in prison. Think how much money the government could save if taxpayer dollars went to Child Protective Services to take care of the little ones *before* they're abused instead of just building more and more prisons to house 'em in *afterward*." He shook his head slowly and sighed in disgust. "Hell, I'm just preachin' to the choir, ain't I? Sorry. I reckon I'd best climb down off this soapbox and get back to work."

"No, no, you're right, PoPo," Ronni said quietly. "Look at these reporters. They see this story as a way to sell papers or get people to watch their newscasts—or, shoot, just to tear Carolyn apart for the fun of it. But they're missing the real crux of the matter, aren't they? The story they *should* be telling is about the mental and emotional damage that's done when a child is abused, and then that child grows up and inflicts it on society or passes it down to his own kids—sometimes in ways that we don't see until it's too late. How many people do you think are in prison today because nobody got involved when they were children?"

"Is that a rhetorical question or do you want an answer?" Larry interrupted, waving a thick packet of paperwork in the air. "Because if you don't want an answer, you might be interested in some of the medical reports we're getting in from nearly ten years ago."

"Like what?" PoPo asked.

"Well, here's one from Dr. Javier Zapata, a psychiatrist Carolyn saw for a few months in Houston along with a social worker back in 1979," Larry replied. "I remember him, but he never said anything to me about this. He says here that her *profile type is fertile ground for...dissociative phenomena...* Does anyone know what that means?"

"I think that's like where you leave in your head and go someplace else you'd rather be," Ronni answered with a grin. "You know, kind of like *Sybil*— only not as bad."

Carolyn snorted in disgust. "Sybil was a multiple personality. My personality is more than enough all by itself. I don't need more than one. What else does it say, Larry?"

"Well, in Dr. Reid's report he talks about fugue-like dissociative episodes, too, sometimes involving amnesia—but he also says that they're difficult to corroborate. He mentions... let's see, where is it... 'At times she experienced what I perceived to be brief episodes (sometimes lasting one to two days) of lost contact with reality...' "

Carolyn was acutely humiliated when everyone at the table turned to stare at her. She felt the blood rush to her face. "He's talking about the night I thought all the men in the ward lobby were child molesters," she muttered. "I went nuts, I admit it. I did."

Larry ignored her embarrassment and continued reading: "'It is important to note the consistency and similarity between testing done in 1979 and these results. The intelligence testing and MMPI support the chronicity of this defendant's disorders, and, along with the corroborating history from past psychotherapists, suggest that her current symptoms have not been merely created in response to the current charges...' "

"That's important, Carolyn!" Ronni interrupted in excitement. "He's saying that none of this psychobabble and mumbo-jumbo is being coughed up now just to get you off! He's showing the judge that these professional opinions are almost ten years old. It just doesn't get any better than this!"

"Carolyn," PoPo interjected in his typically calm voice, "did anyone ever tell you this stuff before? I mean, have you ever heard the term *dissociative* before?"

Carolyn stared at him, wide-eyed and fighting tears of panic. Suddenly her entire body started shaking; her hands felt like ice. She took a deep breath. "I don't think so," she whispered, "but maybe I have... I don't know..."

Then, unbidden and without warning, those enormous black-and-purple bruises she had discovered on her body while she was in Orleans Parish Prison slammed back into her memory and once again she heard her cellmate Chandra Greene's voice.

*"Who got you, girl? What in hell did you do?"*

And once again she remembered that, like so many times in the past, she hadn't known the answer...

But now, unlike all those times in the past, Carolyn finally recognized that she was in real trouble. Now she desperately needed help.

She was also absolutely positive that she wasn't going to get it.

"Are you listening to me, Ronni?" Gazing at her friend's terrified face through the bullet-proof glass in the holding cell on the top floor of the New Orleans Federal Courthouse, Carolyn tried to swallow her own panic and sound in control—maybe for the last time in her life. "It's going to be all right. They'll let me out in three months, you'll see. I'm only going to Lexington Penitentiary for a medical and psychiatric evaluation, remember? George says the judge had to do this—we had so much publicity that he couldn't just let me walk out. Do you hear me?"

"I hear you."

"Okay." Carolyn's voice softened and she placed one hand against a square screen in the center of the glass. Ronni pressed her own hand against it. "I've got to say this fast. I want you to know how much you've meant to me. I've never known anyone in my whole life who's been as good a friend to me as you have." Her voice cracked for the first time. "Don't leave me, Ronni. I need you now."

"I'm here, Carolyn. You know that. I'll always be here."

"You'll look after Larry and Audra for me, won't you?" Ronni nodded.

Carolyn pressed her hand even harder against the screen. "There's one more thing, Ronni. It means more to me than anything else in the world."

"What?" she whispered.

"Write my story. Please, Ronni. No one else knows me like you do. I want people to know my story. I want people to know who I am. I want people to understand how this happened. I don't want to go down in history as this crazy woman who tried to kill her husband. Not after everything I've been through..." Her voice trailed away.

"Please, Ronni...please help me. You're a writer—you can do this. You know what happened. You were there. If you don't write this, it won't get written. I won't allow anyone else that much access to my life."

Ronni was silent for a long moment before she finally nodded and said quietly, "I will, Carolyn. I promise I'll write it. Later. But I'll write it."

Carolyn was nearly overwhelmed with relief. Still, once Ronni had let herself out of that cramped metal room, Carolyn gave in to the tears and the panic. Moments later, when Larry came in, she looked at his sweaty, stricken face and tried desperately not to despise him for his cowardice. When PoPo finally squeezed his tall, lanky frame into the tiny room, she stared hard at the old man and tried to memorize his features just in case he died before she saw him again. She begged him to look in on her Audra, whispered that she loved him, and then prayed for courage as her arms were pulled behind her back and handcuffs locked tightly around her wrists.

"Where are we going now?" she asked a heavy-set woman in a gray uniform.

The woman gave Carolyn a sweetly maternal smile that made her feel a little safer. "You'll spend tonight in jail, honey, and then you'll be on your way to Kentucky."

Carolyn's mouth went dry and the blood drained from her face. "Jail?" she whispered in terrified disbelief. *"I have to go back to Orleans Parish Jail?"*

"Just for tonight, honey, that's all."

*Oh, God, I can't go back there… Please don't send me back there…*

Orleans Parish Prison was just another, newer location in her nightmares, right up there with locked closets in Beaumont and dead blonde babies on the floors of gymnasiums. It was dark and dank and sweltering hot inside, and there were so many roaches in the mattresses that you could actually *watch* the material undulate…

*Oh, God, if I can really dissociate, let me do it now… please, please let me do it now…*

But she couldn't. And she didn't. Apparently, this time, God intended for her to stare reality right in the face.

"PoPo and I had a real interesting conversation with a guy waiting up there to see his brother while you were visiting with Carolyn," Larry said, strapping his seatbelt tightly across his protruding belly. He looked at me in concern. "Are you all right, Ronni? Here, let me help you…"

"I hate to fly," I muttered, locking my own seatbelt and closing my eyes as the plane's engine revved up. "I just hate it. Talk to me. What guy?"

"I don't know his name—didn't catch it—but he said he was in the courtroom when Carolyn entered her plea."

"So? A lot of people were." The plane lifted off and so did my stomach. I kept my eyes closed and fought nausea as a cold sweat broke out on the back of my neck. "You'd have thought it was a movie set with all those reporters and broadcasters…"

"Well, anyway, one of the things you may not have known about was that the federal prosecutors promised us that they wouldn't fight for any prison time if Carolyn would cop a plea…"

"Of course I knew about it," I snapped. "We all knew about it. They lied. And George is an idiot. What kind of attorney doesn't get a promise like that in writing?"

PoPo yawned, removed his glasses and rubbed his eyes. "An attorney that relies on his friendship with the other side, that's all. George is a good attorney, Ronni. He was just too trusting this time."

"Then he's not a good attorney. A good attorney doesn't trust anybody. Ever."

"Listen to me, Ronni," Larry interrupted. "I think this guy we were talking to might have explained a lot. He said that the federal prosecutor, John

Volz, is a real important guy in New Orleans, but he's got egg on his face right now and Carolyn fell right into his hands."

Larry paused dramatically, but I just gave him a blank look. "What are you talking about?"

"Well, Volz was the lead federal prosecutor in two trials against Louisiana's governor—I think his name was Edwards or something like that—on charges of racketeering and fraud. Apparently Volz went on television all the time bragging about how this was an open-and-shut case and the governor didn't have a chance. Well, the first trial ended in 1985 with a hung jury leaning toward acquittal, and the second one ended with a full acquittal in 1986. Apparently everyone knows this governor is crooked, but Volz is now the laughingstock of New Orleans because he can't sink him..."

"What's this got to do with Carolyn?" I interrupted impatiently. "She's not hanging out with the governor, is she?"

PoPo patted my hand soothingly. "Calm down, Ronni. Carolyn's case was real public, so she played right into this prosecutor's game, see? If she didn't get any time at all, Volz would've looked worse to the people than he already looked, so he had to put Carolyn away... That's the way politics works down here, you know."

I gaped at PoPo and felt even sicker to my stomach than I had before, but now it had nothing to do with flying. "Are you saying that they ignored all the evidence about the cases she was working on, *and* all the medical reports, *and* all the proof about her childhood just because this jerk had to win a case to save his own bloody career? Just to make him look good?"

"Well, that might be true," Larry interjected smoothly, "but we can't prove it. Still, it could play well for us when Carolyn comes back from Lexington in three months..."

"*Us?*" I demanded furiously. "What are you talking about, *us*? This is about Carolyn, not *us*!"

Larry gave a deep sigh. "I know that, Ronni. All I mean is, when Carolyn comes back, the case won't be nearly as big as it is now and the feds can just quietly disappear into the woodwork without anyone noticing. Then the judge can do the right thing and send her home with me and I can get her the help she needs."

I glared at him head-on and dared him to look back at me, but of course he didn't. What do you care about doing the right thing? I asked him in silent fury. What do you even *know* about it? The right thing would have been for you to get on that stand this afternoon and tell the court the truth! *That* might have saved her—if you had told the story of how what you did in front of your own little girl might have actually sent your wife over the edge! *That* would have been the courageous thing to do...*that's what a real man would have done...*

Or you could have even written that confidential letter to the judge… that letter you promised you'd write and didn't…

But, hey, what difference does it make? Now you get to go home and play the White Knight all over again while Carolyn spends the next ninety days behind locked iron doors, terrified because she can't get out…

Larry put his hand on my arm. "I know what you're thinking, Ronni, I do."

I jerked away, blinked back tears and shook my head. "No, you don't. You don't have a clue."

"Ronni, we can talk about this later…"

"I never want to talk about this at all."

PoPo cleared his throat uncomfortably. "S'cuse me, Larry, but don't you need to call Carolyn's mom when we get to San Antonio?"

The old man looked so miserable that I was ashamed of myself. He deserved better than to get stuck in the middle of a stupid argument between Larry and me over something he knew nothing about. Carolyn was *The Kid* to PoPo, another one of his beloved children, and I knew his heart was breaking…

Larry gulped. "Oh, God, I forgot! What am I going to tell Betty? I promised her that Carolyn wouldn't get any time and I just don't know how I'm going to explain this."

I tried to smooth over the rough waters between Larry and me, if only for PoPo's sake and if only for this moment. "She's been a victim of the legal system far more than we have, so she'll take this in stride. But don't worry about it, Larry. I'll talk to her."

"Will you really?" He went pale with relief. "I can call her just as soon as we land…if that's all right with you."

I shrugged. "Sure. That's fine."

As the plane bounced and skidded down the runway of the San Antonio Airport, I closed my eyes and prayed fervently that we would make it through this landing in one piece. As we disembarked and I saw Kevin waiting with our lovely Michaela across from the roped-off *American Airlines* lobby, I was filled with such joy that I could hardly contain myself. Just the sight of them let me know that I was safe and secure in their love, immune from the tragedies and chaos that made up Carolyn Huebner's life…

"Can you call Betty for me, Ronni?"

"In just a minute, Larry."

Swallowing my irritation, I marched away from him and found myself engulfed in Kevin's powerful arms. Planting a huge kiss right on my lips, he lifted me off my feet and swung me around like I had been gone for months instead of just a weekend, and in the background I heard Michaela squealing with excitement. The radical difference between my warm relationship with my family and Carolyn's icy one with hers didn't escape me, and for the hundredth time since this had all begun, I was deeply grateful for their loving support.

"I have to call Carolyn's mom," I finally told Kevin breathlessly. "I promised Larry I would. I won't be but a minute."

His eyes widened. "She doesn't know?"

"No."

"Okay, go on. We'll meet you down by the baggage pick-up, all right?"

I nodded, stood on my tip-toes for one more kiss, and then walked toward the phone booth where Larry and PoPo were waiting.

"Is this Mrs. Shaw?"

A smoke-husky voice answered rather nervously, "Yes?"

"Mrs. Shaw, you don't know me... My name is Ronni Hoessli and I'm a very good friend of Carolyn's."

"Oh, yes! I know who you are. In fact, I was hoping I'd get a chance to talk to you at some point."

"Really?"

"Yes, I just wanted to thank you..."

Suddenly her voice thickened, then broke, then trailed away completely. I held my breath in astonishment. Good Lord...this ice-cold woman...was she crying?

"For what, Mrs. Shaw?" I asked gently. "I haven't done anything you need to thank me for."

She took an audible, shaky breath. "That's not true. You've been there for Carolyn, and we... and I..."

I rescued her. "That's what friends are for, Mrs. Shaw."

She seemed to pull herself together and once more became quite controlled. "What happened in court today?" she asked in the distant, don't-touch-me voice that Carolyn had often described.

"Well, Mrs. Shaw, I'm afraid the news isn't good—although it could be worse. They're sending her to Lexington Penitentiary for three months to undergo medical and psychiatric evaluations, and then they're bringing her back to New Orleans for the judge to deliver his final sentence. So it's not over yet. We still have a little time."

When Betty Shaw groaned, low in her throat like a severely wounded animal, it was a heart-wrenching sound that scared me half to death. "Oh, my God," she whispered, "what have I done? This is my fault...all my fault..."

I was silent for quite awhile simply because I didn't know what to say. As far as I was concerned, she was right—or very nearly right. Carolyn's life would have turned out so differently had this woman not blamed an innocent child for something she hadn't done and couldn't change.

But the truth was that Betty Shaw had felt cheated out of the perfect 1950s life she had envisioned for herself, her husband, and their 2.4 children. Then, just when she had thought the mess couldn't get any worse, her granddaughter had had the audacity to *need* her, to drag her beyond those pretty picket-fence boundaries and force her to confront an ugly reality that couldn't be whitewashed. To Betty Shaw, this was the final and unforgivable sin.

Finally I looked at Larry, who was watching me anxiously, and spoke loud enough for him to hear. "It's not *all* your fault, Mrs. Shaw," I said deliberately, staring straight into Larry's eyes. "There were lots of people that let Carolyn down. Lots and lots of people…"

As Carolyn sat on the cold concrete floor, all alone in her cell, she struggled to keep her sanity. Somewhere nearby she could hear the scratching noises of scurrying rodents, maybe hiding in corners, maybe burrowing into bedding…or perhaps there were hundreds of cockroaches scrabbling about in this cell just as there had been up in The Clinic. Carolyn shivered.

Orleans Parish Prison was famous—or infamous—for being one of the biggest, vilest, most brutal county jails in the country, with a flood of unrepresented poor whites and African-Americans being hauled inside every single day and then forgotten. The Texas correctional facilities were often mentioned as the worst in the nation, but Carolyn knew that wasn't true. The worst correctional facility in the country wasn't a *facility* at all—it was an overpopulated hellhole located in the heart of New Orleans.

For the first time in years, Carolyn allowed herself to think about the *Yellow Brick Road* and how she had so often followed it home when she was little. She thought about her visiting Angels and her vision of the illuminated Christ hovering over the silks in the cornfields. And even though she had been alone in her Beaumont prison back then, locked away and in the dark, she still didn't have the sense of isolation and shame that she experienced now. Now she felt utter panic. She felt sheer terror. She felt absolute horror. Now all she could think was, *What are you doing here, girl? What are you doing here?*

That was the moment when she truly understood that God was demanding she stop all her craziness and let Him have her full attention. She could feel His healing presence seeping through her terrified spirit and she knew that she had to somehow salvage her tattered relationship with Him. Somewhere, perhaps hidden away in the darkest recesses of her soul, she had to find a tiny root of faith and connect to it. She had been so destructive most of her life that she had pretty much devastated anything aboveground as far as her commitment to God was concerned, but she hadn't realized it. After all, that had been the only way she could live in her wickedness and do exactly what she wanted to do. She had thought she had all the answers, but they weren't God's answers.

In her haste to live the way she wanted to live, Carolyn realized now that she had burned through that little root. She had cut it out of the earth. She had so thoroughly trashed it that now she was scrabbling in the dirt hungrily seeking just a fragment that might finally begin to grow.

With tears streaming down her face and shivering with fear, Carolyn drew her knees to her chest, wrapped her arms around them and began to rock back and forth, praying with all her heart to a Being whose presence she knew she wasn't worthy to be in. But He hadn't ignored her when she was a child—in fact, He had come to steal her away more times than she could remember—and she knew He wouldn't ignore her now. He would hear her pleas for His help, for His love, for His divine guidance, and for His forgiveness. He would hear…

Then, in a voice small and timid and little more than a whisper, Carolyn began to sing. It was an old Gospel song she had learned in Ohler's church, and it had comforted her raging spirit when she had first sung it. And even though she wasn't quite sure of the words or the tune, she was absolutely certain of the meaning…

*Trouble in my way… I gotta cry sometime.*
*Trouble in my way… I gotta cry sometime…*

Then, when she heard an answering rich African voice singing a response from a cell nearby, followed by another voice and then another, filling the floor with rapturous melody, Carolyn became quiet and just listened…

*Trouble in my way… I gotta cry sometime.*
*Trouble in my way… I gotta cry sometime.*

Smiling, Carolyn took a deep breath and sang her own soaring response through tears—tears that offered her respite and joy beyond anything she had ever felt before in her life. Voices all up and down the floor joined in, resonating with the elation that Carolyn felt as she sang, echoing the words…

*I lay awake at night… But that's all right*
*Because I know Jesus… Jesus will fix it…after while.*

Then, as her voice faded away, so did the others. Finally, after each glorious round of voices softened and gradually floated away, the floor fell silent once again.

# CHAPTER THIRTY

The United States prison system had never been designed for rehabilitation or therapy. It had been designed to punish, no matter who the inmate was or where he had come from, and Carolyn had always understood that. She had even appreciated it. In fact, she had done more than her share to help put criminals behind bars...but because those criminals had committed crimes against children, she hadn't given them a second thought once those iron doors had swung closed behind them.

Well, she sure thought about them now. *Payback's a bitch, ain't it?*

Once Carolyn had undergone the mandated three-month psychiatric evaluation at Lexington Federal Penitentiary, performed by a "psychology trainee" with a Master's degree in art who had never even seen a patient before, she had known it was all over for her. She wasn't surprised when the trainee's pre-sentencing investigation report—filled with inaccuracies and ridiculous suppositions—claimed that Carolyn was a cold-blooded killer suffering from a borderline personality disorder. She also wasn't surprised to find that this trainee's so-called professional recommendation was that Carolyn serve out her full sentence in Lexington, a minimum security facility that was supposed to have the best medical and psychiatric facilities in the entire federal system.

In her day, Carolyn had read numerous pre-sentencing investigation reports about other people, and never once had she questioned the qualifications of the professionals writing them. Now she did. Now that she was on the other side of the fence, she was livid with the legal system—which should have cut her a little slack, enraged with Larry—who should have been man enough to make a public confession instead of letting his wife go down alone, and incensed with life itself—which had been out to get her from the moment she was born. Even God, whose comforting Presence she had experienced that night in Orleans Parish Prison, seemed to have deserted her.

In other words, it was much easier to blame everyone else for what she had done than it was to face herself. She was still a long way from admitting that the final decision to call a contract killer and put a hit out on her husband was hers and hers alone.

But the Honorable Judge Morey L. Sear had had no such difficulty. On January 13, 1988, he slammed down his gavel and threw the book at Carolyn Huebner, giving her the most time he could under her plea agreement: five years for using an interstate phone line in commission of a felony, and two-and-a-half years for the solicitation of a murder, to be served concurrently at a facility like

Lexington that would give her, he said, the maximum possible treatment. Then, apparently as an afterthought, he had fined her $100.

Even when she boarded the U.S. Marshall's Air Service (called "Con-Air" by the inmates) for the long flight back to her new home in Lexington, Carolyn continued to tell herself that all she had *really* done was to try to be a Super Hero, determined to save the children from all the evil bogeymen out to get them, and if other people couldn't understand that, then that was their problem, not hers.

Even Larry's confidential letter, which George Simno had hand-delivered to the judge the day before her sentencing, didn't move anyone at all. And, once Carolyn had read a copy of it, she hadn't been surprised. In fact, she had been unable to do anything at all except shake her head in amazement.

If she lived to be a hundred years old, she would never forget this portion of that letter:

> January 12, 1988
> Dear Judge Sear,
>
> As both Carolyn Huebner's husband and the "victim" of this case, I sincerely appreciate the sincere and thorough attention you are giving the matter before you.
>
> There is some additional private, personal information which may give you a better appreciation of Carolyn's plight, which if grasped by the media in any fashion would further destroy chances for any career or personal life for Carolyn, Audra, and particularly me.
>
> When Audra, our daughter, was about three (about three years ago), there was an incident wherein I went to bed and Audra bedded herself down at the foot of our king-size bed. Carolyn went downstairs and remained for some reason. The lights were out, and I assumed Audra was asleep. I then committed an act of poor judgment, masturbated, and was caught by Carolyn when she entered the room turning on the lights.
>
> I was simply releasing my sexual frustrations alone, as Carolyn was not at this time in a cooperative mood. I was not in any way stimulated by Audra's presence. I did not then, nor have I ever touched or exploited Audra (or anyone) in any indecent manner.
>
> Naturally, Carolyn was tremendously upset. We sought the counsel of friends and associates to work through this matter. Carolyn did not 'kick' me out of the house or file for divorce. Carolyn and another trained in interviewing children talked to

Audra who corroborated the facts that I <u>never</u> touched her, and that she actually didn't know what happened.

Although Carolyn knew nothing improper ever occurred between Audra and I, this masturbation incident could have contributed to Carolyn's confusion due to her personal childhood experiences, her current work, and her obsession for aiding exploited children. At this same time, Carolyn was involved in a frustrating child abuse case. The child looked <u>identical</u> to our child, Audra...

The letter had gone on and on—for three whole pages—and for the most part Carolyn had to admit it was a pretty good letter. But she didn't see it as an attempt to keep her out of prison. Rather, she saw it as Larry's attempt to downplay his own culpability while trying to make her feel like he was coming to her rescue, but she wasn't buying it. After all, he hadn't copped to anything except what he called *an act of poor judgment,* and this, he claimed, was only because *Carolyn was not at this time in a cooperative mood*—thus placing the blame squarely back in her corner. He also made it sound like every normal man masturbated in front of his children, and that Carolyn couldn't have been nearly as upset as she was had she not been under so much pressure everywhere else.

But what Carolyn found most ironic was that he honestly didn't seem to understand that had she chosen to press charges against him back then, he might well have found his own butt in the same sling hers was in now...

Still, by the time the plane containing about twenty new shackled inmates came to an easy landing near Lexington Federal Penitentiary on January 27, 1988, Carolyn had finally managed to face one brutal fact more urgently important than anything else:

*This is nobody's problem but mine. No matter who else is involved in this, I'm the only one serving time and I need to make the most of it.*

*And...if there's a good shrink in here, I sure as hell better find him...*

After she had been strip-searched, given a nine-page packet of rules and regulations put together by the Bureau of Prisons (BOP), and issued an identifying number as part of her processing into the largest women's unit in Lexington Penitentiary, Carolyn began to understand that no one—at least for the length of time that she was in prison—was lower or of less value to the world than she was.

For example, Judge Sear had placed in with her final commitment papers a Special Protective Order designed to shield her from the media, as well as from attacks by inmates or staff who might take offense at her former work in law enforcement. But, upon her arrival, Carolyn was shocked to discover that someone had anonymously sent newspaper clippings about her case ahead of her arrival so that everybody already knew all about her. Even so, no one was impressed. If anything, they were determined to prove to her that she was no better than anyone else, and someone even began spreading the rumor that she was psychotic and dangerous. Probably all that saved her was that she had once worked to protect children, so that maybe a few of the more forgiving inmates could sort of forget about the "cop" part...

Not long after Carolyn arrived at Lexington, it became clear that the prison was being elevated to a higher level of security, and the increasing violence of the newly arriving female inmates further diminished what tenuous hold Carolyn was managing to keep on her mental stability. Once the feds began moving the male inmates to other institutions, installing more razor fencing, and building an outside guard tower, Lexington Penitentiary began to look more like San Quentin than a minimum security prison. Not, Carolyn was sure, what Judge Sear had had in mind when he had sentenced her to a facility where she could receive the treatment she needed...

Carolyn had a hard time not laughing out loud when she remembered that every doctor involved in her case had claimed that her breakdown was stress-related and the only way she was going to even *begin* to heal was to live in a stress-free environment. Right, she often thought, so send me off to a calm and soothing place like Lexington Federal Penitentiary... Now *that's* going to make a world of difference. No stress here...

Still, Carolyn knew that the only way she could maneuver her way through this alien atmosphere and survive it was to take full advantage of the therapy Judge Sear had mandated. No one could take the place of her psychiatrist back home, Dr. Reid, but even she had begun to finally realize that when it came to the help she so desperately needed, she had to start somewhere.

It was strange that the place where she had to start was inside prison walls. It didn't take long for her to recognize that incarceration created its own kind of sickness, and that achieving any sort of mental health in this environment was probably *never* going to happen.

Still, as Carolyn saw human beings adapt to circum-stances they were never meant to live in, she was impressed by their resiliency and ingenuity. Individuals that had once worked in high-paying, responsible jobs now made 12 cents an hour and felt lucky to get it—people like Carolyn herself, who proudly worked at Unicor, the prison industry corporation, sewing boxer shorts for the military. She was even able to joke about the work, writing in a letter to Ronni that Unicor was responsible for covering the Army's ass. Hand-picked by the head of the textile department, Carolyn worked there until her hands broke out in an allergic rash caused by the dye in the underwear. Then, telling everyone with a laugh that the boxer shorts were just too hot to handle, she moved into ADP-Unicor and began sitting at a computer terminal all day, entering military data.

As hard as it was for her to admit it, Carolyn had completely lost control of her life and there was no way she could get it back. She was invisible in a sea of faceless women; she felt as if she no longer existed. If she tried to call the shots in this place, they'd throw her into lock-down and wouldn't let her out until they were good and damned ready. She had already seen it happen to other women, and it wasn't going to happen to her.

Consequently, when she presented herself to the psychologist assigned to her case, Mark Simpson, PhD, she liked him right away because he was young and well-mannered, dressed neatly, and didn't try to intimidate her. But she also recognized within the first two weeks that hell would freeze over before she got through one full session without any interruptions. It wasn't Simpson's fault and she didn't blame him, but she was shocked at how emotionally debilitating it was to begin digging through all her personal baggage, perhaps igniting a memory or an emotion she had forgotten, only to find that her hour was up, or he had to take a telephone call, or someone else needed his attention. She was invariably left feeling angry, or drained, or impossibly depressed.

There had been a time when none of this would have bothered her because she had always been so expert at playing games with therapists and counselors, but those days were long gone. Now she *wanted* to work. Now she *wanted* to understand why she had done what she had done. Now she *wanted* to get well.

As the weeks went by, Carolyn discovered that the memories she continually conjured up in Mark Simpson's office, as well as the emotions that accompanied them, remained with her night and day, practically suffocating her because they came without warning or provocation. Even though Carolyn had spent most of her life being afraid of *something*, nothing in her past had ever terrified her as much as the visions and night terrors that relentlessly assaulted her now.

The voices had returned as well, but at least this time they didn't frighten her. They weren't the voices of strangers. They were recognizable voices from her past that came any time of the day or night, and they only lasted for a few moments before they disappeared. Sometimes she heard her mother calling her name; sometimes she heard her own childish voice crying out for her mother. Usually when she heard the voices, she felt as if she were zooming right out of her body, like she had somehow split away from the present and become stuck in the past. Then, like so many times before, Carolyn would lose herself—as well as an entire block of time—only to reawaken somewhere else...

But that wasn't all. Added to that constant sense of emotional unfinished business was the very real fear that someone was going to hurt her. She woke up every single morning wondering if this would be the day that some lesbian inmate attacked her for some imagined slur against a lover, or some warden demanded a sexual favor in exchange for a tiny necessity of life, or some piss-ant administrator decided to change an obscure rule and deny her a little pleasure because she hadn't been properly awed by his power...

If Carolyn had felt helpless before, it was nothing compared to what she was feeling now. Now every move she made was dictated by other people, none of whom cared a flying flip about her. All they cared about was *punishing* her and seeing to it that she paid back her debt to society.

Even Mark Simpson, psychologist or not, was to Carolyn's untrusting mind, a *fed, BOP, the enemy...* Carolyn would never, ever, *ever* count on him the way she knew she needed to count on her therapist—the way she still counted on Dr. Reid.

"You need to remember, Carolyn," Simpson had told her once, cutting short a particularly illuminating session because he had to see an inmate on suicide watch, "that Lexington is a *prison*, not a ritzy mental hospital where every patient has a private doctor. While you're in here, I'm all you've got."

So, in an effort to protect herself she reverted back to all of her old coping skills and did everything she could to hide what was happening to her. She stayed away from cellmates as much as possible and ignored them when they claimed she was causing problems she knew she had nothing to do with. She wrote letters to everyone and read her Bible and called her friends and family as often as she was allowed. She watched television in the evening and listened to her radio late at night and tried to blend in with everyone else.

Yet, behind that façade of normalcy and in the only way she knew how, Carolyn was fighting for her survival. She was a long way from giving up. Every chance she got, she pushed Larry to go after another legal angle that might get her released—or at least shave some time off her sentence. It was important to Carolyn's sense of control that she battle for her own freedom, not totally relying on Larry, or George Simno, or even Ronni. She had to be in charge.

Consequently, Carolyn drove everyone within her support system completely crazy, and somewhere in the back of her jumbled brain she was aware of it, but she couldn't stop. Just as in the past, when she had taken on more cases to fight the confusion in her head, she now pushed everyone else to their limits. She fought with George to get a very important sentencing amendment finished on schedule, then pleaded with him to file a *Rule 35*, a legal appeal that she had researched and was sure she could win. It requested a reduction of her sentence for several legitimate reasons, the main two being that the government had broken its promise to "keep silent" on prison time, and she wasn't getting the psychiatric assistance that Judge Sear wanted for her...

But George, for some reason that Carolyn couldn't understand, wasn't as interested in her case as he had been previously and didn't make himself available to either her or Larry. He didn't take their phone calls and he didn't answer their letters. This only frustrated her further, increased her stress level to a fever pitch, and made her more difficult than ever to deal with.

Larry, on the other hand, probably because he knew he was no longer in any danger of losing his job or his reputation, continued to fight valiantly alongside her. Once again he was her Knight in Shining Armor.

He proved his loyalty beyond any shadow of a doubt when he rode his white horse into Lexington Penitentiary in June 1988 to accompany his wife to her first parole board hearing. Carolyn, seated before two panelists at a conference table and struggling to answer questions that she interpreted as being argumentative and accusatory, dissolved into tears within the first five minutes and ceased making sense not long after that. She could tell by the expressions on the interrogators' faces that they didn't have a clue what she was talking about and cared even less. Finally, and very gradually, her voice trailed away.

One of the panelists—an unsympathetic man who had introduced himself at the beginning of the hearing as Mr. Hayworth—began to speak.

"What we're talking about today is punishment for a crime. Of course, whether or not you're a danger to the community is always a concern to us, but generally people who plot to kill their own spouse are not dangerous to people in the community. It's usually directed to one person for personal reasons, or for monetary gain. But the punishment range for engaging in a conspiracy to commit a murder is a minimum of 100 months with no maximum limit at all. But you've only got a five-year sentence and nobody can hold you here past forty months, unless you substantially violate the rules of the prison. So, what this means is that you're going out five years *below* your guidelines in the first place. However, we are required by law to see you every eighteen months until you get out, so if this doesn't go the way you want, you can come back in December, 1989."

Larry spoke up. "Sir, may I interrupt just a second?"

"No. Now the fact that your husband didn't want you prosecuted doesn't have a lot of bearing on the case. I can understand his concern for you and that he's willing to forgive you, and apparently *has* forgiven you. But, thank goodness, the government wouldn't permit that and prosecuted you because he has no authority to give you permission to commit murder—even if *he's* the intended victim. That's a law made by society, not by your family. You've been prosecuted, you must be punished, and this is the punishment range. Did you understand all that?"

Carolyn stared down at her hands and nodded. But what she really understood was, this man wasn't going to let her go anywhere.

"Your background in so many respects is good," Hayworth continued, "and you've done competent work... certainly vigorous, enthusiastic work with that program to locate missing children. You've operated at a level at times that, quite honestly, makes me think you might fall back on the psychological problems when times of stress come and you need an excuse for what you did— because you've done too well at other times. It's not like you're in such bad shape emotionally that you can't function in the community."

There had been a time when she could have taken on this man and an army of others just like him, but now she couldn't. The words didn't stay in her mind long enough to come out of her mouth coherently and she couldn't speak past the lump in her throat anyway. Besides, it was quite clear that he thought she had been given a more than reasonable break to begin with and he had no intention of adding to it.

"Are you involved in any program activities you want to mention today?" Mr. Hayworth asked finally.

Carolyn took a shaky breath. "Well, I...I go to chapel every Tuesday. Larry and I did Marriage Encounter in May... um...I-I'm directing a religious play right now. I go to a counseling session with a Dr. Simpson here that's about forty-five minutes on average once a week on Tuesday mornings... I've taken a couple of psychology courses...um... One was an eight-week course called *Communication in Relationships* that I took last fall and in November I took one called *Surviving Child Abuse*, which was for the adult. I'm also in the *PAC Program—Parents and Children*. I took my GED and passed that with the second-highest score in the group."

Apparently no one was impressed. "Is there anything you want to add, Mr. Huebner?"

Carolyn closed her eyes and bowed her head as Larry began to speak. As usual, it seemed to take him forever to get to his point; it was all she could do not to jump up and start screaming.

"I need for you to bring this to a close..." Mr. Hayworth finally interrupted.

"I know, just hang on, I understand." Larry mopped the perspiration from his forehead with a dark blue handkerchief and shoved it back into his coat pocket. "I appreciate your patience, I really do. I've heard a lot about creative sentencing aspects and creative probation and parole aspects that are being applied these days. House arrest, intensive supervision—I feel this case warrants consideration of something possibly unique to really help Carolyn get treatment, rather than just strict punishment. Carolyn has realized that she *does* need help in reuniting her family... She *has* been punished, gentlemen. Help her. Help us."

"All right. We need to talk a few minutes while you wait in the hall," Mr. Hayworth responded brusquely. He looked at Carolyn. "Are there any questions or comments you thought of while we were talking?"

Carolyn knew that this was her last opportunity to fight for herself. She lifted her chin, met Mr. Hayworth's icy gaze head-on, and somehow managed to articulate how she felt just as effectively as she had in the old days.

"I want to make it clear that while I've been in this institution, I've sought repeatedly to obtain proper psychological treatment. I've made a true, sincere effort. I've asked everybody to please give me more time. Dr. Simpson has been the only established contact I've had, and he has just flat-out said, "There is no more time to give you." If you were to let me go home on parole, I would seek, out of my own desire, through Dr. Reid, the help that I need. When I got out, Dr. Reid helped me pick up my life, helped me see things that I never saw before." Then, once again, Carolyn began to tremble. She took a deep breath and fought those irritating, ever-present tears. "I have a good heart! I do. As God is my witness, I have a very good heart! And I can be a very good person. And I'm asking both of you...please... please...let me go home..."

But of course they didn't. Carolyn's parole was denied. When the written report arrived a few weeks later, the reason cited was quite simple:

"The instant offense involves a detailed, serious plan for this subject to have her husband murdered. From reading the PSI, it appears that there is little doubt he would have been killed if the FBI had not been involved. The panel finds no reason to recommend parole below the guidelines in this case. Subject has been determined to be competent by the court and her past record in the community as an adult shows that she has functioned at a very normal level most of her adult life."

Carolyn ignored the fact that she had already been given a break in her sentencing by Judge Sear; she felt no gratitude for it. Instead she zeroed in on the excuse she was always seeking and usually found: *They didn't give me parole because I functioned too well in society...*

Then, just one day after her parole was denied, Judge Morey L. Sear himself turned down the Rule 35 that they had barely managed to get to him by deadline.

...and Carolyn knew what that meant. It meant that she was out of options. There was nothing left for her to do except... her time.

Carolyn sat at her work terminal, fingers flying over her keyboard as she entered military data into her computer without even paying attention to the information she was recording, and glanced up at the clock on the wall. It was nearly lunchtime, which was a good thing since her stomach was growling so loudly she was afraid it could be heard on the other side of the room, and then later this afternoon, after work, she had an appointment with Mark Simpson. A little smile played around the edges of her lips as she thought of him. They had come a long way since she had taken her first tentative step into his rather dark, closet-like office, and Carolyn was encouraged by their progress…

Their relationship had really begun to click when her back had gone out a few months earlier. In so much pain she could hardly move, Carolyn had found herself being pushed in a wheelchair by a doctor and an orderly from an x-ray room to an unfamiliar medical area on the second floor. Carolyn had immediately panicked because she didn't know where she was, and tried to stand up. A strong but gentle pair of hands held her in the chair.

"Now calm down, Carolyn," the doctor said quietly, "there's nothing to worry about. We're going to put you into this room here just so you can get some rest without anyone bothering you—I'd like you to stay here for a couple of days. That bruised muscle in your back is going to hurt for awhile."

But Carolyn knew that these rooms, comfortable though they might have been, were dark, tiny, and locked down at night. Still she had done her best and had gone into the room, trying to ignore how it seemed to grow smaller and smaller, then darker and darker, until she couldn't even breathe. Her panic finally exploded and she cried out for the doctor, begging and pleading for him to let her go…

Eventually she had ended up back in her dorm where she had remained in bed for the next three days, exactly as she had promised the doctor. When she was finally able to return to Mark Simpson's office for a regular session, he had pulled out his chair and sat down so that he was facing her. His dark eyes seemed magnified behind the thick lenses of his glasses.

"You shouldn't have had to go into that room, Carolyn," he said quietly. "I'm sorry that happened to you."

"It's okay." Embarrassed, she looked away from him. "My daddy used to take the locks off the doors in our house when I was little to make things safe for me."

"Did he? I want to make things safe for you here, Carolyn. Right now." He held out his hand, palm up. "Give me your hand."

Obediently, her heart in her throat, Carolyn had touched his fingers with hers. She said nothing as he held her hand firmly and waited for him to speak. She knew that Mark Simpson seldom made an unplanned move or gave a spontaneous comment. Reaching out to her was something he had made a conscious decision to do.

"Carolyn, listen to me. I'm not going to hurt you. I'm not the enemy, even if I *am* BOP. I'm here for you and I can help you—if you'll let me…"

Carolyn had pulled her hand away from his grasp; she felt strange and breathless. He had never touched her before—in fact, *no one* had touched her in months and she hadn't realized how much she had missed the contact...

Suddenly he stood up, walked to his office door and opened it. He had turned back to her with a grin. "See? It doesn't lock from the inside. You're safe with me..."

Spine-chilling screams exploded through Carolyn's consciousness, jerking her back to the present and bringing her to her feet. The scene around her blurred...moved so fast that she couldn't make sense of it all. When she saw a woman struggling on the floor, blood splattering everywhere, she couldn't take it in. A slender figure straddled her, arm pumping up and down with something in her hand...slicing, hacking...a knife...no, several knives...

The attack, which had come out of nowhere, didn't last long. The assailant was wrestled to the ground by other inmates, but Carolyn—who, at one time, had always been at the center of everything—couldn't move. She stood paralyzed, hands clasped tightly in front of her, and stared at the blood pooling like sticky red syrup on the floor.

Finally, pulling herself together, Carolyn excused herself and found her way to the restroom where she promptly got sick. Eventually, after managing to splash her face and rinse her mouth out with icy water, she looked at her reflection in the mirror. The image gazing back at her was unfamiliar, with blurred edges and translucent skin and a soft blue blanket around its face...a baby...a baby boy with wide, staring eyes...

Carolyn turned and ran mindlessly, without permission, straight for Mark Simpson's office.

"Mrs. Eberhardt has already been here," Mark said calmly, pulling Carolyn into his office and leading her to the uncomfortable chair she always hated sitting on. "She told me everything. Carolyn, I want you to consider getting a transfer out of here. This place is too violent and you don't need to be here. Look into Marianna, or Alderson down in West Virginia... I can help you."

Carolyn clung to his hand. "I know, I know. It was bad—but that's not why I'm upset."

"No?"

Once again the misty image of a tiny baby boy waved back and forth in front of her eyes, almost ghost-like, before it disappeared in a flash of light. Carolyn shook her head. "No. I saw… I don't know… I saw…something…"

"I'm here. Tell me."

Carolyn closed her eyes and took a deep breath and recoiled from the memory, from the pain it brought with it, from the terror she was living all over again…

*A girl-child is in a room—hot, dirty, frightened, hungry… She hurts. She's crying…*

Carolyn fought the vision, struggled to come out of it, but she couldn't. She was there, with the child…she was locked in… she *was* the child…

Far, far away she could hear a man's voice, soothing, deep. "It's all right, Carolyn…you're safe…"

*She returns to the room and then she sees the window. She goes to the window and rubs her tiny fist against the dirt-covered glass so she can see outside into the back yard. She sees a man she's never seen before, and she sees Rose walking beside him. Rose. Fat…ugly…Rose is carrying a blue blanket, a tiny blue blanket. There's a garbage pile that's going to be burned later and the man begins to dig beneath the garbage. A hole. He's digging a hole. Rose takes something…what is it?…something…out of the blanket and buries it in the hole and covers it up…*

*It's the baby…the baby boy in the mirror…*

Carolyn whimpered like a hurt child, the pain coming from somewhere deep in her spirit, and fought her way back from the memory. Gradually, little by little, she came to herself and concentrated on the sound of her own breathing. It was irregular, it was too fast, but it was the sound of life, of *now*, and it meant that she was all right…

Even if she *was* lying on the floor in a corner of Mark Simpson's office.

# CHAPTER THIRTY-ONE

"Here, let me have this, too, please." I grabbed the September 5th issue of *People Magazine* off the rack and gave it to the cashier with a grin. "It's great bathtub reading."

"You're right about that. Anything else for you today, Mrs. Hoessli?"

"No, thanks. That'll do it."

I heard the phone ringing when I pulled into the driveway, but I wasn't about to answer it. There was nobody I wanted to talk to right now. I poured myself a glass of iced tea and carried my "bathtub reading" into the living room.

Curling up on the sofa, I thumbed through the pages, skimming the gossip columns and book reviews without much interest. But when my gaze fell on the section labeled *Trouble* and I read the title of the article—*Harassed by an Unknown Author of Vicious Rhymes, Ruth Finley Confronts the Stranger Within Herself*—I frowned and my heart began to beat just a little faster.

In the article, writer/editor Gene Stone tells the story of a middle-aged lady, Ruth Finley, who lived with her husband, Ed, in Wichita, Kansas in the late 1970s when the BTK Strangler was on the prowl and had already murdered several women. When Mrs. Finley started receiving menacing anonymous phone calls and sadistic poetry in the mail, no one could figure out why. But officials took the threats seriously, thinking they could be related to the Strangler.

It took the police three years and $370,000 to determine the identity of Ruth's persecutor.

During these years, Ruth claimed to have been kidnapped from downtown Wichita by two men she couldn't describe and was driven around for four hours before she escaped. She was admitted to the hospital with three knife wounds, one of which could have killed her. The Finleys' telephone wires were cut; a knife wrapped in newspaper and addressed to Ruth was found near her office, and the Health Department was notified that Ruth was spreading venereal disease.

Eventually the police figured out that Ruth Finley was attacking herself.

As the article began to explore the reasons why, it was clear that we were heading into some horrific child sexual abuse. The poor woman bore all the signs. One of the symptoms I recognized was her inability to verbalize feelings about her molestation with her therapist, yet she could be quite descriptive and even hate-filled in her verse. Poetry was the tool that her doctor, Andrew Pickens, ultimately used to help her to face the truth.

But what jumped out at me in this story, at least as I was reading it the first time, was Ruth Finley's utter determination to destroy herself. The route she had chosen was far more violent than Carolyn's—one of self-inflicted pain—but her ending destination was the same.

*Why would a supposedly normal, well-adjusted woman work so hard to bring herself down?*

I wasn't a doctor. I didn't know the answer to that. But then, when I read the following clinical explanation, all the pieces began to fit:

" '...Ruth's reaction to the rapes at the time was,' says Dr. Pickens, 'similar to that of other sexually abused children. In her own words, she remembers "floating off to heaven" during each assault. "I could see what was happening to this little girl beneath me," she says. But "somehow it wasn't so bad if it wasn't me. I was just watching it." In clinical terms, this is called a dissociative reaction, a split in the conscious mind in which one group of mental activities breaks off to function as a separate unit, as if belonging to another person. Unlike schizophrenia, a dissociative reaction will often not be evident to another individual; it comes into being only when the subject is alone at a time of great emotional trauma.

"For nearly 50 years, Ruth Finley had no cause to fall back on this psychological defense mechanism. But in 1978 a series of events combined to make her feel especially seared and vulnerable. Ed Finley was hospitalized for a possible heart attack (it proved to be a false alarm) and the BTK Strangler was stalking the community and may have triggered subconscious fears in Ruth. 'Like a weakened bridge,' says Pickens, 'Mrs. Finley's defenses held up until an oversized truck came along and the bridge couldn't handle the weight anymore.

" 'Suddenly, emotions that Ruth had repressed since her childhood began breaking through, and she reacted to them as she had as a girl: She dissociated, creating a fictitious person, the Poet, to help her deal with her threatening feelings.

" 'It's just like riding a bicycle,' Pickens says of the dissociation. 'She learned how to do it as a child, and it just clicked back into place.' "

I started to shake; I felt sick to my stomach. Setting the magazine aside, I walked into the bedroom and opened the top drawer of my dressing table. I had told no one except Kevin about the contents of this letter because I just didn't know what to do with it. Now I was afraid that I had made a terrible mistake. The contents of this letter might well hold the key, not only to what was wrong with Carolyn, but to what might actually bring her home. She had written:

> ...Tonight I watched *The Color Purple*. I've seen it three times now and I still cry...
>
> ...I have a little ritual each weekend. I stay in bed all day and night on Saturday. Sunday I do my laundry. Isn't this exciting! Last night though I broke my routine. Me and Betty, my roomate

(sic), jumped the fence and went downtown. Spent all night drinking cheap liquor. Went to another place with two dudes to go dancing but all they wanted was to fool around. I tried to explain that I was a married woman and just out with my girlfriend. On the other hand Betty was really living it up. I could hardly get her out of that joint. By the time we got back to the fence it was 4:00 a.m. I had to shove her over and she hit the ground with a thud. Thank God she was so drunk she didn't even feel it. Anyway she has a hangover today. Of course we usually don't do these kind of things, but we really needed a break from this place. Prison can really get to you!

When I had first received this, I hadn't understood it and thought that it was just another crazy example of Carolyn being...well, Carolyn. But I was certain now that this had been a full-blown dissociative episode. When she had written this, she was simply relating to me something she really thought had happened. Yet if I asked her about it today, I was positive she wouldn't remember a word of it.

Could watching a powerful movie about child abuse like *The Color Purple*, perhaps combined with something traumatic that had recently happened to her, actually *trigger* a dissociative episode that no one was aware of, including her? Is that what had happened here?

And was this episode anything like the confusion she experienced when she placed that phone call to Johnny Bartlett, changing his victim from Harold Best to Larry Huebner?

*For God's sake, is this what's been going on with Carolyn? Is this what her doctors have been talking about?*

The jangling telephone dragged me back to the situation at hand. Before I even picked up the receiver, I knew who the caller was.

"Will you accept a collect call from Carolyn Huebner?"

"Sure." There was a long silence on the other end. I could hear her breathing, but she didn't say a word. "Carolyn? Are you all right?"

Her voice sounded tight and strained, like she could hardly force it out of her throat. "Go to the ice house and buy this week's issue of..."

"*People Magazine.* I just read it."

I heard her draw in a ragged, shuddering breath. "Oh, God, Ronni...what if..."

I sat on the edge of the bed and stared at the letter I still held in my hand. My fingers tightened on the receiver and I cleared my throat.

"Carolyn, can you get in to see Simpson today?"

"I have an appointment in an hour."

"Good," I said softly. "Sweetie, I need you to hear something you wrote…"

Finally, after thirteen months, on a perfect morning in October, Carolyn transferred out of Lexington Penitentiary. Dressed in street clothing, unshackled and without handcuffs, she rode a prison bus 290 miles east to FCI Alderson, a minimum security women's campus nestled in the mountains of West Virginia. She had been so excited that she hadn't slept a minute the night before, but it didn't matter. She wasn't tired at all. In fact, she couldn't have closed her eyes if she had wanted to. Even though there was heavy-gauge grating on the bus windows, she could see the cloudless pink-and-blue sky as the sun came up and watch the landscape fly past—just like a hundred years ago, when she had been allowed to take a day trip all by herself.

For just a few hours, Carolyn could pretend she was free.

As the bus traveled over the highway into West Virginia, Carolyn was completely overwhelmed by the beauty everywhere she looked. It had been so long since she had seen real autumn colors like back home in Pennsylvania. Carolyn couldn't remember when she had last caught even a *glimpse* of crackling crimson and gold leaves wafting gently toward the ground. Even the air had a different, more natural fragrance; it was fresher somehow, cleaner…sort of like the crisp smell of new snow.

Whatever it was, it was pure heaven to be outside, to witness it all…especially after what Lexington had turned into…

Carolyn clamped her mind closed against her ghastly memories of being confined in a maximum security prison. She wasn't ready to deal with them yet—maybe she never would be. All that mattered to her was that she had had a friend. Mark Simpson had fought right alongside of her, just as he had promised, and he had kept her safe.

He had made it possible for her to speak periodically with her personal psychiatrist, Dr. Reid, which may have been one of the main reasons she hadn't gone completely nuts, especially after the stabbing she had witnessed. He had assured her that he believed her flashback of Rose, the strange man, and the dead infant was a *real* memory, not something she had just imagined—and that reassurance meant more to her than she could have ever told him.

When Larry had hired a special attorney to file an appeal for Carolyn's parole denial, Simpson had never stopped encouraging her to believe that it might actually happen. When she had wondered aloud whether or not they should put the *People Magazine* article about Ruth Finley into the appeals package,

Simpson thought it was a good idea. And even though they still hadn't received an answer, she continued to hope just because Simpson did.

But Carolyn, ever cautious, never told him about the letter she had written to Ronni.

And when the word had finally come down that Carolyn could be transferred to Alderson, which was actually closer to her mother (who had visited just once when she had first arrived in Lexington), Simpson was almost as happy as Carolyn was. In her therapy journal about her work with Mark Simpson, Carolyn had written as her final entry:

MS provided the only true safe place in my nightmare at Lexington. I'll miss him.

To her mind, leaving that nasty cell in the Orleans Parish Prison and closing the steel doors of Lexington Penitentiary behind her was the end of an era. Nothing that she was heading toward could be worse than what she had left behind. Even though she had doubted Him many times, God had remained by her side, brought strangers into her life to help, and led her out of the darkness. She was a long way from healthy and she was still in trouble, but He had given her this beautiful, crisp, autumn morning to enjoy in comparative freedom and He was leading her to a place where she could begin to heal.

Alderson, West Virginia was the beginning of hope.

There were unthreatening chain-link fences around Alderson, just like the fence she had around her own back yard, and it was called a *campus* because that's what it was like—a college campus. If there hadn't been a wrought-iron gate with *Federal Industrial Institution for Women* engraved on a brass plaque in the middle of it, a visitor could easily forget that this was a prison.

Whenever Carolyn looked out of the window of her new home in Cottage #2 and later in Cottage #8, or walked across the beautifully landscaped grounds, or sat on a bench outside to watch the birds preparing to fly south for the winter, she felt like she was just over the hill from her home. Everything was so familiar to her—even the old coal stack at the power plant that provided the electricity for the facility, and the train that rolled alongside the Green Briar River...

She also liked her new therapist, Douglas Hawkins, who was tall, handsome, and only about ten years her senior. Her first session with him had run about two hours, which was a gift in itself, and she appreciated the way he had come out of his office to introduce himself to her—like she was his equal and not just another crazy inmate he had to keep in line. He had seemed even more nervous than she was, but he hung in there and kept visiting with her until they were both comfortable. He had a gentle manner, which was very important to her, and his calm, deep voice soothed her jangled nerves.

Over time, Carolyn had found herself talking to him about issues she had seldom had time to discuss with Simpson. She talked to him about Dr. Reid and told him how important the psychiatrist had been to her from the time she had been arrested until this very day, and how she still spoke to him on as regular a basis as she could, BOP permitting. Hawkins had promised to see to it that those calls could continue and he had kept that promise.

Gathering a little more confidence with each session, Carolyn spoke tearfully about her concern over Audra's escalating separation anxiety and her latest tendency to call every woman she met *Mommy*. She talked about Audra's wild rebelliousness at both home and school, which had become so insane that Larry had nearly run out of private schools that would take her. Even Ronni, who was doing everything she could to help the Huebner family, had told her outright that Audra was more than she could handle.

To Carolyn's increasing exasperation, Larry's response to his daughter's refusal to obey was to continually negotiate with her, writing disciplinary contracts that meant nothing to the child and that he had no time to enforce. He would finally end up whining on the phone to either his wife or Ronni that he didn't know what to do because nothing he did worked.

Finally, Carolyn had become secure enough to tell Hawkins about her conflicting emotions for her husband—something she had never told anyone because of the nature of her crime. But now she told the truth. Now it seemed to her that the stronger she became, the more determined he was to aggravate her.

"If I say the sky's blue, he says it's not. If I suggest he try something with Audra, he tells me I'm in prison and I don't know what's going on at home." Carolyn shrugged in irritation. "Well, he's right. I'm in prison, that's for sure. I'm in prison because I did something bad, and I'm in prison because my brain wasn't working right when I did it. But that doesn't mean that I don't know my child or that I don't have any ideas worth mentioning."

Even Ronni was puzzled by Larry's behavior. "When he asks me how he should say something to you and I tell him what I think, he turns right around and does the exact opposite. It's weird, Carolyn. I don't understand it. Why does he even bother to ask?"

Hawkins just said that the whole situation was very difficult for everybody and that they all needed to be very patient with each other.

He had asked her questions about the Harold Best case during their very first session. "I know what the FBI says happened," he had told her, waving the *FBI Statement of Facts* in the air, "but I want to know what *you* say."

For some reason, Carolyn had been sure that he would be sympathetic, so she had told him honestly everything she could remember about what had happened. To her surprise, his answer was typical BOP. In fact, all he did was parrot Mark Simpson. "The sooner you accept responsibility for what you did, Carolyn, the sooner you're going to get well. Stop making excuses, okay? I'm not saying that you're not telling the truth. I'm just saying that it doesn't really matter here. And if you don't stop, if you don't try to adjust, we'll have to send you back to Lexington."

She didn't like the threat, but he was right. She had been playing roles to suit other people her whole life, so why should it be any different in prison? She could accept responsibility for every bit of this crime if that's what it took for her to get out. She could *act* any way they wanted her to act ...

Carolyn stopped abruptly. It was keeping secrets and playing parts and remaining silent that had made her nuts and gotten her in here in the first place. If she hadn't learned anything from her time in prison, she had learned that.

Finally, even though Carolyn realized that early impressions could certainly be deceiving especially when it came to doctors in the BOP, Hawkins fit the mold of the caring therapist and she was comfortable with him. In fact, she figured he wouldn't last in the Bureau of Prisons because he just had too much heart. It wasn't long before Carolyn had given him an affectionate nickname, which she nearly always did with people she cared about; almost immediately— at least in her mind—she called him *Hawkeye*.

Although Carolyn liked Alderson as much as anyone could like a prison and she looked forward to seeing her therapist, she didn't socialize much with anyone else. In fact, she essentially isolated herself—primarily because most of the other women had actually developed "play families" where they had mothers, fathers, sisters, brothers and even babies. It was all too insane for Carolyn. However, it wasn't long before she understood that they did what they had to do to survive—just as she had—and she was in no position to judge.

Carolyn's main source of company was her little radio and she listened to it every night. She had located a real down-home, country western station that reminded her of Texas and it comforted her.

One night around Thanksgiving, just before Carolyn turned off the radio and went to bed, an unfamiliar voice came across the airwaves. "My name is Jim Franklin. Welcome to *Songs in the Night*."

Something in the man's deep, gentle voice seemed to immediately pacify all the turbulence in Carolyn's spirit. She settled back in her bed and closed her eyes...

*Songs in the Night* introduced Carolyn to southern Gospel music and, oh, what music it was! It lifted her soul in a way it hadn't been lifted in years. Jim Franklin played songs by the greatest Gospel singers in the world—Vestal Goodman, the Blackwood Brothers, Dottie Rambo—and from his heart he spoke words of comfort that wrapped themselves around her loneliness and pain like a warm blanket. He shared such personal parts of his life with his listeners that Carolyn felt not only like she knew him but like he *wanted* her to know him. He didn't preach; he just comforted and told stories and played wonderful music. Then, at the end, right before he gave his address in Milton, West Virginia, he prayed for everyone in his radio listening area.

Well, Carolyn didn't have any idea where Milton was, but she wrote him a letter anyway and thanked him for being in her little room and coming out of her little radio. She told him what great comfort he had given her, and she promised that she would listen to him the following Sunday and every other Sunday until she was finally released from her home, the federal camp for women in Alderson, West Virginia.

It had been a long time since Carolyn had looked forward to anything, but the following Sunday night she eagerly turned on her radio. She couldn't wait to hear that wonderful music, and Jim Franklin didn't let her down. She sang along with the songs when she knew them and listened closely when she didn't, committing them to memory so she could sing them during the week until *Songs in the Night* came on again. Finally, after those magnificent voices faded away, Jim Franklin spoke. "I'd like to read you a letter I found in my mailbox this week..." he said without preamble.

When Carolyn realized that it was *her* letter he was reading, she started crying and couldn't stop. And then, when he asked his listeners to write to her, Carolyn buried her face in her hands and sobbed. She didn't know how she knew it, but she knew that God had *moved* Jim Franklin to reach out to her. God was speaking to her through this man, and He was telling her that He was paying attention. He knew exactly where she was and He hadn't forgotten her.

For the first time in Carolyn's adult life, she truly *felt* the presence and the unconditional love of God. It was real, it was there for her, and more than anything else, *it was personal.* Carolyn embraced that certainty with everything she had. It gave her a peace and hope she had never felt in her entire life, and she knew she was going to be all right.

Whatever happened, whatever it took, she was going to be all right.

Within a week, hundreds of cards and letters began pouring in. There was such an outpouring of unconditional love from total strangers that Carolyn knew it could only have come from God. The people who wrote to her didn't judge her, they didn't care, they didn't even *ask* why she was in prison—it just didn't matter. Carolyn answered every single piece of communication that she received, no matter how small, and she loved doing it. The lift it brought to her soul was indescribable... the way that it strengthened her faith and her relationship with God was beyond words.

Every couple of weeks or so Carolyn boxed the letters up and mailed them home to Larry so they would be safe. She had no intention of ever forgetting these wonderful people, or what their words had actually told her during one of her darkest hours…

In His own way and in His own time, God had come down and met Carolyn Huebner in that little room—and He had brought friends to give her strength. And in that cottage, when she lay alone in the dark, listening to the radio, she could still hear Him say, "Carolyn, I am with you here. I haven't forgotten you. I am here."

Now, for the first time, Carolyn realized that she had to begin dealing with her own transgressions, and she had to stop blaming everyone else for things *she* had done.

When she wasn't working in the sewing room, she spent quiet hours sitting on a hilltop, watching the train wrap its way around the valley and pass the smokestack beside the river, just talking to God and taking a hard look at what was inside of her. Carolyn didn't like what she saw. She was ashamed of the way she had lived her life—incidents she remembered and incidents she didn't.

Carolyn knew she had to change, and she knew she couldn't do it alone. She also knew that even the best doctors in the world couldn't change her, either.

Only God could change her, and He wouldn't do it unless and until she turned herself over to Him. When Carolyn thought about this, she couldn't help but grin. How many jailhouse conversions had she snickered at over the years? To her embarrassment she didn't know, but this wasn't a conversion. It was more a jailhouse *surrender*. God had *always* been a part of her life. He had shown Himself to her when she had been a very little child, and He had even taken her to sleep among His Angels when she had needed Him most. She had just forgotten Him for awhile.

Two days before Christmas, Carolyn's parole appeal was denied. Larry took it much harder than Carolyn did. She was more caught up in her spiritual journey than she was in this latest disappointment. She knew that she would go home when she was supposed to and not one minute before.

Carolyn had finally learned the most important lesson she could learn in prison, and she passed it on in a letter she wrote to Ronni: *I have to do the time, girlfriend. I can't let the time do me.*

In April, 1989, Dr. Reid wrote that he could no longer counsel her because he was leaving San Antonio to take on a very important administrative position. But she could still write to him, he said, and he would do everything he could to find her another psychiatrist that would be right for the kind of work they needed to do. Like anyone else in her situation would have been, Carolyn was devastated—but not for long.

And so she found peace in Alderson—and she learned how to handle adversity without falling apart.

Still, things weren't all bad in her life. In May, because she had come so far in her therapy, Carolyn had asked Hawkeye if he would accompany her to her next parole hearing, which would come somewhere toward the end of the year. She was overjoyed when he had instantly agreed. In August, Carolyn was permitted to leave the campus and go shopping with one of the administrators—it was the first time she had felt normal in two years.

And at the end of the month, Ronni had accompanied Larry and Audra to Alderson, surprising Carolyn so much that she almost passed out, and the two women had hugged and talked and carried on like a couple of idiots for three whole days.

Then, in early September, Ronni sent her copies of several articles she had clipped from the *San Antonio Express-News* and attached this little note to them:

> Carolyn, no matter what happens with this—and probably nothing will—you are hereby vindicated! Lord, this feels good!
> Love,
> Ronni

Carolyn opened the clippings and nearly had a heart attack. Dated September 1, 1989, the main headline blared: *Jury indicts attorney in witness tampering: District Attorney's Office accused of cover-up in case.*

The opening paragraphs of the article summed up everything Carolyn had said about Ray-Don Leonard and Fred Rodriguez from the very beginning…

> A Bexar County grand jury—saying it was outraged by what it saw as a District Attorney's Office cover-up—Thursday indicted attorney Ray-Don Leonard on a charge of witness tampering.
>
> Meanwhile, the assistant district attorney whose work helped lead to Leonard's indictment was fired by District Attorney Fred Rodriguez.
>
> Rodriguez accused the grand jury of playing politics and said his office would not prosecute Leonard because there was insufficient evidence…

Carolyn placed the clippings carefully back into the large manila envelope and slipped it into her desk. Strangely enough, all she could think of was the handwritten letter from Ray-Don Leonard to Fred Rodriguez asking him not to prosecute Harold Best, but to *give him time to clear up this misunderstanding...*

That was where it had all started—on a piece of violet-hued paper.

The current case that had brought all this about, specifically a murder case in which the defendant was a client of Ray-Don Leonard's, didn't interest Carolyn at all. Nothing interested Carolyn now except that some poor assistant prosecutor had had the nerve to go after the corruption that she, Carolyn, had witnessed, and she had lost her job for her trouble.

But Ronni was right. It was out there now. The people of San Antonio were aware of the influence peddling that Carolyn had claimed from the beginning was an integral part of the district attorney's office. All this latest case did was prove one very important fact—at least to Carolyn.

It proved that Carolyn Huebner might have been a lot of things, but she wasn't a liar.

The day of Carolyn's parole hearing was right around the corner and she was nervous, but it wasn't like the last time. She was far more in control of herself this time; Larry wasn't involved, and Hawkeye was going to speak for her. His words *had* to carry weight, Carolyn believed, but if they didn't...well, they didn't.

Hawkeye knew about Larry's incident with Audra, but Carolyn just couldn't tell him about the letter she had written to Ronni. It was too humiliating; she couldn't face strangers with it. If she had her way, she'd take that letter to the grave with her.

On November 15, Carolyn and Hawkeye went before the parole board. Although he looked very professional, he was pale and clearly more nervous than she was. She was well-groomed, but her once stylish, curly hair now waved smoothly in an almost matronly fashion to below her shoulders; the color had gone auburn with a few strands of silver. Even though there was a quiet wisdom in her fine blue-gray eyes and her complexion was still flawless with faintest blush on her cheeks, she looked older than her thirty-two years. Still, even in prison, she had aged gracefully and well.

When the panelists began their interrogation, Carolyn said a quick, silent prayer and then answered their questions confidently. She expressed her remorse without making excuses, and told them once again why it was so important for her to return home. She explained that her child had already spent two months in a hospital because her emotional problems were so severe, and that her husband needed her. She told them that she had a job lined up at a lovely bed and breakfast inn belonging to some close friends, and she could begin work right away.

Finally, she tried to make clear that she longed to begin long-term therapy with a San Antonio psychiatrist recommended by Dr. Reid named Dr. George Meyer, who was an expert on post-traumatic stress disorder. Carolyn had already begun having some therapy sessions with him on the telephone, wrote him often, and truly believed that he could help her if she could just see him regularly.

This was where Hawkeye came in—and he came in with a passion. His eloquence was far more than Carolyn could ever have asked for. After he told the panelists about her perfect behavior record and how much she had improved since she had first arrived in Alderson, he stated frankly that further punishment would only exacerbate her mental problems and that he was unable to do anything more than keep her stable until she could finally go home.

In less than an hour it was over. Carolyn received word that the board recommended a four-month cut off her sentence, and wanted her to return to a halfway house in San Antonio in February, 1990. She should remain there for six months, they said, so that she could gradually integrate herself back into her community as well as her family, and she should also begin her therapy immediately. Of course, they reminded her, their recommendation could be overturned by the National Parole Board, but that very seldom happened.

It was the perfect result, Carolyn thought, shaking hands with the panelists, unable to stop smiling. It was everything she had prayed it would be. When she called Ronni, then PoPo, then her brother Bob, and then Larry, all she could do was cry. She was overwhelmed with joy, breathless with anticipation…

It was over. She was finally going home.

On December 28, 1989, the National Parole Board rescinded Carolyn's four-month cut and informed her that she would serve out the remainder of her full sentence at Alderson. It was all Carolyn could do not to lose her mind.

But she managed. As the weeks marched interminably onward, toward the date when she would finally close the door on Alderson and Hawkeye, Carolyn spent as much time being terrified about going home as she was excited…and the more stress she endured, the more chaotic and jumbled her thoughts and memories became.

What if the media swarmed her when she hit the streets of San Antonio? She couldn't handle crowds anymore. What if people asked questions that she didn't want to answer? Her brain just didn't work like it had before. How was she going to handle her husband? He made so many demands on her now, even on the telephone, she usually just shut herself off emotionally and waited for him to stop. How was she going to take care of her child? She couldn't even take care of herself...

"I feel like I'm exchanging one prison for another one, Hawkeye," she said one afternoon just a couple of weeks before she left for home, "and I don't know if I'm up for it. I'm still so angry with Larry and I know I'm a control freak ..."

"And you have to deal with that, Carolyn," Hawkeye interrupted seriously. "That control thing is a survival mechanism with you and it's one of the main reasons you've lasted in here. But part of living and loving is giving it up and learning to trust. That's why I knew I could never enter into any real therapy with you because in order for it to be effective, you'd have to let your guard down. I never wanted you to do that in a place like this. But you *have* to do it when you get home. If you don't, you'll never get well."

"But, Hawkeye... Hawkeye...I don't know if I *want* to go home! I don't know if I *want* to live with Larry... I might just get Audra and go back to Pennsylvania..."

"Take it slow, Carolyn. It's too soon to make a decision like that. Just take it slow."

Now, just a few evenings before she was due to depart, Carolyn sat quietly in her room, her eyes closed, and reflected on the last three-and-a-half years of her life. She had learned what she was capable of—more than she ever would have believed. She had learned what friendship was from people she had never met, and she had learned the meaning of true compassion from a doctor who had given her a reason to go on living. She had even learned where God was—right here in this little room...

Carolyn yawned and went into the bathroom. It was getting late and she needed to get to bed. Processing out of prison, she was learning, was just about as tiring and complicated as processing in. Finally, after washing her face and flossing her teeth, she began brushing her hair with long, solid, soothing strokes. She looked at her reflection in the mirror...and frowned. There was a flash of light, a blurred image, then, somehow, the blending of faces...

She closed her eyes, opened them again...

Carolyn, the woman, was gone.

Carolyn, the child, appeared. Big-eyed, white skin stretched taut across protruding cheekbones, matted hair once red-gold... A razor-sharp image of a pleading smile and trembling lips...

Then, gently, like a cotton-soft cloud, the child and the woman merged in the mirror and became one.

*I saw her today for just a moment*
*She was very young and afraid*
*Held out her hand to me*
*I reached and she was gone.*

*I heard her voice the other day*
*She was very sad and lonely*
*Cried out loud to me*
*I answered but she was gone.*

*I felt her spirit late last night*
*She was lost and very cold*
*Prayed out loud to God*
*I prayed but she was gone.*

*I watch for her*
*I listen for her*
*I search for her*
*I pray for her.*

*Someday I will find me.*


**Carolyn Sue Huebner**
**FCI Alderson**
**1990**

# PART SIX

*Bring me out of prison,*
*That I may give thanks to thy name!*
*The righteous will surround me;*
*for thou wilt deal bountifully with me.*

**Psalms 142:7**
**(Harper Study Bible, Revised Standard Version)**

# CHAPTER THIRTY-TWO

Despite all the media fascination with Carolyn Huebner's case when the story first broke on May 24, 1987, and despite her worry about being swarmed by the press when she came home, not one reporter or television personality met her at the airport when she and Larry finally returned to San Antonio in June 1990. The city's Golden Child had sunk to the bottom of that cesspool for fallen celebrities like a brick.

At first Carolyn had been a little disconcerted, even disappointed, that no one seemed to know or care that she was home. After all, she had worked very hard for that position of prominence in her chosen field and she had loved the limelight. But then, as soon as she saw Kevin waving to her from the airport lobby and Ronni standing there with her arms outstretched, Carolyn was infinitely grateful that this was a private moment.

However, as it turned out, *all* of Carolyn's moments were private. She spent the next six months in the halfway house near the lovely bed and breakfast where she worked, and was grateful that she didn't have to deal with the domestic responsibilities that Larry would have given her had she gone straight home. She was able to pick up Audra after school each afternoon and take her back to work with her; this routine task helped her to settle back into life as she had once known it. It also allowed her to spend precious one-on-one time with her child, who had become a rip-roaring terror in her absence, and this was something she had never before been inclined to do. She did everything she could to blend into the general population, unnoticed and unrecognized, and she did it because, for the first time in her life, she was determined to get well.

Carolyn would never forget the very first time she had walked into Dr. George Meyer's office and met the man she prayed would be her liberator. He had walked across the room with a welcoming smile on his face, took her hand in both of his, and greeted her with such warm enthusiasm that she immediately felt at home.

"Ah, Carolyn, how wonderful to finally meet you in person!"

Shyly, she met his gaze for a brief moment. "I'm happy to finally meet you, too."

She liked the way he looked—like somebody's grandpa. He was slightly built, with thinning silver-streaked hair accentuated by a silver-and-turquoise bolo decorating the collar of his western shirt. His smile was warm and his touch gentle, both extremely important attributes as far as Carolyn was concerned.

He sat back down and gestured toward a large southwestern-style leather sofa near his chair. "Won't you sit down?"

Carolyn obeyed and clasped her hands tightly in her lap.

"How was your trip home?" he had asked.

"It was fine, thank you."

"Did you fly by yourself?"

Carolyn shook her head. "No, Sir. My husband came out and flew home with me. Then my best friend, Ronni, and her husband, Kevin, met us at the airport."

"Ah, yes, Ronni... I met her about two weeks ago, you know, when she came in to...what was it she said?...to check me out."

Carolyn blushed furiously, "Oh, I'm sorry! That was very rude. She shouldn't have put it that way."

"Well, I think Ronni pretty much says what she wants, don't you? And it's perfectly all right. I completely understand." He had given her a conspiratorial grin. "I got a much clearer picture of you, too, just because she knows you so well and wasn't shy about answering all my questions. I think the meeting benefited all of us. Apparently Ronni was your lifeline while you were in Alderson, yes?"

"Yes. I couldn't have made it without her."

He removed his glasses, closed his eyes and rubbed his temples for a moment. "Well, if Ronni was your lifeline," he asked abruptly, "what was your husband?"

"Excuse me?"

"What was your husband to you while you were in there?"

Carolyn sighed. "He did the best he could, I guess."

"The papers all said that he stood by you and wanted you to come home. That sounds pretty important to me."

"That was for his benefit, not mine. That was to make *him* look good."

"Tell me about Hawkeye. He sounds like he meant a great deal to you."

*Good Lord, he switches subjects fast...* She could hardly keep up.

But she liked to talk about Hawkeye. "He fought for me. I made him a medal after he spoke for me at the parole board hearing, and I read him a little speech that I wrote just for him. He kept the medal right up in his bookcase where everyone could see it—he was really proud of it. He told me the last time we met that I was the most professionally and personally rewarding case he'd ever had—or something like that. I cried. I think he tried not to. I'll never forget Hawkeye. He kept me safe."

"Where did he get that nickname, *Hawkeye*?"

"I gave it to him. I give most everyone I know a nickname."

He cocked an eyebrow. "Do I have one yet?"

Looking at him sheepishly, Carolyn blushed. "Yes, Sir."

"I do, really? What is it?"

"I've… I hope you don't mind… I just call you *Dr. George.* Is that okay?"

"I'm flattered," he answered instantly. "Dr. George it is then. Now, Carolyn, let's talk about how I can help you."

Her heart sped up and her mouth went dry, but she nodded. "Yes, Sir."

"First of all, let's drop the *Sir* and keep the *Dr. George,* all right? I like that much better. Now, we're going to be partners on a very exciting journey. We're going to work together, and we're going to work hard, and it's going to take time. Maybe a long time. Are you ready for that?"

"Yes, Sir."

"You can't back out when it starts to get rough, Carolyn—like I think you've always done before. You have to work through it, no matter how hard it is or how much it hurts, because once you work through it, you'll find that it's over and then you'll let it go. And it'll let go of you."

"Yes, Sir."

"I think we need to start at two-hour sessions at least twice a week. How are you sleeping?"

Carolyn's eyes filled. "I don't *sleep.* I sleep*walk.* I have nightmares, and night terrors… I still do. I thought that would stop if I could just get back home, but…"

"Okay, I want to start you on some medications that I think will help you sleep as well as keep you emotionally level. That might take a little time, too, but we'll figure it out. You'll have every phone number for me that you need and you call me any time of the day or night. I mean that, Carolyn. You call me and I'll be there."

She had battled a boulder-sized lump in her throat; tears had streamed down her cheeks. *He was going to help her. He could make her well…*

She took a shuddering breath. "Dr. George, I need to understand something before we start this."

"Of course."

"You know how I…forget things. Ronni showed you the letter…" For a moment Carolyn thought she was going to be sick she was so embarrassed, but she battled on. "The letter I wrote her…"

"I read it."

"Do you think I'm crazy, Dr. George?" she blurted. "Only a crazy person would write something like that!"

He had held up his hand and chuckled. "You're no crazier than I am, Carolyn. In fact, I think you're very intelligent and creative. You taught yourself a coping skill years ago that worked for you when you were a little girl, but it just doesn't work for you anymore. That's all. We're going to teach you coping skills that will work for you now."

"How?"

"Ah, I can't lie to you about that, Carolyn. That's the hard part of this journey. Intensive psychotherapy means *re-experiencing and then re-defining the experience.* In other words, you *remember* it, then you *relive* it, and then you *redefine* it..."

Carolyn didn't like the sound of that kind of therapy. She shook her head. "I don't think I want to do that."

"Of course you don't. Not yet. But you will. You see, you've spent your whole life *leaving* a place, or a traumatic event, or a person you're afraid of... You've spent your whole life *dissociating* your mind from whatever you couldn't handle. What a blessing that was for the little Carolyn! But once you trust me enough, I'm going to take you back there. You're going to learn that a memory can't hurt you. In the beginning you're going to be terrified, but that's all right. Eventually you'll realize that you're safe and then you're going to *want* to do this. You're going to *beg* me to help you do this because, for the first time, you're going to see your life for *exactly* what it is and you're going to know *exactly* who you are."

But Carolyn couldn't join in his professional excitement; her mind was locked in on something he had said in the very beginning. "You're going to take me *back* there?" she whispered, wide-eyed.

"I am. But I want you to understand something, Carolyn. Memories are strange, and your mind protects them in strange ways. In fact, your mind has been protecting *you* for years and you never even knew it. You're going to have memories—maybe you already do—that don't make sense to you. Or you're going to *know* for absolute certain that you did something, or said something, or witnessed something, or experienced something—but it's gone now. It's like falling through ice. It's disappeared into a black hole somewhere in your mind and it's just gone. We'll deal with that if and when it happens, but sometimes it's just best to let it go.

"And while you're going through this, you have to have a strong and powerful support system: your best friend, your therapist, your daughter, your husband... Take your pick, but try to have more than one person in your corner. Like legs on a stool, we'll all hold you up. And when it's all over, it will have been worth it. Do you understand what I'm saying?"

"I'm scared," she whispered, "I'm so scared..."

"Of course you are, but that's all right. You're not alone, and you can do this."

She had been in therapy with Dr. George for nearly two years now and she knew she had come a long way, but she still had a long way to go. She had begun taking Audra to see Dr. George's wife, Paula, who was a therapist skilled in working with emotionally traumatized children, and slowly but surely Carolyn could see her little girl blossom. Several times she invited Larry to join her and Audra in family counseling with Dr. George, which Carolyn believed was crucial to the success of their marriage, but Larry was very busy at Valero and only accompanied her a few times.

Still, every time life threw Carolyn a curve, she was proud to find that she handled it a little better, became a little stronger, and gradually began to regain her confidence.

The one person in her life that she had thought would give her all the support she needed was Larry, but she was wrong. He was either determined to sabotage her progress, she decided, or he just expected more than she could give. From the moment she had left the halfway house and walked in her front door, he had dumped everything he had been handling while she was in prison—except his responsibilities at Valero—onto her fragile shoulders and walked away. He refused to change his style of parenting (such as it was), so the screaming fights within the Huebner household between father and daughter never ceased. And, as he was an only child, Larry also had to care for his terminally ill, elderly parents. But he was too busy—so that responsibility also fell to Carolyn.

Sometimes it was more than Carolyn thought she could handle, especially as she delved deeper and deeper into her therapy.

But that therapy, as painful as it was, was her salvation. The more she was able to face and accept in her past, the stronger she became about the hectic and emotionally draining life she was leading now. And Dr. George, always so soft-spoken and gentle and unruffled, was helping her to acknowledge and even *admire* the creative power of her own mind.

Finally, because she and Dr. George had never thoroughly discussed it, Carolyn just *had* to come right out and ask the question she had longed to ask from the very earliest days of her therapy.

"Do you have a diagnosis for me, Dr. George?" She held her breath.

*Please, God, please don't say Multiple Personality Disorder... Please don't tell me that I'm like Sybil...or Trudi Chase... I couldn't take it if you said that...*

"I do. I believe that you're suffering from post-traumatic stress disorder with dissociative features."

"Huh?"

"Post-traumatic..."

Carolyn interrupted, "You don't think I have multiple... you know...multiple..."

"No, I don't think so."

"What's the difference between... post-traumatic stress..."

"And alters?"

"Whatever."

"Okay, listen to me. I don't think you have multiple personalities, Carolyn, although I *do* think that your personality has been fragmented for many, many years as a self-defense mechanism that you created when you were a child. Instead, I believe that you have gone into *dissociative fugue states* more than anything else.

"Now, that's not as scary as it sounds and it's not all that unusual. People who are in a fugue state, which Dr. Reid even mentioned in his medical report about you for the court, can fail to remember any or all of their past. They often experience confusion about their identity, or even leave home and take on a whole new one—but they're not actually suffering from MPD, which I believe is very rare.

"Traumatic events can often trigger a dissociative episode, like Ronni suggested may have happened when you saw *The Color Purple* and then wrote your letter. People who are in a dissociative state usually appear normal to everyone else and don't attract any attention. Once they return to the pre-dissociative state, they have no memory of what they did or what happened. It's very real.

"On the other hand, in MPD, each *personality* or *alter* has a real personality that's consistent throughout the relationship. Alters are sort of like imaginary playmates. Children have imaginary playmates for years, right? This is very normal, very common, very healthy—often a child is lonesome and this is their friend. But real alters aren't normal or common, and they certainly aren't healthy.

"Some psychiatrists don't even believe in alters, or multiple personalities, but I do. An alter may represent a portion of the personality that can be very frightening, very unhealthy. An alter can truly have power over the individual and say to the individual, "Hurt yourself, cut yourself... Go kill somebody..."

"An alter is a living being for that individual. It's not imaginary. It's a consistent, living being that begins to have power. It's not somebody that the individual feels comfortable with. If a child talks to an imaginary playmate—well, that could easily be the child's best friend. But an alter isn't usually your friend. An alter is usually what we call *ego dystonic*, which means that the alter acts out in a way that's completely foreign to your core or fundamental belief system.

"In other words, this isn't normal, so you feel guilty about it and you think, everyone's going to say I'm crazy. I'm not going to tell anyone about this. So you keep it to yourself and you keep getting sicker and sicker. Of course, you did this over the years, too, but I really believe you were just dissociating and going into self-protective fugue states, not actually morphing into other full-blown personalities."

Once Carolyn realized that she only seemed to dissociate when she was stressed-out and probably wouldn't do it as long as she was calm and rested, she began to relax.

And so, as she began to understand herself a little better every day, she entered a quiet time in her life. After Larry's parents both passed on in 1993 and 1994, within sixteen months of each other, Larry seemed to come into his own as well. He seemed less inclined to spend all his time at work and became more emotionally accessible to his wife and child. It seemed easier for him to laugh and have a good time and actually take some pleasure in his days. Even their love life, although far from perfect, gradually improved.

He and Carolyn purchased a large pontoon boat, then a weekend house near Lake McQueeney, and enjoyed night fishing. They bought a travel trailer and took mostly weekend trips with Audra around Texas. Many weekends he worked on his father's farm, which he had inherited, hoping to build it up so that it might become another source of income for his family. He and Carolyn even began working on the blueprints for a lovely new home they wanted to build on the property…

Carolyn couldn't believe how fast time was flying by. Ronni and Kevin's daughter, Michaela, married her childhood sweetheart as soon as she turned eighteen, and, Lord, what a beautiful bride she was! Carolyn had sung *Wind Beneath My Wings* at the wedding, and Larry proudly ushered Grandma down the aisle while Audra sat in the congregation with Ohler, looking like she was mad at the world.

Carolyn became interested in antiques—originally Czechoslovakian pieces like those passed down in Larry's family—and began learning as much as she could about them. She branched out into art, then furniture… That was one thing about Carolyn that hadn't changed. She still gave 100% to whatever she was interested in.

Since the Hoesslis were now happy *empty nesters,* the four friends finally managed to find a whole weekend to spend together down at Port Lavaca. This meant the world to Carolyn because they had never done such a thing before—Ronni had finally told her that Kevin never liked the way Carolyn had treated Larry and had refused to socialize with them. Carolyn understood and didn't blame him.

But now it was different. Carolyn actually felt *normal,* like every terrible thing that had ever happened to her had happened to someone else. Now Audra and a friend laughed and played and ran along the beach like all the other kids, while Ronni and Carolyn sat outside of their RVs and watched from their lawn chairs. Kevin and Larry marched down the pier hauling heavy tackle boxes and oversized fishing poles, like they expected to catch sharks or something equally impressive, but then they had barbecued chicken legs (because no one caught *any* fish) and drank Yellow Birds and swapped fishing lies...

It was a perfect weekend, and Carolyn felt so blessed to have had it—for a very simple reason.

The next Saturday, on October 22, 1994, following a major heart attack while he was working out at the farm, Larry Huebner died.

Carolyn fell completely apart. She was panicked and inconsolable. Even though their marriage had been rocky in the best of times, Larry had been the one constant in her life. Larry had always been there—and now, like a flash of lightning, he was gone.

There was nothing I could do to help her.

Carolyn was so ignorant about their finances that she couldn't even withdraw money from their bank account—she had to borrow cash from a friend to get through the weekend. She was afraid to be alone but didn't want to be with anybody, either. She didn't eat, and couldn't sleep, and grieved from the very depths of her soul. She cried and sobbed and shrieked and wailed...

But she didn't hear voices, and she didn't dissociate, and she remained firmly in control.

Kevin and I took Audra away for a few hours, and I decided that the child was in shock. Now twelve years old and certainly old enough to express herself, she showed no emotion whatsoever. She didn't shed a single tear and acted as if nothing out of the ordinary had happened. It was eerie and unnerving, and I didn't like it a bit.

Carolyn's brother, Bobby, flew in from Pennsylvania for a couple of days to "represent the family," he said, and I was happy to finally meet him. Jim Rankin telephoned his condolences and seemed pleased when Carolyn told him that she hoped to come home for a visit around Christmas. It meant so much to Carolyn to have old friends and family nearby; she told me several times how much it helped. So, she was crushed when Bobby left early in the morning without even saying good-bye.

No matter what they had gone through over the years as a couple, Carolyn was now determined to honor her husband. The funeral, held at the church Larry had attended as a child, was attended by most of Valero, members of the Optimist Club, a few of his closest friends—and it had Carolyn's unique fingerprints all over it. She even managed to sing one of his favorite hymns at the end—although most of the buttoned-down congregation really didn't appreciate the effort it took for her to accomplish that. Audra seemed oblivious to everything.

Then Travis Koehne, the district attorney in Bellville, contacted Carolyn and told her that he intended to investigate Mr. Huebner's death. Considering her history, Koehne said, he was going to have Mr. Huebner's body exhumed from his grave at Wesley Cemetery to be sure he hadn't been murdered.

At first I thought it was all a joke, but it wasn't. It was another nightmare in a long series of nightmares, but Carolyn still managed to keep it together. PoPo accompanied her to the exhumation, dressed out in his official Texas Ranger badge. She stared, puzzled, at the deputies standing graveside with shotguns leveled and wondered how many guns it takes to shoot a dead man.

"This lady ain't goin' nowhere, fellas," PoPo told them quietly. "So why don't you just put them guns away?"

Carolyn then walked up to Travis Koehne, looked him straight in the eye, and said, "As long as I live, I will never forget what you have done here this day." The district attorney stood silently...and said nothing.

But, ultimately, the autopsy showed that Larry Huebner had died of a massive coronary caused by a congenital heart defect in which an artery behind the heart was too small. His sedentary lifestyle probably hadn't helped, plus his love of rich foods and even the stress of the last years, but he certainly hadn't been murdered.

Carolyn had had it with the drama in her life. She knew she needed to rest and recuperate, so she decided to pack up Audra and take her back to Pennsylvania. She didn't know what she was going to do with the farm or her huge old house, but she did know that Texas had never given her one minute's peace.

She had had enough of San Antonio and it was time to put it behind her. She needed to go back home.

The day after Christmas, when Carolyn and Audra arrived at Betty Shaw's house on Mohawk Street in White Oak, Pennsylvania, memories washed over her with the vengeance of a tsunami. Some were good and some were bad, but it was all right. She just let them flow. She wasn't afraid of them anymore. She had finally come to realize that a memory was fleeting, it was intangible, and it couldn't hurt her...

She remembered her rides with her mommy and daddy for ice cream, and dancing with Maureen in the living room to the latest rock'n'roll record, and chasing Bobby around the house while they played cowboys and Indians... Oh, there were so many memories.

"Carolyn! Jim Rankin's on the phone!"

"Okay—sorry!" Embarrassed, she grabbed the receiver out of her mother's hand and gave her a quick apologetic peck on the cheek. "Hey, Jimmy," she said breathlessly, "how are you?"

"I'm good. How are you?"

"Fine, thanks."

"Well, listen. I'm not going to beat around the bush, Carolyn. Are you free for dinner tonight?"

There was something about his deep voice that sent a little shiver through her, but she didn't know if it was excitement or fear. She knew the old saying about people being unable to go home again and she knew it was probably true, but there was something about his voice that was just so familiar...so warm... The mere sound of it brought with it a sense of safety.

"Yes. Yes, I am."

"Good. I'll pick you up at 7:00..."

"Jim," she interrupted, "I'll drive, okay? I'd feel better..."

He chuckled. "Whatever you say, Carolyn. I'll see you at 7:00."

When Carolyn had answered the door and invited Jim inside, her gaze had started at the ground and worked its way up...and up...and up. *Little* Jimmy Rankin had certainly grown; he was now about 6'2", with broad shoulders and slender hips. His once-red hair was now a deep auburn, more like burnished copper, but his eyes still danced as he looked down at her.

"Good Lord," she breathed, her gaze finally fixing on his face, "little Jimmy Rankin...look at you! You're so handsome!"

Jim had blushed faintly. "Thanks. You don't look any different at all. You're still beautiful. I like your dress."

"Oh...Audra picked it out. Thank you."

He had looked around the living room. "Where *is* Audra?"

"Oh, she's hiding and she's watching you from somewhere, but you'll never get her to come out." Carolyn had picked up her handbag and took her car keys from a front pocket. "Are you ready to go? I'm starving."

Now Carolyn and Jim sat at a corner table in *The Lemon Tree*, a restaurant that Jim's father and Carolyn's Uncle Artie had helped to build, so deep in conversation that they seldom noticed when the waitress continually came around to refill their glasses. Listening as Jim brought her up to date on what had happened in his life while she had been away, Carolyn rested her chin on her hand, luxuriating in the quiet serenity that had always seemed to surround him. She couldn't help but think how different he was from Larry.

"So, anyway," Jim was saying, "I left college and came home to help with the farm. I went to work at the paper and I've been here ever since."

"I haven't seen Grandma Rankin yet, but I'll visit her first thing tomorrow. Is she all right?"

"Oh, you know Grandma. She's tough as nails. She can't wait to see you."

Carolyn nodded but said nothing. Unspoken words were hanging between them—words so powerful and tantalizing that they threatened to steal the oxygen right out of the air. She could tell by Jim's dancing eyes that something was amusing him, but she couldn't begin to figure out what it was. To Carolyn, nothing was amusing. Her heart was pounding so hard she could barely breathe.

Finally, Jim broke the silence. "I want to tell you something, Carolyn."

Here it comes, she thought. This is where he says that he's really sorry that I screwed up my life so bad and I went so crazy and if I'd stayed up here with him, everything would've been different...but I didn't, so it isn't...

"I want you to know that I've never stopped thinking about you." He cleared his throat. "I wouldn't be saying this except that your husband's gone and I want you to know how I feel before any more time passes. I want to be completely up-front with you."

Tears blurred her vision and she blinked them away. For some reason she felt totally bereft, like he had already walked away from her. "Oh, it's okay, Jimmy. You don't have to say anymore. I understand..."

He shook his head. "No, you don't. I've loved you for my whole life, Carolyn. Even when we were kids, I loved you. When I fished you out of that pond, I loved you, and when my dad ran you out of town, I loved you, and every time you came back and I didn't see you, I loved you, and...well, I still love you."

Carolyn stared at him in stunned disbelief. "Oh, my God..."

Jim gave her a crooked grin and flushed. "I'm sorry. I guess it's way too soon... I do that, you know. I don't like secrets."

"No! It isn't that. It's just that...well, so much has happened in my life that you don't know anything about, and if you did, you'd probably change your mind." Carolyn laughed nervously. "I mean, I wouldn't blame you..."

Jim reached across the table and took her hand in his. His intense gaze never left her face. "Try me," he said calmly.

As Carolyn stared down at their entwined fingers, she couldn't help but wonder where this was going. She didn't want to make any mistakes this time. She didn't want to be with this man, or any other man, for any reason other than the *right* reason. She didn't know what it felt like to have a relationship with another human being only because God had ordained it, and not because she had an ulterior motive, but it was an experience she longed to have.

"Let's go somewhere that we can talk," she said, gently removing her hand from Jim's grasp. "You said you don't like secrets, and all I've ever done is keep them." She slipped her handbag over her shoulder and stood up. "For the first time...I think *ever* in my life...I'm ready to be honest."

As Carolyn and Jim sat in the warmth of her Suburban at the top of a hill, they looked out over a snow-covered, moonlit valley as she told him the highlights of her life. Every once in awhile he touched her hand in encouragement, but he never said a word. Finally, when her voice had trailed away, he gently pulled her toward him.

Cupping his hands around her face, his lips met hers for just the second time in their lives—but Carolyn felt as if she had never left his arms. His warm, protective embrace was where she should have always been. Little Jimmy Rankin's kiss reached down into her soul and held it close; it literally stopped her world. For the first time in her life, she felt something *real* down deep in her spirit, something secret that belonged only to her...like God's fingers, moving over her heart. And then, because she didn't know what to do with so much overwhelming joy all at once, Carolyn began to cry.

Instantly, Jim released her. "I'm sorry..." he whispered, "I'm sorry. I shouldn't have..."

She shook her head. As she pulled him back into her arms, tears of happiness still streaming down her cheeks, she laughed softly. This man still didn't understand how far she had come, but he would one day—and Carolyn already did.

Through the Grace of God and just as He had always promised, she had come full circle.

She had finally come home.

*I will restore to you the years*
*Which the swarming locust has eaten,*
*The hopper, the destroyer, and the cutter,*
*my great army, which I sent among you.*

*You shall eat in plenty and be satisfied,*
*And praise the name of the Lord your God,*
*Who has dealt wondrously with you.*
*And my people shall never again be put to shame.*

**Joel 2:25 & 26**

# EPILOGUE

By:

James D. Rankin

Okay, take a breath. For those who have finished this book and are still struggling with the idea that—despite profuse documentation—this story is just too fantastic to be true, let me share that early on in our relationship, Carolyn sat me down and told me the condensed version of her life after White Oak, hitting the key points. I suppose she figured it would be best to hit me with her past now, just in case I was the type to go running off screaming, before we got in too deep.

But I had quite the opposite reaction; this story was too fantastic *not* to be true. I would later learn the full account and meet some of the major players in her life and her recovery. I have been privileged to witness the final stage of her therapy with Dr. George Meyer, and I have been a witness to how the Lord has brought her to the place where she is now.

I have noticed how, in some cases, God brings a person back to who they were before things got off track…or, in this case, before the train of Carolyn's life was derailed by people who were cruel, self-absorbed and evil. Many of us who have given our lives to the Lord go through a similar restorative process as God cleans away the tarnish and the crusting. But in Carolyn's case it was far more dramatic because there was so much ground to cover to get her back to her sense of who she truly is—not just at her core, but in His eyes and His will.

I never became a physician, but as I write this I am in my tenth year of teaching Science, Human Anatomy and Physiology at one of the high schools in San Antonio, (hopefully) getting other doctors started on their careers. When I'm not doing that, I preach in church and write articles for the website of Rankin Family Ministries, Inc.

Carolyn's new career is that of a certified personal property appraiser, a kind of one-woman Antiques Roadshow educating people on their possessions and helping elderly clients get the best possible deal when it comes time for them to downsize and part company with their treasures. This is another link to her core that God has given her, as she developed a love for antiques while she spent time with my grandmother. In her job, she not only gets a chance to work for the rights of her elderly clients (a minor flashback to her crusading days), but also to share the Gospel with others.

Now, this being real life, the ending is not quite as neat as it would be if this were fiction. To this day, Carolyn has no explanation for the knife terrors or the full story of the baby wrapped in a blue blanket that she saw Rose and the man disposing of. Those memories, which Dr. George assured her are real, have simply disappeared and Carolyn has no desire to retrieve them.

And life, of course, goes on. Fred Rodriguez was defeated as Bexar County district attorney in 1991, after serving only one term. In an ironic twist of fate, he was replaced by Steve Hilbig, the court-appointed defense attorney for the notorious child molester Ray Moberg—whose case actually triggered Carolyn's breakdown.

Carolyn's beloved PoPo, retired Texas Ranger Jerome Preiss, the last of the actual cowboy Rangers, passed away in 2004 at the age of 80.

Carolyn and I were married on March 21, 1998, in San Antonio, where we still live, but it wasn't just Carolyn and I who married. God began the process of building a family that day, and our Audra was part of the ceremony as well, receiving her own ring and a separate vow. In 2000, at her request and even though she was legally an adult, I formally adopted her. To my great joy and honor, she added the name Rankin to her own.

Over the years, Audra's relationship with her mother has healed and she has blossomed into a young woman who closely resembles her in many ways. When I first met her, I was astonished at how much she looked like her mother as a child. Now, I see that she also has much of Carolyn's courage and spirit.

As for families, most of what remained in Pennsylvania is no more. Cancer claimed Bobby Shaw in 2002, and Betty Shaw passed away in 2004 at the age of 86. Maureen and her sons still live in White Oak and vicinity. All of them lived to see Carolyn's recovery and the Lord's restoration of the years the locusts have eaten. Sometimes the knowledge led to full restoration of their relationship with Carolyn, but in other cases it did not. People are still people, and God still respects the free will He gave us in the first place.

A significant part of that restoration, ironically enough, came from Larry Huebner himself. A few years after his passing, Carolyn discovered hundreds of taped recordings of telephone conversations Larry made over a period of at least three years with Carolyn and anyone connected with her, accompanied by diaries of Carolyn's actions. The reasons for this documentation are still unknown, but whatever his intent, Larry provided Carolyn (and Ronni) with an enormous resource of material to not only confirm her history but to help write this book...finally proving, once and for all, that God does, indeed, work in mysterious ways.

Our beloved Leola Seay (Ohler) passed away in 2008. She was in her 90s and living with family in California. Despite her physical problems, she remained active in her church and was a living example of how God uses anyone He pleases to carry out His greater purpose and plans. Her introduction of Carolyn—and, by extension, me—to the Church of God in Christ (and their unconditional acceptance of us and Audra) was a key turning point in ultimately bringing Carolyn back to a relationship with Him, and in His plans for my life as well.

Obviously, this is by no means the conclusion. What you have just read is "the story so far," and where things go from here is up to God. In making this public, we realize that we are leaving ourselves open to the scrutiny of others, for good or for ill. But in opening ourselves like this, our hope is that the unseen Hand always at work behind the scenes is also now clearly visible, as is the inescapable fact that God has a plan for every life.

Every person is valuable in God's sight. You are not misbegotten, you are not a loser. If anything, what you have just read is an example of how far God is willing to go to restore people unto Himself. Carolyn's story is an extreme example, perhaps, but sometimes extreme actions are warranted in extraordinary lives. Whatever you may have done, whatever you may have gone through in your life, the only thing keeping you away from His love and His guidance and His help…is you. And He loves you enough not to force Himself upon you.

He simply waits for you to make the next move.

*THE END*

Breinigsville, PA USA
21 February 2011
256070BV00004B/1/P